STRESS

STRESS
Myth, Theory and Research

Fiona Jones and Jim Bright

With contributions from Angela Clow, Lucy Cooper, Gail Kinman, Ben Newell and Ben Searle

An imprint of **Pearson Education**

Harlow, England · London · New York · Reading, Massachusetts · San Francisco
Toronto · Don Mills, Ontario · Sydney · Tokyo · Singapore · Hong Kong · Seoul
Taipei · Cape Town · Madrid · Mexico City · Amsterdam · Munich · Paris · Milan

Pearson Education Limited
Edinburgh Gate
Harlow
Essex CM20 2JE
England

and Associated Companies throughout the World.

Visit us on the World Wide Web at:
www.pearsoneduc.com

First published 2001
© Pearson Education Limited 2001

ISBN 0-130-41189-2

British Library Cataloguing-in-Publication Data
A catalogue record for this book can be obtained from the British Library

Library of Congress Cataloguing-in-Publication Data
A catalog record for this book can be obtained from the Library of Congress

10 9 8 7 6 5 4 3 2 1
05 04 03 02 01 00

Typeset by 35 in 10/12pt Janson Text
Printed in Malaysia, LSP

CONTENTS

PREFACE

IN the last few years a great deal has been written on the topic of stress. Self-help books can be found in every bookseller and articles on coping with stress are perennial magazine features. The academic literature on the topic is similarly vast and presents a complex and often contradictory body of evidence. This book stems from ten years of research and lecturing in this topic during which time we came to realise that, despite all that has been written about stress, there are few accessible published books for the student, researcher or intelligent layperson. Hence this book aims to meet the need for a concise but critical account that attempts to bridge the gap between the popular press and research journals.

Given the depth and breadth of research on the topic of stress, it is not possible to provide anything approaching a comprehensive review of all the relevant literature. An attempt to do this would produce several volumes. Instead, we introduce issues that we see as key to gaining a grasp of this area. This includes introducing theoretical approaches, methodologies and selected examples of research findings. We also aim to help readers adopt a critical approach to the literature so that they are able to distinguish unsubstantiated and often sensational claims about stress from the often more complex but nonetheless interesting findings that have emerged from this area of study. In other words, our aim is to enable the reader to distinguish myths about stress from statements that can be supported by research. For more serious students, we aim to provide a starting point to help them to find their own way through the mass of academic research. The book will provide references to specialised texts and research articles providing a source book for further study.

As stress researchers ourselves we have a particular interest in the methodological problems that beset this area. We have therefore included discussions of measurement issues and information on specific measures which may be of use to those wishing to undertake their own research either in academic or applied settings, e.g. conducting organisational stress audits.

A number of people have helped considerably in the process of writing this book. In particular, we would like to acknowledge the excellent work done by those who wrote whole or part chapters. We would also like to acknowledge the contribution made by Linda Miller in reading and commenting on drafts; Nicky Payne who helped with literature research in the early stages and Avis Cowley for her work on the reference list. Also, many thanks to John R. Bright (Jim's father), for playing host to him on his stay in the UK whilst we completed the book.

Fiona Jones and James Bright
May 5th 2000

ACKNOWLEDGEMENTS

We are grateful to the following for permission to reproduce copyright material:

Box 2.2 reprinted from *Journal of Psychosomatic Research*, Vol. 11, Holmes *et al.*, from Social readjustment rating scale, 1967, with permission from Elsevier Science; Fig 3.4 from 'Physiological Psychology' by Smock, © 1999. Reprinted by permission of Prentice-Hall Inc., Upper Saddle Riber, N.J.; Box 5.2 from *Human Memory: Theory and Practice*, reprinted by permission of Psychology Press Limited, Hove, UK, (Baddeley, A. 1990); Figure 6.1 from *Stress, Type A, Coping, and Psychological and Physical Symptoms: a multi-sample text of alternative models, Human Relations*, Tavistock Institute, (Edwards, J. R., Baglioni, Jr, A. J., and Cooper, C. L. 1990); Figure 8.1 from Stress, social support, and the buffering hypothesis in *Psychological Bulletin* 98, p. 313, copyright © 1985 by the American Psychological Association. Reprinted with permission, (Cohen, S. and Wills, T. A.); Box 8.1 from Academic Stress, Social support and secretory immunoglobin A, in *Journal of Personality and Social Psychology*, 55, p. 806, copyright © 1988 by the American Psychological Association. Reprinted with permission, (Jemmott, J. B. and Macgloire, K.); Figure 9.1 from Job Demands, Job Decision Latitude, and Mental Strain: Implication for Job Redesign in *Administrative Science Quarterly*, Vol. 24, p. 2, © Administrative Science Quarterly, (Karasek, Jr. Robert A. 1979); Figure 9.2 from Job Stress, employee health, and organizational effectiveness: a facet analysis, model and literature review in *Personnel Psychology*, 31, p. 676, © Personnel Psychology, (Beehr, T. A. and Newman, J. E. 1978); Figure 9.3 from *The Management Guide of the Occupational Stress Indicator*, © C. L. Cooper, S. J. Sloan and S. Williams 1988. Reproduced by permission of the Publishers, The NFER-NELSON Publishing Company Limited, Darville House, 2 Oxford Road East, Windsor, Berkshire SL4 1DF, England. All rights reserved; Figure 9.4 from The measurement of well-being and other aspects of mental health, in *Journal of Occupational Psychology*, Vol. 63, Part 3, p. 195, reproduced with permission from the Journal of Occupational Psychology, © The British Psychological Society, (Warr, P. 1990); Box 9.4 from *Handbook of Work and Health Psychology*, reproduced by permission of John Wiley & Sons Limited, (Shabracq, Winqubst and Cooper, 1996); Figure 10.1 from Effects of short-term role overload on marital interactions in *Work & Stress*, 6 (2): 119, (web site: http://www.tandf.co.uk/journals/tf/02678373.html), Taylor & Francis Ltd., (McEwen, K. E., Barling, J. and Kelloway, E. K. 1992).

Whilst every effort has been made to trace the owners of copyright material, in a few cases this has proved impossible and we take this opportunity to offer our apologies to any copyright holders whose rights we may have unwittingly infringed.

PART 1

WHAT IS STRESS?

This section provides an introduction to many of the concepts and methodologies that are fundamental to understanding the concept of stress. It is also intended to provide a useful resource for students and others trying to find their way through the stress literature and perhaps trying to conduct their own research in this area for the first time.

The first chapter considers the concept of stress and how it is defined. It examines the growing popularity of the concept and questions some of our current assumptions about increases in stress in modern life. The potential impact that the growth of stress research itself has had on the ways people perceive their experiences is also considered.

Chapter 2 discusses some of the more popular theoretical approaches to stress and the methodologies associated with those approaches. This includes the study of major life events and daily hassles.

The final chapter in this section, Chapter 3, aims to provide a basic understanding of the processes that are studied by researchers looking at the physiological stress response. This is crucial to a thorough understanding of research into the links between stress and disease. Overall, these chapters provide the basic grounding in theoretical and methodological issues underpinning issues discussed in subsequent sections.

CHAPTER 1

STRESS: THE CONCEPT

This chapter introduces the notion of stress in terms of its history and the ways in which it has been defined. The chapter discusses why, given rising standards of living and reduced mortality, we perceive life to be so stressful. Finally psychological research in the area is introduced and the role of this research in popularising the concept are considered.

EVERYDAY USE OF THE CONCEPT OF 'STRESS'

IMAGINE how you might feel in each of the following situations:

- You are stuck in a traffic jam and are about to be late for an important meeting.
- You are about to stand up and give a public address to 200 people.
- You work on an assembly line in a noisy factory, doing the same boring routine task repetitively every two minutes.
- You are asked to help someone with a psychological study, you do not know what it is about, but you are asked to complete mental arithmetic tasks.
- You have to go to hospital for a major and risky surgical procedure.
- You are having your family to stay for Christmas.
- Your partner for the last 20 years has just announced that they are leaving you to go to live with your best friend.
- You are caring day in, day out for an elderly and demanding relative.

It is easy to imagine a range of reactions to all these situations. However a survey of popular literature will soon reveal that all these events or experiences (and many more) can be summed up by the word 'stress'. In addition, it will be suggested that if you are the kind of person who always expects the worst to happen or you tend to push yourself very hard and have high expectations of yourself, you may be suffering from stress with very little external provocation. Herein lies one of the major problems with the concept of stress. It can be caused by almost any event as well as chronic circumstances such as poor work conditions or poor housing. Stress sometimes seems to be an almost inevitable spin-off of just about all aspects of modern life, yet at the same time there are huge and largely unexplained individual differences in people's susceptibility. Furthermore, it is claimed that stress can manifest itself in the form of an incredibly wide range of negative feelings and lead to an even wider range of outcomes. For example, a women's magazine suggests that it leads to:

> Nailbiting, irritability, loss of libido, withdrawal from friends and family, and food cravings. Then to more serious symptoms of burnout: anxiety and depression, panic attacks, exhaustion, high blood pressure, skin complaints, insomnia, sexual dysfunction, migraine, bowel problems and menstrual disorder. It may eventually lead to potentially fatal conditions like heart disease. (*Marie Claire*, October 1994)

This quote illustrates the popular perception of stress as pathological and in need of treatment and cure. In response to the apparent 'stress epidemic' there has been growing popular interest in the phenomenon over the last 20 years and a growing industry in instant (or not so instant) cures for the stress of modern life. These include medical remedies (such as Prozac), psychological therapies, alternative approaches such as aromatherapy and laughter therapy and more extreme approaches such as 'dropping out' and following alternative lifestyles. A wide range of consumer products is also marketed as potentially offering stress relief, including bubble baths, electric massagers and food products. In addition there is a large number of self-help books that seek to help people to 'cure' themselves. While most of these books treat stress as something that is bad for you, an alternative approach can also be discerned suggesting that stress can be a positive force and that stress can be utilised to improve performance.

A fundamental problem is that stress has been inadequately differentiated from such concepts as 'strain', 'pressure', 'demand' and 'stressors'. Sometimes it is used to describe something external in the environment (a stimulus or stressor), for example, 'She has a stressful job'. Other times it is used to describe an internal feeling (a response or strain): 'He is stressed out'. Frequently it is used to imply some combination of both stimulus and response, for example 'I have too much to do in too little time and it's making me feel tense' (or 'my stressful job is making me stressed'). However, it may also be used, on occasion, as being synonymous with pressure, as in 'A certain amount of stress makes me perform better', and leading to the view suggested above that stress can be positive. The term 'eustress', invented by Selye (1956), also sometimes appears in the popular literature to describe this type of stress. Generally, this confusion in popular perceptions reflects the lack of clarity in definitions in the academic literature.

ACADEMIC USE OF THE CONCEPT OF 'STRESS'

History of the concept

The term stress first appeared in the index of *Psychological Abstracts* in 1944 (Lazarus and Folkman, 1984). Some writers (e.g. Pollock, 1988) argue that use of the term as we know it is relatively recent. She suggests that although it was used to some extent throughout the 19th century and was loosely associated with ill health, it is only in the last few decades that it has really become an established term. Newton (1995), however, disagrees that the term is of recent origin, having found definitions of stress in the *Oxford English Dictionary* which are very close to our present understanding of the term dating back to the 16th and 17th century. Nevertheless, there seems to be a general consensus that popularity of the concept gained ground from the Second World War onwards (Kugelmann, 1992; Newton, 1995).

Most attribute the popularisation of the stress concept to Hans Selye who has been a prolific writer on the topic of stress over the last 50 years (see Newton, 1995, for a detailed discussion on the historical development of the concept). Selye's background as a biologist led him to view stress in physiological terms as the non-specific response of the body to any demand made upon it (Selye, 1993). By this he meant that there is a common response to different types of stressors, and he named this set of responses the general adaptation syndrome (GAS). The term non-specific refers to the fact that a wide variety of demands or stressors, including positive factors such as novel events, bring forth a common response. He identified three stages in the GAS each associated with changes in nervous and endocrine functioning: the alarm reaction, the stage of resistance and the stage of exhaustion.

Selye described the demands that bring forth the stress response as stressors, the implication being that something is a stressor if it brings forth the stress response (Selye, 1993). Such definitions have been criticised as circular (Lazarus and Folkman, 1984). The notion of specificity has also been challenged (Hinkle, 1973; Mason, 1975). Hinkle suggests that detailed responses may in fact be highly specific. To the extent that there is a general adaptive response he suggests that it is difficult to imagine a state of stress which is different from any other state of being alive, since all normal activities require metabolic activity and adaptation.

To add to the confusion Selye himself has since stated that his use of the term 'stress' to apply to the response alone was due to the fact that his English was not sufficiently good to distinguish between the word 'stress' and 'strain' (Selye, 1976). While the physiological responses to stress are now understood to be considerably more complex than Selye suggested, his work has been extremely influential in promoting the current popularity of the concept.

More recent definitions

Gradually, the growth of the study of psychology has led to a proliferation of definitions which has not necessarily helped to clarify the meaning of the term. Over 20 years ago Kasl (1978) listed a range of conceptualisations, from the highly specific to the extremely general, encompassing both stimulus and response. For example, stress was sometimes conceptualised in terms of environmental conditions which were considered stressful (Landy and Trumbo, 1976), or in terms of 'frustration or threat' (Bonner, 1967) or more advanced conceptualisations incorporating the stimuli and response and the relationship between the two. Here Kasl cites the popular definition by McGrath (1976) who suggested that stress was 'a (perceived) substantial imbalance between demand and response capability, under conditions where failure to meet demand has important (perceived) consequences' (p. 20). This diversity of conceptualisations has persisted over the years. Jex, Beehr and Roberts (1992) searched issues of six major journals in organisational behaviour from 1985 to 1989. Each article in which the word 'stress' or 'stressful' appeared was assigned to one of four categories. Of 51 articles, 41% used the word to refer to stimulus conditions, 22% to responses, 25% implied both stimulus and response conditions and the remaining 14% were unclear.

Whether the definition of stress relates to the stimulus or to the response, the stimulus–response (S-R) approach dominates much stress research, including occupational stress research. Research in the occupational field typically seeks to relate external environmental factors (such as workload) to outcome measures (such as anxiety). Often this involves little or no consideration of the process, beyond the inclusion of variables such as the availability of social support which may moderate the stressor–strain relationship (see Chapter 2). However, in recent years there have been moves towards a more detailed consideration of the nature of the processes involved. For example, Lazarus and Folkman (1984) define stress as 'a particular relationship between the person and the environment that is appraised by the person as taxing or exceeding his or her resources and endangering his or her well-being' (p. 19). This draws attention to the processes whereby people appraise their environment as stressful and away from the assessment of the nature of environmental stressors. This approach is known as the transactional approach. Differences between the traditional and transactional approaches and their implications for interventions will be discussed further in the next two chapters.

Some writers even disagree with the idea that there is disagreement about the concept of stress. For example, Cox (1993) criticises the 'unfortunate but popular misconception that there is little consensus on the definitions of stress as a scientific concept or, worse, that stress is in some way undefinable and unmeasurable' (p. 8). However, the definition he offers suggests that the goal of a clear conceptualisation remains as elusive as ever. He states that 'stress can be defined as a psychological state which is part of and reflects a wider process of interaction between individuals and their work environment' (Cox, 1993, p. 29).

The term 'stress' is so vague in definition that it has been suggested that perhaps the most useful approach to stress would be to regard it not as a variable but as a 'rubric consisting of many variables and processes' (Lazarus and Folkman, 1984, p. 12). They further suggest that researchers should adopt a systematic theoretical framework encompassing relevant antecedents, processes and outcomes. One such framework is Lazarus and Folkman's transactional theory which is discussed further in the next chapter. However, within this all-encompassing approach to stress would also fall a wide range of other theories and studies, each of which looks at relationships between objective and/or perceived environmental factors and one or more of a wide range of physiological and psychological outcomes and variables that moderate those relationships. This brings a wide range of studies within the aegis of this book, many, perhaps most, of which might not explicitly refer to the concept of stress or employ any measure of perceived stress.

HOW PREVALENT IS STRESS? IS IT INCREASING?

There is a commonly held view, prevalent not just in newspapers and magazines but supported by some academics and by official reports that, despite the relative prosperity and good health experienced in the Western world, stress has increased throughout this century and currently continues to increase. Cary Cooper (one of the most vociferous and prolific stress researchers of the last decade) sums up this view in a radio discussion programme:

> Stress is endemic to the human condition. We've had it this century and we've had it centuries before. But what . . . is unique (now) is, we no longer have the extended family. We no longer have a sense of community. We are a highly mobile society, so the natural therapists in our society – the extended family, the neighbours, the friends, the people around you – we no longer can turn to. . . . In the 1990s we have a unique problem as well. The 1980s had stress but it was self-imposed stress – individuals trying to achieve during the enterprise culture. During the 1990s we have imposed stress. We have massive downsizing of companies in the public and private sector, we have heavier workloads on a reduced number of people. We have the reduced number of people feeling extreme job insecurity and at the same time as this is happening we have more women entering the workforce so we have the changing nature of the roles between men and women. When you stir that pot you end up with stress related illness. (BBC Radio 4, *All in the Mind*, September 1995)

Similar ideas are also commonly advanced in self-help books. For example, Livingston Booth (1985) atttributes an increase in stress to such factors as people being removed from their roots and traditional means of family support, and to the speed and pace of change. Even those who recognise the undoubted stressors of earlier ages inevitably emphasise the negative aspects of modern life (Jones, 1997). It is common for an increase in stress to be attributed to the pace of modern living (e.g. see Pollock, 1988).

However, given the high levels of mortality and morbidity in many non-industrialised societies, it is very hard to see any basis for the claim that such a lifestyle is any less stressful (Pollock, 1988). Averill (1989) highlights improvements in life expectancy over the last few hundred years. He suggests that, looking at factors such as threat to life, rapid social change and economic fluctuations, it is hard to find historical periods less stressful than the present. Cooper, nevertheless, conjures up an image of a golden era when life was simple and stress free. In fact, it is not possible to resolve these conflicting views. The measurement of stress is very complex and trying to accurately compare different historical eras is probably not a meaningful exercise at all.

Pollock (1988) describes an unusual study that tried to investigate perceptions of stress. In interviews with people who had moved from poor and overcrowded terraces to modern spacious estates, those surveyed did indeed talk about life in the terraces with nostalgia and typically thought there was more stress in the world today.

> Life was felt to be conducted at a quicker, noisier, more pressurised intensity than formerly. . . . Nowadays, it was commonly said, nobody had time for other people. (p. 383)

The study participants often associated improved living standards with 'a fragmentation of social relationships and a breakdown of community feeling (p. 383). However, asked if they preferred the present way of life or the previous life on the terraces, Pollock reports:

> Almost everyone said they preferred the estates, and the way things are now to the past. Similarly, people rarely maintained the close family connections that had apparently been a feature of their youth. Once again, however, the majority preferred their present arrangements, as if, given the chance to be independent of family and neighbours, most people were glad enough to take it. (p. 383)

Since the awareness of stress is a fairly recent phenomenon, it is perhaps not surprising that we cannot conclusively demonstrate whether the move from small close knit communities and the decline of extended family networks has led to any increase in stress. It should perhaps be easier to demonstrate trends in stress incidence over the last 20 years or so, yet this is still problematic. Estimates of the incidence of stress often focus specifically on work stress and reports of the effect it has on productivity and absenteeism can be found frequently in both the media and in academic articles. However, given that there is such a wide range of meanings of the term 'stress' in use, we cannot give much credence to claims of increases in stress unless we know that specific and measurable variables are used. For example, how are we to interpret statements such as 'At least 40 million working days are lost each year to nervous or other ailments associated with or exacerbated by stress' (Lee and Reason, 1988).

Serious attempts to measure work-related disease show just how difficult it can be to assess the extent of stress related illness. For example, in a recent study of self-reported work related illness (HSE, 1998) large numbers of respondents said that they had diseases caused or made worse by stress. However, it was suggested that the recent increase in illness attributed to stress may be due in part to the raised awareness of stress over the past few years. In the HSE report therefore stress was considered a legitimate cause only if there was both reasonable scientific evidence that stress could cause the illness reported, and if the individual sufferer was in a position to know whether their particular illness was caused by stress. Hence self-reports of heart disease caused by stress were not taken as a reliable indicator of the extent of work related heart disease. To properly assess the contribution of workplace factors to such illnesses as heart disease, large scale longitudinal studies are needed, using both well-defined predictors (e.g. clearly specified measures of workload) and data on illness outcomes. It is perhaps even more difficult to assess the extent to which stress at work is related to minor illnesses such as colds or flu. Absenteeism records may be inaccurate or non-existent and the causes of short-term absenteeism (where medical certificates are not required) are inevitably highly dependent upon people's self-reports. These may be influenced by changing beliefs about disease causation, media coverage given to such issues as work stress or even by changing views about what constitutes an acceptable excuse for a day off. Thus it is clearly very difficult to assess the effects of stress at work. If we try to envisage a study which might quantify the extent of the problem of stress beyond the workplace the problem becomes much greater. Here the number and variety of potential stressors are much greater and we lack even such unreliable indicators as absenteeism.

However, there is some evidence that people perceive themselves to be under ever increasing levels of stress, particularly in the workplace, in recent years. Workplace surveys typically reveal reports of increased perceptions of stress. For example, managers reported increasing workload over a one-year period (Charlesworth, 1996) and workplace representatives claimed their employees have increased stress compared with five years ago (MSF, 1997). A large UK survey (Buck et al., 1994) found decreasing psychological well-being (measured by a self-report scale) over a one-year period from 1991 to 1992. Concerns have also been expressed over the poor levels of well-being amongst occupational samples compared to community samples (Jenkins, 1985), though a follow-up study in the civil service found levels remained constant in this sample over a seven-year period (Jenkins et al., 1996). Studies using a popular measure of psychiatric well-being (the General Health Questionnaire, see Chapter 2) at different periods of time in similar occupational groups have tended to report higher levels of symptoms in

9

the more recent studies. Similarly there is evidence that sickness absence due both to cardio-vascular disease and psychiatric disorders is increasing (Cox, 1993) but, as Stansfield *et al.* (1995) suggest, there may be a range of explanations. In the case of psychiatric disorders, there may be a genuine increase or there may simply be increased recognition or reporting of these disorders, or it may simply be that there are now more employment opportunities for those with psychiatric disorders. A further factor that may apply here is an increase in accuracy of the reporting of absenteeism figures in many occupations.

Thus while there is a general acceptance that stress levels are increasing, and data can be found to provide some circumstantial evidence to support this (at least in relation to the last few years), it is surprisingly hard to find strong evidence. Cultural changes, rather than genuine increases in the pressures of life, may lead to our perceiving and reporting greater feelings of stress. Not only is it likely that the growing popularity of the stress phenomenon means there is less stigma associated with admitting to feelings of inability to cope, but it has been suggested that this may have a more fundamental effect in leading us to view and interpret events and emotions in terms of an increasing perception that life is stressful (Pollock, 1988). The notion that the study of stress has been partly responsible for shaping the phenomenon it sought to observe is examined in more detail in the next section.

IS STRESS A PRODUCT OF CULTURAL EXPECTATIONS?

Pollock (1988) argues that the now common perception that people have of stress as 'an integral part of their daily lives', is due to the efforts of social scientists who have been spectacularly successful in popularising stress theories. She suggests that:

> While distress of various kinds is assuredly an integral part of the 'human condition', why should it necessarily be considered pathogenic, rather than, for example, as has been the case elsewhere, an act of God, a spur to intense creative activity, a necessary test of moral fibre, or even simply as the norm? (p. 381)

She goes so far as to suggest

> that 'stress' is not something naturally occurring in the world, but a manufactured concept which has by now become a 'social fact' (p. 390)

This is perhaps an extreme view. It seems hard to believe that the concept would have so captured the public imagination were it not something that they could easily relate to and recognise. Newton (1995) takes a more moderate view, disagreeing with the notion that 'stress' is the invention of social scientists and suggesting rather that 'social scientists feed off and feed into the existing social landscape' (p. 50). This has been described as the 'double hermeneutic', whereby through the publication of work on stress, social scientists encourage the popular adoption of the concept and as a result alter the phenomenon they set out to study

10

(Barley and Knight, 1992; Giddens, 1984). Averill (1989) suggests slightly different cultural influences. He argues that it is the professionalisation of stress treatments (including the growth in professional psychology) together with a general view of stress as ennobling which have created an environment where an interest in stress can flourish. He argues that 'Stress has become legitimized. For many people it is now more acceptable to admit to being stressed than it is to deny it' (p. 30).

While psychological researchers may often be aware of these cultural phenomena, they work within theoretical frameworks and use methodologies that cannot easily take account of the cultural context. In a diffuse area of research it is often necessary to limit the focus of research and make some assumptions regarding theoretical issues. However, it is also necessary to step back from time to time and to re-evaluate such assumptions. Barley and Knight have observed that most analysts writing about stress suggest that we need tighter definitions, better specified models, better measurements and better research designs. They suggest that, while all of these may be sensible suggestions, they are based on the assumption that 'stress is primarily a psychophysical phenomenon whose etiology can be adequately explained by theories implicitly modeled on the notion of a functional disease' (p. 6). Such models may be useful at an individual level, but Barley and Knight argue that they cannot explain either why stress has become so salient in modern society or why reports of the experience of stress do not always coincide with the presence of a psychophysiological process. They point out that these arguments for the cultural influences on perceptions of stress are not intended to undermine psychophysical theories, but rather, to supplement them.

However, cultures (and subcultures) within society are very diverse and, to the extent that perceptions of stress may be culturally determined, they are likely to lead to a wide range of different perceptions of the nature of stress. For example, cultural expectations may differ between different occupational groups. Van Maanen and Barley (1984) suggest that the 'stress rhetoric' is likely to be adopted by some professions more than others. They suggest that the strategy of claiming work is stressful is likely to be useful to establish solidarity amongst a professional group and that it may provide a credible basis for claiming benefits such as higher pay. They suggest this strategy is likely to be particularly useful to the semi-professions that are aspiring to establish higher status. This would certainly seem to be consistent with the findings of a large survey in the UK which reports a spread of self-reported incidence of stress, anxiety and depression across occupations (HSE, 1998), teachers and nurses reporting the highest levels.

Briner (1996) suggests that cultural influences may operate at a number of different levels:

- general beliefs in society about the nature of stress;
- stress beliefs which are specific to particular occupations or professions;
- stress beliefs which are specific to a particular organisation.

The notion that people have different cultural understandings in different occupations or even organisations is seldom investigated. However, Meyerson (1994) provides an interesting attempt to examine different organisational perceptions in her study of social workers. This study focused on ambiguity (a common stressor) and burnout (one manifestation of stress) and found that social workers working in hospitals where a medical ideology predominated viewed ambiguity as undesirable and burnout as 'a pathological condition to control, a disease that one caught and tried to cure' (p. 17). Those working in institutions where the social work ideology prevailed viewed ambiguity as normal and to some extent sometimes as a positive factor, and burnout as equally normal, unavoidable and even a healthy response. Meyerson suggests that these differences reflect two different cultural beliefs about control, and a greater willingness in social work to let go of control.

Psychologists, because of their largely individualistic approach, have tended to ignore issues of culture which are traditionally the province of sociologists and anthropologists. Arguably, however, psychologists have been much more successful than sociologists at selling their viewpoint through the media and translating their professional jargon for public consumption. This has had the result that the assumptions underlying their work have seldom been questioned.

IS IT A USEFUL CONCEPT? SHOULD IT BE ABOLISHED?

In spite of the fact that the concept of 'stress' has become highly fashionable, some have questioned the usefulness of the construct. For example:

> The 'stress concept' was heuristically valuable in the past, but it is no longer necessary, and it is in some ways hampering in the present. (Hinkle, 1973, p. 31)

> the inclusive label, 'stress', contributes little to an analysis of the mechanisms that may underline or determine the organism's response. In fact, such labelling, which is descriptive rather than explanatory, may actually impede conceptual and empirical advances by its implicit assumption of an equivalence of stimuli, fostering the reductionist search for simple one-cause explanation. (Ader, 1981, p. 312)

> I suggest that the term itself has become so vacuous that it represents an obstacle rather than an aid to research, and that further investigation of the relationships which the stress theory attempts to elucidate would get on better without it. (Pollock, 1988, p. 390)

However, vacuous or not, the stress concept has taken a tenacious hold on our society and is likely to be around for some time to come. Part of its appeal may be its versatility in that the various different definitions and approaches can be adopted to locate the source of physical and psychological problems wherever is most convenient. Trade unions can blame work conditions, employers may look to individual inability to cope. Whether the critics are correct and the concept has outlived its useful life, and whether any alternative more useful conceptualisation can be offered is an issue to which we will return later in the book. An appraisal of the methodological approaches and research progress to date using current conceptualisations and theories will leave readers in a better position to judge for themselves whether the concept has helped, hindered, or indeed been largely irrelevant to progressing knowledge.

PSYCHOLOGICAL RESEARCH ON STRESS

Growth in research interest

In line with the increased popular interest in stress, there has been a rapid growth in research activity. The increase in the number of articles on the topic that can be found in the *Psychological Abstracts* over the last 25 years is shown in Figure 1.1. This is based only on articles that appear in academic journals in the psychology area which use the word 'stress' in the abstract. These are likely to be just a fraction of the total publications on the topic. The indications are that research in stress may be past its peak but still remains at high levels.

Figure 1.1   Number of articles in *Psychological Abstracts* featuring the keyword 'stress' in the title.

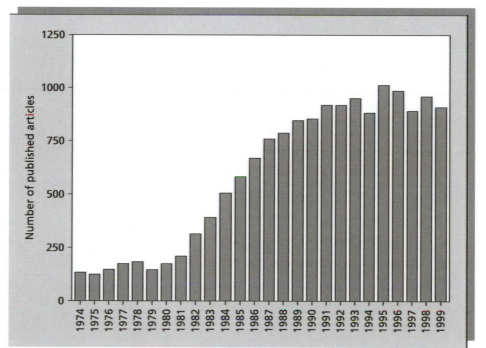

Introducing psychological approaches

As might be expected from the diversity of potentially stressful events and reactions, stress researchers have tackled the issues using a wide range of approaches, from examining the effects of the most minor of short term stressors to that of major life events such as bereavement. An important focus for occupational psychologists has been stress in the workplace and how to alleviate it, while researchers in the medical field have adopted the concept of stress as a basis for examining the role of psychological factors in disease causation and progression. Within this book 'stress' is regarded as an umbrella term or rubric (as suggested by Lazarus and Folkman, 1984) which encompasses a wide range of research into the effects of various psychosocial and environmental factors on physical and mental well-being. This means that the term 'stress' is used to include a range of environmental stimuli or 'stressors', stress responses and other factors that influence the relationship between the two (including personality factors). The concept of 'stress' itself is not a sufficiently precise variable to allow reliable measurement. Thus, research covered within this book uses a large number of different variables which can be more clearly conceptualised and measured than 'stress'. Some of the most important of these variables are shown in Box 1.1.

Some of the research in this book has undoubtedly been conducted by researchers who would not consider themselves to be 'stress researchers' as such and who would

Box 1.1   Some typical variables included within the stress rubric.

Stressors	Intervening variables	Strains
Major life events, e.g.	Personality	Psychological effects
• Marriage	• Type A	• Psychological well-being
• Bereavement	• Locus of control	• Anxiety/depression
• Marital breakdown	• Pessimism/optimism	• Moods
• Illness	• Negative affect	• Job satisfaction
Daily hassles	Coping styles and strategies	Physiological functioning
• Arguments	• Emotion-focused	• Heartbeat
• Car breakdowns	• Problem-focused	• Blood pressure
Chronic stressors	Environmental factors	• Adrenaline secretions
• Workload	• Social support	Disease
• Role	• Control	• Coronary heart disease
Ambiguity/conflict		• Colds and flu
• Poor housing		Behaviour
Laboratory stressors		• Work performance
• Mental arithmetic tasks		• Smoking /drinking

not use the term 'stress' in the course of their work. Nonetheless, their work can be considered within the scope of this concept.

It is the case that most of the research presented in this book comes from a psychological (and sometimes medical) tradition of empirical research. This takes a predominantly positivistic approach focusing on a relatively circumscribed set of factors in the person's immediate environment, sometimes taking into account the individual differences in, for example, personality or coping. Much of the research on stress has focused on identifying the types of phenomena that are related to a range of physical and psychological outcomes. These may be major or minor and may be short term or long term (chronic). Further efforts are devoted to identifying intervening variables that lead some people to respond more negatively to such stressors than others. The type of stressors studied and the methods used are closely linked to the particular theories preferred by the researcher. Most of these approaches do not take into account either the cultural issues or the double hermeneutic effect discussed above. The reader needs to keep in mind the issues discussed in this chapter and to evaluate the extent to which these will have influenced the findings in any particular studies.

CHAPTER 2

APPROACHES TO STUDYING STRESS

Fiona Jones and Gail Kinman

> This chapter provides an introduction to some of the more popular theoretical approaches and methodologies used in stress research. These include looking at major life events or daily hassles, studying stress by the use of retrospective questionnaires or by experimental methods. Some of the conceptual and methodological problems associated with these are discussed. The chapter aims to provide the background frameworks needed to help the reader evaluate the stress literature encountered in this book and when consulting original sources.

A newcomer to stress research might imagine there is nothing very complicated about measuring stress. Stress researchers are frequently contacted by students and practising psychologists wanting a simple measure of stress in the workplace or in the family and expecting to receive a short questionnaire that will solve their problem. This chapter will clarify why there is no such easy solution, and will introduce to you some of the available options.

Chapter 1 outlined the wide range of variables that are encompassed within the stress concept. The chapter demonstrated the need to measure environmental factors (stressors), intervening variables and outcomes (strains). However, this is by no means straightforward. When considering the thorny issue of how to measure stressors, for example, it may not seem unreasonable simply to ask people to rate how stressful they regard particular events or situations or how stressed they feel themselves to be. Box 2.1 discusses why this might not be the good idea it first appears to be.

In fact, because of the considerations outlined in Box 2.1, Jex, Beehr and Roberts (1992) recommend that the word 'stress' be avoided in all measures of stress! However, this leaves the

Box 2.1   Is it meaningful to ask people how stressful an experience is?

Perhaps an obvious way to measure stress is simply to ask people by giving them items such as 'To what extent is your job stressful?' or 'To what extent does your life away from work cause you stress?' However, just as there are many different definitions of stress, so people are likely to use such items in many different ways. For example, in the context of work, one person may rate their job as stressful when they mean that they are merely under pressure whereas another may not even start to rate pressure as 'stress' until it is starting to cause them difficulties. Equally some may rate a job as stressful on the basis of how they perceive the objective nature of the job (the stimulus); others will only concern themselves with how it makes them feel (the response). Thus it is hard for a researcher to interpret the meaning of such ratings (Jex, Beehr and Roberts, 1992).

In addition to highlighting this difficulty with the use of stress measures, Jex *et al.* (1992) suggest there are other, more technical, difficulties. In a study which aimed to examine the implications of such items, they used measures asking people to rate various stressors (e.g. workload, or conflict), measures of psychological strain (e.g. anxiety or depression) and items which contained the word 'stress' such as the one given above. The study found that the items rating stress correlated with both stressors and strains but the strongest correlations were with the anxiety measure. This suggests that the way in which people rated the 'stressful' items had more in common with the way they rated anxiety than it did with the way they rated the more objective measures of job features. Thus, it is likely that rating work as stressful may be a function of your own anxiety at least as much as, if not more than, your perception of the job's features. In other words using such items will lead to confounding of measures. Worse still, it is not unknown to find that a researcher has measured stressors using items asking people to rate job features on the extent of stressfulness and then used a strain measure which includes items asking how 'stressed' people feel. As Jex *et al.* point out, this leads to the worst confounding of all.

researcher with a complex problem of how else to measure stressors. How to resolve this, and the kind of measures and methodologies to use, is a key focus of this chapter. To start to tackle this issue it is necessary first to consider some of the theoretical frameworks and assumptions that underlie stress measurement.

WHAT THEORY? WHAT MEASUREMENT?

Scientists aim to develop theories which are simple, true and have a high degree of explanatory power (Popper, 1959). The notion of developing and testing theory is fundamental to the scientific method. However, stress research is an area where few have let the absence of good theory dampen their enthusiasm to collect data! Nevertheless, it is often the case that, while the theoretical basis of research is seldom made explicit, certain theoretical assumptions can be identified as under-pinning the research.

Early approaches used a simple *input–output* (*or stimulus–response*) approach, in which researchers looked at the extent to which major life events or features of work design predict an outcome such as cancer or cardiovascular disease. While such an approach is simplistic and ignores individual variation in response, it may be justified where, for example, researchers are looking at general trends such as overall effects of working long hours on health. However, in general such research has produced inconclusive results and therefore researchers have become increas-ingly interested in studying the specific conditions under which stressors lead to strain. Such approaches have included looking at how factors in the individual (e.g. personality, see Chapter 6) or the environment (e.g. the availability of social support, see Chapter 8) interact to determine the level of ill effects experienced. A variety of theoretical approaches have been developed to suggest ways in which such factors interact with stressors. An example of this kind of *interactional approach* is Cohen and Wills (1985) 'stress buffering hypothesis' which suggests that social support 'buffers' the effects of stressors.

Typically research using such interactional approaches uses three types of measures:

- *Measures of environmental events or situations* often referred to as stressors (or sometimes 'antecedents'), e.g. the number of life events one has experienced or the extent of one's workload.
- *Measures of intervening variables* such as individual difference, e.g. personality traits or the different coping strategies people use to combat stress.
- *Measures of strain outcomes* such as anxiety or physical symptoms.

In general, it has been recommended (e.g. Kasl, 1978) that all three types of vari-able are assessed in ways which are independent from each other. This means that there needs to be as little overlap in the content of the items used to measure the different variables as possible (thus avoiding the problems described in Box 2.1). He further suggests that measures should be as objective as possible, even where, as is often the case, self-report measures of stressors are used. This means that people are asked to report, for example, whether or not they have experienced certain life stressors, such as divorce, or whether they experience overload at work. They are not asked for any cognitive evaluation of the stressor (such as how intense or how stressful was the experience). Indeed some researchers, e.g. Fletcher (1991), consider that it is not necessary for an individual to perceive a stressor as unpleasant or stressful for it to have a negative effect.

Lazarus and colleagues have criticised this approach and argued that items cannot be conceptualised as stressors independently of a person's reaction to them

(Lazarus *et al.*, 1985). Thus moving house may be a stressor for some people but not for others. Whether or not it is a stressor is therefore not a feature of the environment *per se* but of the environment as appraised by the individual. Thus he suggests you cannot separate the environment from the individual character-istics of the person exposed to the environment without destroying the concept of stress. Lazarus has proposed the *transactional theory* which leads to a rather dif-ferent approach to measurement than that described above. As we have seen in Chapter 1, Lazarus and Folkman (1984) define stress as 'a relationship between the person and the environment that is appraised by the person as taxing or exceed-ing his or her resources and endangering his or her well-being'. The emphasis here is shifted from the relationship between objective stressors and strains (perhaps mediated by other variables) to the process whereby an individual appraises a situation as stressful:

> Once a person has appraised a transaction as stressful, coping processes are brought into play to manage the troubled person–environment relationship, and these processes influence the person's subsequent appraisal and hence the kind and intensity of the stress reaction. (Lazarus, 1990, p. 3)

Thus, Lazarus views stress as a complex, multivariate process. This poses great difficulties as we now have an even larger number of potential influences to take into account, including the environment, personality factors, the way people appraise the environment, the ways in which they cope and the ways in which all these change over time. While this approach has been very popular and has an intuitive appeal, it also is very complex. The advantages and disadvantages are further discussed in the section on daily hassles below and in Chapter 7 on coping.

Which of these types of theoretical approach researchers use may in the end depend on the focus of their theoretical interest or on the applied purpose of the research. The stimulus–response and interactional approaches, reducing the focus of interest to an input (or stressor) and an output (strain), essentially examines the *structure* of the relationships (with or without taking individual differences into account). So, for example, from an employment policy-making point of view, whether relocating employees to a new area causes poor health outcomes for large num-bers of people may be an important question to answer regardless of how people appraise the stressor. Looking at intervening variables such as social support, and whether those with more support cope better, may give broad insights into how to direct interventions. In contrast Lazarus' transactional approach sees stress as a shifting *process* which changes over time and is dependent on how individuals appraise the stressors and the coping strategies they use (Lazarus and Folkman, 1984). Thus this approach would take a different type of strategy that might involve repeated measures to find out patterns of stress and coping over time as people adjust to relocation. Such results might lead to more detailed understanding of individual psychological functioning of less immediate practical use to the employer formulating policies but may be more useful to a counsellor seeking to provide individual help and support to those undergoing a move.

Apart from the decision about the theoretical perspective, a number of other questions need to be considered when measuring stress. What kind of environmental factors are of interest? Are they major or minor, acute or chronic or intermittent? What kind of impacts might they have? Are the relationships immediate or long term? The number of potential stressors and strains and their temporal relationships are huge. The methodologies used to measure whether minor stressors, such as mental arithmetic tasks, provoke rapid changes in blood pressure, will be different to those used to investigate whether a heavy workload is related to raised levels of absenteeism. Different again will be those used to investigate what types of job lead to increased coronary heart disease. In the next section some of the major approaches to measuring stressors, strains and intervening variables will be considered.

CONCEPTUALISING AND MEASURING STRESSORS

Life events approach

This approach is one of the first well-established approaches to conceptualising stressors. The idea of a change being stressful and requiring adaptation is central to the approach. Hence the construct of a 'life event' has been defined as:

> a discrete change in the subject's social and personal environment. The event should represent a change, rather than a persistent state, and it should be an external verifiable change, rather than an internal psychological one.
> (Paykel and Rao, 1984, p. 73)

The work of Holmes and Rahe has been particularly influential in this area. In 1967 they published a major paper presenting their Social Readjustment Rating Scale (SRRS) which established a self-report measure of life events. They collected a list of 43 events from clinical experience and then asked 394 people to rate them on the degree of 'social readjustment' they required. This meant taking into account the intensity and the length of time taken to adjust by the average person, regardless of the desirability of the event. Participants were told marriage had an arbitrary value of 500 and they were asked to assign values based on comparing the adjustment required for each life event with that of marriage. The mean across the sample was then divided by 10 to produce the life change unit (LCU) score. See Box 2.2. To calculate an individual's score on this measure they should simply tick each event they have experienced in the last year on the following list and add together the number of life change units associated with each.

An LCU of over 150 in one year was defined as a life crisis (Holmes and Masuda, 1974), 150–199 being mild crisis, 200–299 a moderate crisis and over 300 a major crisis. An early retrospective study reported by Holmes and Masuda (1974) found that a minor crisis in the preceding year was associated with health change for

Box 2.2   Social readjustment rating scale (Holmes and Rahe, 1967).

Rank	Life events	LCU score
1	Death of spouse	100
2	Divorce	73
3	Marital separation	65
4	Jail term	63
5	Death of close family member	63
6	Personal illness or injury	53
7	Marriage	50
8	Fired at work	47
9	Marital reconciliation	45
10	Retirement	45
11	Change in health of a family member	44
12	Pregnancy	40
13	Sex difficulties	39
14	Gain of a new family member	39
15	Business readjustment	39
16	Change in financial state	38
17	Death of a close friend	37
18	Change to a different line of work	36
19	Change in number of arguments with spouse	35
20	Mortgage over $10,000	31
21	Foreclosure of mortgage or loan	30
22	Change in responsibilities at work	29
23	Son or daughter leaving home	29
24	Trouble with in-laws	29
25	Outstanding personal achievement	28
26	Wife begin or stop work	26
27	Begin or end school	26
28	Change in living conditions	25
29	Revision of personal habits	24
30	Trouble with boss	23
31	Change in work hours or conditions	20
32	Change in residence	20
33	Change in schools	20
34	Change in recreation	19
35	Change in church activities	19
36	Change in social activities	18
37	Mortgage or loan less than $10,000	17
38	Change in sleeping habits	16
39	Change in number of family get-togethers	15
40	Change in eating habits	15
41	Vacation	13
42	Christmas	12
43	Minor violations of the law	11

Reprinted from *Journal of Psychosomatic Research*, Vol II, p. 216, Holmes *et al.*, 'Social readjustment rating scale', 1967, with permission from Reed Elsevier Science.

37%, a moderate crisis was associated with health change for 51%, but for major crises the figure was 79%. Retrospective studies in the 1970s by Rahe and colleagues showed positive relationships between life changes and sudden cardiac death (Rahe and Lind, 1971) and myocardial infarction (Rahe and Paasikivi, 1971; Theorell and Rahe, 1971). However, prospective studies have had more mixed results. Further studies using these measures are discussed in Chapter 4.

This approach generated a huge amount of research and many publications over the last 30 years. The questionnaire or similar adaptations are still found in many self-help publications and magazines. It represented a significant leap forward in researchers' ability to measure life events and assess their impacts. However, inevitably the approach has also generated a great deal of criticism. For example:

- *It does not discriminate between positive and negative events.* The theory suggests that *any* change has the potential to damage health because it involves readjustment (regardless of whether it is positive or negative). However, many now argue that it is the *quality* of the event that is crucial and that it is changes which are 'undesired, unscheduled, non-normative and uncontrolled which are most harmful' (Pearlin, 1989).
- *It ignores chronic or recurrent conditions.* Lazarus (1990) points out that much stress may be associated with more minor stressors (or 'daily hassles') not just major events.
- *It ignores individual differences.* It ignores the different significance of life events to people with varying priorities, motivations and coping styles (Lazarus, 1990). Furthermore events which require a similar response to the check-list may be highly variable. For example, the 'death of a close friend' may refer to someone who is seen every day or to a childhood friend who has not been seen for 20 years (Dohrenwend *et al.*, 1990).
- *Events may be symptoms of being ill and not causes.* Dohrenwend *et al.* (1974, 1993) suggest that many life event items such as 'changes in sleeping patterns' may be *symptoms* of illness rather than antecedents.
- *Reliability and validity of reports.* When asked about events in the past year people may simply not remember very accurately. Not surprisingly, therefore, the reliability and validity of retrospective reports of life events has been questioned (that is, do they measure consistently if repeated after a time interval and do they actually measure what they are intended to measure?). Estimates of test–retest reliability do vary widely depending on the time interval between administrations of the questionnaire (Rahe, 1974). Perhaps more importantly, there are concerns that retrospective reports may not be valid. For example, Brown (1974) suggests that people may feel the need to find explanation for their illnesses, leading them to report more life events than those who have no illness. He cites an early study (Polani *et al.*, 1960)

suggesting the importance of psychological factors in causation of Down's syndrome (a hypothesis now long rejected). In this study parents of Down's syndrome children reported more 'shocks' during pregnancy than controls (22% versus 6%) and that more occurred in early pregnancy. He suggests that the inflation of reports was a result of people searching for explanations for the disorder.

* *Relationships may be spurious.* Brown (1974) suggests that the relationship between life events and illness may result from a third variable such as anxiety. Thus, those with high levels of anxiety may be particularly liable to report life events and be particularly prone to illness (see Chapter 4).

A major issue for debate surrounds whether it is the objective presence of life events that should be the focus of interest or the person's appraisal of them as being stressful. While in recent years, Lazarus (see above) has been the most vociferous critic of methodologies which seek to rule out the effect of appraisal, early life events researchers also debated these issues. As a result adaptations to life event measures have been made which ask individuals to rate events for impact (Sarason, Johnson and Siegel, 1978). However, Dohrenwend and Dohrenwend (1974) suggest that while taking into account the extent to which individuals perceive events as upsetting may increase the extent to which events predict illness, this may not demonstrate just the effect of the event, but also the effect of a particular type of perceptual response.

In recent years, the debate has continued (Lazarus, 1990; Brown, 1990). Brown suggests that interviews using his Life Events and Difficulties schedule (LEDS) offer a position midway between Lazarus and colleagues' (1985) plea for the inclusion of appraisal and Dohrenwend and colleagues' (1984) request for measures which are independent and uncontaminated by the psychological response. Brown's approach achieves this by using semi-structured interviews to get individuals to describe life events. Each event is then rated taking into account the person's situation and history but using normative ratings of the likely appraisal of a typical person in those circumstances rather than the actual appraisal of the individual in question. Studies using this have shown large associations between a range of psychiatric and physical conditions (Brown and Harris, 1989). The measure seems to be an improvement on check-list approaches, however, by incorporating contextual factors, it still has the disadvantage that it is difficult to disentangle the effects of the actual event and other personal variables (Dohrenwend *et al.*, 1993).

Daily hassles – the transactional approach

Overall, Lazarus and colleagues have criticised life events research on the grounds of its limited ability to predict illness and because it said nothing about the processes by which life events may impact on health. An attempt to address these issues, coupled with a view that the comparatively minor stresses and pleasures of everyday

24

life were important for health led to the development of the 'daily hassles and uplifts' approach. Hassles are the 'irritating, frustrating, distressing demands that to some degree characterise everyday transactions with the environment' (Kanner et al., 1981, p. 3). Thus they may include being stuck in a traffic jam or having an argument, for example. 'Uplifts' are the opposite, that is the minor positive experiences of daily life. While hassles are clearly different from major life events, it is certainly the case that a major life event such as a divorce may increase the likelihood of minor hassles. Kanner et al. therefore suggest that they may mediate the life event–health relationships (that is, life events may lead to minor disruptions in routines and coping processes which then lead to poor health). However, other hassles may be a function of personal style or an individual's environment and therefore exist regardless of major life events. Kanner's measure goes beyond simply asking about the existence of such hassles by asking people to appraise the severity and frequency of each. More recently a shorter measure, 'The hassles and uplifts scale' (DeLongis et al., 1982) lists variables such as 'your children', 'your fellow workers', 'your health' and, like the earlier measure, asks people to rate both the *severity* and *frequency* of stressors associated with each. These two ratings can be combined to give a measure of intensity.

It has been suggested that hassles are a more useful measure than life events and are more closely related to disease (See Box 2.3).

DeLongis et al. (1982) suggested that hassles will have a stronger relationship with health outcomes than major life events because they are 'proximal' measures whereas life events are 'distal'. The proximal–distal dimension refers to the extent to which various environments have a conceptual closeness to the person's experience and psychological response. The country you live in is a distal environment, the room you are in at this moment is proximal. DeLongis et al. (1982) suggested that, from a stress perspective, 'a proximal environment consists of person–environment transactions that the person appraises as harmful, threatening or challenging' (p. 121). Thus, measures of life events tend to be more distal because they frequently only measure the existence of the event and not its significance, whereas hassles have been measured in ways that include perceptions of the amount of distress associated.

Strangely, for a measure generally referred to as assessing *daily* hassles, people are often asked to rate hassles retrospectively for the past month. Lazarus (1990) suggests that such aggregated scales are justified when looking at long-term health outcomes. Where shorter-term outcomes are the focus then versions of the measure assessing stressors on a daily basis have been used (DeLongis, Folkman and Lazarus, 1988).

An alternative approach which measures stressors every day is the assessment of daily experience (ADE; Stone and Neale, 1984). Here people rate events that have happened that day on dimensions such as desirability, change-stability and meaningfulness. This measure also allows people to write in any other stressors they may experience – thus rare but major events can also be recorded. Such

Box 2.3   Are hassles or life events more predictive of illness?

A number of studies have examined whether daily hassles are more predictive
of illness than are major events. These tend to suggest that hassles are more
predictive of symptoms (e.g. Kanner *et al.*, 1981) (DeLongis *et al.*, 1982).
For example, Delongis *et al.* looked at the relationship between daily hassles
and uplifts and life events with health status and symptoms (measured at the start of
the study and one year later). They found that, while life events in the 10–36
months before the study predicted health status at the end, the measure
of frequency and intensity of hassles accounted for more of the variance. It is
interesting that in this study not only were uplifts found to be not greatly related
to positive health (in fact the frequency of uplifts was related to an increase in
somatic symptoms), but also that uplift frequency was very highly correlated with
hassles frequency (n = 0.66). The two intensity measures were similarly highly
correlated, suggesting that those people who have a lot of hassles also have
many uplifts. The authors suggested that one possible explanation for this may
be a response bias, such that some people tend to endorse a lot of items on any
measure whereas others only endorse a few. This ignores the possibility that
demanding times in a person's life may in fact often be associated with high
rewards as well as hassles, whereas calmer spells may be relatively free of either.

Delongis *et al.*'s study was replicated and expanded by Jandorf *et al.* (1986)
using Stone and Neale's (1982) ADE and measures of symptoms taken daily. The
results were similar, with the daily events predicting more of the variance in
symptoms than the major events. Undesirable daily event scores were, however,
highly correlated over time (0.92) raising the question that they may be measuring
some stable individual difference variable.

measures have been used to look at the ways in which fluctuations in stressors
may precede the onset of colds for example.

Overall, it is generally the case that measures of daily hassles have been found
to be more strongly related to strain outcomes and disease than major life events
(see Chapter 4). However, hassles measures have also been criticised as confounded
with self-report measures of psychological distress.

Chronic stressors

The emphasis in both life events and daily hassles research is biased towards events
(of either a major or minor nature) which are to some extent out of the ordinary.
They may therefore fail to capture the essence of many lifestyles that may be
perceived to be stressful, for example the chronic stress of caring for an elderly
relative. This may include stressors that are always present but may not seem a

particular hassle from day to day, for example, low income or never being able to go out. They may also fail to capture the chronic nature of many work stressors, such as a heavy workload or having a job that allows little control. While there has been a great deal of debate about measurements of life events and hassles, there has been relatively little discussion about how to conceptualise and measure such chronic factors. This may be because some chronic stressors are objectively verifiable states such as unemployment, low income and poor housing. However, such measures may be crude indicators of the actual stressors experienced. In the occupational stress literature, more attention is paid to the measurement of chronic stressors and there are well-established measures of chronic work stressors such as role conflict (Rizzo, House and Lirtzman, 1970) and job control (Jackson *et al.*, 1993) (see Chapter 9).

It should be noted that the distinction between hassles, life events and chronic stressors is by no means always clear-cut. For example, Hahn and Smith (1999) point out that it is not uncommon for the same variable (e.g. illness of a family member) to appear as a hassles item in one study and as a chronic stressor in another.

CONCEPTUALISING AND MEASURING STRAINS

The main emphasis on the above approaches is on conceptualising and measuring stressors. Conceptualisation of the outcomes (commonly referred to as strains) seldom seems to be explicitly discussed in the research literature. However, it tends to be assumed that strains may include all types of physical and mental disorder ranging from minor to major illness and death, trivial mood swings to major psychiatric disorder. They may also include a range of behavioural indices such as work performance or health behaviours such as drinking or smoking. Some examples are discussed below but many more may be found in the literature.

Physical symptoms

The assumption underlying much stress research and widely accepted by popular opinion is that 'stress' causes disease. The relationship between stress and disease is made explicit in many of the frameworks for stressor/strain relationships found in the literature (Cooper and Marshall, 1976; see also Chapter 9). Various indicators relating to disease are used, including self-report measures, physiological indicators or medical diagnosis.

Self-report measures may include simple unvalidated indices of headaches or other symptoms or more complex validated scales such as the Cornell Medical Index (Brodman *et al.*, 1949). However, some researchers cast doubt on the accuracy of such self-reports as there is a tendency for those with high level of neuroticism (or negative affect) to report more symptoms (Costa and McRae, 1987, and see Chapter 6) and those who are optimistic may tend to report fewer symptoms

(O'Brien, Vanegeren and Mumby, 1995). Costa and McRae advise researchers to use objective measures or to measure and control for the effects of neuroticism. (See Chapter 6 for further discussion of the effects of neuroticism.)

Generally, objective physiological measures tend to be regarded as superior to the above measures (Jex and Beehr, 1991). These have included measures of physiological changes believed to be precursors of disease conditions, for example cardiovascular symptoms (blood pressure, serum cholesterol level) and biochemical symptom (catecholamines, cortisol and uric acid) (Fried, Rowland and Ferris, 1984, and see Chapter 3). While such measures seem more objective and rigorous than self-report questionnaires, they still nevertheless have many associated problems. Jex and Beehr (1991) point out that it may be difficult to control a number of factors that affect such measurements. These include stable factors, such as age and genetic tendencies, and transitory factors, such as room temperature or extent of physical exertion before the measurement is taken. Physiological measurements are also often not consistent with people's self-reports, for example, reports of anxiety, taken at the same time. McGrath and Beehr (1990) suggest that this may be because of the different temporal properties of the measurements such that blood tests may reflect reactions to a stressor the previous day, whereas self-reports may be based on anticipation of a future stressor.

While the above measures tap variables related to disease, clearly many studies (such as those looking at major life events) also attempt to tap relationships with actual disease outcomes, ranging from colds to cancer and mortality. These outcomes are considered more in Chapter 4.

Behavioural manifestations

A range of behavioural outcomes are also important in stress research. For researchers interested in disease, health behaviours such as smoking, drinking and exercise are important. Often researchers have little choice but to rely on self-report measures, the reliability of which may be questionable. While researchers have reported reasonable reliability and validity for self-reports for alcohol and drug use (Brown, Kranzler and Delboca, 1992) and for some measures of smoking (Kozlowski and Heatherton, 1990), there are a number of reasons why some people may be prone to misreport health behaviours. They may deliberately lie or at least be inclined to 'be economical with the truth', in order to give a more socially desirable response. They may also demonstrate the well-established phenomenon of optimistic bias (Weinstein, 1983) which leads people to perceive themselves to be relatively less at risk than others and may lead them to over-report health behaviours (O'Brien et al., 1995).

For researchers interested in work stress, the relationship between stressors and work performance is crucial, although other behavioural measures are also likely to be important (e.g. turnover, absenteeism and accidents). It is therefore surprising, as Jex and Beehr (1991), report that 'by far, behavioral reactions to job-related stressors have been the least studied of all outcomes' (p. 337). Furthermore, with the possible exception of some specialised areas (such as the research into stress in pilots and air traffic controllers (e.g. Caldwell, 1995; Raymond and Moser, 1995; Tattersall and Farmer, 1995), there seems little evidence that this has changed in recent years. One reason for this is that self-reports of variables such as performance and absenteeism are likely to be inaccurate. However, more objective organisational indicators may be difficult to obtain. In many cases there may be no accurate performance measures, or even absenteeism records, kept for individual employees. Where they do exist their use is problematic. Most research in companies relies on the use of anonymously completed questionnaires for ethical reasons and to encourage honesty amongst respondents. However, such anonymity ensures that there is no way of checking whether those experiencing high levels of stressors are persistent absentees or poor performers.

Despite these difficulties, some researchers have successfully used supervisor's ratings of performance (e.g. Motowidlo, Packard and Manning, 1986; Guppy and Marsden, 1997), and have found them to be related to other indicators such as job stressors. However, Jex and Beehr (1991) point out that employers may show negative bias in rating the performance of employees who they perceive as showing some negative reactions to the job. Nevertheless, for many jobs, supervisor's ratings may be the best available performance measure. Because of such difficulties the use of simulations and laboratory studies may be particularly useful in this area (Parkes, Styles and Broadbent, 1990; Searle, Bright and Bochner, 1999; and see Chapter 5).

Psychiatric symptoms

In the absence of good behavioural and physiological measures, researchers often fall back on the much easier option of using self-report measures of psychiatric symptoms. In fact measures of anxiety and depression symptoms are so commonly used that it has been suggested that high scores on such measures '. . . have come to be adopted by investigators in this area as *prima facie* evidence of the presence of stress' (Derogatis and Coons, 1993, p. 207).

While these variables are of interest in their own right they may also be used because of the (as yet unproven) assumption that such variables are related to, and precursors of, both diminished performance and physical illness. While some studies look at the major psychiatric disorders as diagnosed by physicians, most rely on a number of self-report measures that have typically been developed to be used clinically as screening instruments. Such measures are validated using clinical samples, and scores can be compared with such samples to assess the number of respondents who have scores that are at a comparable level. Examples of these measures are the General Health Questionnaire (GHQ; Goldberg, 1972), the Crown–Crisp Experiential Index (CCEI; Crown and Crisp, 1979) and Beck's Depression Inventory (BDI; Beck *et al.*, 1961). One of the most commonly used measures, the GHQ, is discussed further in Box 2.4.

Box 2.4   The General Health Questionnaire (GHQ).

The GHQ was originally developed as a self-administered screening test for minor psychiatric disorder in community and medical settings. It is considered reliable and correlates well with clinical assessments (Goldberg and Williams, 1988). It assesses perceptions of general strain, depression, anxiety, somatic symptoms, insomnia, ability to cope and social dysfunction. Items consist of a series of statements each followed by a four-item response scale, e.g. 'Have you recently lost much sleep over worry?' to which the respondent has to endorse one of the following, 'not at all', 'no more than usual', 'rather more than usual' or 'much more than usual'. High scores indicate a greater likelihood of clinical disorder and scores above a certain threshold level are often designated 'cases'.

Several versions of the GHQ are available (consisting of 60, 30, 28 or 12 items). While it is most commonly used to produce a single score, the longer versions can be used to measure a range of different dimensions including anxiety and depression. Since the early 1980s, the 12-item version (GHQ-12) has been widely used in the workplace as a measure of strain in response to occupational stressors (Banks et al., 1980) and a considerable body of norms has accumulated for various occupations (see Mullarkey et al., 1999). Examples of studies that have used the GHQ to measure work stress can be found in Chapter 9. The GHQ is also commonly used in both large-scale epidemiological research such as the Whitehall Studies (e.g. Stansfeld and Marmot, 1992) and in longitudinal surveys such as the British Household Panel Survey.

Although the GHQ is a popular measure of psychological ill health the validity of the instrument in assessing reactions to stressors is potentially problematic in a number of ways. In particular, it is unclear whether it is sensitive to chronic and/or acute psycho-social stressors. For example, in asking whether over the past few weeks the person has been more or less unhappy than usual, the measure appears to be assessing a relatively transient state. If an individual had been feeling unhappy for several months or years then they may well say they are no more than usually unhappy – the same response as a perfectly happy individual. As a result the GHQ may miss cases of a more chronic nature which might, in fact, have become the individual's 'normal' state.

Paradoxically, however, there is also evidence that it might in fact be assessing a 'trait' (a relatively stable personality characteristic). For example, Deary et al. (1996) reports high correlations between measurements of trait anxiety and GHQ scores. Although a number of studies link major organisational change with higher levels of psychological ill health (e.g. Ferrie et al., 1998), Moyle (1995a) found that GHQ-12 scores were relatively stable over a period of 12 months, and failed to register affective reactions to business process re-engineering. Whilst these workers might have been under chronic pressure, one would expect some change in psychological health under such conditions. These results suggest that the instrument might merely measure a tendency towards negative affectivity, which challenges its usefulness as a true measure of transient strain.

Despite such disadvantages, the GHQ is very popular – particularly in occupational stress research. Occupational studies that use the General Health Questionnaire as a measure of strain arising from work-related stressors often report significantly higher 'caseness' rates than community samples (e.g. Jenkins et al., 1996). 'Caseness' rates amongst human service professionals such as nursing and social services staff have been found to be particularly high (Tyler and Cushway, 1995; Caughey, 1996).

One limitation of such self-report measures is that they tend to be highly transparent to the respondent and easy to fake. For example, Furnham and Henderson (1983) randomly assigned participants to three conditions; the first two groups were instructed to fill in the GHQ giving the impression that they were: (a) psychologically ill, and (b) very well. The third condition was a control group where participants were asked to complete the questionnaire as honestly as possible. Participants had no difficulty in faking a 'healthy' or an 'unhealthy' response. This may have implications when such measures are used in circumstances where participants may be motivated to appear healthy (e.g. in studies of work stress).

The risk of particular response sets in completing measures of psychological health was recognised by Goldberg (1972) who developed the GHQ. In order to reduce the likelihood of response bias, such instruments were originally devised to be used in conjunction with a clinical interview.

Studies showing positive relationships between this kind of symptom measure and various environmental stressors, particularly at work, are the bread and butter of stress research. Much of the evidence underpinning the overwhelming belief that work stress is damaging seems to come from studies of this nature (e.g. see Chapter 9). While the sheer volume of studies seems compelling, many are cross-sectional with all the problems this methodology brings (see pages 35, 40–43).

Perceived stress

We have seen, in Box 2.1 that asking people their perceptions of stress is problematic. However, there is a measure, called 'the perceived stress' scale (Cohen, Kamarck and Mermelstein, 1983), which is frequently used in studies looking at the effects of psychosocial factors on physical health (see Chapter 4). This may for example be used to separate out the effects of the actual existence of an objective stressor, such as looking after an Alzheimer's patient (Esterling et al., 1994) from the experience of distress. However, despite its title, the items in this scale typically ask about feelings of upset, feelings of not being able to cope and feelings of having uncontrollable difficulties as well as the opposite feelings of being in control and 'on top of things'. Some of these items are not dissimilar to those included in symptom scales described above.

Other psychological strains

Whilst the majority of stress research has focused on depression and anxiety as outcomes, a wider range of moods and emotions (both positive and negative) are beginning to attract attention. Measures of mood and emotion tend to be collections of adjectives, presented in a check-list format to measure current or recent states. An example, the profile of mood states (POMS) which measures six different mood states, is discussed in Box 2.5.

Box 2.5   Profile of mood states (POMS).

POMS (McNair, Lorr and Droppleman, 1981) is a self-report check-list comprising 65 adjectives that reflect six broad affective states:

- Tension–anxiety;
- Depression–dejection;
- Anger–hostility;
- Vigour–activity;
- Fatigue–inertia;
- Confusion–bewilderment.

Respondents are requested to assess the extent to which they have experienced each mood *during the past week including today* on a five-point response scale ranging from *not at all* to *extremely*. Alternative time scales can also be used, for example, 'today' or 'right now'. The POMS is often used in the area of health and sports psychology for example in studies looking at the effects of exercise (e.g. Berger *et al.*, 1998). It has also proved to be a sensitive measure of psychological adjustment to extreme environmental stressors: for example, Palinkas, Suedfeld and Steel (1995) assessed the impact of stress coping patterns on psychological adjustment in seven members of an Arctic expedition team. Each team member completed a POMS questionnaire prior to departure and after reaching the destination. Good psychological adjustment was associated with declines in factor scores for tension–anxiety, fatigue, and confusion and the use of problem-solving coping strategies.

   Whilst POMS appears to be a valid and comprehensive measure of mood and emotion, the length of the scale (65 items) can limit its use, especially when: (a) questionnaires are already fairly lengthy; and (b) when multiple assessments of mood are necessary, such as in daily diary studies.

While perhaps not central to stress research, measures of satisfaction often also appear in studies in the general area of stress research. Work stress studies commonly use measures of job satisfaction. Satisfaction in other areas of life is sometimes also considered (Judge and Watanabe, 1994; and see Chapter 9). Stress and satisfaction cannot, however, be assumed to be opposite ends of a continuum. Measures of job distress and job satisfaction seem to be quite inconsistently related (Barling, 1990). Thus employees may report that their job makes them anxious but still find it satisfying, for example.

CONCEPTUALISING AND MEASURING INDIVIDUAL DIFFERENCE VARIABLES

While moods are discussed above as indicators of psychological strain, some measures of mood such as the positive and negative affect scale (PANAS, Watson, Clark and Tellegen, 1988) are designed to be used in both trait and state response formats, by varying the instructions. Thus they measure both strains and individual differences and allow the researcher to investigate the effect of stressors on psychological well-being while controlling for stable dispositional tendencies, such as the tendency to experience a negative affect. See Chapter 6 for further details.

A wide range of other individual difference variables has also been used in the stress literature. These include genetic variables (such as gender) and dispositional variables (such as personality factors). These are discussed in further detail in Chapter 6. The approaches to measurement will clearly depend on the type of variable. Some, such as gender, are in most instances straightforward to measure. Others such as personality characteristics are complex though many validated measures of personality exist.

There are also a number of acquired individual difference variables including a range of environmental features that are believed to intervene between stressors and strains. Coping mechanisms, social support, work–family conflict are all variables that fall into this category. The ways these variables have been conceptualised and measured and their hypothesised relationships with stressors and strains are discussed elsewhere in the book (e.g. Chapters 8, 9 and 10). Overall, the stress researcher has a wide range of choice of variables and measures. The decision as to which are used will be determined by the research question and the theory used, but will also need to be appropriate for the methodology of the study.

KEY METHODOLOGIES USED IN STRESS RESEARCH

A basic introduction to a few of the more popular methodologies used in stress research is provided in this section. This aims to help the reader to evaluate the stress literature encountered in academic journals. More comprehensive coverage of psychological research methods for the potential researcher can be found elsewhere, e.g. Robson (1993). A common element to most of the studies of stress referred to in this book is the use of quantitative methodologies. These have a number of advantages. They are more objective than methodologies that are dependent on the subjective interpretations of researcher (for example, interviews or observations). They also enable data to be collected on large numbers of people representative of the population of interest. This has the further advantage that complex statistical analyses can be performed that may reveal trends and relationships which would not otherwise be obvious. However, there are many social scientists who reject the quantitative approach and advocate qualitative research (relying on narrative accounts often collected during interviews). The debate between opposing factions has been intense and complex (e.g. Glassner and Moreno, 1989) and among psychologists there are increasing numbers who challenge the rigidly quantitative approach. There is also a growing trend toward using a range of methods, including both qualitative and quantitative elements within a single investigation. Both types of approach are discussed below.

Quantitative methods

The following sections attempt to give a flavour of some of the quantitative methods commonly used: epidemiological research, survey methods (including daily questionnaires) and experimental methods. These should not be seen as mutually exclusive. Questionnaires are the key element in survey studies but commonly are also found in epidemiological and experimental studies. A single research question can sometimes be addressed using a number of different methods. The following sections demonstrate this by using an example taken from the occupational stress literature. Here a key research question relates to whether a high level of work demand, coupled with little control is damaging for physical and psychological health (based on the work of Karasek, 1979).

Epidemiological studies

Epidemiology may be defined as 'the study of the distribution and determinants of health-related states and events in populations, and the application of this study to the control of health problems' (Last, 1983). Epidemiological methods are therefore distinguished by their focus on disease outcomes and may use a range of methodologies. This includes descriptive studies based on analysis of patterns of mortality (for an example see Chapter 10, Box 10.2). It also includes case-control studies in which a sample of people with the disease of interest are compared to a sample of people without the disease but who are as similar as possible in other respects. This kind of approach has been used to compare samples of people with breast cancer to those without, to see who has experienced most stressful events (see Chapter 4).

Perhaps most important for the study of stress, however, is the prospective study in which a sample of people are followed up, sometimes for decades, to see who becomes ill. These are commonly used in the study of the impact of stressors on health. Examples can be found in Chapter 4 which examines stress and disease and Chapter 8 on social support. A number of epidemiological studies have also looked at the impact of job control and job demands. A recent example of this kind of study is one by Amick et al. (1998) in the USA. They took a large existing data set of 3,575 males who had been followed up from the early 1970s through to 1987. Five hundred and nineteen had acquired heart disease during this time. Although individual respondents had not been questioned about their job characteristics, job scores for demand and control were allocated based on occupational titles using methodology developed by Schwartz, Pieper and Karasek (1988). This method of scoring used information derived from other surveys about the amount of demand and control typically found in a range of jobs. This study found no increased risk of heart disease for jobs which were high in control and low in demand – a finding which was the opposite of that found in similar studies in other countries (e.g. see Schnall, Landsbergis and Baker, 1994).

Studies such as the above can give us information about broad trends and relationships. However, they cannot show conclusively whether high levels of control and low demand do or do not cause heart disease. Clearly there could be other explanations for the links between certain jobs and mortality. For example, it is difficult to disentangle the effects of job control from those of social class. Typically those in higher socio-economic groups have higher levels of job control and better life expectancy. While recent studies such as that by Amick *et al.* have taken steps to control such factors, studies may vary in the extent to which they are successful. This may account for the often contradictory findings. In the above case, the method of assigning job control and demand scores based on job titles is also crude. Thus other methodologies are necessary to further test the hypotheses.

Epidemiological researchers will often use survey methods in their case-control or prospective studies. However, these are also the mainstay of stress researchers concerned with other outcomes apart from physical illness.

Surveys

Surveys are the most commonly used approach to stress research and are often used to collect data on stressors, strains and other intervening variables (though they may also be used in combination with more objective data such as physiological measures). These studies may be cross-sectional (in which all measures are taken in one survey at one time) or longitudinal, in which case measures of stressors may be taken at one point (or several points) in time and then individuals will be followed up over time to look at future strains. *Cross-sectional studies* are by far the most common, perhaps because it is probably the easiest way of collecting data in an applied setting. An example of such a study is Fletcher and Jones (1993) which was a large survey in which 3,000 people completed questionnaires including measures of work demands and control, job satisfaction, anxiety and depression. Blood pressure measures were also taken. The study found that while high levels of job demand and low control were related to higher levels of satisfaction, anxiety and depression, relationships with blood pressure were consistently in the wrong direction. Thus those with supposedly more stressful jobs tended to have lower blood pressure.

Cross-sectional data such as those described above tend to be based on an assumption that work stressors *cause* the high levels of anxiety. However, it may be that people with high levels of anxiety or low levels of satisfaction are more likely to rate their jobs as having less positive characteristics.

Since cross-sectional studies cannot determine causation, *longitudinal studies* are often advocated as a superior approach. Many longitudinal studies using survey methodology are discussed in this book. However, while these may be able to show that stressors precede strains, this does not necessarily mean the stressors cause strains. Usually in surveys conducted in real-world settings there are too many other external factors that are not controlled to be able to establish causation with any confidence. Furthermore, for many people, stressors (such as unemployment) and psychological disorder may both have existed concurrently for a long time and even longitudinal studies cannot tell us which came first (Depue and Monroe, 1986).

Daily diary questionnaires and experience sampling

These can be regarded as an adaptation of the survey approach, except that people are asked to complete repeated ratings of questionnaires on a daily (or even more frequent basis). We have already seen one example of this in the daily hassles approach, when it is adapted for daily use. Studies using daily measures are relatively unusual in psychology but are particularly relevant to the study of stress as they allow the researcher to look in detail at the processes by which stressors and strains are related. This includes offering the scope to look at lagged relationships (that is, whether stressors may affect mood on the following day rather than the same day for example). Methodologies have been developed to analyse such data (Bolger *et al.*, 1989; Caspi, Bolger and Eckenrode, 1987). However, a difficulty with this approach is that it produces complex data that is difficult to interpret in the absence of good theories and hypotheses relating to these detailed relationships. An example of a version of this type of methodology, known as experience sampling, involves obtaining self-reports at varying or random intervals by providing participants with radio-controlled beepers or pagers, or pre-programmed watches (e.g. Marco and Suls, 1993). Unlike other methods that usually rely on retrospective recall, experiential sampling can capture current activities and transitory moods. See Box 2.6.

Experiments

The use of experimental methods, in which psychological phenomena are measured in a controlled environment, is fundamental to much of psychology. Such studies allow researchers to manipulate only the variables of interest while controlling other factors. This therefore makes it possible to draw conclusions about cause and effect. This is not possible in field studies in real-world settings. For example, many studies in the workplace have shown that job control is related to poorer well-being.

Box 2.6   Experience sampling.

Marco and Suls (1993) used experience sampling methodology to assess how everyday problems impact on mood – during the same day and over subsequent days. Forty employed males wore signal watches which were activated eight times a day for eight consecutive days. When the signal was heard, respondents were instructed to record in a check-list diary:

- details of their current location (e.g. home, car or work);
- details of their current activity (e.g. reading, working, watching TV);
- whether a problem had occurred during the previous 30 minutes;
- the amount of distress engendered by the problem rated on a four point scale;
- their current feelings.

Findings revealed that prior mood and concurrent problems impacted on mood during the same day. Interestingly, mood in response to a current problem was worse if the individual had previously been relatively problem-free than if the preceding period had been rated as stressful. Results also indicated that people high in negative affectivity were more distressed by current day problems and were slower to recover from problems of the preceding day.

The effects of the kinds of stressors studied here were small and short-lived. However, compared with major life events which are comparatively rare, these are the stuff of everyday life. The authors argue we need to study these experiences if we hope to understand how stress impacts on mood and emotion. This kind of approach may also shed light on the longer-term effects of chronic but minor stressors.

However, it is not normally possible to randomly allocate workers to high or low control jobs, so we cannot tell whether the lack of job control is harmful or whether those who select low control jobs are people who have poorer well-being at the outset. They may, for example, be from different social class backgrounds that are associated with different types of diet and lifestyle. These factors may cause the increased symptoms in low control workers. Thus it has been suggested that many studies of the relationship between job control and health are *confounded* by social class (Fletcher, 1991).

In experimental studies, individuals can be randomly allocated to different groups. Laboratory conditions can also be controlled so that no unintended stressors, such as noise or temperature, confound the results. Perhaps most important of all, they do not need to rely on self-report measures of job control, instead tasks can be designed with *objectively* different levels of control. For example, Steptoe *et al.* (1993) randomly allocated 40 men to carry out experimental tasks in either a self-paced (high control) or externally paced (low control) condition for five-minute periods.

Those who were in the externally paced condition had higher levels of blood pressure and heart rate during the session. However, participants were also asked to rate their perceptions of control and demand and it was found that physiological responses were particularly pronounced for those in the externally paced condition who perceived their work to be high in demand and low in control. It is suggested that this might clarify the mechanism whereby such job features may be related to cardiovascular risk. While experiments allow the researcher to control for the effects of such factors, they have the disadvantage that findings in the artificial setting of the lab may not apply to the outside world (that is, they may not be ecologically valid). Field studies may therefore also be required to confirm the applicability of experimental findings.

Work discussed in Chapter 5 has used experiments to look at stress, anxiety and cognition. This chapter further explains how such experiments may suggest mechanisms whereby stressors affect performance and well-being.

Qualitative methods

Perhaps as a result of the complexity and methodological difficulties of the available quantitative methods there has been an increase in popularity of qualitative approaches, such as the use of interviews and case studies. The increased complexity of existing statistical approaches may also tempt the less numerate psychologist to look to qualitative approaches as an easy option. However, good qualitative data is time-consuming and difficult to collect and analyse. It is also the case that many qualitative researchers in psychology will categorise responses and apply frequency counts and even statistical analyses, although to others this may be seen to be anathema (Robson, 1993).

Qualitative methods of stress research are perhaps more commonly found amongst sociologists or anthropologists working in this area (such as Pollock's, 1988, study described in Chapter 1). However, qualitative methods are gaining in popularity in psychology. One such example is Firth-Cozens' (1992b) paper describing a number of case studies. These give in-depth descriptions of the meaning of occupational stress to individual employees. Such reports do certainly add to psychological understanding of individual processes. However, many feel that the main strength of psychological methods is in their attempt to apply scientific rigour to the study of human behaviour, involving the use of quantitative methods and statistical methods to test hypotheses, thereby enabling findings to be generalised beyond the sample studied.

Combined methods

Given that no methodology is completely without flaws and limitations it is often appropriate to combine a number of different methodologies to address a research question. These may be combined within a single study for example, qualitative methods may be used in the early stages of an investigation and form the basis for the construction of questionnaires. In investigations of stress in an occupational setting, a small number of employees are often interviewed to explore the concerns of the workforce and help determine the factors to be investigated further using rating scales. Open-ended questions requiring descriptive responses are also often used alongside rating scales in questionnaires to gain more detailed and informative responses.

In providing an adequate test of a major hypothesis or theory it is usually the case that many different studies are conducted by different researchers. Typically a range of methodologies may be needed to ensure that the findings are not just a quirk of using one particular methodology (that is, a methodological artefact). For example, in some areas of applied psychology, problems or hypotheses are commonly identified in the field setting, tested using experimental methods in laboratory settings before returning to the field to confirm the findings. This approach offers the potential to make progress in hypothesis testing and developing theories with practical relevance. However, it seems to have been seldom used in stress research. Commonly, in the study of stress, researchers have relied far too exclusively on survey methods. These have often been atheoretical and have led to a plethora of isolated and unconfirmed findings. The development of testable hypotheses and good theories is needed to allow more rapid development in this field.

Reviews and meta-analyses

Where many different studies have been conducted to test a single theory or a hypothesis (such as the relationship between the amount of control someone has at work and their susceptibility to heart disease) it can be very useful to look for a review article or book which summarises the main points of these findings. However, many review articles are quite subjective and can be dependent on the doggedness of the author in tracking down relevant articles, their particular theoretical standpoint and their interpretation of findings. Recently the development of the systematic review represents an attempt to apply a somewhat more objective approach which usually involves making much more explicit the search strategies used to access literature and the criteria for inclusion in the review. Results are tabulated in a systematic fashion. An arguably even more rigorous approach is meta-analysis, which involves a systematic review of the literature but uses statistical methods that quantify the magnitude and significance of the effect across a number of comparable studies to arrive at an overall effect size.

The existence of a meta-analysis supporting a hypothesis usually constitutes fairly powerful evidence. However, even here there is room for controversy. Two researchers may use different criteria for including studies within their analysis, different methods of weighting the importance of the studies, and different statistical strategies to summarise findings. Thus two meta-analyses of the same topic may on occasion reach somewhat divergent conclusions (e.g. see Chapter 6).

39

METHODOLOGICAL PROBLEMS IN THE
STRESS LITERATURE

A number of key methodological problems that have attracted particular attention in the literature are discussed in the following sections.

Can we rely on self-report measures?

It is clear from the above that the vast majority of studies in stress research are dependent on self-report measures. It is sometimes possible to get objective measures of outcomes, for example, physiological measures or physical illnesses, but where the focus of concern is minor physical symptoms or psychological distress then there is little alternative but the self-report. All kinds of stressors (work stressors, hassles and life events) are also typically measured using self-reports. Thus in many studies stressors, strains and intervening variables are all measured by self-report alone in a simple cross-sectional survey. This clearly places a great reliance on the accuracy and reliability of such reports which has been questioned by a number of writers. How good are people at reporting their perceptions of stressors and strains? Lazarus and Folkman (1984), for example, suggests that appraisal of stress may not be conscious. Yet the self-report questionnaires used to measure appraisals are completely dependent on conscious reports – which must therefore reduce their validity.

In some areas of stress research it is possible to get ratings from different sources to try to validate the self-report measures, for example in the assessment of work stressors. One of the few studies which attempts this, by Spector and Jex (1991), found only limited relationships between the individuals' ratings of their job characteristics and ratings obtained from job analyses conducted by independent raters. However, objective raters may also be prone to bias (Frese and Zapf, 1988). Hence it is not necessarily clear which type of rating is more accurate. However, the conclusions we draw from research into people's perceptions of their work stressors tend to be based on an assumption that these correspond to some kind of objective reality. To the extent that they are reflections of individuals' idiosyncrasies, in either the ways they interpret or the ways they respond to questionnaire items, then we have a problem. This may be the result of individual differences (see Chapter 6) or may be a function of poor questionnaire design.

Some researchers have also used observers to assess strain outcomes such as mood by obtaining ratings from spouses, friends or co-workers. For example, Stone and Neale (1984) obtained self-reports of daily events and mood (negative and positive) from 50 married men up to a period of 21 days. Daily ratings of husbands' moods were also provided by their wives. In general, spouses' opinions tended to converge, but some differences were also observed. Same day associations between negative events and negative mood were found in husbands only, whilst their wives failed to register their male partners affective reactions to these events until the following day. Interestingly, wives were fairly consistent in rating their husbands' as being in a less positive mood than husbands rated themselves. However, there seems no good reason to assume that an observer's report of someone else's mood is superior to the rating of the person concerned. Such ratings are therefore only likely to be used to complement and not replace self-reports.

The problem of common method variance

The problem of 'method variance' or 'common method variance' is one that is a particular problem for stress research using self-reports. The problem comes about if both stressors (such as daily hassles) and strains (such as anxiety) are measured using the same method (e.g. a self-report questionnaire). In these circumstances, relationships between the stressors and the strains may be the result of the method rather than the actual constructs of interest.

One reason this may occur is due to response biases, that is a tendency of individuals to always respond to questionnaire items in a positive or negative way. Spector (1987) attempted to explore the extent of this problem by reviewing studies using self-report measures of affect (for example, job satisfaction) and perceptions of the work environment. He tested for the tendency for different traits measured with the same method to correlate more highly than different traits measured with different methods. He found little evidence for method variance in the studies evaluated, which used well-validated scales with sound psychometric properties. However, he points out that method variance may well be more of a problem with single items or poorly designed scales. Spector's findings were criticised on methodological grounds and a re-analysis of their data using confirmatory factor analysis did find evidence of method variance (Williams, Cote and Buckley, 1989). This issue, like many others in this area, remains unresolved in the literature. However, Jex and Beehr (1991) in a review of evidence conclude that while 'method variance may well be a problem in some cases, it is clearly not pervasive enough to use as a basis to dismiss all correlations between self-report measures' (p. 352).

Another cause of common method variance problems is that conceptually similar items are used to measure both stressors and strains. This problem has already been introduced in Box 2.1. As we saw earlier in the chapter, the criticism that stressors and strains are conceptually confounded is one that has been particularly directed at Lazarus and his transactional approach to stressor measurement (Dohrenwend *et al.*, 1984; Dohrenwend and Shrout, 1985). Lazarus' view of stress hinges on the notion of *appraisal*. This leads to the measurement of stress in terms of, for example, the hassles scale as discussed above (Lazarus *et al.*, 1985) which asks people to rate the extent they feel hassled by certain events. Such items may sometimes be quite similar to items contained within self-report anxiety scales used to measure strain outcomes, leading to spuriously high correlations between stressors and strains. This problem also occurs in other areas of stress research, for example work stressors may be measured in ways that encompass appraisals. The problem is summarised in the much-quoted statement by Kasl, who states that such theoretical formulations fall into

> a self-serving methodological trap which has tended to trivialise a good deal of the research into work stress and role stress: the measurement of the independent variable (for example, role ambiguity, role conflict, quantitative overload, etc.) and the measurement of the 'dependent' variable (work strain, distress and dissatisfaction) are sometimes so close operationally that they appear to be simply two measures of a single concept. (Kasl, 1978, p. 13)

There is therefore quite a gap between the view of stress researchers such as Lazarus who think that the idea of stress is meaningless without including appraisal and those who, like Kasl and Dohrenwend, hold that self-reports of stressors need to be as objective as possible do avoid the problem which has been labelled the 'triviality trap' (Frese and Zapf, 1988), Frese and Zapf support the latter view and suggest that for a measure to be objective it means that 'a particular individual's cognitive and emotional processing does not influence the reporting of social and physical facts'. They suggest that any kind of subjective questionnaire report can be placed on a continuum from low to high in terms of its 'dependency on cognitive and emotional processing'. Hence, in their terms, some self-report measures can constitute objective measures of stressors. However, while some variables such as workload may be easily measured in a relatively objective way using self-reports, concepts such as role conflict are likely to always be highly dependent on individual perception and cognitive processing.

These two fundamentally different approaches to stressor measurement continue to co-exist in the literature and whether the advantages outweigh the disadvantages depends largely on the aims of the study.

Direction of causation

A further problem particularly associated with cross-sectional studies is that it is not possible to determine the direction of causation. Thus while it may seem logical to assume that the perception of stressors has caused the strain, the reverse may also be the case, e.g. feeling depressed might negatively bias perceptions and recall of stressors. For some time now it has been known that individuals are likely to retrieve memories that are emotionally congruent with their current mood state (e.g. Bower, 1981). Thus Bower found that individuals who were experimentally induced to have a depressed mood remembered more negative personal events than those in a happy mood. Induction of a happy mood has the reverse effect. This may account for Firth-Cozens and Hardy's (1992) finding that, following psychotherapy, clients showed more positive perceptions of some job characteristics, particularly perceptions of the extent of job control and skill use, although nothing was done to change the nature of the job.

In a laboratory study, people's perceptions of their job characteristics have also proved very easy to manipulate. Adler, Skov and Salvemini (1985) conducted a study in which participants were randomly told they had either relatively high or relatively low scores on a job satisfaction measure. Those told they had high scores subsequently rated features of the task and the environmental conditions more positively. This does not mean that task characteristics do not cause dissatisfaction or distress but that the direction of causation may not simply be uni-directional.

As a result of the difficulty in overcoming the above problems, West *et al.* (1992) state that:

> cross-sectional surveys, based on single samples and where all variables are self-reported, tend to reveal interesting patterns of statistical relationships between variables, but now advance understanding about behaviour to a very limited extent. (p. 1)

Some academic journals (e.g. *The Journal of Occupational and Organisational Psychology*) now usually refuse to consider cross-sectional studies for publication.

What time intervals are important?

Clearly in experimental studies we are usually looking for stress effects that are manifested almost instantly. However in most non-experimental studies researchers are looking at longer-term outcomes. Here the expected time lag between experiencing a stressor and the appearance of a strain outcome (such as CHD) is seldom explicitly addressed. Where studies follow people over time, the time elapsed between measurements may be determined on some common sense basis or for organisational or administrative reasons. Thus studies looking at daily stressors may be looking at stress outcomes that are short term or manifest within days (e.g. studies of colds), whereas with chronic or major life stressors outcomes may be examined over months or years. Frese and Zapf (1988) draw attention to the fact that low relationships between stressors and strains may be due to the wrong time lag being selected. However, it is not just the length of time lag that is important, but also the *nature* of the relationships over time. Frese and Zapf describe five types of possible temporal relationship between stressors and strain.

1. The stress reaction model – whereby the impact of the stressor increases strain with exposure time. When removed the strain reduces.

2. The accumulation model – whereby the strain is the result of an accumulation and does not go away if stressors are removed.

3. The dynamic accumulation model – whereby strain increases even after stressors are removed, perhaps because of lowered resistance.

4. The adjustment model – whereby initially there is an increase in strain but after a while the person adjusts and strain decreases even though the stressor is still present.

5. The sleeper effect model – whereby the dysfunctioning may appear a long time after exposure to the stressor such that the stressor may no longer be present when the strain is manifest (e.g. post traumatic stress).

Zapf, Dormann and Frese (1996) point out that most research studies currently do not take into account these possible variations, looking typically only at linear relationships, and are therefore likely to underestimate the true strength of relationships.

Is the published literature a biased sample of research?

A further element of bias can creep into the scientific literature as a result of the review and selection process that takes place before articles are published. This is a problem in all research, not just research into stress. The typical process is that articles are reviewed by 2 or 3 experts in the field, usually academics publishing in the same field as the author of the article. The process is known as peer review. Reviewers will make recommendations to the editor about whether the article should be accepted or rejected or whether it should be amended and resubmitted. While in theory, this process should be fair and impartial, the process has been criticised on a number of grounds. For example, reviewers have been accused of being unwilling to recommend publication of non-significant results (Kupfersmid, 1988) and replications of previous studies (Neuliep and Crandall, 1993b). Bornstein (1991) reviews the evidence from a number of studies and concludes there is strong evidence of bias against the publication of non-significant results. This clearly could have major implications for the advancement of knowledge. Statistical significance testing means that there is always some possibility that significant results are due to chance. While it is possible one study based on data that owe much to chance may be published supporting an incorrect hypothesis, it is much less likely that studies testing the same hypothesis with non-significant (but correct) results would ever be published. Whether replications in general are less likely to be published is less clearly established (Neuliep and Crandall, 1993b).

CONCLUSION

This chapter has provided a rapid tour through the theoretical and measurement issues and the methodological approaches that are needed for a critical appraisal of the stress literature. It has highlighted the complexity relating to the conceptualisation and measurement of stressors, strains and intervening variables. Theory

44

and measurement go together, and it is the case that the lack of good theoretical frameworks to guide research in this area has made integrating findings difficult and hampers future research. Nevertheless, some dominant theoretical and methodological approaches have been identified. Subsequent chapters will draw on these approaches, for example, in looking at the relationships between stressors and health.

CHAPTER 3

THE PHYSIOLOGY OF STRESS

Angela Clow

This chapter describes the complex psychophysiological systems that are implicated in the physiological 'stress' response. An understanding of the physiological reactions to stressors provides insights into the mechanisms whereby psychological reactions may have consequences for health.

PSYCHOPHYSIOLOGISTS try to explain the relationship between psychological state and health status (both mental and physical). To understand this relationship, which underpins much stress research, it is necessary to appreciate the anatomical and physiological systems involved in what is known as the 'stress response'. It is the purpose of this chapter to outline these links and explore the physiological consequences of exposure to stressors. As such, this chapter examines 'stress' in terms of internal reactions to a situation, rather than the situation itself (stressor). Individual responses to the same situation may vary considerably so that a stimulus that induces a stress response in one person may not induce the same response in another individual. Indeed this individual variation in responding forms the basis of the 'diathesis–stress' models for vulnerability to psychopathology and physical illness. These models propose that individual predisposition (diathesis), which is dictated by genetic and developmental influences, interacts with the intensity of the external stressor to dictate the intensity of the stress response and thus the threshold for illness.

We tend to assume that 'stress' is bad for health, however, many of the physiological responses to stressors have evolved to promote survival at a time of crisis. Indeed we share our stress response systems with other species where they continue to function to the animals' advantage. The problem with the human condition is that the behavioural response required to many stressors in the modern world (e.g. problematic personal relationships or lack of job control) does not require the same

47

physiological demands as the stressors experienced by a wild animal, for example being sought by a predator. However, humans continue to experience the same dramatic physiological stress responses as other species. In short, the body's response to a stressor prepares it for rapid physical action (fight or flight). While there are situations where these responses might still be critical for survival, in many circumstances in modern life, other responses such as negotiation might be more appropriate. Furthermore, the animal's stress response is designed to combat relatively infrequent and life threatening events, whereas the types of events humans commonly call stressors are much more frequent but very rarely immediately life threatening. The consequence of this is that the human stress response systems are repeatedly activated. Here arises the problem. Such frequent activation can lead to dysregulation of responses and it is under these circumstances that the body's own response system (rather than the stressor) potentially presents the greatest threat to well-being.

There are two basic physical response systems to stressors which can be differentially activated or dysregulated depending on the severity (mild versus severe) and the duration (acute versus chronic) of the stressor. Initially the body needs to identify the stressor. This process requires higher brain processes such as sensation and memory. The brain integrates the information regarding the stimuli and, if they are perceived to be threatening, emotional responses are generated in the limbic system. The limbic system comprises such areas as the hippocampus and amygdala and is evolutionarily old. It is this system that is responsible for directing behaviours required for survival such as sexual reproduction, fear and aggression. The limbic system can activate an area of the brain known as the hypothalamus. The hypothalamus is uniquely placed to orchestrate the appropriate physical responses required by the emotion of the moment. The hypothalamus can control both of the stress response systems namely the *sympathetic adrenal medullary (SAM)* response system and the *hypothalamic-pituitary-adrenal (HPA)* axis. Together these systems regulate activity in the cardiovascular system (heartbeat and blood pressure) and the immune system (number and activity of circulating immune calls). It is by modulation of these systems that the psychological reaction to stressors has a direct impact on the body and, under certain circumstances, health. Thus one can see the beginnings of a link between the higher brain processes involving the perception and appraisal of a threatening stimulus, the emotional response to the stimulus, such as perhaps fear, and finally the impact on the cardiovascular and immune systems. These processes are described in further detail below.

ORGANISATION OF THE NERVOUS SYSTEM

The role of the nervous system is to detect what is going on outside and inside the body, interpret that information and orchestrate an appropriate response. To this end the nervous system is made up of many millions of specialised cells called neurones. There are neurones designed to sense what is going on in and around us, and others designed to initiate different processes. The sensory neurones can be found in the body's internal organs (e.g. the heart), the sense organs (e.g. the eyes) and more generally under the skin. These sensory neurones relay information to the brain where many other neurones integrate and make sense of the input. Yet other different neurones effect the appropriate response by activating the body's organs for instance to make the heart beat faster, the glands to release chemical messengers called hormones into the blood or the muscles to produce a behavioural response. In very simplistic terms neurones are organised in relays or circuits and communicate with each other via neurotransmitters: chemicals that are released when a chemical fires. These chemicals transfer across the synapses (gaps) between neurones and have either an excitatory or inhibitory effect on the likelihood of the next neurone firing. The inappropriate activity of some of these circuits has been associated with various disorders such as depression, which in part can be treated by drugs that influence (amongst other things) the production, release or reuptake of neurotransmitters.

The nervous system is extremely complex and it helps in understanding how it works to categorise different functional subsystems within it. In simplifying the description of the system like this, it is easy to forget that these subsystems are part of an integrated whole and do not act independently. That said, the most simplistic way in which to subdivide the nervous system is into the central and peripheral components. All parts of the *central nervous system* are encased in bone: the brain in enclosed within the skull and spinal cord within the backbone. Thus the central nervous system comprises the brain and spinal cord and is well protected from damage. In contrast the *peripheral nervous system* is not encased within bone, it projects to and from the central nervous system connecting all other parts of our bodies: the internal organs and glands as well as skeletal muscles.

The peripheral nervous system can be further subclassified into the parts that we have more or less control over. The part of the peripheral nervous system that controls our skeletal muscles is called the *'voluntary' nervous system*. We have conscious control over activity of this branch of the peripheral nervous system. We can activate muscles as and when we decide to, so that we can communicate through speech and expression (facial muscles) as well as move our limbs to walk, run and do what ever else takes our fancy. In contrast, that part of the peripheral nervous system that regulates our internal organs is not (normally) under our conscious control. Throughout our lives our bodily functions go on without conscious instruction. For example our hearts beat, our food is digested and we regulate our body temperature completely automatically. These processes are under the control of that part of the peripheral nervous system called the *'autonomic' nervous system*.

The autonomic nervous system is really our 'survival' nervous system. Without the efficient running of this branch of our nervous system there would be no need for higher mental process like communication and voluntary activity as we would be dead, or at the least very ill. To effect the most efficient organisation of this

Figure 3.1   Summary of the processes in the ANS.

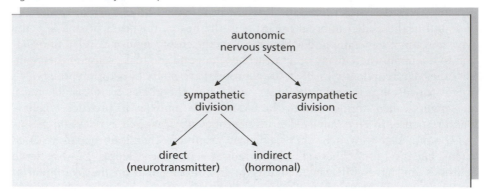

onerous task the autonomic nervous system itself has two branches: the *sympathetic and parasympathetic nervous systems* (SNS and PNS, respectively); see Figure 3.1. We need not dwell on the detailed differences between these branches (see any standard physiology text). It is sufficient here to identify the most crucial facts: different emotional states cause differential activation of these branches of the autonomic nervous system. In short, relaxation is associated with domination of the PNS whereas arousal and feeling anxious or 'stressed' is associated with domination of the SNS.

THE SYMPATHETIC ADRENAL MEDULLARY (SAM) RESPONSE SYSTEM

If an animal is under threat, for whatever reason, its sympathetic nervous system is activated. This activation occurs virtually instantaneously. The organisation of the SNS is such that branches of it reach out to virtually every organ and gland within the body. Mostly this is achieved by branching neurones directly influencing the organs. Noradrenaline (also known as norepinephrine) is the neurotransmitter released by the SNS to activate the internal body organs. However, there is an additional mechanism that ensures harmonious and simultaneous alerting of the animal and this is the release of adrenaline (or epinephrine) into the bloodstream. Once in the body, adrenaline is transported rapidly and unimpeded throughout the body to prepare the animal for fight or flight. The system that releases adrenaline into the bloodstream is called the SAM: sympathetic adrenal medullary system. As the name suggests the SAM system is under the regulatory influence of the sympathetic nervous system but also the adrenal medulla. An appreciation of the adrenal glands is vital for any individual striving to understand the physiology of the stress response; they are central to both the SAM and HPA stress response systems.

Figure 3.2   An adrenal gland.

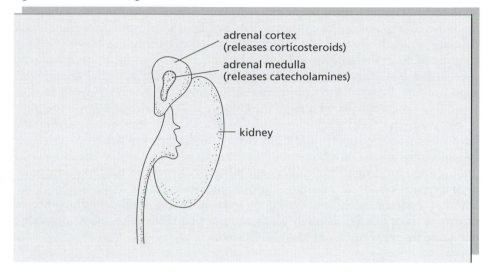

There are two adrenal glands in mammals, one located on top of each kidney (Figure 3.2). Each adrenal gland has two distinct functional zones. At the core is the medulla and around the outer area lies the cortex. The inner medulla is directly innervated by the neurones of the SNS such that when activated adrenaline is released into the blood supply. Once in the blood, adrenaline has widespread and rapid effects on physiological systems. Hence this system is the sympathetic adrenal medullary stress response system. (Later in this chapter we will discuss the role of the adrenal cortex in release of glucocorticoids as part of the HPA response system.)

THE SNS/SAM SYSTEMS AND CARDIOVASCULAR ACTIVITY

The immediate stress response system, mediated by the SNS and SAM systems, concentrates its efforts on changing activation of the cardiovascular system. In the face of danger the body's most immediate concern is to provide sufficient oxygen and energy to the brain and muscles so that the animal can survive the emergency by either running or fighting – both of which are physically demanding activities. The first thing that happens is that the heart beats faster, thus ensuring a more copious and forceful supply of blood to the essential organs. It has been calculated that during a maximum stress response the heart can increase its output of blood by five times compared to its resting state. In addition changes occur in the blood vessels themselves. This is possible because the walls of the main arteries (those vessels taking oxygen and energy rich blood from the heart towards the organs

51

of the body) are wrapped in tiny circular muscles. These muscles are innervated by the SNS. During a stress response the SNS constricts these muscles, narrowing the lumen of the vessels. As a direct result the blood is delivered faster and blood pressure is raised, which is why many stress researchers measure blood pressure. In order to direct this copious and forceful supply of blood to the most appropriate sites in the body the SNS also changes blood flow. For example, the arteries supplying the digestive system constrict sufficiently so as to divert the main flow away. In a similar way blood flow to the kidneys and skin is reduced, whereas flow to the brain and skeletal muscles is maximised. Perhaps it is worth mentioning here that in addition to reducing blood flow to the kidneys the stress response system causes release of a hormone (vasopressin) which works on the kidneys to inhibit urine formation. Remember that urine is a filtrate of the blood. In times of emergency we aim to maximise the volume, power and efficacy of the blood. It is not a good idea to be reducing these by producing urine. The urgency to urinate at times of crises is solely a way of removing dead weight waste, in reality our urine *formation* (in the kidney) is reduced.

Cardiovascular disease

The physiological processes outlined above are all ideal and adaptive for survival in stress responses requiring an energetic behavioural response. However, as pointed out earlier, modern human life rarely requires such levels of physical activity. The problems for health arise when the stress response system is repeatedly activated so that the cardiovascular system suffers from unnecessary wear and tear. The increase in blood pressure, caused by sympathetic nervous system activation, can cause turbulence in the blood flow and physical damage to the delicate lining of some blood vessels. The points where vessels branch into two (branch points) are particularly vulnerable. The smooth vessel lining may be torn allowing access to fatty acids and glucose (also increased in availability by the stress response, see

Figure 3.3 Drawing of a cross-section through (a) a healthy and (b) an atherosclerotic human artery. Note the fatty deposits (plaques) attached to the inner wall, reducing the width of the channel.

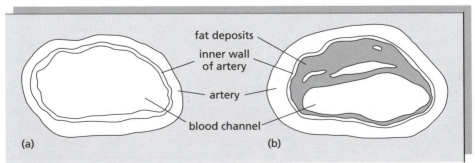

later). The result can be a build-up of these fatty nutrients underneath the tear, in the walls of the vessels. This process gives rise to what clinicians call atherosclerosis, or plaques lining the blood vessels (Figure 3.3). Plaque formation can have severe health repercussions. If they occur in the arteries supplying the heart, they can lead to heart attacks. If they occur in the lower part of the body they can lead to 'claudication', which means that legs and chest become painful during even moderate exercise, due to impaired oxygen supply caused by obstructed blood flow to the periphery. If the plaques obstruct blood flow to the brain the result can be a stroke (see Fuster *et al.*, 1992).

THE HYPOTHALAMIC-PITUITARY-ADRENAL (HPA) AXIS RESPONSE SYSTEM

The other stress response system, activation of which is thought by many to be synonymous with a stress response, is the HPA axis. In actuality arousal and pleasure, as well as strain, activate the SNS/SAM systems. Hence it is not possible to use activation of these systems as diagnostic for a stress response. In contrast, activation of the HPA axis is much less easy to achieve. Activating the SNS/SAM can be likened to lighting a match whereas activating the HPA is like lighting a fire. Lighting a match is easy, has an instant effect and the effect does not last long, whereas lighting a fire takes a lot more effort and its effects last much longer. The HPA axis is only activated in extreme circumstances. Individual differences in threshold for HPA activation are thought to be part of an individual's diathesis (i.e. susceptibility or predisposition) upon which external challenging events (stressors) can impact. The more readily the HPA axis is activated the more impact the stress will have on both physical and mental well-being. However, as was the case for the SNS/SAM systems, activation of the HPA axis can be induced by purely psychological stressors, even though its adaptive value lies in its ability to equip for fight or flight.

Let us now examine this system in greater detail (Figure 3.4). At the beginning of this chapter it was pointed out that stressors are perceived in higher brain centres (cerebral cortex), processed in the evolutionarily old limbic regions (including the hippocampus and amygdala) and relayed to the hypothalamus. In reality, the hypothalamus receives inputs from many different brain pathways. It is vital that this region is well regulated as activation can have widespread impact on a host of physiological and psychological processes. The hypothalamus provides the 'H' of the HPA axis. If, as a result of the aforementioned integrative processes, a particular area of the hypothalamus known as the paraventricular nucleus is activated, this causes production of a chemical messenger called corticotrophin releasing factor (CRF). Newly formed CRF passes into the local blood supply that feeds directly to the anterior lobe of the pituitary gland that lies immediately beneath the hypothalamus. The pituitary supplies the 'P' of the HPA axis. On arrival in the anterior lobe of the hypothalamus the CRF acts as a messenger to cause production of yet another chemical messenger, called adrenocorticotrophic hormone (ACTH).

Figure 3.4 *The HPA Axis.* Endocrine systems are feedback regulated, meaning that existing endocrine products stimulate or inhibit further production of themselves. In one example of a negative feedback system, the hypothalamo-pituitary adrenal (HPA) axis, the adrenal steroid cortisol inhibits further production of itself by crossing the blood-brain barrier and shutting off the first step of its production cycle.

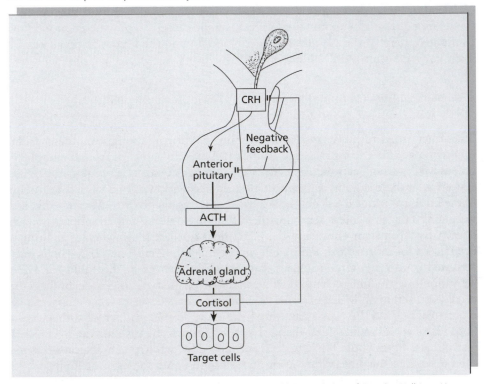

From 'Physiological Psychology' by Smock, © 1999. Reprinted by permission of Prentice-Hall Inc., Upper Saddle River, N.J.

This time the messenger (ACTH) is secreted into the general circulatory blood system. The targets for this hormone are the pair of adrenal glands located over the kidneys. As previously discussed the adrenal glands are central to stress response systems: the medullas provide the adrenaline for the SAM system whereas the outer cortex responds to the ACTH by secreting the glucocorticoid cortisol (in humans) again into the general circulation. This is why cortisol is often measured in stress studies (see Chapter 4).

Regulation of cortisol secretion

Secretion of cortisol (in humans) from the adrenal cortex is also under the regulation of the body's own biological clock. Levels of circulating cortisol are at their lowest during night time sleep but the act of awakening is a powerful stimulus to the HPA axis: levels can rise three-fold within the first 30 minutes after awakening (Pressner *et al.*, 1997). This abrupt rise is relatively short-lived; levels fall to something like the first waking value within about an hour. Throughout the rest of the day, there is a continuous and steady decline in circulating cortisol concentration. Thus, the daytime secretion of cortisol comprises two main components: the awakening response and the underlying diurnal fall. The nature of the continuous decline in cortisol makes it difficult to assess basal levels using a single spot measure; basal measures are best determined by multiple sampling over the day, synchronised to awakening. Stress-induced activation of the HPA axis is superimposed upon this background activity. An acute stressor will activate the production of CRF in the hypothalamus and then ACTH from the anterior pituitary to induce an additional burst of cortisol secretion from the paired adrenal cortex. It takes about 20–30 minutes for this response system to be complete; typically, circulating cortisol levels rise sharply 20 minutes after an acute stressor. However, levels remain high for only a limited period. The HPA axis (under normal circumstances) is very efficient at regulating itself. Both the hypothalamus and pituitary gland have receptors (special recognition sites) that detect circulating levels of cortisol. If levels go above the norm for the time of day, they initiate a down-regulation in cortisol secretion. This system is akin to the working of a thermostat on a central heating system. As the temperature rises, the thermostat cuts in to reduce the heat output. In the same way, cortisol secretion is inhibited when levels rise. Consequently, circulating cortisol levels return to their norm within about one hour of any acute rise. The mechanisms to keep cortisol in check are usually very efficient. Cortisol is a steroid and as such its chemical nature ensures it access to every part of the body. It freely passes into the brain and all other body tissue. In these tissues, it has powerful effects (see later) so it is vital that it is carefully regulated. As we shall see later the effect of repeated activation of the HPA axis, as may occur in chronic uncontrollable stress, can lead to a dysfunction of the regulatory mechanisms so that raised levels are not adequately detected. The result is that levels remain high and unchecked. The outcome of this situation can have significant effects on both physical and mental well-being.

Cortisol, energy and the cardiovascular system

Let us now discuss the effects of cortisol on body function. Activation of the HPA axis, in common with that of the SNS/SAM systems, has evolved to promote survival in animals when under challenge. These systems work together. Different stressors can activate these systems to various degrees and in slightly different time courses. Thus the orchestration and patterning of responses tends to vary from stressor to stressor and across different individuals, but together these two response systems constitute the main infrastructure of stress response capability. As such, it should be no surprise that their functions are somewhat synergistic.

The accelerated heartbeat and blood pressure needs to deliver energy (as well as oxygen) to the muscles and brain. One of the main functions of cortisol is to liberate the body's stored energy reserves. In a crisis, energy is needed immediately. Excess energy previously consumed (in the form of starch, sugars and carbohydrate) will have been stored in muscle and liver as glycogen (long chains of glucose). (The hormone that stimulates the storage of these reserves is insulin, hence the high blood glucose levels of untreated insulin-deficient diabetics.) The role of cortisol first and foremost is to stop any further storage from occurring and secondly to activate the liberation of these stores. Thus the glycogen is liberated and broken down into its constituent glucose parts ready for use. In the same way, stored fats and proteins can be liberated during times of strain. These processes ensure adequate energy to the muscles and brain.

If the body is exposed to repeated stress activation of the HPA axis, the result is repeated liberation of energy stores which, by the very nature of modern-day stressors, are not usually utilised. This excess glucose (and free fatty acids released from stored fat) clogs up the blood vessels contributing towards formation of atherosclerotic plaques, as described earlier. Such plaques restrict blood flow to organs such as the brain and heart leading to possible stroke and heart attack.

STRESS RESPONSES AND IMMUNE FUNCTION

Thus far, we have focused our attention on the relationship between activation of stress response systems and cardiovascular function. However, both stress response systems also have direct effects on the activity of the immune system. The autonomic nervous system sends nerves directly to the tissues that form, or store, the cells of the immune system. Furthermore, cells of the immune system are sensitive to circulating cortisol, the main stress hormone. So, the infrastructure is in place for a direct relationship between stress, immune function and a range of other diseases not associated with cardiovascular function. The main function of the immune system is to protect the body from infectious agents such as viruses, bacteria and parasites. The immune system can fail us in two main ways: (a) it may *not be vigilant* so that the infections agents gain entry to our bodies and organs such as to cause the infectious disease, or (b) it may be *over vigilant* such that the immune system itself (rather than an infections agent) causes the illness. Stress has been associated with both types of immune dysfunction (see Evans, Hucklebridge and Clow, 2000).

Types of immune function

In order to understand the relationship between the stress response and immune-related illness we need to appreciate, at the most basic level, how the immune system operates (see Mair and Watkins, 1998). The body is capable of utilising two strategies to ward off infection (Romagnani, 1997). The first (known as humoral immunity) involves the secretion of antibodies. Antibodies are proteins that bind to invading pathogens so that they are inactivated and then rapidly cleared from the body. This type of defence is suitable to ward off pathogens that remain outside the body's own cells. The second strategy (known as cell-mediated immunity) is a more aggressive type of defence whereby the immune cells, after making contact with the invading pathogen, actively destroy it. Most often, this type of defence is used to ward off pathogens that have already entered the body's cells (such as viruses). During cell-mediated immunity, destruction of the pathogen is associated with destruction of the host cell also.

The cells of the immune system that circulate in the blood are white blood cells called leukocytes (see Kiecolt-Glaser and Glaser, 1993). Leukocytes are produced in the bone marrow where some remain to mature but some migrate to the thymus gland, the spleen or peripheral lymph nodes for storage. The cells that remain in the bone marrow become B cells (B for bone) whereas the others are known as T cells (T for thymus). The two classes of immune cells are the basis of the two types of immunity outlined above. The B cells give rise to the antibodies of humoral immunity. This type of immune activity is also known as 'Th2'. The T cells are those responsible for the more aggressive cell-mediated immunity, known as 'Th1'. Th1 immunity is very important in attacking cancer as well as viruses. Natural killer (NK) cells are also part of the Th1 armoury and, by definition, work to fend off cancer cells as well as viruses.

To some extent this dichotomy of immune function is counter regulatory. Each branch, when active, produces chemicals (called cytokines) that down regulates the alternative branch. Over 24 hours the typical person fluctuates between night-time cell-mediated (Th1) immunity and daytime humoral (Th2) immunity (Petrovsky and Harrison, 1995). In addition to this daily fluctuation, some individuals may be biased towards one or other strategy for fighting off infection. Stress can influence this balance. It is simplistic to describe stress as being merely immunosuppressive as suppression of one branch would likely liberate the alternative to be overactive.

Chronic and acute responses

The physiological stress response can be accurately described as disturbing the fine balance in the regulation of these two branches, or strategies, for fighting off infection. In summary, a chronic (or repeated) physiological stress response is associated with down regulation of cellular (Th1) immunity and has either little effect on, or up regulation of, the humoral type (Th2) immunity. This shift seems primarily to be orchestrated by raised cortisol levels: cortisol is quite a potent down regulator of cell-mediated immunity but can enhance humoral (antibody-mediated) immunity. Acute stress, in contrast, may be associated with some transient up-regulatory effects on cell-mediated immunity (Dhabhar and McEwan, 1997). These effects are probably mediated by direct sympathetic innervation of the immune system and can have short-term value in helping protect the animal during an emergency.

The appreciation that chronic stress, which is accompanied by repeated HPA activation and a milieu of high circulating cortisol, is associated with a shift away from cell-mediated (Th1) immunity towards humoral (Th2) immunity is critical. This disturbance in the fine balance of the immune system is fundamental to understanding how stress can lead to both types of immune system disorders: *lack* of vigilance and *over* vigilance. For example chronic stress has been associated with impaired ability to ward off cancer (less efficient cell-mediated immunity) but at the same time a greater propensity to atopic disorders, such as asthma (over reactive humoral immunity).

The secretory immune system

The immune system operating via the blood is only part of the body's defence system. In addition the 'mucosal surfaces' are protected by the 'secretory' immune system. Mucosal surfaces are the linings of the passageways that run through the body, e.g. the gastrointestinal and urinogenital tracts. In fact these surfaces are outside the body but enclosed within it. Unlike the rest of the outside of the body, which is protected by resilient and tough skin, the mucosal surfaces have no physical barrier to the passage of infectious agents. Physical barriers are not a design possibility as the function of these surfaces is to permit the rapid and easy transport of bodily essentials such as digested food or air. Indeed these surfaces are moist and warm and present an ideal environment for infectious agents such as bacteria and viruses. Furthermore, these surfaces, which are highly convoluted, have an estimated surface area of more than one hundred times that of the external surface area of the body. The body's way of preventing infection from entering the body via these surfaces is to provide them with a 'barrier cream' of antibody. Antibodies, made from the B cells, are transported across the mucosal surface from within the body to the outside cavity and as such act as the first line of defence against invasion. The main antibody to protect the mucosal surfaces in this way is secretory immunoglobulin A (sIgA). Levels of sIgA are dependent upon two main mechanisms: (a) availability from the B cells and (b) rate of transport across the mucosal surface. As such sIgA does not represent either the Th1 or Th2 branch of the immune system but if collected in the correct way (see later) levels in saliva reflect those of the entire mucosal immune system (Mestecky, 1993). Psychoneuro-immunologists have demonstrated that levels of sIgA are particularly sensitive to both very acute and chronic stressors and that these changes are important in vulnerability to infection (see Evans, Clow and Hucklebridge, 1997). Such studies have shown that chronic stress tends to cause sustained reduction in levels of sIgA whereas an acute laboratory challenge in healthy individuals can cause a transient rise in sIgA (e.g. Willemsen *et al.*, 1998).

STRESS RESPONSES AND DEPRESSION

The association between exposure to repeated uncontrollable stressors and depression, in particular melancholic mood, is well documented in the clinical literature. This leads to a discussion of yet another physiological effect of cortisol. Cortisol can pass freely into the brain where it can affect levels of the brain neurotransmitters responsible for mood. In particular high levels of cortisol can reduce availability of tryptophan in the brain. Tryptophan is the immediate precursor of serotonin (also known as 5HT), low levels of which are known to be associated with depressed mood (the popular anti-depressant drug Prozac works to increase availability of brain serotonin). Thus not only does repeated HPA activation and high cortisol predispose to cardiovascular disease or cancer (depending on genetic predisposition and environmental influences), it also increases the likelihood of depressed, melancholic mood (see Dinan, 1994).

PHYSIOLOGICAL MEASUREMENTS

This brief section has merely set out to highlight some important issues for psychophysiologists with regard to commonly used measures of stress response in humans. Of course there are many more ways to assess these responses in animal models, e.g. brain neurotransmitter levels and receptor populations, but these are beyond the scope of this chapter. Of particular importance for psychologists are non-intrusive measures that can be taken without causing distress for the participant. Of particular use in this regard is the increased use of saliva as a medium for investigation.

As we have seen the physiological response to stress is variable between individuals and orchestrated by a combination of mechanisms. The sympathetic nervous system (SNS) and sympathetic adrenal medullary (SAM) system work in harmony to increase heart rate and blood pressure. Many studies have been undertaken to examine the extent of these changes in relation to individual differences and eventual health outcomes (e.g. Uchino, Cacioppo and Kiecolt-Glaser, 1996). These studies are relevant but can be hindered by the very readiness of such responses. In addition these responses are not specific to any particular emotion, being equally intense with pleasurable emotion as negative emotion (see also Krantz and Manuck, 1984).

Measurement of hypothalamic-pituitary-adrenal activity provides a better index of negative emotion as it has been shown to be sensitive to a limited number of negative stimuli: novelty, unpredictability, uncontrollability, anticipation and ego involvement. In fact, it can be quite difficult to elicit a HPA response. As discussed earlier this system is much harder to initiate, only kicking into action under quite severe perceived threat. The most usual way to study the HPA axis is to examine its excitability. For example, researchers may study the extent of its activation in response to a psychosocial stressor such as the Trier social stress test which involves public speaking and mental arithmetic in front of an audience (Kirschbaum, Pike and Hellhammer, 1993). Levels of the end-point of HPA activation, i.e. cortisol, are determined before and after the test. Levels usually peak about 20 minutes after an acute stressor and return to normal within an hour. Cortisol (or its precursor ACTH) can be measured in the blood but this requires blood sampling, which itself can be a stressor and difficult to repeat in order to examine time course. More preferable for psychophysiologists is its measurement in saliva samples. Cortisol (but not ACTH) moves freely into the saliva and can easily be measured there. Levels are not affected by rate of saliva flow and once collected levels remain stable for some hours at room temperature. Furthermore, measurement of salivary cortisol has a definite advantage over blood. In the blood, about 90% of total cortisol present is bound to large proteins (cortisol binding protein and albumin) and only the remaining 10% is unbound and physiologically active. Thus blood cortisol determination provides a measure of total cortisol concentration (bound + unbound). Only the 'free' cortisol (unbound) can pass into the saliva and thus salivary cortisol provides a reliable measure of the physiologically active component of cortisol (Kirschbaum and Hellhammer, 1989).

Measurement of sIgA in the saliva is somewhat more complicated than measurement of cortisol. Cortisol is passively passed through the saliva glands as a filtrate from the blood. In contrast, sIgA is actively transported from the saliva glands across the mucosal surface. In addition, not all the saliva glands transport sIgA to the same extent. The most significant saliva glands with respect to sIgA production are those that lie under the tongue, i.e. the sublingual and submandibular glands. The parotid glands that have their ducts in the cheeks produce copious volumes of saliva during chewing but are not important suppliers of sIgA. Thus, the method of collection of saliva for determination of sIgA in psychophysiological research is critical. Flow of saliva should not have been stimulated (by either chewing or chemicals) as this enhances parotid flow and dilutes the concentration of sIgA being produced from the glands under the tongue. The best way to make the collection is to place an absorbent cotton roll under the tongue for a timed (usually about two minutes) period and allow saliva to passively pass into the roll. Presentation of results of changing levels of sIgA should always show the volume of saliva collected over a timed period, concentration of that saliva as well as the amount of saliva produced over a unit of time (i.e. concentration of sIgA × volume of saliva/time of collection). Research that does not take these issues into account is seriously flawed; these methodological problems did cause much confusion in the early days of research in this area.

Measurement of indices of immune function from the circulation is more complex and to a large extent beyond the scope of this chapter. Indeed, use of saliva as a substitute medium for psychophysiology research has been well discussed (see Nishanian et al., 1998; Kirschbaum, Pike and Hellhammer, 1993). However, measurement of circulating measures falls into two broad categories, i.e. background activity and response to challenge. Commonly used is a measure of the number of specific immune cells in the circulation. Automated cell counters can distinguish between the different types of cells and express their number per ml of blood. It is also possible to test the capacity of immune cells to proliferate (a process required for activation). This type of assay requires a blood sample to be taken and the immune cells within the sample to be challenged *in vitro* with a known activator. Degree of proliferative response can then be measured. Another approach is to quantify the chemicals (cytokines) released by the immune cells. This can be done in two ways: either measurement of circulating basal levels or increase in levels following challenge. Circulating antibodies can be measured; IgE is particularly useful here as raised levels give quite a useful indicator of Th2 activity. In contract, a raised number of NK cells, or NK cell activity, provides a useful index of increased Th1 activity. The interested reader is recommended to explore these topics further in the excellent text by Kuby (1997).

CONCLUSION

This chapter has examined 'stress' in terms of internal reactions to a situation, rather than the situation itself (stressor). It has not explored the basis for individual differences in these responses but has explained the mechanisms whereby a perceived threat can have widespread effects on the cardiovascular and immune systems as well as brain neurotransmitters responsible for mood. Typical stress response-inducing situations in human everyday life are often associated with interpersonal relationships and finance rather than true life-threatening situations. However, our stress response systems have evolved to serve us in just such life threatening situations, which in the wild would be rare events. It is the repeated activation of these stress response systems that potentially poses a significant health threat.

PART 2

WHAT EFFECTS MIGHT STRESS HAVE?

This section looks at some of the main outcomes that stress researchers have examined. We have already established that stress is such a general and diffuse term that measurement is not a simple matter. Definitions of stress (e.g. Lazarus and Folkman, 1984) often use individual well-being as a criterion, an approach which potentially brings any area of well-being into the remit of stress research. This may encompass a wide range of physical ailments, psychological states and cognitive processes as well as behaviours. Consequently, a large number of potential outcomes have been considered in the literature. Only some of these can be considered in detail here.

Key issues concerning research into the links between stressors and physical and psychological well-being are introduced in Chapter 4. This presents evidence relating to specific examples of links that have been a particular focus of research, for example the research looking at the relationship between life events and breast cancer. The chapter also considers psychological illness and symptoms and their relationships to stressors.

Chapter 5 will introduce a more cognitive approach to stress. This examines the possibility that specific cognitive and performance effects may stem from impaired psychosocial well-being and anxiety. It draws on work from the field of cognition and emotion that is not typically presented in the stress literature but suggests mechanisms whereby psychological reactions to stressors and impaired performance may be linked.

CHAPTER 4

STRESS: HEALTH AND ILLNESS

Do psychosocial factors (including life events and job demands and the psychological reactions these produce) lead to physical or psychiatric illness? Why has it proved difficult to establish these links? What mechanisms might be involved? The chapter will consider evidence in a limited number of specific research areas including research on the effects of stress on immune functioning.

THE view that stress leads to illness is fundamental to much that we read or hear about stress, so much so that it is often assumed that conclusive evidence exists. For example Pollock (1988) in an interview study of 114 people in the UK, found that there was a general belief that stress could be a direct cause of illness. Two specific conditions were thought to be most strongly associated with stress, 'heart attacks' and 'nervous breakdowns'. Situations (e.g. in the workplace) were typically thought to cause heart attacks, whereas people were thought to cause nervous breakdowns. An archetypal heart attack victim was seen as an executive or businessman under pressure. More minor symptoms such as headaches or stomach aches were also thought to be related to stressors or worries. Since Pollock's study it is unlikely that these beliefs have changed greatly. Statements about the contribution of 'stress' to disease appear regularly in the press as well as the academic literature serving to confirm the belief that 'stress' causes disease.

In fact, given the vagueness and generality of the term 'stress' it would appear that the question 'Does stress lead to illness?' is problematic. Indeed, Briner and Reynolds (1993) go so far as to suggest the question is 'naïve and trivial'. To even begin to consider the issues underpinning the question we need to consider a large number of different questions. Some of the more obvious that are listed below:

- Does exposure to a range of demanding stimuli (stressors) lead to psychiatric and/or physical illness?
- If so, what kind of stressors (major life events, chronic stressors, hassles)?
- Are stressors related to all illnesses or just some?
- Is it the existence of stressors or the feeling of being 'stressed', anxious or depressed that leads to illness?
- Why do only some people seem to be affected?
- What are the mechanisms?

There is a large amount of research addressing these questions, some of which will be discussed in further detail in other parts of the book, for example, the role of individual differences and chronic work stressors.

Despite the volume of research it has nevertheless been surprisingly difficult to establish a link between psychosocial factors and disease. Evidence comes from a wide range of sources and different types of study published in both the medical and psychological literature. For many years the focus of this research was on major *life events*. Many studies have been conducted into the relationships between life events and both physical and psychiatric disorders with often conflicting conclusions (e.g. Dohrenwend, 1998; Miller, 1989). Studies now often also look at *daily hassles* and *chronic stressors* (see Chapter 2). All three approaches can be seen in studies discussed in this chapter.

Before considering the links between psychosocial factors and specific illnesses we look briefly at why research in this area might be difficult.

WHAT DIFFICULTIES ARE THERE IN ESTABLISHING RELATIONSHIPS BETWEEN PSYCHOSOCIAL FACTORS AND DISEASE?

We have seen in Chapter 3 that the reaction to stressors has been associated with a variety of different physiological changes, for example in immune functioning. Frequently psychophysiologists look at relatively short-term changes in physiological indicators such as sIgA or cortisol (see Chapter 3). However, it cannot necessarily be assumed that these changes are of significance in causing disease. To confirm this we need to look at effects of stressors and diseases such as cancer in the real world. There is then, however, the complication that many other potential confounding factors cannot easily be controlled. Furthermore, the possible short and long term links between different stressors and different diseases that can be investigated are almost unlimited. In many cases the evidence, as we shall see, is ambiguous. Lazarus (1992) suggests that there are a number of reasons why a relationship between psychosocial factors and health (and by implication, illness) might be difficult to establish.

- Health is affected by a great many factors, including genetic influences and accidents. There may be little variance left to be accounted for by factors such as stress.
- Health is generally fairly stable and slow to change, making it difficult to demonstrate that psychosocial factors lead to changes in health.
- To demonstrate that stress affects long term health it is necessary to measure what is happening consistently over time. This may require repeated sampling and is likely to be costly, although it can and has been done over relatively short periods of time (months rather than years) examining illness symptoms or colds (e.g. DeLongis, Folkman and Lazarus, 1988; Evans and Edgerton, 1991).
- The criterion of health is unclear; for example a criterion of longevity would exclude some quite debilitating diseases whereas a criterion based on social functioning would lead to a conclusion that the person with high blood pressure is healthy.

These factors make it very difficult to establish the relationship between psychosocial factors and health. As we shall see, in the following sections, some researchers feel that we cannot claim to have established with any degree of certainty the extent and nature and even the existence of the relationship.

STRESS AND PHYSICAL ILLNESS

It would be a vast undertaking to review the large number of studies that exists in both medical and psychological literature on the role of life events, hassles and chronic stressors in a huge range of illnesses. This chapter will focus on three different aspects that serve to illustrate the diversity of approaches.

Early researchers focused predominantly on the effect of major life events (see Chapter 2). One area considered below, which has attracted a great deal of attention, is the relationship between stress and breast cancer. Here the debate for and against the influence of psychosocial factors has been particularly fierce. A second aspect that will be considered here is the influence of the chronic stressors of job control and job demands. The relationship between this factor and cardiovascular disease has been a particular focus of attention. The third aspect of physical illness highlighted in this chapter is the common cold. Because of its prevalence and the fact that it is a minor illness it is more amenable to research than other diseases.

Life events and breast cancer

There is widespread belief in an association between stressful experiences and the onset of breast cancer amongst both the general public and the medical profession. For example, a study by Baghurst, Baghurst and Record (1992) reports that

40% of South Australian women hold this belief, while Steptoe and Wardle (1994) found that almost half of a sample of medical experts were either undecided or confident of the role of stress in the causation of breast cancer.

The belief that emotionally distressing events are implicated in all types of cancer can be traced back to medical literature from the 19th century. There were numerous anecdotal reports in the literature commenting on the frequency with which negative events, grief and depression were associated with the onset of all kinds of cancer (see LeShan, 1959). The first statistical study of this association is attributed to Snow (1893) who studied 250 cancer patients in London and reported that in 156 of them there was some 'immediately antecedent trouble', frequently the loss of a close relative. LeShan suggests that the idea disappeared in the literature in the early part of the 20th century, as the developments in surgery and radiation offered the most promising hope for an answer to the problem of cancer. The notion of the importance of loss in cancer causation emerged again in the second quarter of the century. Again most studies were based on clinical observations. Nevertheless LeShan remarks on the consistency with which 'in different countries and at different times' physicians independently described their patients using descriptions such as 'despair', 'hopelessness', 'loss of a child', 'loss of a spouse' or 'afflictions that appear insurmountable'. In his own work, LeShan also found that cancer frequencies and age-adjusted mortality rates were higher amongst groups who had experienced loss, e.g. the highest incidence was found in the widowed, followed by divorced, married, then single people (LeShan and Worthington, 1956).

More recent work focusing specifically on breast cancer, rather than cancer in general, has also produced many studies which show associations (e.g. Cooper, Cooper and Faragher, 1989; Geyer, 1991; Chen et al., 1995). For example, Cooper, Cooper and Faragher (1989) studied 1,596 women attending breast screening clinics with symptoms of breast lumpiness or tenderness, as well as 567 controls. Prior to being examined and diagnosed, they completed a questionnaire which asked about life events in the previous two years. This design is known as a 'limited prospective study'. They found that some life events, including the death of a husband or close friend, were associated with breast disease and its severity. More recently, Chen et al. (1995) investigated 119 women who were referred for biopsies. They were interviewed using Brown and Harris's (1979) life events and difficulties schedule (see Chapter 2) before they received a definitive diagnosis. They found that 19 out of 41 women with cancer had 'greatly threatening life events' during the five years before diagnosis compared with 15 out of the 78 controls. There was also increased risk associated with moderately threatening events but none with minor events.

However, persuasive as these results are, there are many studies that have used similar approaches and failed to confirm these findings (e.g. Muslin, Gyarfas and Pieper, 1966; Greer and Morris, 1975; Protheroe et al., 1999). Over the years, while isolated studies continue to find links, reviews of the literature (e.g. Stolbach and Brandt, 1988) have tended to conclude that there is little evidence for an association. Genuine prospective studies (which follow people from before the appearance of symptoms) are rare, but one was conducted by Jones, Goldblatt and Leon (1984) who investigated the notion that widows, having experienced loss, should be more prone to breast cancer than others. They followed up a 1% sample of the UK population and found that, although there was a slight increase in breast cancer mortality amongst widows this was not significant.

More recently, meta-analyses have been conducted to try to reach conclusions from this conflicting evidence. Petticrew, Fraser and Regan (1999) considered 29 studies of the association of life events and breast cancer. Studies are described as of 'variable design' but all included controls. Assessment of events was typically based on check-lists (e.g. the SRRS) or interviews (e.g. LEDs; see Chapter 2). Overall, they concluded that there was 'no good evidence for a relationship' between negative life events and cancer on the basis of analysis of better quality studies. However, the meta-analysis did suggest that breast cancer patients were more than twice as likely than controls to report negative life events, though there was no greater likelihood of them reporting bereavement. They suggest however that this result may be due to methodological flaws. When only the five highest quality studies are considered, they found no significantly increased cancer risk.

Petticrew, Fraser and Regan (1999) further suggest that there is some evidence of publication bias (see Chapter 2) in this area and that non-significant studies are less likely to be published. Published studies that have found a relationship (e.g. Chen et al., 1995) are also more likely to get media coverage, thus fuelling public beliefs.

A further meta-analysis has also been conducted by McKenna et al. (1999). They considered a smaller and largely overlapping sample of studies and found a significant relationship between the development of breast cancer and both severe life events and loss experiences. However, they too go on to criticise the method-ological approaches used and to argue that the associations found are 'draped with much qualification'. They conclude that 'results overall support only a modest association between specific psychosocial factors and breast cancer' but also, somewhat ambivalently, 'that results speak against the conventional wisdom that . . . stress factors influence the development of breast cancer' (p. 528).

Reviewers frequently identify methodological flaws and these may certainly account for the relationships that have been found in many studies. As we saw in Chapter 2, methods that rely on retrospective recall (e.g. case-control studies) may be biased as those who are diagnosed with cancer may be inclined to search hard for life events to explain their illness. The use of limited prospective studies (such as that of Chen et al., 1995, described above), assessing life events just before diagnosis, is a methodological improvement on the early retrospective studies. Nevertheless, these are still open to the criticism that people with symptoms that are later confirmed to be cancer may already have a strong suspicion of their diagnosis. Hence they may be subject to the same biasing factors as retrospective studies.

Overall, given the contradictory findings in the literature and the somewhat marginal and confusing findings from the meta-analyses it is difficult to avoid concluding that, as yet, we simply do not know for sure whether or not life events cause breast cancer. However, it also seems likely that if there is an effect it is likely to be very small compared to the influence of biological factors. Methodological flaws are often blamed for inconclusive results, but this is because it is extraordinarily difficult to control all possible confounding variables. What seems to be required is a large scale and long term prospective study assessing (objectively) a range of events or stressors prior to the occurrence of symptoms. A study of this sort would be extremely costly and may still not settle the issue conclusively. For example, McGee (1999) points out that causative factors may be operating years before diagnosis, thus it is difficult to rule out the possibility that life events accelerate development of cancer or influence the likelihood of diagnosis.

Similar debates have raged concerning whether life events influence not just the initiation but also the development and recurrence of breast cancer. Here again the results are inconclusive (Jensen, 1991).

In addition to the effects of life events, much interest has also focused on the related topic of the importance of affective states (e.g. depression) or personality characteristics such as the repression of emotion in the causation and recurrence of breast cancer. Detailed review of this research is beyond the scope of this chapter, however, the meta-analysis by McKenna *et al.* found no support for the hypotheses that breast cancer patients experienced heightened anxiety or depression or that they had difficulty expressing anger. They did find a significant effect size suggesting those with breast cancer tended to cope by denial or repressive coping but they also highlight the methodological flaws and suggest more research is needed. Mixed findings also exist concerning the success of psychosocial interventions in reducing mortality. This is discussed further in Chapter 11.

One difficulty researchers have in assessing the effect of life events is (as McGee, 1999, points out) the very vagueness of the hypothesis. Life events and even the single event of bereavement encompasses a very broad range of experiences. The next section looks at some rather more focused research on two chronic work stressors.

Chronic work stressors and cardiovascular disease (CVD)

There is a great deal of research looking at the relationships between two particular aspects of work stress (job demands and control) and health. This largely stems from the popularity of Karasek's job strain model that suggests that these two aspects are particularly important for predicting strain. According to Karasek, a job which is high in demands (workload and pace of work) and in which employees have little control (e.g. over what they do and when they do it) will be a high strain job. (The model and its importance for work stress research is considered in further detail in Chapter 9.) Early epidemiological studies by Karasek and colleagues (e.g. Alfredsson, Karasek and Theorell, 1982; Karasek *et al.*, 1981) suggested that the combination of these two variables did indeed predict heart disease. These variables

are now frequently used in studies in both the medical and psychological literature generating a large and complex body of research. This includes work on
psychological well-being (see Chapter 9), musculoskeletal disorders (Skov, Borg
and Orhede, 1996; Krause *et al.*, 1997) adverse outcome of pregnancy (Brandt
and Nielsen, 1992), cancer of the colon (Courtney, Longnecker and Peters, 1996),
periodontal disease (Marcenes and Sheiham, 1992) and drug use (Storr, Trinkoff
and Anthony, 1999).

However, the largest number of studies has considered the relationship between
these work stressors and cardiovascular disease (CVD) and its associated risk
factors (e.g. raised blood pressure). A number of large epidemiological studies
have now related the incidence of heart disease and mortality from CVD to type
of employment. Frequently these studies assess people's work stressors using a
methodology that classifies individuals on the job strain dimensions (in terms
of level of demand and control) according to their job title. Thus, for example, all
waiters might be classified as having low control, high demand jobs. Alternatively,
some studies have assessed job stressors using the more subjective method of
asking individuals to rate their levels of demand and control. Using the former
method, Alfredsson, Karasek and Theorell (1982) found that hectic work combined
with low control was associated with higher incidence of heart disease. Using the
latter method, Johnson, Hall and Theorell (1989) found the greatest risk was in
high demand, low control isolated jobs.

There is also a large number of studies relating job features to risk factors that
are implicated in cardiovascular disease (see Chapter 3) such as high blood pressure (e.g. Brisson *et al.*, 1999; Fletcher and Jones, 1993; Fox, Dwyer and Ganster,
1993) or measures of adrenaline and cortisol (e.g. Pollard *et al.*, 1996; Fox, Dwyer
and Ganster, 1993). Fox, Dwyer and Ganster, in their study of nurses found that
the combination of high demands and low control predicted both blood pressure
and cortisol levels. However, Fletcher and Jones in a sample from heterogeneous
occupations found no relationships between control and blood pressure and where
demands showed relationships these were in the opposite direction to that predicted (i.e. those with lower demands had higher blood pressure).

In addition there are a small number of experimental studies that have manipulated levels of job strain in the laboratory and examined the relationship to
short-term physiological indicators which are implicated in CVD development (see
Chapter 3). These include heart rate levels and cortisol (Perrewe and Ganster, 1989;
Steptoe *et al.*, 1993). For example, Steptoe *et al.* found that middle-aged men showed
greater changes in blood pressure when they could not control the pace at which
they performed laboratory tasks involving problem solving and mirror drawing.
However, pacing had little effect on cortisol, suggesting work pace has a specific
effect on cardiovascular functioning.

A comprehensive meta-analysis or systematic review is perhaps overdue but
given the different measures and lack of comparability between studies it would
be very difficult to achieve (Kristensen, 1995). However, the literature in relation

to CVD has been reviewed by Schnall, Landsbergis and Baker (1994). They state that the literature 'strongly suggests a causal association between job strain and CVD'. However, when the main effects are examined, 17 out of 25 studies found significant associations between job decision latitude and outcome, whereas only eight out of 23 studies showed significant relationships between demand and outcome. Since this review, a further large study by Alterman *et al.* (1994) also suggests the greater importance of control in coronary heart disease mortality. A few recent studies have also found an effect for demands opposite to that predicted (e.g. Alterman *et al.*, 1994; Hlatky *et al.*, 1995; Steenland, Johnson and Nowlin, 1997).

Until recently most studies used male samples and it has been suggested that the model is less applicable for women, but here again there are conflicting results. For example, Weidner *et al.* (1997) found that having a high demand/low control job was unrelated to standard coronary risk factors in both sexes but that it was related to increased medical symptoms and health damaging behaviour in a sample of men but not women. However, a more recent study by Amick *et al.* (1998) did find that high demand and low control, together with low support, predicted poorer health status in women. Furthermore, Brisson *et al.* (1999) found a combination of large family responsibilities and high strain jobs was related to raised blood pressure in well-educated women in white-collar jobs.

There have inevitably been numerous criticisms of this literature. For example, the accusation is often made that the research fails to adequately take into account the influence of social class (Muntaner and O'Campo, 1993). Others have criticised the ways in which the core constructs of demand and control are operationalised suggesting that they are too vague and all encompassing (e.g. Jones *et al.*, 1998). In addition, Kristensen (1996) points out that the two methods of assessing job strain classify the same people very differently. Further criticisms are discussed further in Chapter 9.

Thus overall, deriving a clear message from this literature is difficult. However, a review by Van der Doef and Maes (1998) which does not separate the effects of demand and control, concludes that across different populations, measurement methods and job designs, there is substantial support for the hypothesis that high demand, low control jobs lead to increased CVD. Our view is that where evidence exists this primarily seems to point to the importance of job control rather than demands. While evidence here is mounting, further work is needed (including more laboratory studies) to find out what specific aspects of control may be important, for example, is it control over pace of work that is important or does more general involvement in decisions about work have an impact?

Psychosocial factors and the common cold

The mounting evidence for the influence of stressors on immune functioning has resulted in an increased interest in the effects of factors such as life events, hassles and perceptions of stress and infectious diseases (Cohen and Williamson, 1991). Cohen and Williamson point out that in order to successfully predict the occurrence of a disease from these variables, it is necessary to have a reasonably high incidence of the disease in the sample studied. This has led to an emphasis in the research literature on the study of common diseases such as colds, influenza and herpes.

It should be noted that in the study of infection, there is a distinction between the presence of infection and the presence of actual symptoms. In the case of the common cold, a clinical cold only develops in a proportion of those infected. Evidence of infection can be found by analysing blood samples. Evidence of the presence of clinical colds is dependent on the assessment of external symptoms, either reported by the participant or by, for example, measuring mucus weight (by weighing used tissues).

A large number of studies using different types of methodology have demonstrated a relationship between stressors and colds. Prospective studies using measures of family stressors (such as life events) and family functioning have shown these predict the frequency of occurrence of verified colds and influenza in family members (e.g. Clover *et al.*, 1989; Graham, Douglas and Ryan, 1986). Daily stressors have also been studied by Evans and Edgerton (1991) who got 100 people filling in daily questionnaires for 10 weeks, during which time 17 developed a cold. They found that desirable events decreased in frequency in the week just before the onset of a cold (referred to as the four-day desirability dip) and there was an increase in hassles or negative events. Specifically, there was lack in social support and intimacy and the most important hassles related to interpersonal problems.

An alternative interpretation for the reported relationships between stressors and colds could be simply that people who are exposed to a lot of stressful events may be more likely to come into contact with a cold virus. One way in which researchers have attempted to gain greater control over possible confounding variables in this area is to use a quasi-experimental approach. Typically, in such studies, healthy individuals complete retrospective measures of psychosocial factors before being exposed to a controlled amount of a cold virus. Such quasi-experimental studies are referred to as 'viral-challenge' studies by Cohen and Williamson (1991) in their review. These have provided mixed and generally rather limited evidence for the influence of stress on susceptibility to colds perhaps because of methodological limitations. However, some more recent reports provide stronger evidence.

In the UK such studies were conducted at the Medical Research Council's now defunct Common Cold Unit in Salisbury. In studies by Cohen and his colleagues (e.g. Cohen, Tyrell and Smith, 1991b; Cohen, Tyrell and Smith, 1993), healthy volunteers were recruited to stay at the unit for a period of weeks. On arrival they completed retrospective questionnaires about major life events, about perceptions of stress and negative affect as well as measures of health practices. Blood tests were also taken for immune assessment. One group of volunteers was then given nasal drops containing a low dose of one of five types of cold virus. The doses were designed to be similar to those experienced in normal person-to-person transmission. A small number in a control condition were given saline drops instead of the virus. Neither investigators nor volunteers knew who had been given the virus and who had received the saline drops. The participants remained in quarantine, either alone or with one or two others, for two days before and seven days after the viral challenge. During this time they were examined daily for signs and symptoms. Twenty-eight days later further blood tests were taken.

Cohen, Tyrell and Smith (1991b) reported that of the 394 participants exposed to the viruses, 82% were infected and 38% got clinical colds. In the 26 people in the control group only 19% were infected and none got clinical colds. The reporting of psychological stress before exposure to the virus (using a combined index based on life events, perceived stress and negative affect) was associated with an increase in respiratory infection in a dose-response manner, that is, for each increase in stress score there was a corresponding increase in the proportion with colds. Stress scores were more strongly associated with infection than with clinical illness. The overall results remained the same when levels of immunity, health practices and personality variables (self-esteem, personal control and introversion/extraversion) were taken into account.

Using the same sample, Cohen, Tyrell and Smith (1993) looked at the separate effects of stressful life events, perceived stress and negative affect. They suggested that different processes mediated the relationships between life events and colds and that between perceived stress and colds.

> Negative life events were associated with greater rates of clinical illness, and this association was primarily mediated by increased symptoms among infected persons. Perceived stress and negative affect were also related to clinical illness, but there associations were primarily due to increased infection. (p. 138)

Cohen *et al.* found that life events predicted illness even when perceptions of stress and negative affect, as well as health behaviours, were controlled for. This casts doubt on the common assumption that the effect of life events influence health via their effect on feelings and emotions. Instead it suggests that life events might lead to colds even though we are not aware of feelings of 'stress', such as anxiety or unhappiness. Whether we need to feel stressed for it to have an impact on our health is an issue that is discussed further in Box 4.1.

Moving on to even more specific examination of the stressors implicated in the common cold, Cohen *et al.* (1998) in research conducted in the US found that particular types of stressor were associated with developing colds. In this study both acute and chronic stressors were assessed using the LEDS. In addition, personality factors were assessed as well as social networks. As in the previous studies participants were then exposed to the virus, with similar numbers showing signs of infection and clinical colds. They found that acute stressors (lasting less than a

Box 4.1   Do we need to feel 'stressed' or anxious for life events and other stressors to be harmful for health?

Yet another problem with the construct of 'stress' is that it is not entirely clear whether we need to *feel* stressed to *be* stressed. Implicit in popular notions of stress is the idea that it is a feeling we can report on. This assumption also underlies the use of self-report questionnaires such as the GHQ. However, many researchers also look at relationships between stressors and health (e.g. whether life events are related to health) without considering appraisals of distress or anxiety. This seems to contradict Lazarus' transactional approach to stress (see Chapter 2), for which appraisal is the central component.

However, a snag with the notion of appraisal and its assessment by self-report measures is that it does require conscious awareness of appraisal, yet Lazarus suggests that 'an individual may be unaware of any or all of the elements of an appraisal'. He suggests that this may operate via a defence mechanism. One example of such a mechanism, repressive coping, is discussed in Chapter 7. If stressors need not be *consciously* appraised then it makes sense to measure the relationship between stressors and strains without necessarily looking at the impact of perceptions of stress or anxiety. Thus the questions 'Do stressors such as life events lead to illness?' and 'Does feeling stressed and anxious lead to illness?' are two different, though related, questions. Unfortunately the vague nature of the stress concept means that this distinction is often not made clear. Self-reports of anxiety and stress are likely to be only one of the pathways by which stressors lead to ill health.

As we saw in Chapter 2, researchers such as Kasl (1978) consider that stressors should be measured independently of appraisals. The value of this approach is demonstrated by Cohen, Tyrell and Smith (1993) (see p. 74).

month) did not increase the risk of colds, but that more enduring, chronic stressors were associated with greater susceptibility. This was primarily due to a greater number of colds developing among infected people. The strongest associations were found for interpersonal conflicts and work stressors (particularly unemployment or underemployment). However, Leventhal, Patrick-Miller and Leventhal (1998) point out that the high level of payment to participate may mean the study attracted people with these problems. There was also some indication that, for those with chronic stressors, having an acute event actually offered some protection, perhaps distracting from the chronic problem. While the study did find that introverts and those with few social networks were more likely to be infected, this did not effect the stressor–strain relationship (i.e. these factors have a direct effect only).

The conclusion drawn by Cohen, Tyrell and Smith, that chronic stressors are the most important type of stressor implicated in the development of colds, contradicts the work of Evans and Edgerton (1991) discussed above which suggests the importance of minor hassles in the days preceding development of colds. Cohen, Tyrell and Smith suggest this may be because of the different kinds of events studied, the acute events measured by the LEDs being much more serious than the minor day-to-day perceptions of hassles.

Some recent studies also suggest that positive life events may be even more important than negative events. Stone *et al.* (1992), for example, have found that positive events rather than negative predict colds while Evans *et al.* (1996) found that only positive events predicted the subsequent occurrence of colds. Like Cohen, Tyrell and Smith (1993) they found that self-reports of perceptions of stress were not related to colds. and that the effect was not explained by health behaviours. Furthermore, they consider that the link cannot be fully explained by those with positive events being more socially active and exposing themselves to more pathogens. The mechanisms for this relationship are therefore unclear. However this study adds further support to the view that the perception of 'stress' may not be a key issue.

Overall, Cohen *et al.* (1998) suggest that studies using sophisticated methodologies provide strong evidence for a dose–response relationship between psychological stress (defined in terms of negative events and the affective states they cause) and risk of developing a cold. Perceptions of stress may not always be crucial. Emotional distress seems to be associated with a greater risk of infection while life events including positive events seem to be associated with actually getting a cold.

What might be the mechanisms underpinning a relationship between stressors and physical health and disease?

Steptoe (1991) identifies two major links whereby stress responses may be linked to health:

- *The cognitive–behavioural pathway.* Steptoe suggests that cognitive, affective and behavioural aspects of the stress response can have an impact on health that is independent of any direct physiological effects. For example, work stressors may lead to a person feeling anxious (affective element), thinking that having a cigarette would help them relax and cope better (cognition) and therefore smoking more (behavioural). Developing a smoking-related disorder is thus an indirect effect of smoking rather than a direct effect of the reaction to work stressors. In the literature this kind of relationship is often described as mediation – that is, smoking *mediates* the relationship between stressors and health. (Mediation is discussed in further detail in Chapter 6.)
- *The psychophysiological pathway.* These pathways are complex and Steptoe has identified three types of physiological process involved. For example, under stress there may be a hyperreactive response, that is an exaggerated

76

physiological response which may be implicated in disease causation (for example, exaggerated blood pressure responses to stress may predict future blood pressure). Secondly, hyperreactivity may destabilise existing disease processes to exacerbate a disease (such as diabetes). Thirdly, stressors may have an effect on the immune response, for example via their influence on endocrine responses. Here stressors are related to illness via lowering resistance.

Many of the studies discussed above have considered the possible mechanisms to explain relationships. Thus, studies such as that by Cohen, Tyrell and Smith (1991b), control for the effects of health behaviours when they look at the relationship between life events and illness. Many studies also take physiological measures such as blood pressure or measures of immune functioning to explore the mechanisms (e.g. Cohen, Tyrell and Smith, 1991b, 1993; Cohen *et al.*, 1998; Steptoe *et al.*, 1993). The next sections consider some possible mechanisms in more depth. Firstly, cognitive–behavioural pathways are discussed. This is followed by an introduction to the psychophysiological pathway associated with immune functioning. This has received a great deal of attention as a possible link between psychosocial factors and disease.

WHAT EVIDENCE IS THERE FOR STRESSORS LEADING TO CHANGES IN HEALTH BEHAVIOURS?

Research looking at the cognitive–behavioural pathways has focused predominantly on whether stressors are linked to the negative health behaviours of smoking and drinking alcohol. Positive health behaviours such as eating healthily and exercising have received relatively little attention, though it is also likely that such behaviours may be disrupted by stressful events. Existing research is typically built on an assumption that the negative effects on health of smoking, drinking and not exercising are well-established. This assumption is reasonably well founded. Certainly the evidence that smoking damages health is now overwhelming (e.g. Dunn *et al.*, 1999) and the value of exercise seems clear (e.g. Blair *et al.*, 1989). Extreme alcohol consumption also has an established damaging health effect, however, the evidence in relation to moderate levels of alcohol consumption is far less clear (see Box 4.2). This factor further complicates the interpretation of evidence in relation to this 'risk factor'.

Generally studies of the effects of stressors on substance use suggest relationships between high levels of life stress and various aspects of substance use such as the initiation of smoking, drinking and drug use (Wills, 1990). Wills also suggests that stressors are linked with an increased amount of substances used by regular users and reduced success in cessation.

One study that supports the notion of a cognitive–behavioural pathway between such substance use and physical health is that of DeFrank, Jenkins and

Box 4.2   The relationship between alcohol and health.

Alcohol consumption is probably one of the most ubiquitous methods that we use to cope with stressors. Some of the effects of alcohol are well known, including mild elation, depression, lack of judgement, temporary and chronic cognitive impairment and loss of coordination. We also know that it is addictive.

Excessive consumption of alcohol is widely agreed to be injurious, however it is not at all clear what excessive means in this context. There are those that argue that any alcohol consumption is bad for you, those that suggest that moderate amounts of alcohol such as 2–3 glasses of wine per day is harmless, and those that argue that much greater quantities (e.g. 1 litre of wine per day) may be harmless. Furthermore there are some groups that suggest that ingestion of alcohol has positive health benefits. Some examples of the complex findings are given below.

Boffetta and Garfinkel (1990) studied 276,802 US men to see whether moderate alcohol drinkers have a lower total and coronary heart disease (CHD) mortality than non-drinkers. The data suggested that alcohol has a protective effect for mortality generally for those drinking one or two drinks a day and a protective effect more specifically for CHD for those drinking considerably more.

However, not all studies have concluded that alcohol has a positive health benefit. A 21-year follow-up study of over 5,000 men found no relationship between alcohol and coronary heart disease once potentially confounding factors were ruled out. However, overall risk of mortality was higher for men drinking 22 units per week and there was a particularly strong association with mortality from strokes (Hart et al., 1999).

Alcohol has also been linked to greater risk of cancer. Merletti et al., (1989) compared 122 cancer sufferers with 606 controls and found that heavy consumers of alcohol and tobacco had very high risks of both oral and throat cancer. Hiatt (1990) conducted a meta-analysis of 21 studies investigating the link between alcohol consumption and breast cancer in women. Hiatt found that there was a 50% increase in breast cancer risk for women who average between one and two drinks per day.

Rose (1987). This study looked at the links between work stressors, social supports, alcohol consumption and blood pressure in a study of air traffic controllers. Their evidence suggested that high levels of work stressors and good social supports were primarily related to greater alcohol use and that this in turn predicted raised blood pressure.

However, the links between stressors and health behaviours are not straight-forward. For example, Cohen et al. (1991a) found gender differences in the pattern of relationships with smoking showing relationships with full-time employment, depression, increased marital conflict and higher numbers of negative life events for women. Depression and marital conflict and the interaction between full-time employment and marital conflict were also related to increased alcohol consumption for women. However, for men only, smoking was related to psychosocial factors. Specifically, it was related to depression and to job demands and job control.

Other studies which have investigated job demands and control support the finding that work features affect the health behaviours of men and women in different ways (e.g. Weidner *et al.*, 1997; Hellerstedt and Jeffrey, 1997). For example, Weidner *et al.* found that demand and decision latitude were related to health damaging behaviour (a combined measure of smoking, drinking alcohol and coffee, and lack of exercise) in men but not women. They suggest that these behaviours may in part mediate the relationships between work factors and coronary risk factors. Other job demands, such as shiftwork, piecework, hazardous exposure and physical load were associated with increased smoking in both sexes (Johansson, Johnson and Hall, 1991).

Not surprisingly the health behaviours of students preparing for exams has also come under scrutiny. The fact that students are a readily accessible sample who are experiencing a common stressor at the same time, means that they have been a popular focus of research. For example, Steptoe *et al.* (1996) compared a group of university students undergoing exams with a group with no exams. Those taking exams were assessed at baseline and then within the two weeks before exams and the control group was assessed at an equivalent interval. As expected measures of perceived stress and distress increased when students were closer to exams. Physical activity decreased nearer to the exams. However changes in alcohol consumption were dependent on level of support. Specifically, there was a reduction in alcohol consumption in students with high social support, while those with low social supports increased their alcohol intake, i.e. the relationship between stressors and alcohol was moderated by social support. (See Chapter 6 for further discussion of moderated relationships.) When smoking was considered, both gender and social support moderated the relationship such that in the exam group, women who had few social supports showed increased smoking between the two assessments whereas men did not. Controls showed no systematic changes in health behaviours between the two assessments. Ogden and Mtandabari (1997) found similar results and in particular report reductions in alcohol use, less exercise and greater numbers smoking.

Thus we see that the relationship between stressors and health behaviour is not a simple one with exam stress often improving one health behaviour (alcohol use) while having negative impact on another. This reduction in alcohol in the face of exam stress is perhaps surprising but makes sense when health behaviours are viewed as coping strategies as has been suggested by Ingledew, Hardy and Cooper (1996). Reducing exercise, increasing smoking and reducing alcohol use can all be viewed as coping strategies that help by freeing up time and increasing concentration. (See also Chapter 7.)

One possibility seldom considered is that, where perceptions of stress are related to health behaviour, it is the poor health behaviour that actually causes an increase in the perception of stress. However, Wills (1990), in his review of substance use, suggests that evidence converging from a number of different types of study indicates that the predominant direction of causation is from perceptions of life stress to substance use rather than vice versa. He suggests two possible models of this effect that could be used to guide future research. These may also apply to other health behaviours:

- *Affect regulation model*. This suggests that under conditions of stress substance use serves a coping function in that it reduces anxiety.
- *Self-control model*. This suggests that stress reduces self-control because it increases cognitive load and reduces feelings of efficacy both of which may impact on maintenance of self-control and resisting temptation.

Of course these models are not mutually exclusive and both may play a part.

Overall, evidence suggests that stressors do sometimes impact on health behaviours but relationships are complex. The extent to which observed relationships between stressors and illness can be attributed to health behaviours is inadequately understood. However, a number of studies reviewed in this book suggest that where there is a relationship between stressors and health, it is only partially explained by health behaviours (e.g. Cohen, Tyrell and Smith, 1993; Evans *et al.*, 1996).

What evidence is there for stressors leading to changes in immune functioning?

The relationship between stress and immune functioning has been a major focus of research in the specialism of psychoneuroimmunology. Acute stressors have been the focus of many such studies (for a review see O'Leary, 1990). This has included the study of dramatic events such as the effects of splashdown on Apollo astronauts (Fischer *et al.*, 1972). However, O'Leary suggests such extreme stressors may confound physiological and psychological effects on immune functioning.

A more everyday, but still relatively acute, stressor is that of college examinations. Longitudinal studies assess immune functioning typically over a few weeks before during and after the exam period. Kiecolt-Glaser, Glaser and colleagues have conducted a series of such studies on medical students and have found immunosuppressive effects such as reduction in the percentages of T cells and in the numbers of NK cells (Kennedy, Kiecolt-Glaser and Glaser, 1988) (see Chapter 3). Exam related immune changes have also been shown to have a dramatic effect on the length of time it takes for wounds to heal. For example, Marucha, Kiecolt-Glaser and Favegehi (1998) inflicted standardised wounds consisting of a punch biopsy on the hard palate of dental students both during the summer vacation and three days before an exam. They found that the wounds took three days (that is 40%) longer to heal in the approach to exams than in the vacation.

It may be, however, that such acute events are less important than the chronic stressors of daily life, including such aspects as marital discord or caring for elderly relatives. The work of Kiecolt-Glaser, Glaser and colleagues has been particularly influential in establishing a link between such stressors and immune functioning. In a study comparing women who had separated from their partners with matched married controls, they found poorer immune functioning in women who had separated in the last year (Kiecolt-Glaser *et al.*, 1987). Of course, it may be the case that separated people have unhealthier life styles; however, they found no evidence to suggest that this was the case. Furthermore, even among the married women poorer quality marriages were associated with some reductions in immunocompetence.

The processes involved have been examined further by Malarkey *et al.* (1994) in a study in which 90 newly-wed couples were admitted to a research unit for 24 hours. Couples were asked to discuss and resolve marital issues likely to produce conflict (e.g. relating to in-laws or finances) in a 30-minute discussion. This was recorded and later analysed. Blood samples were taken before, during and after the discussion and levels of hormones were analysed (e.g. including adrenaline, noradrenaline, and cortisol). They found that marital conflict and hostility was related to changes in levels of all the hormones assessed with the exception of cortisol. They suggest these changes could lead to poorer immune functioning. Women demonstrated greater impacts than men in response to marital conflict. Similar results have also been reported in older couples (Kiecolt-Glaser *et al.*, 1998).

In a further group of studies, this time focusing on the carers of Alzheimer's patients, Kiecolt-Glaser and colleagues have found that carers report higher perceived stress levels and have poorer immune functioning than controls (Kiecolt-Glaser *et al.*, 1991). This effect was still present in the two years following bereavement (Esterling *et al.*, 1994). Caregivers also show slower healing of wounds than controls (Kiecolt-Glaser *et al.*, 1995).

Herbert and Cohen (1993) conducted a meta-analysis of 38 studies looking at the relationship between stressors and immune outcomes in healthy people. They included studies of short-term laboratory stressors (lasting less than half an hour), short-term naturalistic stressors (lasting between several days and a month, e.g. college examinations) and long-term naturalistic stressors (lasting longer than a month, e.g. bereavement or unemployment. Overall, they found substantial evidence for relationships between stressors and a range of immune parameters and that objective stressors were related to larger changes in immune functioning than self-reports of stress. They also found that acute laboratory stressors and long-term real-life stressors showed different immune changes reflecting different processes (see Chapter 3). Furthermore, interpersonal stressors led to different immune effects than non-social stressors.

Overall, this area of research is uncovering potentially important links between psychosocial factors and immune functioning. In this section we have only been able to give a very brief introduction to this complex and expanding area of research, providing a flavour of the complicated relationships between different types of stressors and different immune parameters. What we do not yet know is how important these demonstrated immune changes are in causing disease. However, studies have shown that caregivers and stressed/anxious students show poorer antibody responses to the influenza virus and hence are likely to be more vulnerable to infection (Glaser *et al.*, 1998; Vedhara *et al.*, 1999). This provides evidence of a link between immune parameters and disease. However, whether stress-related immune changes can be linked to more severe illness is unclear. Stein, Miller and Trestman (1991) argue that there is a lack of evidence for a link between depression and stressful events and any increase in mortality or morbidity from disorders associated with the immune system. As we have seen above, for example, there is little evidence that life events or depression are implicated in breast cancer causation. Stein also points out that mortality following the stressful event of bereavement has been linked to cardiovascular disease and not immune disorders (Osterweis, Solomon and Green, 1984). Stein *et al.* suggest that it is important to establish links between psychiatric disorders and/or stressful experiences and specific immune related disorders *before* seeking mechanisms.

Why do some people seem to be more susceptible to the effects of stressors than others?

In so far as there is evidence for a relationship between stressors and disease it is very clear that not everyone who is subject to a particular stressor becomes ill. The diathesis–stress approach introduced in Chapter 3 suggests that whether an individual is affected by stressors will depend on their individual physiological predisposition. However, psychological and social factors may also predispose the individual to be adversely affected, or conversely, protected from the effects of stressors. These may include individual personality factors or factors in the environment, e.g. the availability of resources such as social supports (see Chapter 8). In researching stress and disease, certain personality factors have been researched more than others. The predominant focus has been on those factors that are regarded as being related to dysfunctional coping styles and strategies (see Chapter 7). A cluster of characteristics associated with negative emotions has been particularly related to disease. These include Type A personality (characterised by impatience, irritability, hostility, competitiveness, job involvement and achievement striving) and negative affectivity (the dispositional tendency to experience negative emotions and a negative self-concept). The complex relationship between these factors and strains is considered in detail in Chapter 6. Box 4.3, however, introduces one specific type of approach to examining personality that seems to be related to higher incidence of disease generally.

Box 4.3   Pessimistic explanatory style and disease.

One personality variable, clearly related to negative affectivity, which has been useful in predicting disease is that of pessimistic explanatory style. This work is associated with Peterson, Seligman and colleagues. Peterson, Seligman and Vaillant (1988a) suggests that a person with a pessimistic explanatory style tends to explain negative events by making stable, global, internal attributions. For example, such a person might explain a serious conflict with a friend as something 'which is never going to go away' (stable), 'is going to ruin everything' (global) and 'is my fault' (internal). By contrast a more optimistic person may interpret the event as less long lasting, with much more restricted implications and blame it on the other person or the circumstances. In one study, spanning 35 years, Peterson et al. (1988b) classified the explanatory style of 99 graduates who were at Harvard in the years 1942–45 when they were aged 25. To assess explanatory style they used a method whereby written accounts of difficult war time experiences were content analysed for stable, global, internal explanations. They then measured a range of health outcomes (based on scores from medical examinations) every five years until they were aged 60. They found that pessimistic explanatory style was related to overall health from ages 45 to 60 even when initial health at the age of 25 was controlled for. A number of potential mechanisms are proposed. For example, pessimism may result in passivity in the face of illness and failure to seek medical advice. Alternatively, because they tend to be poor at problem solving they may fail to 'nip a crisis in the bud' and thus may experience more or worse life events. They may neglect health behaviours because they may feel they are not worthwhile or they may be socially withdrawn and lack the buffer of social support.

More recent research has also linked pessimistic explanatory style to immune functioning (Kamen-Siegel et al., 1991) and catastrophising (that is attributing bad events to global causes) has been shown to predict accidental or violent deaths (Peterson et al., 1998).

Other examples of research examining the impact of negative dispositional styles are considered in Chapter 6.

One further way in which individual differences may be important in some studies of illness outcomes is that some people may be more inclined to report illness than others. For example, Feldman and Cohen (1999) have found that personality symptoms such as neuroticism and conscientiousness increased reporting of cold symptoms that had no physiological basis. This effect may influence results in studies that are based purely on self-reports or on physician diagnosis, which may be heavily dependent on patient reports.

Summary

The findings from the studies discussed so far in this chapter are complex. While many interesting links between psychosocial factors and health have been found, the overall evidence for relationships between psychosocial factors and disease is far from unambiguous. At best it seems that public belief in the relationship has raced ahead of scientific evidence. Some researchers have suggested that currently there is still only limited evidence for relationships (e.g. Briner and Reynolds, 1993; Cohen and Williamson, 1991). The evidence we have suggests the relationship may vary dependent on which stressors, diseases and individuals are considered.

For example, evidence seems to support the influence of stressors on the development of colds (e.g. Cohen *et al.*, 1998). This does not, of course, mean that the findings can be generalised to other kinds of disease such as cancer or heart disease (Leventhal, Patrick-Miller and Leventhal, 1998). In considering the broad range of diseases, Cohen and Manuck (1995) have concluded that 'convincing evidence that stress contributes to the pathophysiology of human disease is sparse and, even where evidence exists, relatively small proportions of variance are explained'.

While the link between psychosocial factors and physical illness has proved difficult to establish, it might be expected that it would be easier to prove connections between stressors such as life events, and psychiatric illness. However, this area has similar difficulties.

STRESS AND PSYCHIATRIC ILLNESS

Psychiatric symptoms are frequently measured by stress researchers. This is not just because they are of interest in their own right but also because they are presumed to be the precursors of both physical and psychiatric disorders. While definitions of stress are vague, some kind of manifestation in the form of symptoms, such as anxiety, tension or 'feeling stressed' seems central to the notion (but see Box 4.1). Thus researchers typically use measures of anxiety and depression as a reliable and valid way of assessing these factors (see Chapter 2). A large amount of literature now exists looking at the influence of various stressors on psychiatric symptoms although many of these studies are limited by cross-sectional designs and may suffer common method problems. Examples are found throughout the book (e.g. Parkes, 1991; Fletcher and Jones, 1993). Typically these do show relationships between stressors and levels of anxiety and depression that are comparable with levels experienced by psychiatric outpatients. For example, studies have shown high levels of psychiatric 'caseness' in employed samples (see Box 2.4, Chapter 2). The relationship is so commonly found that it may seem logical to assume that more extreme stressors lead to more serious incidents of verifiable psychiatric illness.

Certainly, it is a commonly held belief that psychosocial factors are related to psychiatric disorders. From analysing the lay beliefs of over 2,000 adults, Ridder (1996) found psychosocial stress to be the second most popular explanation of the cause of mental disorders.

To confirm this view, however, evidence is needed linking psychosocial factors with independently diagnosed clinical illnesses (such as depression and schizophrenia) using designs that can show the direction of causation. Rabkin (1993) reviews this literature and, echoing the kind of statements we have heard throughout this chapter, states that

> In view of this nearly universal conceptualization of stress as a relevant consideration in illness onset, it is all the more surprising that the large majority of studies of stress and psychiatric disorder have failed to demonstrate a clinically significant association, although small, statistically significant relationships repeatedly have been found. (p. 477)

Where studies exist, Rabkin suggests that much of the research has been flawed because stress researchers pay regrettably little attention to the systematic diagnosis of psychiatric disorders, many just assessing the presence or absence of illness on the basis of interviews or global ratings.

In the case of psychiatric illness, Rabkin suggests there is also a particular problem with the assessment of stressors. Frequently it is not possible to tell the extent to which stressful events and experiences in the period before diagnosis have been triggered by the patient's deteriorating state. Thus the direction of causation is frequently unclear. There is also the familiar problem of potentially biased retrospective recall in many studies. As is common in the study of physical illness, many studies use retrospective methodology in which recall of events is likely to be unreliable (see Chapter 2). However, this is all the more likely to be a problem if the patient is seriously depressed or suffering schizophrenia. Nevertheless, it is the case that the most common approach to research has been the retrospective study that assesses the frequency of stressful events in people who are already diagnosed with a disorder. Genuine prospective studies, that follow a cohort of people over time and see who becomes ill, are rare.

Depression

There is much more research relating to depression than other psychiatric disorders. One particularly well-known prospective study by Brown and Harris (1978) found that women who both suffered life events and lacked the support of a confiding relationship were more likely to develop depression. This study is discussed further in Chapter 8. Brown and Harris considered in detail the difficulty in distinguishing between clinical depression and depressed mood and they based diagnosis of depression on a standardised clinical interview including ratings of severity. They established clear criteria for defining cases of clinical depression and borderline cases.

Gruen (1993) reviews research in this area and concludes that 'the results of a large number of studies suggest that life stress is significantly but moderately related to depression' (p. 554). However, Rabkin (1993), in her review, takes a slightly more cautious view stating the effects are small, at best accounting for 10% of the variance. However, stress researchers seldom find psychosocial factors account for much of the variance in any measure of well-being. Given the number of other possible contributing factors (e.g. age, gender, genetic, developmental influences as well as unmeasured psychological factors), even small amounts of variance being explained by a limited number of psychosocial events may be seen as impressive. Frese (1985) argues that such small effects can still be clinically significant. For example, it may mean that over a large population exposed to a major stressor, a considerable number will become depressed who would not otherwise have done so.

However, it is also clear that in the face of the same stressful event most people will not become depressed. As is suggested by Brown and Harris' research, stressful experiences alone seldom explain the onset of depression. Many factors are likely to contribute, for example, some people may be more vulnerable to the effects of stressful events due to genetic pre-disposition or childhood experiences. A lack or interpersonal resources may also have an impact on resistance to stressors. These resources are both external (such as degree of control, social support and income) and internal (such as personality, coping style, interpersonal skills, etc.). See Chapters 6–8 for further discussion of these issues.

Other psychiatric disorders

The evidence relating stressors such as life events to other psychiatric disorders is less strong. For example, the onset of phobic disorders (such as agoraphobia) is often thought to be related to stressful events. Rabkin suggests that a number of studies indicate around two-thirds of patients report a precipitating stressor. However, we do not have sufficient good quality studies in this area to establish a clear link.

In the case of schizophrenia, an aetiological role for stress is less often proposed and more research has focused on the role of stressors in precipitating a relapse. Rabkin (1993) here suggests that there is no positive evidence for any association between stressful life events and the onset of schizophrenia. Evidence arguing against the role of life events is produced by a case-control study by Stueve, Dohrenwend and Skodol (1998) who compared the role of life events in depression, schizophrenia and other non-affective disorder as well as community controls. This found that stressful events were associated with the onset of depression, but not with the other disorders.

There is more evidence that life events may be related to the onset of a relapse (e.g. Birley and Brown, 1970). However, these are like to interact with many other factors e.g. social support (Hultman, Wieselgren and Oehman, 1997).

CONCLUSIONS

Overall, it appears that there is some evidence for stressful events predicting depressive illness but not schizophrenia or other psychotic disorders. Difficulties and lack of clarity about objective diagnosis, coupled with further difficulties relating to self-reports, make this area of research perhaps even more problematic than that of physical illness. However, in both areas it is clear that research is complicated by a range of dispositional and individual differences that may impact the relationships between stressors and strains. These may include psychological predispositions and protective factors as well as physiological factors (including genetic influences). The latter is beyond the scope of this book; however, the rapid progress in the study of genetics opens up new possibilities for stress research. Increasingly individuals can be easily tested for genetic markers for an ever-increasing number of diseases. This gives the possibility of controlling for such factors in studies examining psychosocial factors and offers exciting future possibilities for separating genetic and environmental influences such as that of life events.

CHAPTER 5

COGNITION, STRESS AND ANXIETY

Ben Searle, Ben Newell and Jim Bright

This chapter introduces work from the field of cognition and emotion that is relevant to the study of stress. It introduces a range of theories and experimental paradigms for investigating stress-related phenomena, and describes the effects of stress on various aspects of cognitive functioning including attention, memory and judgement.

IF we accept that stressors lead to behavioural change, then it is necessary to consider the nature of the processes underlying this change. So far we have discussed strain responses in physiological and self-report terms (e.g. blood pressure and responses to questionnaires), but a different approach to strain reactions is to consider how the cognitive system reacts to stressors. Looking for cognitive explanations of strain phenomena has become a popular research approach and there are now journals such as *Cognition and Emotion* that are dedicated to these investigations. However, the scientific evidence connecting stressors to cognitive processes (such as attention and memory) is far from straightforward. This may in part be due to the vague definitions of stress that abound (see Chapter 1). As we have seen in Chapter 2, the term 'stress' is often used to describe a physiological or psychological response to stressors, leading to considerable overlap between popular usage of the term 'stress' and the concepts of anxiety and depression. These latter concepts have attracted a lot of attention in the cognitive literature (e.g. Eysenck, 1992; Beck and Emery, 1985).

Although all these concepts overlap, anxiety and depression are narrower, more clearly defined and thus more easily measured. Because they have been more thoroughly researched by cognitive psychologists, the effects of anxiety and depression on cognitive processes are also more clearly understood. While this area of research is seldom discussed in books on stress

– which usually focus on more applied work – such research has potential to provide greater understanding of the stress process. Thus stress research would undoubtedly benefit from a greater integration of such approaches. The following section provides a brief summary of some key differences between cognitive psychology methods and those used by occupational and health psychologists.

COGNITIVE PSYCHOLOGY

Cognitive psychologists use tightly controlled experimental paradigms and tend to conduct studies in the laboratory where this high level of control is easier to achieve than in field studies. Psychologists in the more applied branches of the discipline, where stress is commonly studied (e.g. health, occupational or clinical psychology) also conduct laboratory studies, but there is a stronger tradition of studying the phenomena in naturally occurring settings. Part of the reason for conducting studies of behaviour in the places where the behaviour is normally exhibited is to capitalise on the very rich and complex environmental cues that may contribute to the phenomena. Consequently, organisational psychologists may study stress in workplaces, and clinical psychologists may study stress in patient groups. Such studies are said to be more ecologically valid than laboratory approaches because the psychologist can see the behaviour in its genuine and full context (i.e. the ecology of the situation is normal). Often, however, gaining ecological validity can be at the expense of tight experimental control. As we have seen in earlier chapters, completely satisfactory control is simply not possible in applied settings. However, laboratory experiments often use both stressors and measures of performance that are very different from those in real life situations. Such studies may therefore be open to criticism on the grounds that they lack ecological validity, that is, they cannot be generalised to the real world. However, because they can control all aspects of the experiment, it is possible to show cause and effect relationships which are not confounded by extraneous variables. For example, rather than waiting for a stressor to appear and then ask a participant how they behaved, in a controlled experiment a stressor can be manipulated in terms of intensity and timing by the experimenter and a participant's response can be measured quantitatively. These studies therefore have the potential to shed light on the mechanisms whereby stressors, emotions (such as anxiety and depression) and cognitions are linked. Further studies may be needed to test the real world applicability of some of the mechanisms first explored in the laboratory.

THEORIES OF COGNITION, ANXIETY AND DEPRESSION

There are many theories that attempt to explain the effect of anxiety and depression on cognition; here we concentrate on three of the most influential theories. These theories refer to both state anxiety and trait anxiety. *State anxiety* refers to the level of anxiety one is experiencing at any given time. *Trait anxiety* refers to the stable characteristic of an individual to experience anxiety; an individual with high trait anxiety is likely to feel anxious much more often than an individual with low trait anxiety. These dimensions are typically measured using Speilberger's state-trait anxiety measure (See Box 5.1).

Box 5.1   The State-Trait Anxiety Inventory (STAI).

The State-Trait Anxiety Inventory (STAI: Spielberger, 1970) is a self-report symptom-mood inventory designed to provide a distinction between anxiety as (a) a state – a transient affective experience, and (b) a trait – a stable and enduring personality characteristic. This measure comprises two sets of 20 statements (both positively and negatively phrased). Respondents are required to respond:

(a) in terms of how they feel *at that moment* i.e. their current *state* (statements include: I am tense; I feel calm; I feel self-confident).
(b) in terms of how they *generally* feel i.e. reflecting the *trait* element (statements include: I feel nervous and restless; I feel satisfied with myself; I have disturbing thoughts);

The STAI is frequently used by stress researchers who, depending on their aims and objectives, might employ either state or trait scales. *State anxiety* is commonly utilised to assess momentary or situational distress, or responses to conditions that threaten self-esteem: for example, performance evaluation (Saunders *et al.*, 1996), although it is also used to assess responses to stressful life events which are likely to be more long-term affective reactions (e.g. Sexton-Radek, 1994). *Trait anxiety* has often been utilised as a measure of negative affectivity (e.g. Steptoe, Lipsey and Wardle, 1998). Some researchers use both scales: for example, Shea, Clover and Burton (1991) assessed the influence of both state and trait anxiety and stressful life events on the immune functioning of medical students leading up to an examination period.

Beck's schema theory

Beck's schema theory of depression and anxiety is based upon an approach to memory that can be traced back to Bartlett (1932). Essentially a schema is a memory store that contains a series of related pieces of information. Beck and Emery (1985) define a cognitive schema as an integrated structure or body of information that is stored in an individual's long-term memory. For instance, a schema for a yacht might include a hull, a mast, a main sail, a foresail, a boom, a rudder, a tiller, and a cabin. Beck suggested that our schemas can affect the way we process new information, and they can direct attentional resources toward new information that is congruent with existing schemas. Schema-consistent information is thus more likely to be detected, encoded and processed through elaboration. Information that is not consistent might be ignored, or else will be processed shallowly and will be forgotten more easily. So if we are interested in going sailing and we arrive at a yacht club, our attention will be more readily focused on objects that match our yacht schema, such as masts, sails and hulls, etc. We may not remember seeing things which are irrelevant to our schema such as children playing on the grass outside the clubhouse, or the parking attendant on the car park entrance gate, etc.

According to this theory, when someone feels anxious they process and encode information from the immediate environment as being 'threatening'. That is to say, they will incorporate current environmental stimuli into their pre-existing schema of threatening stimuli (things that make them feel anxious). This information will be used when that person again encounters such environmental stimuli. Beck predicted that highly anxious people should demonstrate a pre-attentive bias towards detecting, interpreting and allocating resources to threatening stimuli. That is to say, anxious people should detect threat more quickly and easily, and their threat-schema should consist of a large amount of environmental stimuli, including stimuli that less anxious people would consider non-threatening. According to Beck's theory, individuals who suffer from high trait anxiety have maladaptive schemas that direct resources towards rapid and efficient detection and processing of threat-related information. The more this occurs, the more information becomes incorporated into the 'potential threat' schema until the individual interprets ambiguous information as threatening. In a similar fashion, depressed people have schemas that influence them to process information in a negative way. Thus even trivially negative events might assume a disproportionate significance due to the selective processing of the negative material contained in the event.

Bower's associative network theory

Bower's theory draws from the semantic associative network model (Bower, 1981). According to this model, every unit of information is stored within memory as a node (that is, a location in a network). Through learned associations between related units of information, related nodes become connected in a network. When an individual is exposed to external stimuli (or even internal stimuli) that are closely related to a node, that node will pass a critical threshold level of activation. An activated node will spread activation to any connected nodes, although these too must exceed a threshold level before they become activated.

Bower argued that anxiety provokes a bias towards detection of threat-related stimuli, and also that while in an anxious state more information will be processed as being threat-related. Bower's theory derives from the assumption that emotions are also stored as nodes in the associative network. When a person is feeling anxious, this will activate the anxiety node(s) and this in turn will spread activation to related nodes. Environmental stimuli present when the anxiety node is activated will become connected to the anxiety node(s). Bower suggests that individuals who suffer from high trait anxiety experience a greater base level of activation in their anxiety node. In such people, it takes little to trigger activation of the anxiety node and, as a result, it takes little to trigger other nodes associated with anxiety.

Eysenck's processing efficiency theory

Eysenck (1982, 1983, 1992) has proposed a slightly different approach to explain and predict the effects of anxiety on cognition. Eysenck argued that state anxiety is determined by two factors: the situation (or the stressor), and the individual's level of trait anxiety. Eysenck argues that state anxiety levels critically determine current task performance because state anxiety in the form of worry occupies valuable cognitive processing resources. Drawing on Baddeley's (1990) working memory model (see Box 5.2), Eysenck suggests that worrying uses up attentional

Box 5.2 Working memory.

Working memory has been described as the 'desktop of the brain. It is a cognitive function that helps us to keep track of what we are doing or where we are moment to moment and that holds information long enough to make a decision, to dial a telephone number or to repeat a strange foreign word that we have just heard' (Logie, 1999). It is therefore much more than just a short-term memory store, it is fundamental to many cognitive tasks such as reasoning and learning. Baddeley (1990) suggests that working memory relies on different systems to those used in long-term memory, so that amnesic patients may have functioning working memory, while patients with poor working memory may have good memory for past events.

Baddeley proposes that working memory is made up of a controlling attentional system (the central executive) which co-ordinates a number of subsidiary systems. The key subsidiary systems which have been examined are the visuo-spatial scratchpad which is responsible for setting up and manipulating visual images and the phonological (or articulatory) loop responsible for manipulating speech-based information.

A simplified representation of the working memory model (Baddeley, 1990)

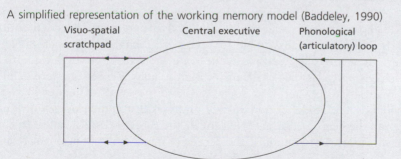

From *Human Memory: Theory and Practice*, reprinted by permission of Psychology Press Limited, Hove, UK, (Baddeley, A. 1990)

resources that comprise the 'central executive' component of the working memory system, and possibly also the 'articulatory loop' component. The extent to which any task requires the use of the central executive or articulatory loop will determine the extent to which state anxiety can influence task performance.

A key aspect of his theory is that there will not be a simple linear relationship between state anxiety levels and performance. Eysenck argues that when processing on some primary task is under threat due to a stressor, the individual can increase their levels of effort in order to maintain performance levels. This additional effort takes the form of using additional processing resources. For this reason, anxiety can impair processing efficiency (use of attentional resources) more than it impairs performance effectiveness (ability to perform the task well). Eysenck suggests that individuals with high trait anxiety are likely to be better at applying these extra resources. This may be due partly to a greater concern with performing poorly and partly to a heightened awareness of the mismatch between desired and actual performance. In one sense you could say that anxious people are better performing under stressful conditions than non-anxious people, as they are used to doing it. However, it is important to remember that the anxious person is putting in more effort just to maintain performance comparable to that of a non-anxious person. The anxious person is a bit like a person who has to run to just keep up with their very fast walking companion. When the fast walking person then begins running, the anxious person cannot run any faster and is left behind. In cognitive terms, when the anxious individual encounters further anxiety-inducing stimuli, they may not have the resources to increase effort any further and so performance deteriorates, whereas the non-anxious person confronted by the same stimuli, probably has enough spare resources to increase effort and maintain performance.

More recently, Eysenck and his colleagues (e.g. Eysenck, 1997; Eysenck and Derakshan, 1997; Derakshan and Eysenck, 1998) have further developed the model to account for the different attentional and interpretative biases observed in different groups of people defined by their levels of trait anxiety and social desirability. Four different groups of individuals were identified by Weinberger, Schwartz and Davidson (1979) along the dimensions of trait anxiety and social desirability. Those low on social desirability and anxiety were classified as low anxious, those high on trait anxiety but low on social desirability were classified as high anxious (these are called 'sensitisers' in some studies). Those high on both of these dimensions were classified as defensive high anxious. Repressors were defined as having low trait anxiety and high social desirability (see also Chapter 7).

Essentially this new model of trait anxiety proposes that high anxious individuals will exaggerate the degree of threat inherent in any threat-related stimuli. In contrast, repressors will tend to minimise the degree of threat inherent in threat-related stimuli.

The common feature of these models is that stressors are represented in memory, and the processing of new information is biased by either the presence of the stressor, or the memory of it. In all of the models, attention is influenced by stressors which in turn influences what is processed. So, in general terms, stress affects both attentional and memorial cognitive processes. At this point it is worth examining what evidence exists in support of these models and the more general contention that stress has a cognitive impact.

EXPERIMENTAL STUDIES ON COGNITION AND ANXIETY ———

The above general theories, in addition to many more specific theories, have been tested through the use of experimental paradigms. Such research allows manipulation of environmental factors in addition to sensitive assessment of cognition and behaviour. A variety of different research paradigms have been developed for examining cognitive phenomena under experimental conditions, and there is now a voluminous literature on this topic. Here we review just some of the key relevant studies, focusing on key aspects of cognition.

Attention

Scanning tasks

Beck and Emery (1985) and other theorists have suggested that anxious people are likely to be hypervigilant for threatening stimuli, meaning that that they will scan the environment for threatening information more rapidly and more thoroughly than non-anxious people. In studies to investigate this phenomenon, Luborsky, Blinder and Schimek (1965) presented participants with pictures that had sexual, aggressive or neutral content. Scanning was measured using eye movement data. Repressors performed less scanning than did sensitisers. This would appear to indicate that trait anxiety is indeed associated with hypervigilance. However, Haley (1974) found that both repressors and sensitisers performed more scanning during a workplace accident film than did participants who were neither repressors nor sensitisers. While this is less supportive of the prediction that anxiety should provoke greater scanning, some evidence in Haley's study suggested that sensitisers were focusing more on the stressful content than were repressors. It is worth noting that in the study by Luborsky, Blinder and Schimek static pictures were used (rather than moving ones which provoke greater eye movement) and repression was assessed using Rorschach inkblot tests, a projective technique which is rarely accepted in modern experimental studies.

Halperin (1986) presented participants with static pictures that had sexual, injury or neutral content. Within the pictures with sexual and injury content there were key areas which were responsible for most of the emotional effect. Halperin found that repressors spent significantly less time fixated on these areas for both sexual and injury pictures than did sensitisers, which suggested that high trait anxious individuals may scan the environment more, but that this increased scanning may not be specific to threatening stimuli.

95

Distractibility tasks

Some researchers (such as Easterbrook, 1959) have suggested that anxiety pro-duces narrowed, or more focused attention, and therefore anxious people should be less distractible than non-anxious people. However, as we have seen, others claim that anxiety produces hypervigilance, and that anxious people are more easily distracted. However, the exact predictions from these theories are not clear. If anxious people scan the environment *for threatening information* more than do non-anxious people, then threatening distractors will more easily distract them. If anxious people simply scan the environment more rapidly and thoroughly than non-anxious people, then any distractor should distract anxious people more easily.

To investigate the distracting influence of threatening and neutral stimuli, Mathews and MacLeod (1986) performed a dichotic listening experiment. Participants were told to 'shadow' (speak aloud) spoken passages that were played through one channel of a pair of stereo headphones. Threatening and neutral words were played through the non-attended channel; post-test investigation revealed that these words had not been detected by the participants. However, Mathews and MacLeod did find that threatening words presented through the non-attended channel impaired performance at shadowing more than did the neutral words. This result was true for anxious participants only, suggesting that anxious people are more easily distracted by threatening stimuli than by non-threatening stimuli, and that this occurs through pre-conscious processes. The effect size for this result was, however, very small, meaning that any performance deficit in the anxious group may not be of practical significance.

Mathews *et al.* (1990) reported a similar effect. Three groups of people (current sufferers of generalised anxiety disorder (GAD), recent sufferers of GAD, and normal controls) were asked to explain words, and they were presented with distractor words that were either threatening or non-threatening. Currently anxious participants were distracted more by both sets of distractor words than were controls, while recent GAD sufferers differed from the controls only for the threat distractors. This sug-gests that high trait anxiety predisposes an individual to increased vulnerability to threatening distractors, but that only current anxiety affects vulnerability to any distractor. However, it would be valuable to check this under conditions where state anxiety could be manipulated.

According to Eysenck's processing efficiency theory, anxious people should more easily be distracted by any distractor. Graydon and Eysenck (1989) found that dis-tractibility seems to be greater when processing demands are high. Eysenck (1992) argued that worries or sensations of anxiety use up attentional resources, with the result that any information processing task becomes more demanding. If anxiety is associated with enhanced detection and processing of threatening stimuli, this should make anxious people more susceptible to any distraction, and particularly to threatening distractors. Evidence for this can be seen in the study by Eysenck and Graydon (1989). Participants were required to read strings of letters and perform numerical operations on them (e.g. JULI + 3 = ? [Answer – MXOL]). The authors found that while there were no differences in distractibility between anxious and non-anxious groups for a meaningless distractor, anxious people were distracted more than were non-anxious people by a non-threatening distractor related to the task being performed.

The Stroop task

Stroop tasks are another form of distractibility task. The original Stroop task uses a word list of colour names (such as 'RED' and 'ORANGE'). These words are printed in a series of different coloured inks, without any relation between the written word and the ink colour of that word. For example, the word 'RED' might be printed in blue ink, while the word 'ORANGE' might be printed in green ink. Participants are asked to go through the list and recite the ink colour that each word is presented in, while ignoring the meaning of the written word. For example, if the word 'RED' was printed in blue ink, the participant would be expected to say 'Blue'. This task is difficult because it requires suppressing involuntary activation of the semantic meaning of the words (Martin, 1978). Despite the fact that identifying colours is normally a quick and easy task, it is easy to be distracted by the semantic meanings.

A common paradigm in cognitive studies of anxiety is the modified Stroop task. In this task, participants are shown a list of words that vary in emotional significance. Again, the words are printed in different colours. Participants are asked to go through the list and recite the ink colour for each word, ignoring the meaning of the written word. Participants appear to take longer to report the ink colour for words that attract the participant's attention. Many studies have indicated that participants suffering from anxiety disorders take longer to respond to threatening words (such as 'suffering', 'wounded' or 'violent') than to neutral words, compared to normal participants (Martin, Williams and Clark, 1991). For example, Mathews and MacLeod (1985) found that patients with GAD were slower to name the colours of threat-related words than were non-anxious people. However, Martin, Williams and Clark found that non-patients with high levels of trait anxiety were faster to name threat words than were non-patients with medium or low levels of trait anxiety. Martin, Williams and Clark showed that patients with GAD were slower to name the colours of threat-related words than were non-patients with the same levels of trait anxiety. This suggests that while anxiety may play a role in distractibility, the presence of GAD itself, or some other factor of being a GAD patient, affected the attentional bias toward threat-related words.

A problem with the modified Stroop is that participants, especially clinical participants, can guess what the expected response pattern should be, and this may limit the reliability of the results. For example, arachnophobes (people with an irrational fear of spiders) may know that it is their phobia that has led them to be chosen for the experiment, and this may consciously or unconsciously slow their responses to certain words. Another problem with both Stroop tasks and dichotic listening tasks is that they require participants to make verbal responses. Verbal responses require a relatively large amount of cognitive activity, and consequently more extraneous variables could affect the experiment. Such knowledge may not affect their pre-attentive biases, but once they have seen and read the word 'SPIDER' this knowledge may affect the speed of their verbal responses. One solution to both problems is to limit the amount of cognitive activity required for a response.

The dot-probe task

One alternative to the paradigms described above is the dot-probe task (MacLeod, Mathews and Tata, 1986). In this task, participants sit in front of a computer monitor and watch for a neutral dot stimulus that appears on the screen. This dot appears in either the upper half or the lower half of the screen. Participants are instructed to press a different button in each case. In addition, immediately prior to the presentation of the dot, a pair of words (one neutral and one threat-related) is presented on the screen. One word is presented in the top half and one in the bottom half. The threat and neutral words appear with equal probability in each half of the screen, as does the dot-probe.

Using this task, MacLeod, Mathews and Tata (1986) demonstrated that anxious participants (GAD patients) were faster than non-anxious people at detecting the dot when it was in the half of the screen that had just displayed a threat-related word. This result indicated that the anxious participants were more likely to attend to the threatening words and were consequently able to respond more quickly if the dot appeared in the same place as those words. These results have been replicated for social threat words, which are attended to more by patients with social phobia than by controls (Asmundson and Stein, 1994).

Once again though one can question the ecological validity of these studies. The word manipulation is very obvious, and it is plausible that the participant may guess that these words have special qualities. In particular, the threat-related words are more distinctive than their neutral counterparts because they all belong to a relatively narrowly defined category – 'threat' – whereas the neutral words are drawn from a much broader category of words. Therefore it is relatively simple for the person to work out that they are seeing a bunch of threat-related words, but it would be much harder to find such a clear pattern in the non-threatening words. Accordingly, the person's behaviour may be influenced by this knowledge. A much more rigorous approach would be to draw the neutral words from a category that is equally narrow, e.g. work-related words (office, desk, factory, word processor, etc.).

Implications of attention experiments

Attention experiments can be very sophisticated. The dot-probe task, for example, involves very little opportunity for influence from extraneous variables. This is extremely valuable for developing an understanding of how anxiety and stress affect fundamental cognitive processes, such as attentional biases and detection of stimuli. Further field research is then required to test out findings that are replicable in a real world setting. Once such studies have been conducted, it may be possible to develop therapeutic approaches. Thus the strength of the cognitive psychologists approach is to test theories and establish basic processes which may indicate directions for applied research.

Interpretation and memory

Interpretation bias

Interpretation bias experiments aim to determine the extent to which anxiety affects how we interpret ambiguous stimuli. The claim is that anxious individuals will tend to interpret ambiguous stimuli as threatening. In studies conducted by MacLeod (1990), anxious and non-anxious participants were played sentences that could be interpreted in different ways depending on the interpretation of a single homophone which could have either a neutral or a threatening meaning (e.g. die/dye, break/brake, etc.). After each sentence was played, participants were asked comprehension questions to assess their interpretation of each sentence. MacLeod's findings indicated that high-anxious individuals were significantly more likely than non-anxious people to make the more threatening interpretation. However, such a procedure is sensitive to response bias; although participants may make similar initial interpretations of the stimuli, non-anxious participants may be less likely to report the threatening interpretations.

Eysenck *et al.* (1991) attempted to avoid response biases in another experiment on interpretation of ambiguity. Anxious and non-anxious participants were presented with ambiguous and neutral sentences. Participants were subsequently given a recognition test, where they were presented with reworded versions of the presentation sentences. The reworded versions were less ambiguous, being closer to either the threatening or non-threatening meanings of the original sentence. Results of the recognition tests showed that anxious participants were more likely to make more threatening interpretations of the ambiguous stimuli than were non-anxious participants. One problem with this finding is that it is impossible to determine whether the anxiety-linked interpretative bias is an 'on line' effect – that is an automatic resolution of ambiguity – or a retrospective process undertaken during the recognition task (Hitchcock and Mathews, 1992). In an attempt to resolve this problem MacLeod and Cohen (1993) tested participants' on line (that is, immediate) interpretation of ambiguous text. Passages of text were used that contained an ambiguous sentence with one emotionally negative and one neutral interpretation, followed by a continuation sentence consistent with only one interpretation. Mathews and Cohen found that, when the continuation sentence was consistent with the neutral interpretation, high anxious participants took longer to comprehend

the passages than low anxious participants, suggesting that high anxious participants had initially imposed the more negative interpretation onto the ambiguous
sentence, leading to longer comprehension times for the sentence that contradicted
their initial belief.

Interpretive bias has become a major focus of research attention in recent
times, as several models of anxiety have interpretation of stimuli as a central
feature (e.g. Eysenck, 1997; Williams *et al.*, 1988, 1997; Mogg and Bradley,
1998; Mogg *et al.*, 2000). For example, according to Eysenck (1997), interpretive
biases between high and low anxious groups should be in the opposite direction.
Derakshan and Eysenck (1997) suggested that this would lead to high-anxious
individuals exaggerating how anxious their own behaviour is in social situations.
In contrast, repressors should have an opposite interpretive bias and underestimate
how anxious their behaviour is. They found support for these predictions in two
experiments.

Memory bias

The previous section has highlighted evidence that supports the hypothesis that
elevated levels of anxiety lead to selective *processing* bias for negative stimuli. It has
also been suggested that anxious people may have better *recall* of negative stimuli
due to a form of mood-congruent memory bias, whereby individuals have better
recall for material that is consistent with their mood at the time of recall.
However, there is currently little support for the notion that bias is also observed
for the recall of emotionally negative stimuli. Indeed a number of studies have shown
that recall of negative stimuli is *impaired* in highly anxious participants (e.g. Mogg,
Mathews and Weinman, 1987). Evidence against the notion of a recall bias comes
from a study by Nugent and Mineka (1994) in which implicit and explicit memory
performance was investigated in groups of high and low trait anxiety participants.
(Roughly speaking, explicit memory refers to memories which can be consciously
recalled, whereas implicit memories cannot but can be shown to exist by, for
example, performance on tasks). In Nugent and Mineka's experiment, participants
rated how much they liked a set of 64 words containing equal numbers of positive, neutral, social threat and physical threat words. Participants were then given
an implicit memory test (word stem completion), an explicit recall test and an
explicit recognition test. In two experiments no implicit memory bias was found
for threat-related words; a bias for threat-related words in the explicit recall test
was found for anxious participants in one experiment but was not replicated.
These findings lead Nugent and Mineka to conclude that the evidence for recall
bias in anxious participants is equivocal at best. This is supported by Mathews
and MacLeod (1994) who point out that depression, but not anxiety, seems to be
associated with facilitated recall of emotionally negative material.

A few exceptions to this pattern appear to have been found for autobiographical memories (e.g. Burke and Mathews, 1992; Richards and Whittaker, 1990) though,

again, recent studies have questioned the reliability of these findings. In studies of autobiographical memory participants are presented with words and asked to recall a specific personal autobiographical memory associated with each word. Typically a combination of negatively valenced and positively valenced words are used and the recall latencies of memories (that is, the time taken to recall) associated with each word are measured. Richards and Whittaker found that high anxious participants were quicker to recall memories associated with anxiety-related words than with happiness-related words. However, when Levy and Mineka (1998) conducted a similar experiment that included neutral words as a baseline condition, they found no differences in high and low anxiety groups on recall latency of memories. Levy and Mineka state that there were many procedural differences between their study and that of Richards and Whittaker. However, the failure to conceptually replicate Richards and Whittaker (combined with the often negative findings of bias in non-autobiographical memory studies) led them to be sceptical of the evidence for mood-congruent memory bias in anxiety.

In a recent excellent review of the implicit memory bias literature, Russo, Fox and Bowles (1999) suggest three criteria that need to be met to demonstrate an implicit memory bias.

1. There should be a significant interaction between anxiety status and word type on the size of the priming effect.
2. High anxious individuals should show more priming for threat-related words than low anxious individuals, and the same levels of priming or worse for neutral words.
3. High anxious individuals should show significantly higher levels of priming for threat-related words compared to neutral words.

From their review of the literature, and from their own experimental work, Russo, Fox and Bowles, conclude that there is no evidence of implicit memory bias in high anxious individuals and furthermore they argue that the implicit memory bias paradigm is not suitable for investigating differences in the integration of information between high and low anxious individuals.

Implications of interpretation and memory studies

These experiments on interpretation and memory rely on tasks with rather more similarity to real life tasks than those examining attention. It is therefore easier to see potential applications. For example, the studies on interpretation bias offer insight into the ways in which an individual who is already under pressure and anxious, for example in the work environment, may perceive apparently neutral events as more stressful (a phenomenon described as secondary stress by Fletcher, 1991). They may further suggest possible approaches to therapy.

Memory bias studies also have potential implications for applied research and for treatment, for depression. For example, Williams *et al.* (1996) have extended the experimental approaches to memory bias in depression by looking at the content rather than just the affective bias of autobiographical memories of suicidal patients. He found they tended to have poor recall of specific events. He suggests this affects problem solving when faced with difficulties as these patients cannot retrieve memories of specific behaviours that may help them cope. This suggests new clinical approaches to working with such clients. In relation to anxiety, the lack of evidence for a recall bias currently leaves researchers without any particular direction for application of the findings in this area.

Judgements, working memory and task performance

Effect of affect on judgements

Another area of research that may aid understanding of stress and anxiety is the more general area of mood states, and how they affect cognitive processes. Forgas (1995) proposed the *affect infusion model* (AIM) to explain and predict mood influences on decision making. The predictions of the AIM have been shown to apply to judgements of the behaviour of others, judgements of one's own behaviour, attribution of success or failure, and a number of other social judgements (see Forgas, 1995, for review).

Forgas argued that people may adopt one of a variety of information processing strategies when making decisions, especially in social situations. The AIM identifies four of these judgmental strategies. Direct access strategies occur where a judgement on the issue has already been made in the past, and the individual simply makes a direct and complete retrieval of that judgement. Motivated processing strategies occur where an individual seeks to achieve a particular goal in the making of the judgement (such as the motivation to make a decision that will make one feel better), and consequently the information processing stage is relatively brief. Heuristic processing strategies occur where the issues are fairly simple, the accuracy of the judgement is less important and when cognitive resources are limited, so the information processing stage is brief. Finally, substantive processing strategies occur where the issues are more complex and there is a perceived need to be accurate, so the individual processes the information extensively.

The AIM predicts that the degree of mood influence on judgements varies along a continuum of these processing strategies. Judgements requiring heuristic or substantive processing are more likely to be 'infused' by affective states than are direct access or motivated judgements. Substantive processing is more likely to be influenced by affect due to the additional processing conducted while vulnerable to mood influences. According to the AIM, stress and anxiety should have relatively little influence on decision making when making a simple decision of slight importance compared to a situation where we wished to make an accurate judgement on complex issues.

The majority of studies that support the AIM have involved inducing mood states of happiness or sadness using such techniques as memory recall for particularly happy or sad events or video recordings depicting happy or sad events. Such techniques inevitably result in only mild and short-lived alterations in mood states, and again it is not entirely clear whether response bias may influence participants in these studies. Even so, the predictions of the AIM are worth investigating further.

However, studies testing the AIM have focused on the mood states of happiness and sadness. A related theory that may be more applicable to anxiety is the *dynamic complexity model* (*DCM*; Paulhus and Lim, 1994). DCM predicts that person-perceptions become less complex and more polarised when people experience physiological arousal. Experimental studies used loud white noise to generate arousal in some participants (a method that is very similar to many manipulations of anxiety). When asked to make personal judgements about famous personalities or acquaintances, Paulhus and Lim found that aroused participants made more extreme judgements than did non-aroused participants. DCM suggests that anxiety may lead to adoption of more heuristic information processing techniques, where shortcuts are made leading to less complex perceptions. DCM seems to be consistent with Zajonc's (1965) social facilitation theory, which suggests that high arousal impairs performance at complex tasks (where the dominant response may not be correct), but that high arousal may actually facilitate performance at simple tasks.

Effects of anxiety on working memory capacity

Eysenck's processing efficiency theory and its relation to Baddeley's working memory model was introduced earlier in this chapter. Central to Eysenck's theory is the finding that anxiety-linked performance deficits are more pronounced on difficult cognitive tasks, and are moderated by the degree to which cognitive tasks can be executed automatically (MacLeod and Donnellan, 1993). As we have seen, processing efficiency theory suggests that this happens because anxiety restricts the capacity of working memory. According to Eysenck (1992), anxiety does not impair automatic processes because they do not engage the resources of working memory. In contrast, difficult tasks that do require access to working memory will be impaired by anxiety if the load on working memory exceeds the available capacity.

The processing efficiency theory has been successful in accounting for many experimental findings; however, as MacLeod and Donnellan (1993) point out, the theoretical value of the research has been compromised by two methodological limitations. Firstly, replications of the two initial findings that motivated the development of the model serve only to confirm that the phenomena are genuine rather than providing experimental tests of the model. The second limitation is concerned with the nature of the task comparisons that have been conducted. Many studies have attempted to contrast performance across tasks that place differing demands upon working memory. However, by concentrating solely on the working memory-demand characteristics of the task, many researchers have failed to take into account other dimensions on which the tasks vary which may explain the differential effect of anxiety on task performance.

MacLeod and Donnellan (1993) report an experiment that solves the problem of working memory-demand being confounded with other (theoretically irrelevant) task differences, through the use of a loading paradigm (e.g. Baddeley and Hitch, 1974). Participants performed a grammatical reasoning task while concurrently remembering a six-figure digit string as a memory load. The load placed on working memory was manipulated by varying the complexity of the digit string to be remembered. MacLeod and Donnellan proposed that the more complex the string, the greater the load on working memory and the less available functional capacity of working memory for solving the reasoning task. They hypothesised that the effect of high concurrent memory load on solving the reasoning task would be disproportionately high for high anxious participants. This is because, according to processing efficiency theory, the effect of anxiety on difficult cognitive tasks and the effect of reduced functional working memory capacity induced by the concurrent load task should interact with each other.

Such a pattern of results is exactly what MacLeod and Donnellan found. All participants exhibited longer decision latencies in the high memory load condition, but the increase was disproportionately high for the high anxious participants. This result, combined with similar findings recently reported by Derakshan and Eysenck (1998), lend weight to Eysenck's original claim that a restriction in the functional working capacity of working memory is responsible for the performance deficits on difficult cognitive tasks that are typically shown by highly anxious people.

Effects of stress on task performance

Karasek (1979) proposed that occupational stress was affected by two job design characteristics: demands and control (see Chapters 3 and 9). Demands refer to the amount of attention and effort required to carry out one's job. Control primarily refers to the decision-making freedom present in a job. Karasek predicted that work was more stressful when demands were higher or when control was lower. Karasek also predicted that demands and control would interact to create an extremely stressful environment. Typically, this model has been tested in field studies with mixed results (see Jones and Fletcher 1996b), however, several researchers have investigated the model in the more controlled confines of the laboratory.

Parkes, Styles and Broadbent (1990) used a simulated mail-sorting task to test this theory. They investigated the effects of machine paced work compared to self-paced work, to see if control over one's work pace affected self-reported stress, arousal and performance. The study also investigated the effects of task demands by including two machine-paced tasks (fast and slow). In this context 'stress' is conceptualised as negative mood and both stress and arousal were measured using the Stress Arousal Check-list (Mackay *et al.*, 1985). This involves rating current feelings in relation to various stress-related mood adjectives such as 'tense' and 'nervous' and arousal-related adjectives such as 'alert'. Participants sorted more mail under the self-paced condition than under the machine-paced conditions, and accuracy was higher in the self-paced condition than in the fast machine-paced condition. While arousal was higher in the fast machine-paced condition than in the slow machine-paced condition, participant self-reports of stress did not differ significantly between the three conditions. As such, Parkes, Styles and Broadbent's results did not directly support Karasek's theory, although there seemed to be a relationship between Karasek's predictions and performance. Higher demands were associated with greater arousal, and they were also associated with poorer performance.

Searle, Bright and Bochner (1999) performed a replication of the Parkes, Styles and Broadbent mail-sort study. Searle, Bright and Bochner used a fully factorial design to compare the effects of high and low demand (fast and slow sorting speed), high and low control (self- and machine pacing) and also high and low social support (present and absent positive feedback and reassurance). As predicted, higher demands produced more negative mood, as did low social support. Task control did not affect self-reported stress, which may explain why there was no interaction between demands and control for stress reports. Participants sorted more envelopes when under high demands, but they made more mistakes at this higher speed. Participants sorted more envelopes when under high control, and they also made fewer mistakes when they were self-pacing their work. There was also an interaction between demand and control, as the difference between low and high demands was greater in machine-paced conditions than in self-paced conditions. Social support did not affect performance. Controlling for pre-task stress and for the experimental conditions, there was no significant correlation between the level of post-task stress and either measure of performance. Consequently, it must be assumed that while self-reports of stress and performance were each affected by task characteristics, feeling under stress itself did not affect performance at this task.

Whilst these work simulation experiments do support theories of occupational stress such as Karasek's model, they do not provide strong support for predictions of the effects of stress on cognitive performance. While the factors that cause stress appear also to impair task performance, there is no clear relationship between experienced stress and task performance. This has important implications for experiments examining the relationship between stress and cognition, as any apparent effects of induced stress on cognition may often be the result of the stress induction procedure rather than the feelings of stress. This does not mean that studies using individual differences (such as trait anxiety) are necessarily superior, as again there may be other factors that affect both trait anxiety and cognitive functioning. These 'other factors' may themselves be theoretically and practically interesting, but they may not be relevant to the investigation of what effects, if any, stress has on cognition. The simple message from this is that when we do look at self-reported stressful mood rather than using specific measures of anxiety, there is little if any evidence that stress directly impairs the performance at simple tasks. Rather, it is more likely that a third factor influences both stress and performance.

Implications of studies of judgements, working memory and task performance

Many of the experiments included in this section are high on ecological validity. The experiments attempt to simulate real judgements that people make or real tasks that people perform. Results from these studies therefore would seem to have the greatest application value. Research indicating that judgements about other people become more extreme when in a state of arousal (or 'stress') have clear implications for the newly developing applied area of the psychology of conflict. The value of arousal reduction in a range of areas of conflict resolution from marriage guidance to international politics could be investigated in the applied arena.

In the occupational area, the mail-sorting studies suggest that feelings of stress increase with increased attentional demands, and this is associated with an increase in work done but a reduction in accuracy. However, while these studies are generalisable to real world situations, this has been achieved at the cost of reduced experimental control. This is an inevitable trade-off and strengthens the argument for the use of a range of approaches, tightly controlled experimental paradigms to test theoretical hypotheses in controlled settings then extending such ideas to more ecological experiments and finally to real world surveys and intervention studies.

CONCLUSIONS

This chapter has examined the claim that stress has an adverse impact on cognitive functioning. We have discussed three theories that present plausible accounts of a cognitive mechanism of stress, and we have presented a series of studies offering varying degrees of support for these theories. Many of these studies appear to suggest that stressed or anxious people perform cognitive tasks differently to non-anxious people. However, when we take a critical look at this research it is by no means clear that stress or anxiety affects all cognitive processes.

What is the balance of the evidence for stress/anxiety affecting cognitive functioning? Largely it seems to indicate that anxiety does affect strategic cognitive processes, including performance on some tasks, as well as certain attentional processes. However, it is less clear that anxiety affects the information we recall.

It is important to consider exactly what these experiments have demonstrated. Many experiments on anxiety use clinical patients (such as those with generalised anxiety disorder) or those who appear to have high trait anxiety, rather than directly manipulating sensations of state anxiety. It is not always clear whether people with trait anxiety think or behave in the same way as people who are currently feeling anxious, or have been made to feel anxious. This is particularly true when indirect or non-standard methods are used to distinguish high and low anxious people (such as identifying repressors and sensitisers, rather than individuals with high or low trait anxiety, especially when this is done using projective tests).

If we wish to explore further the effects of anxiety on cognition, we need to draw some of these results together. In order to do this, it is essential that comparisons can be made between different experiments. For this reason it is important that we use standard methods of *inducing* anxiety. Similarly, we need to use standard *measures* of trait anxiety. Finally, we need to investigate further the relationship between state anxiety, trait anxiety and anxiety disorders. Perhaps it would help to classify individuals into high–low trait anxiety as well as manipulating state anxiety. We need to see if high trait-anxious individuals think and behave the same regardless of state, and how this compares to high state-anxious individuals with low trait anxiety. We also need to compare anxious and non-anxious people who are within the normal range to people suffering from diagnosed anxiety disorders. For example, the study by Martin, Williams and Clark (1991) demonstrates that the modified Stroop effect, commonly attributed to anxiety, is different for GAD patients and non-patients, even though their trait anxiety levels were the same. The crucial point is that when we compare *high to low state* anxious people within the normal population, when we compare *high to low trait anxious people* in the normal population, and when we compare *patients with anxiety disorders to non-patients*, we are making different comparisons. This is particularly important in these experimental paradigms, where ecological validity is often sacrificed for the purpose of increasing experimental control.

In summary, this chapter makes a case for the importance of rigorous experimental paradigms which enable us to isolate clear effects of stress-related constructs such as anxiety or depression. Many studies report differential task performance between anxious and non-anxious groups, for example, which may have important practical implications. Even in the lab setting, however, some studies can be criticised for the lack of rigorous controls, and the sometimes imprecise measures that are used to measure the phenomena. However, where we have tight controls together with clearly defined and specific measures of anxiety or depression (rather than the more diffuse variable of 'stress') we are able to identify clear effects on cognition. A research approach which involves establishing basic effects in the tightly controlled laboratory situation and then taking the findings and testing them again in naturalistic settings may offer the greatest potential for progress in the area of stress.

PART 3

WHY DO PEOPLE REACT DIFFERENTLY TO STRESSORS?

This section focuses on key variables, sometimes referred to as intervening variables, that may have an influence on whether stressors lead to strains in individual cases. It is often stated that people respond differently to stressors and that some people are more susceptible to stress than others. This may be due to physical/genetic factors (see Chapter 3). It may also be the result of differences in variables such as age or gender or personality differences. These latter factors are the focus of Chapter 6, which particularly focuses on the personality characteristic known as negative affectivity. The chapter also introduces the hypothesised alternative mechanisms (direct effects, moderators and mediators) whereby all the factors considered in this section affect the relationship between stressors and strains.

A further set of factors that influence whether stressors lead to strains is the extent to which people differ in the ways they cope with demanding experiences. Chapter 7 provides an introduction to the large and complex area of work on coping. This considers approaches that look at different dispositional tendencies (coping styles) as well as approaches that consider coping in terms of responses to different situations (coping strategies).

Finally, Chapter 8 looks at an equally large and complex area of work on social support as an external resource that may help to minimise the impact of stressors. It considers both the impact of social support on health as well as the effects of illness (such as cancer) on ability to mobilise social support.

CHAPTER 6

INDIVIDUAL DIFFERENCES IN REACTIONS TO STRESS

Lucy Cooper and Jim Bright

This chapter examines the evidence that individuals differ in their reaction and susceptibility to strain. It considers the nature of the evidence that is required to demonstrate individual differences in strain reactions. It contrasts genetic, acquired and dispositional individual differences and uses key examples from each category to illustrate how each is purported to influence strain.

IN a research tradition that places such great emphasis on observations of individuals it is inevitable that there would be great interest in potential differences between people in their tolerance of, and reactions to, stressors. Much of this interest has centred on the commonly held belief that certain individuals are more 'stress-prone' and therefore more vulnerable than others (e.g. the diathesis-stress approach). This view typically sees individuals as being approximately normally distributed along some resistance continuum, implying that there exist some people who are especially prone to stress, and some who are almost immune. In the occupational context, this argument is attractive to organisations interested in selecting employees, because it holds out the promise that they could recruit suitably robust employees, provided they could measure this resistance concept reliably. This potentially renders expensive stress-related compensation claims less likely. In the health field, this idea is attractive because it suggests we can identify vulnerable individuals and provide appropriate interventions to assist them.

The research reviewed here generally has been conducted in real-life settings, and therefore suffers from the usual problems associated with the inability to actively manipulate the key variables. Much of the research has involved comparisons of groups classified using some existing personality construct (e.g. locus of control, extraversion–introversion), however some new constructs have been developed specifically to look at individual differences in relation to stress (e.g. Type A and Type B).

A plethora of individual difference factors have been investigated in relation to stress. Cooper and Payne (1988) classified these into three broad categories: genetic (e.g. gender, physique or age); acquired (e.g. social class, education, social support) and dispositional (e.g. coping style, negative affectivity, Type A and other personality variables). While genetic and dispositional factors are considered to be generally stable traits or characteristics of the individual, those acquired during the person's lifetime can change. However, this distinction is not clear-cut. For example, acquired factors such as social support are likely to have dispositional and genetic components. Factors such as intelligence may have both genetic and acquired elements.

After considering some of the important methodological issues in the next section, the remainder of the chapter will consider in further detail research into some key individual difference variables.

METHODOLOGICAL ISSUES

The individual differences literature highlights quite clearly a key methodological problem related to the way in which reactions to strain outcomes are measured in stress research. The logic of these studies is essentially to compare levels of strain in groups who experience the same environmental stressors but differ on some individual difference measure. The problem with this approach is that the individual difference dimension might bias the reporting of strain. This can be seen clearly in relation to negative affectivity (NA). This is the dispositional tendency to experience negative emotions and a negative self-concept (Watson and Clark, 1984). For example, consider two employees, Molly and Jane. Molly is higher in NA than Jane. When both are faced with the stressor of being made redundant, Molly is likely to report higher levels of anxiety or depression than Jane. However, many studies fail to take into account the baseline level of anxiety. This is important because *Molly would tend to report elevated levels of strain both in the presence and absence of stressors*. The fact that after redundancy Molly has higher levels of anxiety could mean a number of things, for example:

Case A. They both experience a similar increase in strain as a result of redundancy but Molly starts with higher strain, and so her final level of strain is higher than Jane's. Molly's negative affect affects her overall levels of anxiety and depression but has no impact on how she reacts to a specific stressor like redundancy.

Case B. Molly's negative affect leads her to react more severely to the stressor so that her levels of strain increase more than Jane's.

112

Figure 6.1   Alternative models (adapted from Edwards, Baglioni and Cooper, 1990).

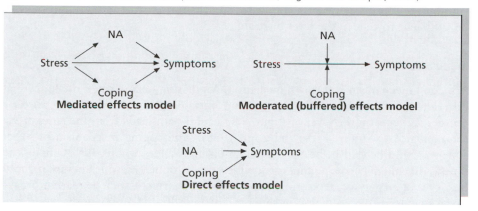

In case A it would be misleading to conclude that NA acts as a reliable marker of individuals who are unduly impaired in the presence of the stressor. This is an important point to clarify not only because this is often overlooked in the litera-ture but also because in terms of research, the mechanisms (e.g. either A or B) through which the variable NA influences the stressor–strain relation will determine what kind of statistical analysis is performed. Furthermore, as will be shown, each mechanism also has different implications for reducing or preventing stress in the workplace. Hence, for empirical, theoretical and practical purposes, just how a variable is proposed to affect the stressor–strain relationship should be established at the outset. Case A describes what is known as a direct effect while case B is a moderated effect. These two mechanisms plus a third common mechanism (medi-ation) are described below and illustrated in Figure 6.1.

Direct effects

The first means by which individual difference factors can influence the stressor–strain relation is in a direct or additive manner. Direct effects occur when the individual difference variable has a direct effect on the level of strain irrespective of the effects of a stressor. In other words, its effect on the level of strain is independent of the stressor variable with both variables contributing independently to the outcome (Parkes, 1994). The description given in example A above is one example of how NA might have a direct effect. For a further example, coping could be said to have a direct effect if it always reduced the level of strain experienced by the individual, irrespective of whether there was a high or low level of stressor in the environment.

(For a more detailed discussion of coping see Chapter 7.) In terms of stress interventions, in this case, increasing or decreasing the intensity of social support would
be sufficient to reduce the level of strain.

Mediators

A second mechanism is through mediation. Mediation occurs when the individual
difference variable acts as an intervening variable through which the stressor
exerts its effects on the level of strain. The causal path leads from the stressor via
the mediator to strain (Frese and Zapf, 1988). The coping mechanism of social
support could be said to be a mediator in circumstances where, for example, the
illness of a child incited a mother to mobilise support resources, which in turn reduced
her level of anxiety or depression. Alternatively, a stressor such as marital break-
down may lead to a reduction in support (through loss of a previously supportive
partner and perhaps the partner's family and friends) that may lead to an increase
in anxiety and depression. A slight variation on this, and one not often considered
in research, is when the stressor mediates the relation between the individual difference variable and the level of strain. For example, in terms of social support, a
high level of social support could incite the individual to expose themselves to more
stressors (such as taking on a difficult job). This in turn might influence their level
of strain. In this case social support has become the independent variable and the
stressor, that is the new job, becomes the mediator.

To establish statistically whether, for example, social support mediated the
relationship between marital difficulties and anxiety, three conditions must be met
(according to Baron and Kenny, 1986). Firstly, social support must be strongly
related to both marital difficulties and anxiety; secondly, anxiety must be strongly
related to marital difficulties; and thirdly, when social support is statistically
removed, the direct relationship between marital difficulties and anxiety should
disappear. Perfect or total mediation occurs when the zero-order correlation
is reduced to zero. Partial mediation occurs when the zero-order correlation is
significantly reduced rather than completely eliminated. It should also be noted
that the predictor (in this case the stressor), must be causally antecedent to the
mediator. As such, only individual difference factors acquired by the individual can
logically function as mediators, i.e. social support can mediate but age cannot.
Personality factors would not normally act as mediators unless it can be argued
that stressors actually influence personality.

Moderators

Moderators, unlike mediators, do actually change the nature of the stressor–strain
relationship by altering either the strength or direction of the relationship. Thus
social support could be said to moderate the relationship between a stressor such
as workload and a strain such as anxiety if, for example, heavy workload led to high

anxiety only in the absence of social support. In the presence of social support, increasing workload may be met with less anxious responses. A moderator such as this, that decreases the strength of the stressor–strain relation, is referred to as a *buffer*.

A moderator that increases the strength of the stressor–strain relation is referred to as a *vulnerability or reactivity* factor. For example, some personality factors are thought to increase vulnerability to stress. Personality could be said to moderate the effect of workload on anxiety if, for example, workload could be shown to lead to anxiety only in those with vulnerable personalities. To those of statistical inclination, both types of moderator effects are demonstrated by the presence of interaction effects in analyses of variance or multiple regression.

In terms of stress interventions, moderators are generally considered to be of greater importance than mediators in reducing strain (Frese and Zapf, 1988). Because moderator variables interact with stressors, it is possible to alter the intensity of the stress response by manipulating the level of either the moderator or stressor (e.g. workload) variable. For example, in the work context, if a stress *buffer* such as social support is shown to moderate the effect of high workload, then developing more effective coping mechanisms could reduce the negative impact of the workload without cutting the volume of work done. Alternatively, to prevent strain from occurring, known *vulnerability or reactivity* factors could be eliminated or reduced. For example, if certain personality types are shown to be more reactive to stressors such as working to deadlines, redesigning a job to reduce the number of deadlines would reduce their strain. In contrast, if this personality characteristic had either a direct or mediator effect then changing the stressor would not change the nature of the stressor–strain relation, thus manipulating the level of stressors would not necessarily have a positive impact on strain levels.

Hence, there are three main mechanisms through which individual difference factors can influence the stress process, each with their own implications for stress interventions. The following section will consider how some key individual differences have been implicated in the relationship between stressors and strains.

THE EFFECTS OF INDIVIDUAL DIFFERENCE VARIABLES ———

Gender

One variable normally considered to have a direct effect on the level of strain is gender. There are well-established differences in health status and mortality between men and women. For example, men are four times more likely to die of coronary heart disease (CHD), five times more likely to die of alcohol-related diseases and have an average life expectancy eight years shorter than females (Ivancevich and Matteson, 1980). However, studies also tend to show that women report more strain symptoms and engage in more health-related behaviours (e.g. visits to clinicians, general practitioners). It is particularly notable that researchers have found that psychological symptoms such as depression are much more likely to be diagnosed in women than in men. Holmes (1994) reports that studies conducted in 30 countries over a period of 40 years reveal a female:male ratio of about 2:1. In terms of less serious levels of psychological ill health, an analysis of two large international data sets by Lucas and Gohm (1999) also concluded that women were more likely to experience negative affective states than men. Similarly, the Whitehall Study (a large-scale longitudinal epidemiological study of London-based Civil Servants) report significantly higher rates of psychological distress (using the GHQ) in women than men (Fuhrer *et al.*, 1999). Not all studies reveal such clear-cut gender differences, however. Recent waves of the British Household Panel Survey (another large-scale longitudinal study that uses the GHQ: $n = 10,000$) found no significant differences (Buck *et al.*, 1994).

It is also the case that factors related to gender are likely to influence self-reports of psychological health status. Diener *et al.* (1999) and Fujita, Diener and Sandvik (1991) both suggest that women tend to feel emotions more intensely and frequently than men. Alternatively, these differences may reflect different cultural expectations for men and women. It is, perhaps, more socially acceptable for women to express negative feelings or admit to lack of confidence and thus women are more likely to endorse items such as 'Do you find yourself needing to cry?' (Crown and Crisp, 1979) or 'Have you recently been losing confidence in yourself?' (Goldberg, 1978). However, it may also be the case that as gender roles equalise fewer studies will find significant differences.

While it may make sense from an experimenter's point of view to control for the sex of participants when looking at the stressor–strain relationship, this does not help us understand precisely how gender may influence these relationships. Individual differences based upon genetics have long been a cause of controversy within psychology and more broadly in society. The major difficulty for anyone wishing to assert that the stressor–strain relationship is affected by a genetic factor, must first establish the impact of co-varying environmental factors. So in the case of gender, it is not clear whether it is the biological sex of the person that influences strain responses or a complicated set of environmental stimuli that cause these differences. For instance, social learning, stereotyping, access to coping strategies, work patterns, social norms of behaviour and power imbalances between men and women may all plausibly contribute to these differences. We have already seen in Chapter 4 that gender moderates the relationship between health behaviours and disease (e.g. Cohen *et al.*, 1991a). However, a whole range of influences both genetic and environmental may contribute to the different relationships between, for example, alcohol and depression for men and women.

Age/health

Age is another individual difference factor which may be implicated in the stressor–strain relationship in ways which are complex. Sometimes, a distinction is drawn between an individual's chronologic and physiologic age. Chronologic age is the time elapsed since birth while physiologic age depends on the amount of wear and tear or stress the individual has been exposed to (Ivancevich and Matteson, 1980). As such, it would seem that chronologic age would be related to the type of stressors the individual is exposed to while physiologic age would be related to the consequence or outcome of exposure to such stressors.

Chronologic and physiologic age are both related to an individual's physique or overall health status. It is commonly observed that more physically robust individuals appear to cope better with stressors or stressful situations than physically weaker individuals. Once again, however, an individual's physical status is likely to be affected by a host of non-biological factors such as previous medical history, personal habits and socio-economic status. Most stress research, however, only considers chronologic age and usually focuses on direct effects.

Research findings on the relationship between age and psychological ill health do not show straightforward relationships. A study of 11,000 healthcare workers by Wall et al. (1997) revealed that younger respondents were in better general psychological health than their older counterparts. Data from the British Household Panel Survey (which spans a wider age range) reveals a more complex picture; well-being worsened in the middle-aged group (35–44) then improved with age only to deteriorate again at 75+ (Buck et al., 1994). Both of the above studies used the GHQ to assess psychological well-being. Warr (1992) looked at work-related well-being in a study of 1,686 workers from a wide range of occupations. The middle-aged workers reported lower levels of job-related enthusiasm and contentment than younger or older workers.

More work is needed on the role of age as an individual difference factor. Relationships are clearly likely to be complex. For example, we saw in Chapter 4 that age may interact with stressors in impacting health (that is it acts as a moderator). This kind of relationship is seldom investigated.

Education and social status

While some individual difference factors (such as gender) are determined by genetic factors, many are acquired over time. Such factors would include resources, such as education or financial assets, social supports or various coping strategies that individuals may develop to deal with stressors. (The extensive literature on the latter two factors are considered in Chapters 7 and 8.)

Education and occupational status, because of their relationship to income, are factors that might be expected to be related to both psychological and physical health. For example, depression has been shown to be related to socio-economic status (Beekman, Copeland and Prince, 1999). The effect of socio-economic status on physical health and mortality is also well established (e.g. Wilkinson, 1997). Large-scale studies investigating occupational stressors and health outcomes usually take such variables into account as they may well be confounded with occupational stressors. For example, those in lower socio-economic groupings are likely to have jobs with less control, a job characteristic which is considered to be implicated in heart disease (Fletcher and Jones, 1993).

However, as in the case of gender, education may influence the reporting of strain outcomes. A national survey conducted in the USA found that men with higher levels of education were more likely to express reactions to environmental stressors in psychological terms (such as feelings of self-doubt, vulnerability, anxiety and 'mental break-down'), whereas those of a lower educational status defined these judgements more in terms of physical symptoms (Bryant and Marquez, 1986).

While control for such demographic variables is important in stress research, more usually, when people refer to individual difference variables, they have in mind dispositional individual differences (i.e. personality traits). These are considered below.

DISPOSITIONAL FACTORS

Several different traits have been linked to stress in the literature, but two stand out as having received particular interest. These are Type A behaviour/hostility and negative affectivity (NA) (e.g. see George, 1992). While the construct 'negative affectivity' is considered one of the 'big five' personality dimensions (Tokar, Fischer and Subich, 1998; see Box 6.1), the Type A behaviour construct grew out of a body of research investigating risk factors for CHD (e.g. Rosenman et al., 1964). Both these variables have received considerable research attention and are consistently included in major review articles on dispositional variables (e.g. Schaubroeck and Ganster, 1991; O'Driscoll, 2001; Parkes, 1994). The role of both in stress will be considered here.

Type A and hostility

The concept of Type A behaviour evolved out of a series of studies investigating risk factors for (CHD) which became known as the Western Collaborative Group Studies (WCGS; Rosenman et al., 1964). After eight years of extensive interviews and observations, a group of behaviours and traits was identified that appeared to distinguish 'at risk' individuals. Referred to as Type A behaviour pattern, the Type A individual is described as impatient, irritable, hostile, competitive, job involved, achievement striving, competitive and deadline focused. The Type B individual is characterised by a relative lack of these characteristics. Even after controlling for traditional risk factors (e.g. blood pressure, cholesterol level, family history), the risk from developing CHD for Type As was reported to be twice that of Type Bs. A number of subsequent studies have also focused on the mechanisms whereby Type A may be implicated in strain outcomes. According to one hypothesis (labelled the *differential exposure hypothesis*, Cohen and Edwards, 1989), Type A individuals should place themselves in situations where they will encounter more stressors through, for example, self-selecting into more demanding jobs, i.e. the relationship between personality is mediated by job stressors. The few studies examining this hypothesis have generally not been supportive. In one study, an analysis of Type A and B by occupation showed both types to be in what are considered 'stressful' occupations (e.g. working on machine-paced assembly lines). Furthermore, Type Bs scored higher on average on scales measuring somatic complaints (Caplan *et al.*, 1975).

An alternative hypothesis (the *differential reactivity hypothesis*, Cohen and Edwards, 1989) suggests that Type A individuals should be more reactive to stressors in the environment, showing a greater strain reaction under stressful conditions, i.e. Type A moderates the relationship between stressors and strains. Once again, support for this hypothesis is mixed, with some studies finding for (e.g. Ivancevich, Matteson and Preston, 1982; Payne, 1988) and some against (e.g. Burke, 1988; Keenan and McBain, 1979) this hypothesis. More importantly, one of the few studies that has sought to test this hypothesis using an objective stressor measure (self-paced versus machine paced) also failed to support the hypothesis in relation to measures of anxiety and depression (Hurrell, 1985).

Generally, there appears to be more evidence suggesting Type A to be a risk factor for physiological indicators of strain than for either psychological or work-related distress (Ganster *et al.*, 1991). On the whole, however, research on Type A is 'plagued by controversy' (O'Driscoll, 2001) with most of this controversy stemming from three factors: the ill-defined nature of the construct, its unidimensionality and the validity of measures of the construct (Parkes, 1994). Firstly, it is debatable whether Type A represents a personality trait or a self-reported behavioural style (Frew and Bruning, 1987; see also Chapter 7). Secondly, the validity of the construct itself has been questioned with factor analytic studies showing it to be composed of a number of unrelated constructs (Parkes, 1994). For example, Ganster *et al.* (1991) concluded that Type A as measured by structured interview (Rosenman *et al.*, 1964) identified three, unidimensional factors: hostility, speech characteristics and answer content. Thirdly, the validity of different means of measuring the construct, particularly the self-report questionnaire measures, has been questioned (Parkes, 1994; Powell, 1987).

The strength of initial findings, particularly in relation to heart disease, was also gradually undermined by a number of studies finding negative results. For example, reviews of this research (e.g. Powell, 1987; Matthews and Haynes, 1986), which included several, large scale prospective studies, found that Type A was significantly related to CHD in just over half the studies examined. A number of meta-analyses (see Chapter 2) have also been conducted (e.g. Booth-Kewley and Friedman, 1987; Matthews, 1988; Myrtek, 1995), which have shown that results varied depending on the methods used. Booth-Kewley and Friedman (1987) concluded that:

> The picture of coronary-proneness revealed by this review is not one of a hurried, impatient workaholic but instead is one of a person with one or more negative emotions. (p. 343)

119

They suggest that this may include someone who is depressed, anxious, angry, aggressively competitive or easily frustrated. The review by Matthews (1988) singled out the hostility component of Type A as particularly important. Dembroski *et al.* (1989) also subsequently found hostility to be more predictive of CHD than a global measure of Type A. Since this time, a considerable body of work has focused exclusively on hostility and this variable has now also been the subject of meta-analyses (e.g. Miller *et al.*, 1996). Miller *et al.* include 45 studies in their analysis and concluded that hostility is an independent risk factor for heart disease. When structured interview approaches to measuring hostility were used then the effects were equal to or greater than those reported for traditional risk factors for CHD such as elevated cholesterol levels, high blood pressure or smoking. Controlling for other risk factors did not reduce this relationship. There is also evidence that a hostility-reduction intervention can be effective in reducing blood pressure in CHD patients (Gidron, Davidson and Bata, 1999).

Interestingly, more recent studies have tended to find weaker relationships than the earlier studies, just as they did in the case of Type A (Miller *et al.*, 1991). Miller *et al.* (1991, 1996) suggest that methodological artefacts account for this and particularly the tendency for more recent studies to focus on only high risk groups which already have some form of CHD. This restricts the range of disease severity and biases the results.

The mechanisms whereby hostility might have an impact remain unclear. It may be that the hostile person provokes more stressors (the differential exposure hypothesis), or that they have worse reactions when faced with stressors (the differential reactivity hypothesis). It is also possible that hostile people are more likely to suffer strains as a result of poorer health behaviour and a less healthy lifestyle. However, the meta-analysis by Miller *et al.* indicates that the latter is not likely to be the sole explanation. The bulk of research considers predominantly direct effects of personality on disease and does not look specifically at the ways in which hostility impacts on stressor–strain relationships. For a discussion of different mechanisms we turn to the literature on the personality construct of negative affect.

Negative affectivity

The dispositional construct of negative affectivity or NA, was first defined by Watson and Clark in 1984. While similar to Type A in that it also evolved out of a body of research, its origins are broader, spanning personality, social and clinical research in addition to stress research. NA as defined by Watson and Clark (1984) is a very broad dispositional dimension reflecting pervasive individual differences in negative emotionality and self-concept. High NA individuals are considered: (a) more likely to report distress, discomfort and dissatisfaction; (b) to be more introspective and dwell more on their failures and shortcomings; (c) to focus on the negative side of the world and, therefore, (d) to have a less favourable self-view and be less satisfied with themselves and with life (Watson and Clark, 1984). A central feature of the construct is that it manifests itself even in relatively benign conditions. This predicts that across time and different conditions, high NA individuals will report greater distress and dissatisfaction on average compared to low NA individuals. As a construct, it is considerably better established empirically and theoretically than Type A and therefore, less controversial. It is also quite highly correlated with Type A (Payne, 1988). Considered synonymous with the Eysenckian construct *neuroticism*, it is a personality dimension identified consistently in studies. It is also one of the five dimensions identified in the five factor model of personality ('the big five'), the personality taxonomy for which there is the most widespread agreement (see Box 6.1). In relation to occupational stress, it is the most studied of all the major personality dimensions with a 'substantial portion of this literature focused on the role of workers' negative affectivity' (Tokar, Fischer and Subich, 1998, p. 133).

How is NA related to other personality factors?

Other personality traits that have been implicated in the stress process, such as locus of control (Rotter, 1966) and hardiness (Kobasa, 1979), are considered to overlap considerably with the major personality dimensions and particularly NA

Box 6.1 Personality theories.

A number of different multi-trait personality theories have been proposed based on the analysis of rating scale data. Cattell, Eber and Tatsuoka (1970) highlight 16 traits in their measure the 16PF. Others, however, reduce the number to a smaller number of 'core' traits.

The two factor model
Eysenck (1953) proposed that personality was adequately described by the two dimensions of extraversion/introversion and neuroticism/stability, though later he added the third dimension of psychoticism (Eysenck and Eysenck, 1976). The earlier two-dimensional version is perhaps better known.

The five factor model ('the big five')
Based on further research using Catell's rating scales, Norman (1963) proposed five core dimensions – extraversion, agreeableness, conscientiousness, emotional stability and culture. These were derived using the statistical method, factor analysis. The importance of five factors have been replicated many times (Hampson, 1988), however the nature of one of the big five factors has been questioned. McCrae and Costa (1985) claim to have discovered a new factor called 'openness', referring to openness to experience, for example, in terms of liberal views, creativity and intellectual and artistic interests. Hampson (1988) suggests that this could also be interpreted as a form of Norman's 'culture' variable.

(Payne, 1988; Tokar, Fischer and Subich, 1998). Locus of control is operationalised along an internal–external continuum, and describes the tendency for individuals to describe events either as under personal control (internal), or under the control of external factors such as fate, chance or luck (Rotter, 1966). Individuals high on internal locus of control are considered to exert greater effort to control their environment, exhibit better learning, actively seek and use information more effectively and focus on information rather than the social demands of situations (Phares, 1976). Not surprisingly, they are also considered to be more resistant to stress. Research has confirmed this supposition with externals reporting both higher stressor and strain levels (e.g. Payne, 1988).

However, there is a considerable body of evidence demonstrating that high externals also tend to be high on NA (e.g. Jolley and Spielberger, 1973; Watson, 1967). It has been found that locus of control generally correlates ($r = 0.4$) with negative affect (Eysenck and Eysenck, 1964) and, unsurprisingly, there is also research demonstrating that controlling for NA reduces the previously significant relationship between LOC and strain to non-significance. In Payne's (1988) study of unemployed men, for example, controlling for NA eliminated the previous significant relationship between LOC and a measure of depression and anxiety. Consequently it has been argued that the observed relation between LOC and strain is attributable to NA.

A similar argument has been raised in relation to the hardiness–stress relationship. According to hardiness theory, the 'hardy' individual is believed to be buffered against stress by virtue of a cognitive appraisal system characterised by three strategies: commitment (a belief that one's life and activities have value and importance); control (belief that one can control events); and challenge (change in one's life is expected and can be beneficial) (Maddi and Kobasa, 1991). However, NA and hardiness correlate reasonably well, leading some commentators to argue that NA subsumes hardiness, with the 'hardy' individual being one low on NA (Funk and Houston, 1987). Finally, it is also suggested that Type A is closely related to NA (Payne, 1988).

It should be apparent by now that NA is a central concept in personality research. The next section therefore considers the relationship between NA, stressors and strain, in rather more detail than has been given for variables discussed so far. This should help give an understanding of the complexity of some issues addressed by researchers trying to disentangle the ways in which individual differences effect the stressor–strain relationship. First, however, the measurement of NA will be considered.

Measuring negative affectivity

Several different measures have been employed in research to measure the construct of NA, with measures of trait anxiety and neuroticism being most frequently used. The concept evolved out of a large body of research demonstrating strong relationships between various measures of negative affect such as neuroticism, trait anxiety, depression, ego strength and general maladjustment (Watson and Clark, 1984; Watson, Clark and Tellegen, 1988). However, when conducting research into stress it is important to select a measure that minimises content overlap with measures of psychological strain. For example, nearly all measures of neuroticism and trait anxiety contain items that are very similar to those contained in measures of somatic complaints. One measure of NA that contains no symptom-related items, however, is the Positive and Negative Affect Schedule (PANAS) developed by Watson, Clark and Tellegen (1988). Designed specifically to measure NA, it requires respondents to indicate how well each of a number of adjectives describes them in general. This is increasingly being adopted as the preferred option in stress research (see Box 6.2).

The effect of NA on self-reports of stressors and strains

Given NA's pervasive influence over a person's cognitive and affective evaluation of themselves and their world it is not surprising that it is considered to have important implications for the experience of stress. From the definition of NA it follows firstly that high NA individuals will view their environment more negatively than low NA individuals. Secondly, it follows that at any one time, high NA individuals will experience greater distress and dissatisfaction than low NA individuals regardless of the environmental conditions. Hence, by definition, it is predicted that high

Box 6.2   The Positive and Negative Affect Check-list (PANAS).

PANAS (Watson, Clark and Tellegen, 1988) is a brief and easily administered measure of mood. PANAS comprises two 10-item scales consisting of mood adjectives that assess the two dimensions. Positive affect (PA) is conceptualised as feelings of enthusiasm, activity and alertness, whilst negative affect (NA) includes feelings of anger, contempt, guilt, fear and nervousness. This instrument has been used with varied time instructions, for example asking the individual to indicate to what extent they 'feel this way right now', 'felt this way during the past week', 'felt this way during the past year'. Alternatively, they can be asked to rate how they generally feel. In this way, PANAS can be used to discriminate between state and trait (Watson and Tellagen, 1985). Watson and Tellagen claim that when used as a 'state' measure, the scale is sensitive to fluctuations in mood in response to environmental change, whilst as a 'trait' measure it is stable over time. The authors consider PANAS to be a valid and reliable measure of psychological well-being. Both dimensions correlate highly with the Beck Depression Inventory (Beck *et al.*, 1961) and the State-Trait Anxiety Inventory (Spielberger, Gorsuch and Luschene, 1983), with NA showing a positive relationship and PA a negative relationship.

NA individuals should report more stressors and greater strain across time than low NA individuals. If you recall our earlier example, both Molly and Jane faced the same stressor – losing their jobs – however it was the high NA Molly and not the low NA Jane who reported the highest levels of strain.

This prediction is supported in the literature with a wide body of research showing NA to be significantly correlated with a range of both work and non-work measures of stressors and strains. For example, occupational research has shown NA to be significantly correlated with a range of work stressors: role ambiguity, role conflict, interpersonal conflict, situational constraints (Chen and Spector, 1991); control, social support (Moyle, 1995b); work demand (Parkes, 1990); and with various strain measures such as turnover intent, organisational commitment (Cropanzano and James, 1993); job satisfaction (Brief, Butcher and Roberston, 1995); absenteeism (Chen and Spector, 1991); burnout (Deary et al., 1996) and general psychosomatic distress (e.g. Moyle, 1995b).

Does high NA really predispose people to greater strain reactions?

While the relationship between NA and self-report measures of stressors and strains is a robust finding in the literature, there is currently much debate as to quite what role NA plays in occupational stress. Specifically, the debate has centred on whether NA functions purely as a partial confound in stress research, or whether it also functions as a substantive vulnerability factor (although other alternative mechanisms such as the idea of differential exposure cannot be ruled out). As a confounding variable NA is considered to spuriously inflate the observed relation between self-report measures of stressors and strains (for example, by leading to negatively biased responses to questionnaire items related to both stressors and strains). As such, it is considered a methodological nuisance factor and should be controlled in stress research (e.g. Brief et al., 1988; Stone and Costa, 1990). This is referred to as the *confound model* (see below). As a vulnerability factor, however, NA is considered to play a substantive role in the stress process. Rather than confounding the stressor–strain relation, it might also act as a moderator by altering the strength of the relationship. High NA individuals would thus be expected to have a heightened reactivity to stressors thereby increasing the intensity of their strain response (e.g. Bolger and Schilling, 1991). Such individuals are therefore considered more vulnerable to occupational stress than their low NA counterparts. This differential reactivity approach is known as the *vulnerability model* of NA (see below).

While these two models of NA have very different theoretical and practical implications, it is important to note they are complementary rather than competing models. Indeed, research to be discussed later provides evidence for NA as both a confound and vulnerability factor in occupational stress. However, as will be shown later, a bias in the literature towards the confound model of NA leaves its role as a vulnerability factor poorly understood.

Confound model

The basic premise of the confound model is that the independent and dependent variables in stress research are confounded by NA. It is argued that self-report measures of stressors and strains are not measuring separate, meaningful constructs but instead are measuring indirectly this dispositional trait (Dohrenwood *et al.*, 1984). For an example of the practical implications of this, see Box 6.3.

Box 6.3   Confound and vulnerability models illustrated.

Fred is high on NA. For Fred the glass is half empty and not half full. He tends to view the world in a negative way. He feels that his office job is very stressful because he does not get on with his boss and he has too much work. There have also been a lot of recent redundancies in his company and Fred is worried that he might be next. As a result Fred is generally very anxious and worried.

Bert works in the same office as Fred and is also high on NA. Like Fred, he too is worried about losing his job and is suffering from similar work problems to Bert.

Both have recently taken part in a stress survey conducted by an organisational psychologist. This included a measure of anxiety. When they were given feedback they both got exactly the same scores. They scored 70 out of 100. They were told that the average score in the company was only 48 out of 100 so they were on the high side.

Soon after this, the boss visited their department and warned the employees about the need to improve performance, and both Fred and Bert were threatened with the sack. The organisational psychologist came back to see them again, and asked them to fill out the anxiety scale again. This time the results showed a marked difference between Fred and Bert. Fred's score was now 80 out of 100, but Bert's was 95 out of 100. In fact most of the people in the organisation got nasty visits from the boss, and the average anxiety levels as a result went up to 58.

For Fred NA was a confounding variable – it made him report greater anxiety than others to begin with, and when he was subjected to the additional stressor of the boss's threats, his anxiety levels rose even further. However, the increase in his level of anxiety (up 10 points) was the same as the average for the company. This indicates that his high NA levels did not make him any more susceptible to stressors, just that he started off from a higher base.

For Bert, NA was a vulnerability factor. Whilst he reported higher than average levels of anxiety to begin with, when put under pressure by the boss, he became extremely worried. His NA made him vulnerable to stressors and his anxiety levels rose 25 points, 2.5 times the average increase.

This model has serious implications for stress research. If the association found between self-report stressors and strains is not attributable to an underlying, causal relationship as is assumed, but to NA, doubt is cast over the conclusions drawn from previous research (e.g. Burke, Brief and George, 1993). In the occupational context this undermines the main assumption underlying occupational stress models, that work stressors are causally related to the level of occupational strain. On a practical level, if most people are like Fred in Box 6.3, this means that eliminating or reducing work stressors will have very little effect in eliminating or reducing occupational strain. If the assumption that work stressors cause occupational strain does not hold, then the principle underlying current workplace stress intervention practices is no longer valid: changing the work environment will be of very little benefit if self-report measures of work stressors and strain are surrogate measures of NA. For any real benefits to be observed on self-report outcome measures, the individual would first need to be changed.

Support for this confound model of NA comes from two main sources. The first is from studies showing remarkable consistency in strain measures across time and situations. For example, job attitudes show remarkable consistency across major career changes (Staw, Bell and Clausen, 1986), and major life changes (Costa, McCrae and Zonderman, 1987). In the nine-year longitudinal study conducted by Costa, McCrae and Zonderman (1987) enduring dispositional factors were found to be a better predictor of future well-being than major life changes (e.g. changes in marital status, employment, state of residence). While individual differences were found to account for 25% of the variance in well-being scores, life circumstances accounted for only 4–6% of the variance. These results suggest an underlying stable trait to be responsible for this relationship, as opposed to environmental variables.

The second source of evidence comes from studies examining the relationship between NA and long-term indices of health. It has been argued that if NA plays a substantive role in causing people to perceive that they are under stress then it should be related to long-term physiological indicators of strain. However, studies generally have not supported this conclusion (e.g. Costa, McCrae and Zonderman, 1987; Watson and Pennebaker, 1989). Watson and Pennebaker (1989), for example, found that while NA was significantly related to various self-report measures of health complaints, NA was related to neither physiological measures (e.g. blood chemistry, blood pressure), nor to behavioural measures (e.g. dietary habits, physical fitness, number of healthcare visits). An extensive review of the literature by Watson and Pennebaker further showed NA was neither related to indicators of cardiovascular health, risk factors for heart disease, heart-related mortality, nor cardiac pathology. Hence, it was concluded that NA is neither a predictor of long-term health nor of health relevant behaviours.

There are presently two accounts of the confound model in the literature. The first treats the confounding of stressor and strain variables in stress research as a measurement issue. The second attributes the confounding role of NA to its dispositional influence on the reporting of stressors and strains. Those subscribing to the first view, that measurement is the issue, argue that measures of stressors and strain variables are confounded with NA because of content overlap between the scales. For example, it has been argued that items on some NA scales, e.g. Eysenck's neuroticism scale (Eysenck and Eysenck, 1976), overlap with symptom items on health complaint and general well-being scales (Payne, 1988). The same argument has also been directed at commonly employed life stressor measures such as life event and daily hassles scales (e.g. Brett *et al.*, 1990). However, content overlap between scales does not provide an adequate account of the confound role of NA. For instance, even when the purported 'overlapping' items have been removed from measures of stressors and strains, their relationship with NA still remains (Burke, Brief and George, 1993).

The second account attributes the confound role of NA to the *disposition of NA influencing the reporting of stressors and strains*. It argues that because high NA individuals perceive and evaluate themselves and their world through a negative cognitive set their reporting of stressors and strains will reflect this bias. Furthermore, given that by definition high NA individuals report greater distress regardless of the situation, this reporting bias will exist even in the absence of overt stressors. This exaggerated reporting by high NA individuals of stressors and strain will act to inflate stressor–strain correlations spuriously (e.g. Stone and Costa, 1990).

This account of the confound model has received the most attention in research. Support for this model of NA can be seen in the well-known study conducted by Brief *et al.* (1988). This study of 497 managers and professionals showed that controlling for the effect of NA on both work- and non-work-related stressors and strains (somatic complaints, negative affect at work, job satisfaction and life satisfaction) reduced 12 out of the 15 initially significant correlations to below significance. The average size of the reduction was 0.22. The authors concluded that:

> NA should not remain an unmeasured variable in the study of job stress. One can no longer assume that simple, zero-order correlations between self-report measures of job stress and job strain are particularly informative. (p. 197)

These findings were supported by Payne (1988) and, for a while, it seemed that the stress researcher would be well-advised to control for NA in all research using self-report measures.

However, evidence for this confound model of NA has now been challenged on a number of grounds. Firstly, Schaubroek, Ganster and Fox (1992) cautioned that the conclusion that there is no relation between NA and physical health was premature. Citing studies that have found a relationship between NA and health indices such as immune functioning (salivary immunoglobulins) and systolic blood pressure, they argued there were enough inconsistencies in the literature to suggest a possible aetiological role in long-term health. Further grounds for challenging this account stem from the inconsistent results that have been obtained from studies following the advice of Brief *et al.* and partialling NA out of the stressor–strain relation. For example, Jex and Spector (1996) and Moyle (1995b) found limited reductions in correlations when NA is controlled.

The whole idea of regarding NA as a bias that confounds the relationship between stressors and strains has now been questioned by Spector *et al.* (2000). They suggest that by controlling for NA in studies of stressor–strain relationships researchers are removing shared variance, however it is caused, rather than investigating why NA inflates relationships. They suggest a number of alternative mechanisms including the vulnerability model (discussed below).

Judge, Erez and Thoresen (2000) also question the notion that negative affect causes bias. They argue that we now have evidence that those with high NA tend to be more (rather than less) accurate at assessing the environment (Alloy and Abramson, 1979), as they lack the positive self-serving biases which we now know characterise 'normal' individuals (e.g. Taylor and Brown, 1988; Weinstein, 1980). They suggest that we have not adequately investigated the effects of such positive biases on stressor–strain relationships. They suggest that self-deception, one form of positive bias, may actually be related to reporting less strain and less health problems. They argue that this variable may be as important as negative affect, opening up the possibility that individual difference variables may have led us to underestimate rather than overestimate the strength of stressor–strain relationships. Judge, Erez and Thoresen (2000) and Spector *et al.* (2000) are in agreement that NA should not simply be controlled for as a confounding variable, rather it should be investigated in its own right.

Vulnerability model

This moderator model proposes NA to play a substantive, aetiological role in the stress process by altering the strength of the stressor–strain relationship. It predicts that under stressful conditions, high NA individuals will have a greater strain response compared to low NA individuals. In other words, high NA individuals are considered to have a heightened reactivity, or a stronger reaction to environmental stressors (e.g. McCrae and Costa, 1991; Deary *et al.*, 1996). It follows from this that the difference between high NA and low NA individuals on psychological, behavioural and physiological measures of strain should be greater under conditions of high demand.

While according to Watson and Clark (1984) this heightened reactivity of high NA individuals is not inconsistent with the definition of NA, it is not generally considered a central feature of the construct and has been inadequately investigated. However, given that trait anxiety is considered to be an indicator of NA, and that by definition, heightened reactivity is a central feature of trait anxiety (e.g. Spielberger, 1983), it is not illogical that heightened reactivity is also a feature of high NA individuals.

It is therefore surprising that the vulnerability model of NA has been so little researched, especially when its important implications are considered. It potentially predicts those individuals most at risk from occupational and other life stressors. For example, according to the moderator model, as work conditions become more demanding, high NA individuals will be the first employees to exhibit symptoms of strain. Hence, NA should be associated with behavioural indicators of occupational strain whereby high NA individuals show greater work performance decrements, increased absenteeism and higher turnover. Thus, this model suggests that high NA individuals will be the more difficult and costly employees. Alternatively, the model also makes the important prediction that stress interventions aimed at alleviating or reducing work stressors should be effective in reducing the level of strain of high NA individuals.

The few studies that have tested both the vulnerability and confound models have generally obtained support for *both* models (e.g. Morrison, Dunne and Fitzgerald and Gloghan 1992; Marco and Suls, 1993). However, it should also be noted that results from studies that have tested for interaction effects are far from conclusive. Firstly, when interaction effects have been obtained they are generally of small magnitude and explain only a small portion of the variance in strain outcome measures (e.g. Cassar and Tattersall, 1998). Secondly, and as indicated in the above study, interaction effects tend not only to be small but also inconsistent. NA appears to moderate only certain stressor–strain relationships. This is shown clearly in the occupational stress literature. For example, Parkes (1990), in a one-year longitudinal study, found different models of NA were appropriate for different work stressor and strain relationships. She found the moderator model best explained the relationship between work demands and well-being and the confound model best explaining the relationship between social support and well-being.

Results from a more recent study, by Moyle (1995b), further complicate the situation by indicating that the nature of the strain dimension must also be considered. In this study, while NA was observed to moderate the relationship between work stressors and general well-being, it did not moderate the relationship between these same stressors and job satisfaction. In other words, it would seem that different strain outcomes are also predicted by different models of NA.

Further approaches to NA

It would appear from these results that the role of NA in stress research is complex. The few studies that have examined both the potential roles of NA (as confound or vulnerability factors) have found inconsistent results with different models of NA predicted by different stressor–strain relations. The situation is yet more complex when other possible models of the relationship between stressors and strains are considered. For example, Spector *et al.* (2000), referring primarily to the work context, suggest a number of other possible mechanisms on which there has been limited research.

- The selection mechanism. They suggest that those with negative affect may be selected into more stressful jobs (a differential exposure hypothesis).
- The stressor creation mechanism. People high in NA may actually create more stressors, for example, by getting into more conflicts, which may lead to them having higher objective stressors rather than biased perceptions. This is another form of differential exposure hypothesis – the stressor mediates the relationship between NA and strain.
- The mood mechanism. Mood, and not the disposition of NA, reduces stressor–strain relationships by influencing reporting of strains, stressors and NA.
- The causality mechanism. Exposure to job stressors actually increases NA. (Here NA mediates the relationship between stressors and strains.)

They suggest that these are all plausible mechanisms to explain the relationships between NA and stressors and strains and further efforts need to be made to understand the role of NA and other personality variables in the stress process. Furthermore the practical significance of these models and their implications in terms of developing interventions needs to be investigated. For example, cognitive behavioural strategies to promote more positive thinking are frequently advocated as part of stress management training but we need to unpack the mechanisms whereby this might work. Does it simply induce a general positive bias that does not actually make any difference to the extent of reactions to stress, or does it have a real impact on reactions to stress by one of the mechanisms discussed above?

CONCLUSIONS

This chapter presents the common-sensical argument that people differ in their responses to stressors. However, researchers have only just begun to unravel the complexity of these relationships and there are numerous mechanisms whereby a range of individual difference factors may impact on perceptions of stressors and strains, physical health and the relationships between these variables. We can, as yet, draw few clear conclusions about the importance of individual differences. Early research suggested Type A was a major predictor of CHD. This research has subsequently been criticised and more recently a narrower focus on hostility has shown promise in having a direct effect on CHD. However, there is limited evidence supporting the effects of these variables on stressor–strain relationships. Researchers looking at the impact of individual differences on the stressor–strain relationship have more frequently focused on the role of negative affect. Here we have seen that, while NA seems to have an impact in many situations, it is far from a simple relationship and there is a need to investigate a number of alternative models.

There is also a need to extend research to include a much wider range of personality variables. As we have seen, Judge, Erez and Thoresen (2000) have suggested the importance of a general tendency to engage in positive biases. Miller *et al.* (1996) also recommend the study of a larger number of variables and recommend greater investigation of personality variables derived from the big five. Many of the issues discussed in relation to negative affect may also apply to other personality variables. Relationships are likely to be complex and a number of alternative models will need to be investigated.

COPING

This chapter introduces theoretical approaches to coping. This includes various dispositional approaches (such as repressors/sensitisers, monitors/blunters) and the relationship between personality traits and coping. These approaches are contrasted with Lazarus' transactional approach which views coping as a shifting process whereby the individual responds to different situations. The relationship between situational and dispositional approaches will be debated and their relationship to health and other outcomes considered. Finally some alternative approaches to coping will be introduced.

THE number of books now written on the topic of coping is enormous. A quick search of one university library gives an indication of the number of aspects of life we now need to cope with. It is possible to find books offering advice on coping with ageing parents, chronic illness or cancer and coping with dying as well as those on coping with violence, coping with difficult bosses and coping with peak hour traffic congestion. If your problems do not fall into any of these categories you may find help in 'coping with research' (Calnan, 1984). In short, there seems no limit to the problems that we may need help to cope with.

Coping is also central to stress research, particularly to Lazarus' transactional approach that will be discussed further in this chapter. As with research on stress, there has been a vast increase in research on coping in the last 30 years with large numbers of studies of coping with various illnesses, life events and chronic stressors. However, in spite of the volume of studies, it has been suggested we still know little about how a given individual can best cope with a particular situation and we still have few interventions that will make a real difference (Costa, Somerfield and McRae, 1996). It is also the case that research on coping has focused almost exclusively on what we do to cope reactively when pressures or difficulties arise (Pierce, Sarason and Sarason, 1996; Newton, 1989). It is often the case that by anticipating events we may avoid the problem but we know little about why and how some individuals are able to anticipate difficulties and therefore 'cope' by preventing the stressor arising in the first place. These are issues we will return to later in the chapter, after examining historical and current trends in coping research, including trait approaches to coping and ways in which people cope in different situations.

EARLY APPROACHES TO COPING

The origins of modern coping research can be traced back to work done in the late 19th century by psychoanalytic theorists, and Freud in particular. Much of Freud's work focused on the ways in which individuals deal with unpleasant feelings and emotions by either repressing them (so that they are no longer consciously aware of them) or using other defensive manoeuvres. These include rationalisation, sublimation (whereby unacceptable urges may be directed towards socially acceptable goals) or projection (for example, the attribution of aggressive impulses to an outside person) (Brown, 1964). Freud's daughter, Anna Freud, took up her father's ideas and expanded them, suggesting that individuals may have preferred defence mechanisms or a preferred defensive style (Freud, 1946) and, furthermore, that particular types of defence might be linked to specific psycho-pathologies (Parker and Endler, 1996). For example, she suggested that denial in fantasy may be linked to delusions. While this latter idea has not stood the test of time, many of the defensive mechanisms suggested by psychoanalytic theories are reflected in modern ideas of coping.

It was not until the 1960s that the term 'coping' started to be used to describe certain defence mechanisms (Parker and Endler, 1996) and gradually the coping literature developed as a more or less distinct field of research. However, there is still confusion about exactly what counts as 'coping' and what is 'defence'.

Freudian ideas influenced some subsequent approaches to coping such as the influential work done in the 1960s and 1970s on reactions to one's own impending death or the death of others (e.g. Kubler-Ross, 1970; Parkes, 1972). For example, Kubler-Ross (1970) suggested that people facing their own death go through a number of stages, which are characterised by forms of coping reminiscent of earlier work on defence mechanisms. An initial stage of denial gradually gives way to the second stage characterised by anger and resentment. This is followed by the third stage involving bargaining. For example, a dying person may try to enter into a bargain with either medical staff or with God. Eventually, the person will no longer be able to deny reality and will move into the fourth stage, which is characterised by depression and a sense of loss. Finally, if the person can work through this stage, they may finally come to a stage of acceptance. Parkes' model consists of broadly similar stages though it is based on interviews with the bereaved. However, the

134

stage approach has been criticised. For example, Corr (1993) argues that early research did not support the model and 20 years on there is still no evidence for the validity and reliability of the stages. He suggests that there is no reason to think that there are only five ways in which individuals cope or that they form stages in a process. Despite these criticisms, these frameworks seem to have an intuitive appeal and still feature strongly in literature for counsellors and caring professionals.

In contrast, in the psychological literature on coping, little attention is paid to stage approaches. Indeed many psychologists are very critical of psychoanalytic ideas and reject any links with a theoretical approach which is seen as fundamentally untestable using scientific methods (e.g. Eysenck, 1990). Nevertheless, the impact of psychoanalytic ideas has been so powerful that echoes of these approaches are inevitably present in modern psychological theories.

The emphasis in psychology has been predominantly on two main approaches discussed below. The first, referred to as the *dispositional approach*, looks at whether there are specific coping styles or dispositions that enable people to cope better across situations. The second, the *situational approach*, looks at the process of coping and whether there are specific strategies that are useful in different situations.

THE DISPOSITIONAL VIEW OF COPING

Those who take a dispositional view focus on relatively stable individual differences in coping. The key issue here is to look at the extent to which certain dispositional tendencies, usually referred to as coping styles, are effective in terms of leading to positive outcomes such as improved health and psychological well-being. One particular dichotomy that has dominated the literature is the distinction between ways of coping which represent *avoidant* versus *approach* ways of dealing with stressors. There are a number of different ways of conceptualising this distinction (Cohen, 1987) but two particularly popular approaches are discussed below.

Repressors/sensitisers

The notion of repressive coping style has clear links to the Freudian notion of repression, one of the most influential aspects of Freudian theory. Freud suggested that repression is a defensive mechanism in which an individual deals with unpleasant memories by banishing them to the unconscious so that they are no longer available to conscious recall and can only find expression through indirect means, such as symptoms or certain character traits (Brown, 1964). Repressive coping style has been identified as an individual difference variable by researchers such as Byrne (1961, 1964). Repressors are people who have an avoidant style of coping typified by the avoidance of negative feelings. A distinction was originally made between repressors and sensitisers (Byrne, 1961). According to Byrne (1964), repressors react to anxiety-arousing stimuli and their consequences by avoidant behaviour (including repression, denial and rationalisation) whereas sensitisers attempt to reduce anxiety by approaching or controlling such threats (e.g. by intel-lectualisation, obsessive behaviours and ruminative worrying). However, on the whole, the term 'sensitisers' is no longer used in the repressive coping literature.

It is clearly difficult to measure repression using questionnaire measures and an early measure (the repression–sensitisation scale by Byrne, 1961) was highly correlated with trait anxiety. This meant that a low anxious person would be likely to be classified as repressive, when in reality, they may simply not be anxious! To overcome this difficulty, Weinberger, Schwarz and Davidson (1979) developed a more sophisticated way of measuring repression. Under this approach, to be defined as repressors, people had to score low on anxiety but also high on a measure of defensiveness. The measure of defensiveness often used is a measure of social desirability that assesses people's tendency to respond to questionnaires in socially acceptable, rather than strictly accurate, ways (Crowne and Marlowe, 1964). This includes items such as 'I don't find it particularly difficult to get on with loud-mouthed obnoxious people' or 'I never resent being asked to return a favour' to which the respondent has to endorse either 'true' or 'false'. Those who claim a large number of such items are true are assumed to be defensive. Three other groups can be identified using this method: low anxious people (low on trait-anxiety and low on defensiveness); high anxious people (high on trait anxiety and low on defensiveness) and defensive high anxious (who are high on both measures). An alternative approach to measurement has also been developed which involves measuring distress and self-restraint (Weinberger and Schwartz, 1990). Both types of measure are currently in use.

Research has linked repression with a range of negative outcomes such as poorer immune functioning (O'Leary, 1990; Jamner, Schwartz and Leigh, 1988; Jamner and Leigh, 1999), poorer outcome amongst cancer patients (Jensen, 1987) and asthma (Mathe and Knapp, 1971). It has also been linked with increased coronary heart disease risk factors such as high cholesterol (Niaura *et al.*, 1992).

However, from the stress researcher's point of view, one of the most interest-ing factors is the effect that repressive coping style may have on the validity of using self-report questionnaires to measure stressors and strains. The psychology of stress is largely constructed around an assumption that people can more or less accurately report their feelings and symptoms. However, as we have seen there is evidence that repressive coping is related to negative outcomes where physiolo-gical or health outcomes are used, yet repressors answer self-reports in a positive way and on these measures they report less negative affect and fewer symptoms (Myers and Vetere, 1997; Myers, 2000). Thus this group may pose a serious threat to the validity of research based on self-reports of well-being and symptoms and thus to the validity of much stress research. The presence of repressors may also be responsible for the tendency for self-reports of stress reactions and physiological indicators to show little relationship. This is explored further in Box 7.1.

Box 7.1   Dissociation between verbal and autonomic responses.

It is a problem for stress research that measures of physiological activity which are taken to be indicative of stress are often not accompanied by corresponding reports of emotional affect. Equally, self-reports of feeling stressed may not be linked to changes in physiological activity. The two responses are said to be dissociated. One explanation for this dissociation is that repressive coping is responsible for self-reports failing to reflect physiological change. This has been confirmed in a number of studies. For example, Asendorpf and Scherer (1983) found that when faced with a stressful task, repressors showed greater increases in heart rate and showed more anxiety in their facial expressions than low anxious people, yet these increased responses were discrepant with low self-reports of anxiety. Newton and Contrada (1992) conducted a study which suggests that the picture is rather more complex. They recruited three groups of participants: repressors, high anxious and low anxious participants to take part in an experiment about the relationship between feelings and physiological reactions. They were asked to prepare and give a speech about the most undesirable aspect of their personality. Half of the participants delivered their speeches in private to one researcher and half to a group of three. Heart rate and blood pressure were recorded in addition to self-report measures of affect. The researchers found that repressors exhibited raised levels of physiological activity but no associated heightened levels of negative affect. However, this effect only occurred in the presence of the audience. The highly anxious participants showed an opposite dissociative effect, that is, they had heightened levels of negative affect but no similar increases in physiological activity.

The authors suggest that differences in self-concept concerning emotionality may be at the heart of the difference in coping strategies between these groups. They suggest that repressors have a 'stoical' self-concept and highly anxious people (sensitisers) have an 'emotional' self-concept. The reporting of emotional experience is biased by such self-concepts. They suggest that the discrepancy may only occur in the public condition because, for the repressor, the psychological threat posed by greater self-awareness produced by the public condition may cause greater internal conflict between their emotional response and their view of themselves as stoical and unemotional.

For these reasons, Myers (2000) suggests that self-report measures are an unsatisfactory way of obtaining information from this group, who may constitute around 10–20% of the population. She suggests overcoming this by using more than one method of data collection, and some evidence suggests that interviews may be more appropriate for this group. It may also be important to examine repressors as a separate group and evaluate their impact on research results.

Monitors/blunters

The distinction between a monitoring coping style and a blunting coping style appears to bear some superficial resemblance to the repressor/sensitiser distinction, but focuses more specifically on information-processing behaviour of people under threat. In fact it has been found to be unrelated to both the repression/sensitisation dichotomy and to state anxiety (Miller and Mangan, 1983). This approach has been applied particularly in research trying to determine the optimal form of medical information to give to patients. Originally the view was that people could be classified as either monitors or blunters on the basis of the way in which they deal with threat-related cues, that is, monitors will seek out threat-relevant information while blunters will avoid this information (Miller and Mangan, 1983). Miller and Mangan suggested that patients' level of arousal was lower when the level of information given was consistent with their coping style. Thus, blunters had lower arousal with low information and monitors had low arousal with a high level of information. However, more recent work has suggested that there is not just one dimension (Miller, 1987) and that it may even be possible to be high (or, indeed, low) on both monitoring and blunting – a phenomenon which has been labelled dispositional conflict (Rosenbaum and Piamenta, 1998). This has added considerably to the complexity of work in this area and the difficulty of interpreting the findings.

Research suggests that these coping styles do seem to have important implications for health. For example, Miller, Summerton and Brody (1988) found that high monitors tend to go to their doctors with less severe medical problems than low monitors but they complain of equal levels of discomfort and distress and are slower to report improvement or recovery. They also demand more tests, information and counselling. Perhaps surprisingly, however, monitors and blunters also differed in the role they wished to play in treatment. High monitors seem to prefer a passive role, suggesting that they wanted the information to reduce uncertainty – not in order to enable them to take any positive action. Although it seems that high monitors have higher levels of anxiety in the face of uncontrollable stressors such as many medical situations, monitoring is thought to be associated with better health. For example, in a prospective study which followed patients over four weeks, Davey, Tallis and Hodgson (1993) found that blunting was associated with poorer psychological health (recorded using GHQ scores) as well as higher levels of self-reported symptoms such as colds and 'flu. However, despite this relationship for blunting, they found no relationship between monitoring and symptom reports. They suggest that this may be due to the fact that high blunters, unlike high monitors, fail to respond to early illness cues and wait until a later stage in the development of psychological and physical disorders before seeking treatment. In the longer term it has also been suggested that monitoring has positive implications, for example, Steptoe and O'Sullivan (1986) suggest that high monitors and low blunters are more likely to undergo cervical smears and perform more frequent breast self-examinations, preventing more serious health problems in the longer term.

In recent years attention has focused particularly on the process of monitoring with the development of the monitoring process model which looks at how monitors cope with potentially life threatening stressors (e.g. Schwartz *et al.*, 1995; Miller *et al.*, 1996). This indicates that the situation is rather more complex than had been portrayed in the earlier literature. The model suggests that high and low monitors differ in the way they construe these high threat situations. High monitors tend to scan for external and internal threats and access such threats more readily than low monitors. In the face of severe, enduring and uncontrollable stressors they generate what is described as 'intrusive ideation' about the stressor, that is, they have persistent and intrusive thoughts such as reliving the situation, being kept awake by thoughts or dreaming about it. They may also tend to view ambiguous information as threatening and hence exaggerate their risk. All this is likely to generate anxiety and encourage the use of avoidant ideation, including denial and disengagement. Miller *et al.* suggest that 'using such strategies is not ultimately successful because of the continuing partial breakthrough of avoided or denied material into conscious awareness. The cycle of intrusive and avoidant ideation can also interfere with full adaptation to and acceptance of the situation because the stressor is never actively confronted and emotionally processed' (p. 217). They suggest that this pattern is likely to be strongest when the stressor is low in controllability as well as long term and of high intensity (for example, in the case of HIV diagnosis).

The work of Miller *et al.* (1996) suggests that while monitors generally prefer to seek information, under certain circumstances, such as where the threat was severe, chronic and uncontrollable they become more avoidant than most people. Miller *et al.* suggest the need for research to look in yet further detail at patterns of coping in different circumstances. However, while research in this area is highly sophisticated it becomes increasingly difficult to interpret and to draw out clear implications for practice. Furthermore, there is confusion between the monitoring and blunting dimensions, with some studies abandoning the monitoring scale, others treating high monitors as equivalent of low blunters and yet others treating the dimensions as independent (Rosenbaum and Piamenta, 1998). Like many other branches of psychology, this is an area where it is proving difficult to strike a balance between the need for simple practical and useful theory and the need for theory that is complex enough to provide an accurate description of relationships.

Personality traits and coping

If coping dispositions or styles are relatively stable across time, the question arises as to how they relate to personality traits. A number of well-known personality factors, including optimism, negative affectivity and Type A (discussed in Chapter 6), are clearly candidates to impact on the ways in which people cope in particular situations. Some writers even refer to such variables as coping styles (for example, Newton, 1989, refers to Type A as a coping style). Most, however, make a distinction between traditional personality variables and coping styles (e.g. Carver, Scheier and Weintraub, 1989) and seek to study the relationship between the two types of variable.

Hewitt and Flett (1996) suggest that some personality types (for example, neuroticism, locus of control and optimism) have received much greater attention in coping research than others, such as extraversion, openness, conscientiousness and agreeableness – variables that, together with neuroticism, form 'the big five' (see Chapter 6). They suggest that neuroticism is usually linked to maladaptive coping. For example Costa *et al.* (1996) found that people high in neuroticism tend to react badly to stressors, indulging in self-blame, wishful thinking and becoming passive. Unusually, this study also looked at openness and conscientiousness, as well as extraversion, and found that extraversion, as might be expected, is associated with coping by talking, joking and relating to others. Openness to experience is related to coping by seeking new information and trying novel solutions and conscientiousness is associated with perseverance and personal growth.

Hewitt and Flett propose three alternative models for the relationship between personality, coping and maladjustment. These will already be familiar from Chapter 6.

- *A mediational model* whereby personality determines coping style or strategy which then determines degree of maladjustment;
- *An additive model* whereby personality and coping have independent direct effects on maladjustment;
- *An interactive model*, whereby personality variables interact with coping variables.

A number of researchers have tested such models. Bolger (1990), for example, looked at neuroticism and found mediational relationships, such that ineffective coping in the form of wishful thinking and self-blame, mediated the relationship between neuroticism and anxiety (explaining over half of the effect of neuroticism on anxiety). He suggests that, under conditions of stress, neuroticism leads people to adopt ineffective coping strategies and this coping in turn leads to increases in distress.

These studies provide some support for the view that personality and coping are very closely linked and even that 'coping is personality in action under stress' (Bolger, 1990, p. 525). However, some researchers whose work is discussed in the next section dispute this emphasis on the role of personality. They argue that the stressful situation, rather than the individual's personality, is the main influence on the coping response. They further argue that coping takes the form of a wide range of shifting responses to different stressful situations.

THE SITUATIONAL VIEW OF COPING

Lazarus is one of the main proponents of the situational view. His transactional theory focuses on coping as a process and as something that is specific to situations of psychological stress.

Coping is thus a shifting process in which a person must, at certain times, rely more heavily on one form of coping, say defensive strategies, and at other times on problem-solving strategies, as the status of the person–environment relationship changes. (Lazarus and Folkman, 1984, p. 142)

While he accepts that dispositional factors play some part in coping (Lazarus, 1993), Lazarus and Folkman view coping overall in transactional terms as:

Constantly changing cognitive and behavioral efforts to manage specific external and/or internal demands that are appraised as taxing or exceeding the resources of the person. (Lazarus and Folkman, 1984, p. 141)

The emphasis on 'efforts to manage' also means that the definition includes strategies that may not work or that are geared to avoiding or minimising stressors as well as mastering them.

Thinking about any major stressor can clarify this. For example, after the break up of a close relationship or marriage, you may initially feel shock or disbelief. This may next give way to tearfulness or frantic activity, or maybe to efforts to take your mind off the problem by drinking. Later on there may be times of depression when you just feel you need to retreat from the world while at other times managing to get out and put a brave face on things, take up new activities and rebuild a social life. There will undoubtedly be a great deal of mulling over the events of the break up. What went wrong? Was it your fault? Could you have done anything to change the situation? How will you face the future without your partner? This process may take months or even years in the case of a very close relationship and may be very different at different times. In the case of more minor stressors, Lazarus suggests that the coping process will proceed much more quickly. However, he suggests that in all cases there is an 'unfolding, shifting pattern of cognitive appraisal and reappraisal, coping, and emotional processes' (p. 143). This emphasis on process, however, does not deny that the specific pattern of appraisal and coping adopted by the individual may be influenced by dispositional factors, but Lazarus and Folkman (1984) do suggest that dispositional typologies discussed above 'grossly simplify complex patterns of coping'.

The notion of appraisal is central to Lazarus' approach to coping. He describes two types of appraisal: primary and secondary. *Primary appraisal* is the process whereby the person evaluates the potential harm, loss, threat or challenge imposed by the stressor. *Secondary appraisal* is the process whereby the person evaluates what can be done to overcome or prevent harm or improve benefits, i.e. coping options are evaluated. Thus secondary appraisals in the case of the broken relationship discussed above could include the following:

- 'There are lots of other fish in the sea, I must do something to improve my social life and meet new people.'
- 'Relationships are hopeless, I'll try celibacy from now on.'

141

- 'I'm hopeless at relationships, and come to think of it I'm not much good at anything. Everything I do always goes wrong, I might as well sit here and get drunk.'

Clearly the nature of appraisal adopted will affect the type of coping strategy used and the likely emotional response. A further process of re-appraisal may also take place on the basis of any new information, for example the stressor of losing a relationship may be reappraised as less harmful if efforts to improve one's social life prove successful.

Lazarus suggests that the nature of appraisal is important in determining how the individual copes, that is, appraisal mediates the relationship between stressors and coping. In the process of coping itself, Lazarus identifies a crucial distinction between coping which is aimed at actually managing or dealing with the stressor and coping which is directed at dealing with the emotion caused by the stressor. The former he has labelled *problem-focused coping* and suggested it is most likely to be used when the individual appraises the situation as amenable to change (as in the first of our three scenarios above). The latter he called *emotion-focused coping* and argued that this is likely to be used when appraisal indicates that nothing can be done to modify the stressor (as in our last scenario). Problem-focused coping includes a range of problem solving strategies (such as learning new skills or reducing levels of aspiration). There are a vast array of coping strategies that can be viewed as emotion-focused strategies including expressing emotion, using cognitive strategies, such as trying to view the situation differently, or behavioural strategies to take your mind off the stressor (e.g. by exercising, shopping, drinking alcohol, etc.).

Folkman and Lazarus (1988) developed the Ways of Coping check-list for measuring coping in specific situations. This consists of eight subscales measuring confrontative coping, distancing, using self-control, seeking social support, accepting responsibility, escape-avoidance, planful problem solving and positive re-appraisal. In studies using this approach, people were asked to nominate a situation (for example, their most stressful experience in the last week). They then complete the rating scale in respect of that situation. Diverse situations are then pooled to draw general conclusions across situations (e.g. Folkman and Lazarus, 1980; Folkman et al., 1986).

Of course, even within a single situation, such as the break-up of a relationship as discussed above, it is likely that a range of different strategies will be used and that the individual will move between cognitive and emotion-focused strategies at different times. Folkman and Lazarus (1985) demonstrated this by looking at emotion and coping amongst students taking exams. They took measures at three points, during the run-up to an exam, between the exam and results and following the results. They found that combinations of most of the available problem- and emotion-focused coping strategies were used at every stage, but different forms dominated during the anticipation and waiting stages. Problem-focused coping predominated before the exam and the emotion-focused strategy of distancing was more important during the waiting period.

Which strategies are good or bad will depend on the situation and may change over time within a situation. Thus strategies such as denial, which are widely seen as unhelpful, may be useful in certain circumstances (Lazarus, 1993). For example, Lazarus suggests that when experiencing heart attack symptoms, denial may be unhelpful and dangerous in that it may lead to delay in seeking treatment, but in the immediate post-coronary period it may be useful as a way of coping. It may become unhelpful again if it continues for too long, preventing the person changing their life style in order to prevent further attacks.

Lazarus' and Folkman's approach and their Ways of Coping measure have inevitably been criticised. For example, Oakland and Ostell (1996) point out that a number of studies that have factor analysed the items have found anything between 3 and 9 different factors, casting doubt on the distinctive nature of the eight types of coping originally identified by Folkman and Lazarus. Stone *et al.* (1991) have further argued that the items included in the measure are much less applicable to some kinds of events than others. Thus people found most of the scale relevant for problems with boyfriends and girlfriends, but 27% of items were not applicable for health problems. Some items may simply not make much sense in the context of some problems, e.g. 'finding a new faith' as a coping strategy when the car breaks down. Furthermore, they suggest that people may have difficulty in interpreting the instruction to rate 'the extent to which they used an item in coping with the situation'. How, for example, should a person rate the 'extent' to which they 'approached the person who caused the problem'? People are likely to interpret such an instruction in different ways, reflecting perhaps the time it took or the effort they made. Nevertheless, despite such criticisms, the Ways of Coping check-list continues to be widely used.

Coping behaviour or coping style?

It is of course likely that in any real life situation people may use a range of different coping behaviours at different times. They may also have a general dispositional tendency to use certain strategies more often, e.g. in a difficult situation they may tend to try to avoid thinking about the problem or maybe drink more. This in turn may be related to having an overriding style characterised by the use of avoidant rather than non-avoidant methods of coping. Frequently the WOC is adapted to ask people how they 'usually' cope. The question then arises as to whether this is measuring an aggregate of coping behaviours (as researchers sometimes assume) or whether it is measuring a form of coping style (as others have assumed). However, it is argued in Box 7.2 that it may not be a valid way of measuring either behaviour or style.

Box.7.2   What are we measuring if we ask people how they 'usually' cope?

As a quick and convenient way of measuring coping, researchers will often use measures that present people with a range of options and ask them how much they 'usually' use each option. Sometimes this is taken as providing an indication of coping behaviours (or strategies) which are used in specific situations. Newton suggests this approach may, in fact, measure something closer to coping style and that there is likely to be a difference between people's perception of their style of coping over time and how they behave in particular situations. He draws on the work of Argyris and Schon (1974) who suggest that when someone is asked how they would behave under certain circumstances they will give their 'espoused theory' of action or how they think they act. However, the theory that governs their actual behaviour is their 'theory-in-use'. This may be different from their espoused theory and the person may not be aware of the incompatibility between these two theories. Questions asking about generalised situations are likely to assess espoused theories whereas questions relating to coping in real acute situations are much more likely to get close to assessing theory-in-use.

Lazarus is even more critical of questions asking how people 'usually cope', suggesting that it is not a valid way to measure coping styles.

> I think it may be a bad assumption that a subject actually copes in any specific encounter in the way indicated when the word 'usually' is used in the measurement . . . Subjects may be giving nothing more than a vague impression about how they would prefer to cope, perhaps influenced by what they believe is socially desirable or ideal, rather than what they actually have thought or done.
> (Lazarus, 1993, p. 242)

While Lazarus and Folkman argue that adapting the WOC in this way is not a satisfactory measure of dispositional coping, they also criticise unidimensional typologies (such as avoidant/non-avoidant styles) discussed above. They argue that these have had little success in explaining or predicting what people do in particular situations (Lazarus and Folkman, 1984). Lazarus (1993) suggests that a better approach to measuring the influence of dispositional factors is to draw out people's coping strategies from process measures taken on a number of occasions. This approach also offers scope to examine new aspects of coping such as the extent to which people are flexible or rigid, or use simple rather than complex patterns of coping across a number of encounters.

Folkman et al. (1986) used Lazarus' approach to examine coping over five different stressful episodes nominated by participants. They suggested that overall coping processes were 'more variable than stable' (p. 578), but that different coping strategies varied in the extent to which they were stable across situations.

So, for example, in their study, positive reappraisal was the most stable suggesting that this strategy is most related to personality factors, whereas the problem-focused coping strategies of confrontational coping, seeking social support and planful problem-solving were more strongly influenced by the situation.

Schwartz, Neale, Marco *et al.* (1999) go a step further and actually compare Lazarus' recommended approach to measuring coping dispositions with the approach Lazarus has criticised. This involved taking the average of a number of momentary reports of how each individual coped with a variety of stressful situations. These were correlated with a measure based on an adaptation of the WOC, asking how people coped in 'general'. Like Folkman *et al.* (1986) they found that the averaging approach did reveal some, albeit modest, stable tendencies or coping dispositions (particularly for escape-avoidance and religion). However, they also found that the general coping style measure was a very poor predictor of the averaged momentary coping, confirming Lazarus view that this may not be a useful approach.

Despite these limitations, for practical reasons, many researchers in areas of health psychology may wish to include simple indicators of coping when looking at the relationship between stressors and illness. The use of questionnaire measures asking how people 'usually' cope therefore remains common in such situations. This approach is built into one of the most popular and widely used measures – the COPE inventory discussed in the following section.

The COPE approach

The work of Carver, Scheier and Weintraub (1989) builds on Lazarus' theory but suggests that the distinction between problem- and emotion-focused coping made by Lazarus is just too simple. Carver, Scheier and Weintraub argue that within these two broad categories are strategies which are quite different from each other and have different implications. They further argue that previous measures tended to be largely developed by statistical means rather than based on theory. Their measure, the COPE questionnaire, draws on two theoretical frameworks: Lazarus' stress theory and their own model of behavioural self-regulation (Scheier and Carver, 1988). It originally consisted of 13 distinct scales, but more recently the final two scales measuring alcohol/drug use and humour have been added (see Box 7.3). It should be noted that social support appears as both an emotion-focused strategy and as a problem-focused strategy depending on the use made of the social support.

As with Lazarus' approach some of these strategies would appear to be more constructive than others, but they cannot be clearly divided into adaptive and non-adaptive strategies. Each strategy may be useful for some people in some circumstances. For example, using denial as a strategy for coping with financial problems is likely to mean the problem gets worse. However, when facing financial collapse, denial of the enormity of the problem in the initial stages may be useful in minimising distress and facilitating coping. One factor that is thought to influence the usefulness of different strategies is whether the stressful situation is controllable

Box 7.3   Proposed dimensions of coping (adapted from Carver, Scheier and Weintraub, 1989).

Active coping – Taking active steps or initiating direct action to deal with the stressor.

Planning – Thinking about how to deal with a stressor – developing action strategies (occurs during secondary appraisal, not the coping phase, but is part of problem-focused coping).

Suppression of competing activities – Avoiding being distracted by other activities and maybe letting other things slide to let you deal with the stressor.

Restraint coping – Waiting for the right moment to act and avoiding rushing into action too soon.

Seeking social support for instrumental reasons – Seeking advice, assistance or information.

Seeking social support for emotional reasons – Getting moral support, sympathy or understanding.

Focusing on and venting emotion – Focusing on the distress or upset and expressing feelings.

Behavioural disengagement – Reducing efforts to deal with stressors.

Mental disengagement – Using activities to distract from thinking about a problem, e.g. by day dreaming, sleeping.

Positive reinterpretation and growth – Trying to construe a stressor in positive terms.

Denial – Refusing to believe the stressor exists or trying to deny that it is real.

Acceptance – Accepting the reality of a stressful situation.

Turning to religion – Seeking God's help and finding comfort in religion.

Alcohol/drug use – Using drugs as a way of avoiding the problem or to feel better.

Humour – Laughing and joking about the situation.

or not (Folkman and Lazarus, 1980). Carver, Scheier and Weintraub found that people used more active coping, planning and suppression of competing activities in controllable than uncontrollable situations. In uncontrollable situations emotion-focused coping strategies of acceptance or denial were more likely to be used.

The COPE scale was designed to measure both situational responses (strategies) and the underlying dispositional coping styles, depending on whether ratings are requested relating to 'usual' responses or relating to a specific incident. As we have seen in the last section, it is questionable what this kind of measure is assessing. In the context of the WOC we have already seen that such measures are a poor predictor of averaged momentary coping. Carver, Scheier and Weintraub look at how this approach to coping style relates to personality variables and the dispositional approaches discussed at the beginning of this chapter. They looked at the relationship of a range of personality factors (including the monitoring and blunting constructs discussed above) with coping styles measured using COPE (asking people how they 'usually' coped). While there were correlations between some dimensions, e.g. active coping was positively correlated with Type A, optimism and self-esteem, generally such cor-relations were not great, suggesting that coping styles were distinct from personality dimensions. There were few relationships between the COPE styles and the monitoring and blunting dimensions, suggesting that these approaches are complementary. Question marks therefore remain as to exactly what this approach is measuring. However, Carver, Scheier and Weintraub maintain that both approaches to coping, measured by the COPE scale as well as traditional personality traits, have a complimentary role to play in coping research.

Carver and Scheier (1994), like Lazarus and Folkman (see above), have applied their approach to study coping during college examinations. They took measures two days before an exam, in the interval between the exam and the announcement of results and again after the exam results were published. They used the COPE dispositional measure at the start of the study followed by the situational version at each stage. Like Folkman and Lazarus they found that problem-focused strategies (such as active coping, planning, suppression of competing activities and use of instrumental support) were high during the pre-exam period. Some other reactions, such as the use of emotional support, remained high throughout the exam and post-exam period, declining only after the results. Use of one coping strategy, denial, increased across the measurements to become higher after the results than before the exam. They found that coping dispositions were moderately related to situational coping, though in only a few cases did they predict emotion (always being linked with negative emotion). The most striking finding in this respect was that those who reported a dispositional tendency to use alcohol to cope reported higher levels of harm emotions at every stage.

Because it is easy to use and widely available, the COPE scale is now one of the most commonly used measures and a brief version is also now available (Carver, 1997). There are, however, a wide range of other measures, some catering for specific age groups (for a review of alternative measures, see Schwarzer and Schwarzer, 1996). Increasingly, the heavy reliance on the use of check-list measures such as the COPE scale and the Ways of Coping has been criticised. Coyne and Gottlieb (1996), for example, suggest that 'As they are currently employed, conventional check-lists render an incomplete and distorted portrait of coping'. Specifically, these check-lists are grounded in too narrow a conceptualisation of coping which forces respondents to use a framework which may not be appropriate to them. For example, they suggest that check-lists may be based on an assumption that when faced with difficult situations people make appraisals and select coping strategies, whereas often in fact what they do is muddle through with little in the way of appraisal of either threats or resources, until they are faced with a questionnaire which may lead them to retrospectively impose such a structure to events. Coyne and Gottlieb report that they have found discrepancies between what people report in narrative accounts and the items that they endorse when completing question-naires. For example, they suggest that people may endorse items such as 'I tried to see the bright side of things', because they feel that this is something that they generally do, even though it may never have been a conscious strategy used in coping with a particular event. This implies that even situational coping check-lists may be assessing espoused theories of coping rather than actual coping.

Weight has been added to these criticisms by Smith, Leffingwell and Ptacek (1999) whose research raises doubts about the common practice of assessing situational coping retrospectively (e.g. see Chapter 8, Box 8.3). They found great discrepancies between reports of exam coping as the exams occurred and retro-spective reports of the same situation made seven days later. They conclude that people may not be able to give accurate summaries after time has passed. Like Coyne and Gottlieb they also suggest that this situation may lead to people responding in terms of their own implicit theories of how they cope.

As a result of such criticisms there have been calls not only for the development of methods to improve measurement accuracy (e.g. Smith, Leffingwell and Ptacek, 1999) but also for the use of more varied approaches to assessment including qualitative methods (e.g. Coyne and Gottlieb, 1996; Newton, 1989).

Qualitative approaches to coping measurement

Qualitative approaches have the advantage that they can explore the wide range of strategies used. The four items in the COPE measures of active coping or mental disengagement, for example, can give very little insight into the many ways people may problem-solve or distract themselves. Unless much more sophisticated questionnaire measures can be developed, qualitative approaches seem an appro-priate alternative in this area. Some early studies (e.g. Pearlin and Schooler, 1978; Menaghan and Merves, 1984) show the advantages of combining both approaches by using qualitative interviews prior to constructing quantitative measures relevant to the sample being studied (See Box 7.4).

Qualitative approaches to coping, sometimes in conjunction with quantitative measures have also increasingly been used in occupational stress, perhaps because applied researchers in this area have identified the need for more detailed and specific information than can be gained from existing measures (e.g. Oakland and Ostell, 1996; Bunce and West, 1994). Such studies give people open ended questions allowing them scope to explain their own ways of coping which are then typically categorised by independent raters.

For example, Oakland and Ostell interviewed 80 headteachers of schools in the UK using both qualitative and quantitative approaches. They asked not only about stressful situations and coping strategies but also how effective the head-masters felt their strategy was and, where it was not felt to be effective, why not. When the authors considered the simple statements they found the responses fell into the traditional problem- and emotion-focused categories. However, when the

Box 7.4   An early approach to coping by Pearlin and Schooler (1978).

An early study of coping by Pearlin and Schooler (1978) remains something of a classic and is an excellent example of the advantages of combining qualitative and quantitative approaches. The study was ambitious in its scope in seeking to specify the circumstances that people found stressful, to identify coping mechanisms and to assess their efficacy. It further aimed to look at the impact of individual difference variables, specifically the personal resources of self-esteem, self-mastery and self-denigration.

Exploratory interviews with over 100 participants were used to identify people's problems or stressors (which rather confusingly they call strains in this study!) and the coping mechanisms that they used to deal with them. From this they developed questionnaire items of stressors and coping responses which were administered to 2,300 people in the Chicago area. From factor analysis of the coping items they identified 17 different types of coping, each of which applied to one or more of the following domains: marital, parenting, household/economic and occupational. For example, these included negotiation in marriage and punitive discipline in parenting. They suggested that these 'constitute but a portion of the full range of responses people undoubtedly call upon in dealing with life exigencies' (p. 5).

The study looked at how effective coping mechanisms were in reducing distress (labelled 'stress' in this study) as measured using rating items, e.g. when you think of your financial situation how . . . do you feel? (A) worried, (B) bothered or upset, etc. The study found that different types of coping were effective in different domains. In the occupational arena coping mechanisms were relatively ineffective in reducing distress. In the economic area, the manipulation of goals (e.g. telling oneself that money is not that important) is most effective. This latter kind of coping was less useful in marriage, where the rather different strategy of reflective probing was one of the most effective strategies. Also in the area of marriage and parenting self-reliance was more effective than seeking advice.

When they considered the relationships between coping and the individual difference strategies, they found that distress experienced in all areas depended more on self-denigration that the other variables. In all domains except the occupational it was most effective to have both the personal resources and a repertoire of coping responses than either alone. Results suggest that personal resources may be more important in situations where people have little control (e.g. the economic domain) and coping responses are important where they have control (e.g. marital domain).

While this study had limitations in terms of only looking at how people generally cope and ignoring the range of different types of problems and responses that might occur within a domain, nevertheless, such studies made great advances and offered promise that much future research has failed to fulfil.

context was considered it was not so easy to categorise responses meaningfully. For example, coping responses often include seeking advice or information from others. However, they suggest that it was futile to categorise such responses in terms of how often headteachers sought advice, when the crucial factor in terms of outcomes, was not whether the person sought advice but whether the advice they received was useful. Similarly, when dealing with problem-solving and direct action, they suggest the making and implementing of plans was not the key issue in determining outcome, rather, it was whether the plans work. They question the utility of coping questionnaires that focus on coping strategies and look for relationships between the use of these strategies and health and situational outcomes. They suggest that qualitative methods are more useful to explore aspects such as the adequacy of resources and the effectiveness of coping, which may have a crucial effect on appraisal, psychological distress and other outcomes. They also argue that the use of such methods may need to be combined with quantitative methods to 'adequately assess the dynamic, ever-changing nature of the coping process' (p. 152).

WHAT ARE THE OUTCOMES OF COPING?

It is clear from the preceding section that outcomes are not just dependent on the coping strategy used, but are likely to crucially depend on the effectiveness of that strategy (Oakland and Ostell, 1996). However, using current methods of research, this is seldom examined. This may in part account for the general lack of clear findings related to the outcomes of coping. To the extent that there is a consistent trend it seems to be that coping tends to be either neutral or it has a negative effect on outcomes. Thus we seem to know little about effective coping that may lead to positive outcomes. As we have seen, coping styles such as monitoring and blunting have been associated with illness. Similarly, where situational measures were taken on a number of occasions, Folkman *et al.* (1986) found low correlations between coping and health and where significant they were negative, indicative that coping was related to worse health. However, for psychological symptoms they did find that planful problem solving was related to reduced symptoms whereas confrontative coping was related to greater symptoms.

Looking at the much-researched area of exam stress, Bolger (1990) found that wishful thinking, self-blame and even problem-solving strategies increased anxiety. While Carver and Scheier (1994) suggest that though there is some evidence about benefits resulting from task focus and positive reframing, there are far more findings indicating avoidance coping increases distress. Studies of exam stress also suggest that there is little relationship between coping and performance (Bolger, 1990) with the exception of the perhaps unsurprising finding by Carver *et al.* that mental disengagement before an exam has a somewhat negative effect on performance.

COPING: THE WAY FORWARD

The literature criticising coping research and measurement is now substantial, much of it focusing on the fact that the large amount of research has not yielded information on which to base interventions (e.g. Costa, Somerfield and McCrae, 1996; Coyne, 1997; Somerfield, 1997). Critics of existing research have posed a lot of questions that we have not begun to address. These include: how does anticipatory coping work? (Coyne and Gottlieb, 1996; Newton, 1989) and what happens when we cannot use the dispositional styles we prefer or if they are inadequate? (Carver, Scheier and Weintraub, 1989).

A range of theoretical and methodological problems has been highlighted in this chapter. Much of the criticism has focused on the emphasis on the use of questionnaire measures of coping strategies (e.g. Coyne and Gottlieb, 1996; Coyne, 1997; Somerfield, 1997). Coyne suggests that measures such as the Ways of Coping check-list and its revisions should have been seen as 'the first steps' in coping measurement. Instead, the 'mindless repetition' of the use of these measures has led to 'hundreds of studies which tell us little about coping that is not trivial or misleading' (Coyne, 1997, p. 153).

It has been suggested that this lack of progress and development may also stem from a gulf between theory and methodology in coping research (Somerfield, 1997). Somerfield suggests that conceptual models such as that proposed by Lazarus (1990) which portray coping as an interactive dynamic process are so complex that testing them adequately is difficult. Thus, most research has focused on limited aspects of these models such as personal or situational influences on coping and few studies have looked at more complex interrelations among a wider range of influences (e.g. Aspinwall and Taylor, 1992).

Accompanying such criticisms are calls for new approaches. Arguably, the problems with the area are such that a paradigm shift is needed (i.e. essentially a radically new way of framing the issues) rather than minor changes. A number of new ways forward have been proposed, some more radical than others. One approach is that of Somerfield (1997) who proposes the use of more holistic models which take into account a 'multiplicity of personal and environmental factors within a dynamic and interactive framework'. However, to be practically manageable these need to be conducted at a micro-analytic level, that is researchers should focus on coping with specific stressors (e.g. exam stress). He cites an example of research investigating coping with the stress of treatment induced sterility in bone-marrow transplant survivors.

Somerfield argues that a more micro-analytic approach will produce findings that can inform practice. However, it has the disadvantage that it could impede progress towards the development of a broad theoretical framework (Smith and Wallston, 1997). For this reason, Smith and Wallston suggest the use of meta-analyses across studies of different stressors to develop more general theories.

151

Folkman (1997), however, considers there still remains a need for more 'basic research' formulated within the context of theoretical models to address such issues as the principles for determining coping efficacy.

In the quest for progress in such basic research in recent years Lazarus has suggested that stress researchers should focus on the study of specific emotions. For example, he suggests that distinguishing between reactions of anger, anxiety or guilt is likely to be more informative than simple looking at reactions to 'stress' (Lazarus, 1993). This clearly has implications for the study of coping, in that coping is likely to depend on the type of emotion experienced. For example, in the context of marital interactions, he suggests that in an argument with a spouse an individual may cope with anger by attacking, whereas in anxiety-provoking situations they may look for social support. He suggests that very little is known about how coping is shaped by emotion but it is likely that each of the emotions and situations that provoke them would lead to a distinctive pattern of coping. This, however, leaves the rather disheartening feeling that there are so many permutations of coping responses that developing a useful theory of coping to guide interventions is even further from our grasp than we thought.

Costa, Somerfield and McRae (1996) suggest perhaps the most radical approach. They suggest that:

> progress has been hampered and unrealistic expectations have been fostered by the assumption that stress and coping are special processes, governed by their own laws, and lying outside the normal range of human adaptation. (p. 44)

They argue that stress and coping have been defined as a specific aspect of human adaptation that is distinct from both routine processes such as learning and social interaction and from psychopathological responses. They suggest instead that there is no clear boundary between coping and normal experience. For example, they suggest that information seeking is seen as a coping response but it is also clearly part of everyday life. They suggest that the view that coping should be seen as part of the broader field of normal adaptation is consistent with Lazarus' (1990) suggestions that stress would be more usefully replaced by the study of emotion. Viewed in this way it perhaps becomes clear why coping researchers have made little progress. As Costa, Somerfield and McRae (1996) point out,

> The management of distressing emotions is the single most important focus of the disciplines of clinical psychology and psychiatry, which have been grappling with this problem for decades with only modest success. To expect that stress and coping researchers could solve the problem in a few years was quite unrealistic, tenable only under the mistaken assumption of a categorical distinction between normal and abnormal psychological processes. (p. 47)

Even more unrealistic is the assumption that all coping processes could be understood using the same questionnaire methodology.

This new approach may clearly raise considerable difficulties in that it seems to broaden the field of stress and coping to encompass much of psychology. However, Costa, Somerfield and McRae (1996) also suggest that some of the solutions are already out there, as we already know a good deal about normal emotional and behavioural processes. Thus, knowledge in the areas of personality, affect and problems-solving may provide useful insights. They suggest that the most appropriate way forward is not to look at the many ways of dealing with a narrow band of adaptive problems but instead to focus in depth on specific coping mechanisms. The overall implications of these suggestions seem to be that while basic research should focus on and shed light on individual processes (for example, focusing in depth on the processes of mental disengagement or seeking social support), applied research might focus on very specific problems such as coping with specific medical interventions (in line with the suggestions of Somerfield, 1997, discussed above).

CHAPTER 8

SOCIAL SUPPORT

This chapter considers a number of approaches to social support, ranging from studies of the extent of an individual's social networks to much more specific supportive interactions with other individuals. It considers research investigating whether social support is beneficial for health and whether it can buffer the effects of stressors. It further considers possible mechanisms for such effects. Finally, the complexity of social support issues in the real world is considered, focusing on research into social support for cancer sufferers.

SOCIAL relationships are so fundamental to human beings that it comes as no surprise that their effects on well-being have been a topic of interest to social scientists for many years. For example, a classic early study by Durkheim, first published in 1897, suggested that a lack of social ties and low social integration within groups is related to a greater number of suicides (Durkheim, 1952). The emergence of 'social support' as a distinct field of study, however, is a more recent phenomenon commonly attributed to two papers by Cassell (1976) and Cobb (1976). Cassell emphasised the role of social relationships in increasing resistance to disease. Cobb produced an early classification of types of support. Both highlighted the role of social support as a *buffer* or *moderator* of the effects of stressors (see Chapter 6), an emphasis that has clear implications for researchers.

We saw, in Chapter 6, that studies of coping strategies frequently incorporate measures, such as the COPE scale, which include assessment of the extent to which people use social support either in specific situations or as a general dispositional tendency. The approaches to social support discussed in the present chapter are somewhat different and relate to the extent to which social support resources are available or offered by others. The range of conceptualisations of social support and the hypothesised mechanisms by which they may influence outcomes are considered below.

WHAT IS MEANT BY SOCIAL SUPPORT?

Many issues are encompassed within the global heading of 'social support', ranging from studies investigating whether social isolation is related to mortality to studies investigating the nature of specific supportive behaviours that might be perceived as helpful by those suffering irritable bowel disorder. Measurement methods reflect this diversity of issues, with measures ranging from very broad indicators such as marriage or number of family members, to those addressing very specific supportive behaviours (such as offering advice). While some studies have incorporated supports which are not clearly social (such as measures of the availability or extent of financial assistance), generally this chapter will focus on supportive aspects of relationships.

A number of writers have sought to classify the range of approaches to social support that has been used. Some writers make a distinction between *structural* and *functional* measures (Cohen and Wills, 1985; Uchino, Cacioppo and Kiecolt-Glaser, 1996). While structural measures look at the existence of social relationships, which are presumed to provide support, functional measures examine the supportive functions of those relationships. Others have identified further categories of social support. Four categories, based on classifications by Barrera (1986) and Winnubst, Buunk and Marcelissen (1988) are discussed in further detail below. These are social embeddedness, relationship quality, perceived social support and enacted social support.

Social integration or embeddedness

This approach looks at the structure of support and 'the connections that individuals have to others in their social environments' (Barrera, 1986). Barrera suggests that two main approaches to assessing these can be identified in the literature. One involves the use of indicators such as marital status, membership of organisations or numbers of friends. The second uses more complex measures of social networks that take into account such factors as the stability and complexity of social networks. Such measures are clearly quite crude as they can tell us nothing about the quality of these relationships. Nevertheless, they have generally been assumed to provide an indirect indicator of the availability of support.

A classic study, conducted in the USA, which supports the importance of social networks for well-being was conducted by Berkman and Syme (1979). This provided persuasive evidence that a lack of social relationships was a risk factor for health. The study monitored a random sample of almost 5,000 adults (aged 30–69) for nine years from 1965. At the outset a survey assessed the presence and the extent of four types of social ties – marriage, contact with the extended family and friends, church membership and other formal and informal group affiliations. Each type of social tie predicted mortality over the next nine years, as did a combined 'social network' index. The people low on the index were about twice as likely to die as those scoring highly on the index, even after controlling for self-reports of social class, smoking, obesity and health at the outset. The increased risk was not just associated with one cause of death but applied to all causes of death. One limitation of this study was the use of self-reports of health in the initial measurements. However, replication studies using physical examinations have broadly supported these findings, although evidence is less strong in relation to women (e.g. House, Robbins and Metzner, 1982; Schoenbach et al., 1986). In an overall review of a range of studies House, Landis and Umberson (1988) suggested that the evidence consistently supported the view that there is an increased risk associated with having few social relationships even after adjusting for other risk factors. They also conclude that being married has more health benefits for men than for women, and bereavement is more harmful. However, women may benefit as much or more than men from relationships with friends and relatives.

Berkman (1995), in a more recent review of the evidence for the links between social relationships and health, suggests that evidence for the importance of social integration is now so strong that the next step should be to develop interventions to improve social networks. While the development of support groups for patients is now quite common, she suggests that interventions aimed at 'restructuring naturally occurring networks and resources for support will be more effective than those that rely on short-term constructed support groups' (p. 251). Clearly a wide range of action may be needed to strengthen social networks. These may involve economic and political initiatives as well as large-scale interventions focusing on communities or workplaces.

However, improving social networks does not guarantee that individuals will actually receive greater help when needed. Cohen and Wills (1985) suggest that the correlation between the number of social connections people have and the actual functional support they receive tends to be rather low. They suggest that this may be because one good relationship may provide more adequate functional support than is available to someone with many superficial relationships.

Social support as relationship quality

Unlike the above approach which focuses on the number of people available, this approach 'views social support in terms of the subjectively experienced quality of the social relationships of the person' (Winnubst, Buunk and Marcelissen, 1988, p. 513). It is consistent with the idea that one strong relationship may be more important than wide social networks.

In a study exemplifying this approach, Hobfall and Leibermann (1987) studied the impact of the quality of marital relationships on reactions to childbirth stressors. They looked at a group of women who had a normal delivery and those with various forms of stressful delivery, i.e. premature delivery, caesarean section and spontaneous abortions. They investigated the extent to which intimacy with spouse as well as self-esteem moderated the relationship between the stressor and depression. They found that having either high intimacy or high self-esteem limited depression at the time of the event though having both added little additional benefit. However, at three months follow-up, self-efficacy limited depression but high intimacy did not. They argue that self-esteem enables people to resist feelings of failure and a sense of being overwhelmed. A supportive relationship may have similar effects at first. However, once the initial crisis is over and social support subsides then women who were depending on their intimate relationship for support have to fall back on their own resources.

A further example of this type of approach can be seen in the classic sociological study of Brown and Harris (1978) who looked at the origins of depression in a sample of women living in Camberwell in London. Over 400 women were interviewed and asked about life events in the past year. They were also asked to name people with whom they could talk about their worries. The researchers then classified the respondents according to whether or not they had 'close, intimate and confiding' relationships. The quality of relationships was classified according to four groupings: (a) women considered to have a close, intimate and confiding relationship with a husband or boyfriend or occasionally a woman in the same household; (b) those without the above but reporting a confidant (such as a relative or friend) who is seen at least weekly; (c) a confidant seen less than weekly; and (d) none of the above. The study found that the presence of a confiding relationship was a major protective factor. Where women had reported a severe life event or major difficulty, one in ten of those in category (a) developed depression, one in four of those in category (b) and one in 2.5 of those in categories (c) or (d).

One flaw with the above study was that the women described events and supports retrospectively. This was remedied in a subsequent study that followed 303 women (all with children living at home) who did not have depression at the start of the study (Brown et al., 1986). During the 12 months following initial assessment over half had suffered a severe event or major difficulty. Most (91%) of those who became depressed had suffered a severe event in the six months before the depression started. Results in relation to social support were complex. For married women there was actually no relationship between having a close confiding relationship with their partner at the start of the study and the onset of depression after a negative event. However, the presence of support from the husband during the crisis (as measured retrospectively at follow-up) was associated with a lower risk of depression. For single women, however, the presence of a confiding relationship was associated with reduced depression. The reason for the difference between married and single women seemed to be that those who confided in a confidant but then failed to get crisis support (that is they were 'let down' by their partner or friend) had a risk of depression as high as those who had never confided. Sadly, 40% of married mothers were 'let down' by their partners in the sense that they did not receive support during the subsequent crisis. Of course in some such instances, such as the husband's infidelity, the husband was implicated in the crisis event. In others the woman did confide but did not receive support. Brown *et al.* gave the example of a woman who experienced an ectopic pregnancy. Her husband's response was to say he 'might as well leave'. Interestingly, for single women, the presence of confiding relationships at the start was a much better predictor of crisis support when the need arose, i.e. they were much less likely to be let down. Brown *et al.* suggested that these women seemed to have invested more time in the development of such relationships and they had often been well tested over other crises. Overall the findings support the importance of having close confiding relationships but also highlights the complexity of such relationships and the difficulties involved in their study. Like Hobfall and Leibermann's research, this study also looked at self-esteem. They found that this was correlated with measures of social support and predicted later depression.

PERCEIVED SOCIAL SUPPORT

In this approach the person's perceptions of social support from their social networks are examined, for example, by asking people to rate satisfaction, adequacy and availability of supportive relationships, rather than the mere existence of social contact. The numbers of people involved and the quantity of contact they offer is not normally measured. For example, an early longitudinal study of adults in families by Holahan and Moos (1981) looked at support from both family relationships and work relationships at two time intervals a year apart. They asked people to rate family relationships using items such as 'Family members really support each other'. Similarly, work relationships were rated using items such as 'Employees often talk to each other about their personal problems' and 'Employees discuss their personal problems with their supervisors'. This study controlled for social integration (measured as described above) as well as initial levels of perceived home and family support. The findings provided some support for the hypothesis that decreases in perception of family and work support between time one and time two were related to increases in depression and psychosomatic symptoms.

This kind of approach is frequently used in the work context where people are asked to rate the perceived supportiveness of supervisors and co-workers. In fact, one of the most well-known models of work stress – Karasek's demand–control model (see Chapter 9) is now frequently expanded to include perceptions of job-related supports (Johnson and Hall, 1988). There is now a large body of research using this kind of variable in the work context. For example, a study by Fletcher and Jones (1993) found that a measure of social support at work accounted for more of the variance in anxiety than the other work-related variables (demand and control) put together.

While asking people about their perceptions of support is a fairly simple and intuitively sensible way of assessing social support, it is not without methodological problems particularly if they are then correlated with self-report measures of psychological well-being. Such measures are very likely to be positively correlated (e.g. Holahan and Moos, 1981; Fletcher and Jones, 1993) but the direction of causation may be unclear. It may be that lack of social support leads to depression, but it is also likely that being depressed or anxious will lead people to rate their relationships with others, and the support they offer, more negatively. Other problems associated with common methods may also apply (as discussed in Chapter 2). While other self-report methods, such as measures of enacted social support discussed in the next section, do not entirely eliminate these problems, the more specific and sometimes more objective nature of items is an advantage.

Enacted social support

This last category views social support in terms of 'what individuals actually do when they provide support' (Barrera, 1986). Many writers have produced taxonomies of enacted support, and these frequently include factors such as emotional/esteem support, instrumental (or tangible) support and informational support (e.g. Cohen and Wills, 1985). Esteem or emotional support relates to feeling valued and accepted. Informational support includes advice and guidance, while instrumental support includes actual practical help. Cohen and Wills also include an additional category of social companionship, e.g. spending time with others in recreational activities.

Researchers typically use this kind of approach to social support when they are interested in finding out exactly what kind of support is helpful for a specific type of stressor. For example, Dakof and Taylor (1990) interviewed cancer patients about their perceptions of what was the most helpful or unhelpful thing that support providers has said or done. These were coded and categorised according to whether they were (a) esteem or emotional support, (b) informational support or (c) tangible. The study found that esteem/emotional support was the most helpful category of support from family and friends and informational or tangible supports are less likely to be valued. Low levels of emotional support, or inappropriate supports from close relationships were also regarded as particularly unhelpful, for example, spouses who expressed too much worry. In relation to support from other cancer patients and physicians, informational support was seen as helpful by a significant number of people.

A subsequent study by Martin *et al.* (1994) extended Dakof and Taylor's approach to the study of chronic disorders which are not life-threatening. They used the same structured interview approach as above, but with patients suffering either from irritable bowel syndrome (IBS) or headaches. The results for these two disorders were compared with those for cancer patients from the previous study. It was predicted that IBS and headache patients would differ from the cancer patients in their perceptions of helpful or unhelpful supports. In particular, because of the frightening nature of cancer, it was expected that esteem/emotional support might be considered more important by cancer patients. In contrast, the inconvenience of headaches and IBS might lead to tangible assistance being seen as more important by these patients. However, it was also predicted that IBS patients would consider tangible assistance to be less helpful than do headache patients, because of the embarrassing nature of the former disorder.

The main finding of this study was that, as predicted, the headache and IBS patients perceptions of helpful social support placed greater emphasis on tangible assistance and less on emotional/esteem support than did the cancer patients. However, there were fewer differences between the headache and IBS patients who were equally likely to report all three types of support as helpful. Headache and IBS patients, like cancer patients, recalled more incidents of helpful than unhelpful support, although attempts at support which were unhelpful were not uncommon. Together these two studies illustrate the ways in which more specific approaches to social support may be able to offer practical insights into the best approaches to supporting those with debilitating illnesses.

Measurement and relationships between different measures

In line with the diversity of approaches, there are very many measures of social support, administered either by interview or self-report questionnaire. Published research is based on a wide variety of different measures which may not clearly fall into one of the above categories (e.g. see the study described in Box 8.2 below). This makes it very difficult to compare findings between studies. Heitzmann and Kaplan (1988) reviewed 23 techniques and suggests that data on validity and reliability of many is lacking, but that choice is likely to depend on the particular conceptualisation of support favoured by the researcher. For example, a researcher interested in perceived supportiveness of others may use the Social Support Questionnaire (Sarason et al., 1983) which consists of 27 items each consisting of two parts. Individuals are asked to first list the people they can rely on to provide support in a given set of circumstances and then indicate their overall satisfaction with that support.

A researcher interested in actual supportive behaviours may use Barrera's (1981) measure of enacted behaviours which consists of 40 items asking the individual to rate the frequency with which others have done certain activities for them in the past month. Examples of activities included are 'loaned you over $25' or 'comforted you by showing physical affection'.

Box 8.1   A vignette approach to assessing social support (Jemmott and Magloire, 1988).

Ronnie	Stuart	Peter
People are devoted to Ronnie and love him They always support and listen to him and sympathise with him	People are usually fond of Stuart They can be sympathetic but do not always listen to him or support him	People are not devoted to Peter. They do not support and listen to him or sympathise with him. They do not care about him or love him

I'm like Ronnie	I'm halfway between Ronnie and Stuart	I'm like Stuart	I'm halfway between Stuart and Peter	I'm like Peter

A rather different approach was developed by Turner and Noh (1983). This uses vignettes (little descriptions) of individuals, and the respondent has to say which of the individuals described he or she most resembles. The measure also assesses both the amount of support and need or desire for support. An item based on a version of this methodology used by Jemmott and Magloire (1988) is given in Box 8.1.

Similar statements are given about the kind of social support preferred, e.g. 'Kevin constantly needs to feel that people are devoted to him and love him. He constantly needs to feel that people sympathise with him and care about him a lot'. The two items can then be combined to give a measure of perception of support relative to need.

Questionnaires providing thorough assessments of social support are inevitably lengthy and this may preclude their use in stress questionnaires (e.g. in the work setting) where a large number of other dimensions also need to be assessed. Frequently therefore stress researchers use very much shorter measures, for example, brief ratings of the perceived support from colleagues, supervisors, etc. are frequently used in work stress research (e.g. Parkes, Mendham and von Rabenau, 1994; Fletcher and Jones, 1993). However, the ability of such measures to adequately tap the construct of support (i.e. their validity) is likely to be more limited.

Because of the range of approaches available and their lack of equivalence, it is not straightforward to interpret the findings from different studies. In fact, measures of social embeddedness, perceived social support and enacted social support often show only weak correlations with each other (Barrera, 1986). The number of friends and family we can list may have little to do with our general perceptions of how much support we receive, and these in turn may have little to do with the actual enacted support we experience.

Two of the support categories, perceived support and perceived quality of relationships, seem more likely, on the face of it, to be more closely related. However,

Pierce, Sarason and Sarason (1991) compared measures which tap general perceptions of support (including the SSQ) with a measure which looks at support from
specific people. They found that perceptions of support from mothers and friends
added significantly (and inversely) to the prediction of loneliness over and above
the effect of general perceived social support. They conclude that people's beliefs
about specific relationships are distinct from their general perceptions of social
support and they suggest that the latter may reflect personality characteristics. In
particular they suggest that it reflects a 'sense of support', which

> encompasses the belief that one is loved, valued and cared for, and that others
> would gladly do what they can to help regardless of personal circumstances.
> (Pierce, Sarason and Sarason, 1991, p. 1037).

Thus it seems that the different types of support need to be considered separately
and they may affect well-being via different mechanisms. Some of these mechanisms
are considered further below.

HOW DOES SOCIAL SUPPORT AFFECT HEALTH?

There are many questions to be answered about the mechanisms by which social
support impacts on health and well-being. For example, does social support have
an impact only under conditions of stress (a buffering effect) or is it helpful under
all conditions? Are there different effects arising from different kinds of support?
What physiological systems does social support affect? Does it improve health
indirectly because it leads to improved health behaviours? Are there individual
differences in social support effects? Is social support always a good thing? These
issues are discussed below.

Moderating or direct effects?

Cohen and Wills (1985) suggest two different processes by which social support
has a beneficial effect on well-being. One model suggests that social support has
a *direct effect* regardless of whether people are under stress or not. The second model
suggests that support is only related to well-being for people who are under stress,
i.e. social support functions as a *moderator or buffer* (see Chapter 6 for a further
discussion of these terms). Cohen and Wills call this 'the buffering hypothesis'.

In relation to the *direct effects model*, they suggest that a positive effect of social
support could occur regardless of the existence of stressors because

> large social networks provide persons with regular positive experiences and a set
> of stable, socially rewarded roles in the community. This kind of support could
> be related to overall well-being because it provides positive affect, a sense of
> predictability in one's life situation and a recognition of self-worth. (p. 311)

Figure 8.1   Two points at which social support may 'buffer' the link between stress and illness (adapted from Cohen and Wills, 1985).

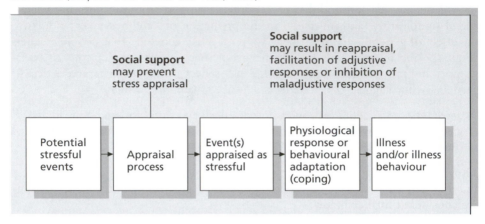

They suggest, therefore, that social support could be related to health via similar mechanisms to those by which stressors may affect health, that is, either via emotionally induced effects on the neuroendocrine or immune system (see Chapter 3) or via an effect on health related behaviours (see below).

To explain the mechanism by which the *stress-buffering model* might operate, Cohen and Wills draw on Lazarus and Folkman's (1984) transactional approach. They suggest that social support potentially may intervene at two stages of the stress appraisal and coping process (see Figure 8.1). Firstly, it may intervene at the stage of appraisal. For example, if a person is aware that others are around who will help with their problem then they may appraise the event as less harmful and themselves as more able to cope. Secondly, social support may intervene at the coping stage by reducing the impact of the stressor on the person, for example, by providing a solution or perhaps by providing informational or emotional support to minimise any effects (see also Chapter 7).

They reviewed the early evidence (up to 1983) to assess whether the direct effects or the moderated effects model was most accurate. They found that there is evidence to support a direct effects model where primarily structural measures are used (assessing integration in social networks), although buffering was sometimes found when close relationships were examined. This latter point was confirmed more recently by Uchino, Cacioppo and Kiecolt-Glaser's (1996) review. This found support for the stress buffering effects of familial relationships (e.g. spouse and siblings) on cardiovascular functioning.

However, more studies have found evidence for a buffering effect of social support when functional measures (e.g. enacted supports), which assess the availability of specific supportive behaviours, are used. Cohen and Wills suggest that, for buffering to occur, a match may be required between the needs associated with the particular stressor and the social support available. They point out that studies of esteem and informational support have been particularly successful in demonstrating buffering effects, suggesting that while these might be relevant in a range of stressful circumstances, social companionship and instrumental support may require a more specific match.

Overall, these relationships seem to make intuitive sense. It is easy to imagine that, in the general run of events, having a lot of friends and family around is better for health and well-being than being relatively isolated. However, in particularly stressful circumstances, such as bereavement or marital breakdown, what may really help is the support of one or two close and long-suffering friends or family members, and the provision of specific practical and emotional help. What is more problematic for researchers is to identify the particular supportive behaviours that might be appropriate in the wide range of stressful circumstances that exist. Support-matching approaches, aimed at doing just that, have been suggested as a way forward.

Support matching

Various authors have emphasised the need for research that matches support to specific stressors (Hobfall, 1986; Cutrona and Russell, 1990). This means that, not only do we need to look at different types of support, but we also need to look at very specific stressors, something which has not been done in most of the studies described earlier in this chapter. Given the number of possible stressors this is clearly a daunting exercise but some have nevertheless attempted to meet this challenge.

For example, Cutrona and Russell (1990) proposed a theory of optimal stressor-support matching, suggesting that matching supports to stressors could enable us to design better support interventions. They have attempted to classify stressors according to whether they relate to one of four domains: assets; relationships; achievement and social roles. They further suggest stressors can be classified according to magnitude, desirability, controllability and duration. A number of researchers have adopted this approach and looked at the effects of different types of supports on specific stressors. For example, Peirce et al. (1996) looked at the relationship between a specific stressor (financial stress) and alcohol use and found only tangible assistance or material aid had a buffering effect. Availability of a confidant or someone with whom to socialise did not.

Effects of social support on physiological functioning

Studies have suggested associations between social support and a wide range of disorders including cancer, coronary heart disease and infectious diseases. Effects on the cardiovascular, immune and endocrine systems are likely to be implicated (see Chapter 3 for discussion of mechanisms). There has been only limited research on the effects of social support on endocrine functioning (Uchino, Cacioppo and Kiecolt-Glaser, 1996), however its effects on the cardiovascular and immune systems are briefly considered below.

Cardiovascular system

The majority of studies of stress and physiological functioning have looked at cardiovascular functioning, typically using blood pressure as an indicator (Uchino, Cacioppo and Kiecolt-Glaser, 1996). Many such studies have used a correlational design and samples with normal levels of blood pressure. Uchino, Cacioppo and Kiecolt-Glaser, review 28 such studies which used a range of approaches to measuring support, including social networks, perceptions of support and enacted supports and reported that while 23 found evidence that social support was associated with lower blood pressure, four found no relationship and one found the opposite. Overall, using meta-analytic techniques to look at the effects of structural and functional measures separately, they found small but reliable effects on cardiovascular functioning in both cases. These effects applied to both men and women. However, the review suggested that men and women may benefit from different types of social support. Specifically, the meta-analysis indicated that social resources may be predictive of blood pressure for men while instrumental support is a stronger predictor of blood pressure for women.

Three out of the four studies that failed to show relationships looked specifically at job supports, suggesting that these may be less beneficial. Kaufmann and Beehr (1986) suggest that one explanation is that the source of support at work may not be independent of the stressor. For example, if support is offered from a boss who has also caused the stress, this offer may in itself be perceived as stressful. A further explanation is the lack of reciprocity in work relationships (see Box 8.2 below), which may lead to the employee feeling guilty or humiliated if they accept support from an employer.

Prospective studies also provide evidence that social support is useful (Uchino, Cacioppo and Kiecolt-Glaser, 1996). For example, Levine *et al.* (1979) allocated 400 hypertensive patients to interventions which consisted of an interview, family support, small groups, a combination of two of these interventions, all three or a control group. Those allocated to all three did best, with the proportion of patients having blood pressure under control increasing by 28% (from 38% to 66%). However, family support alone decreased diastolic blood pressure by 11%. The interventions were also associated with greater adherence to medication and weight loss. These effects were still apparent at a three-year follow-up (Morisky *et al.*, 1985).

The above studies looked at basal levels of cardiovascular functioning. However, *laboratory studies* offer the opportunity to look at the relationship between social support and cardiovascular reactivity under stress (that is the tendency to react to a stressor by increased cardiovascular responses such as increases in blood pressure and heart rate). This is based on the view that such reactivity contributes

166

to the development of hypertension and heart disease, a hypothesis which has received some support (Light *et al.*, 1992).

Laboratory studies allow researchers to have greater control and to investigate the direction of causation in a way which is not possible in studies of major illness or mortality (which are often open to the challenge that illness may lead to a reduction in social support, rather than vice versa). Such studies typically set the participants a task, such as mental arithmetic or public speaking which is conducted either with a support provider (the experimental condition) or alone or in the presence of non-supportive others (the control condition) (Thorsteinsson and James, 1999). For example, a study by Gerin *et al.* (1995) required individuals to play a computer game under high and low stress conditions, with or without social support. In the high stress conditions the experimenter harassed the participants urging them to go faster. In the social support condition another student sat by the participant and tried to convey support without speaking. They found reduced cardiovascular reactivity (based on blood pressure ratings) for those in the high stress supported condition compared to the other conditions.

A meta-analysis conducted by Thorsteinsson and James (1999) considered 22 laboratory studies of social support most of which measured both heart rate and blood pressure. They found considerable variations in effect sizes, perhaps accounted for by variations in methodologies such as differences in type or level of support provided. They suggest that, in some cases, control conditions are problematic as a no-support condition may involve a silent observer who may be seen as hostile rather than merely non-supportive. Observed differences between support and no-support conditions may be due to the negative effect of a silent observer rather than the positive effect of the supportive person. Overall, though, Thorsteinsson and James concluded that social support had a medium-to-large effect in reducing reactivity to stressors.

Immune system

Research into immune functioning also provides some support for the benefits of social support, although the methodological complexities of this research area can make it difficult to interpret and compare studies. As we saw in Chapter 3, there is no single accepted measure of immune functioning and some measures that have been used are now considered to be flawed. For example, Jemmott and Magloire (1988) looked at exam stress and found that students who reported greater support, relative to their needs, had better immune functioning using measures of sIgA. However, they used measures of sIgA in whole saliva – an approach that does not take salivary flow into account and has therefore been criticised (see Chapter 3).

Uchino, Cacioppo and Kiecolt-Glaser (1996) reviewed 19 studies of the relationship between social support and immune functioning, excluding studies such as Jemmott and Magloire's which they considered to be flawed. They suggest that 12 showed social support to be related to improved immune functioning. For example,

167

Kiecolt-Glaser *et al.* (1991) studied carers of people with demented relatives over a period of 13 months and compared them with demographically matched controls. Carers generally had fewer social relationships than controls and received less support from those they had. They found that the caregivers showed deterioration on three measures of immunity compared to controls, as well as more days of infectious illness such as colds. Carers who reported lowest levels of social support at the start showed the greatest decline in immune function. While such studies provide powerful support, seven of the studies reviewed by Uchino, Cacioppo and Kiecolt-Glaser failed to support the association. They suggest methodological reasons may account for the lack of relationships in some of these studies.

A meta-analysis of the studies reviewed by Uchino, Cacioppo and Kiecolt-Glaser found a significant effect size and, overall, they argue that there is 'relatively strong evidence' linking social support to aspects of immunological functioning with particularly clear evidence in the case of emotional support. They further argue that, as in the case of cardiovascular functioning, close relationships such as family members may be particularly important. It is not yet clear whether social support has a direct or a buffering effect in the case of immune functioning. Overall, these effects potentially implicate social support in both the causation and likely progression not only of colds and infectious diseases but a much wider range of health problems. For example, Spiegel *et al.* (1998) suggest that social support may increase cancer resistance by facilitating the recovery of immune mechanisms.

Health behaviours as mediating variables

One potential explanation for the effects of social support on both immune and cardiovascular systems is that this support leads to improved health behaviours. For example, those with good social support may be more likely to give up smoking (Barrera, 1986) or drink less (Steptoe *et al.*, 1996). However, a number of researchers have found significant relationships between social support and physiological measures of both immune functioning and cardiovascular functioning even when controlling for health variables (see Uchino, 1996, for a review).

Furthermore, evidence for the benefit of social support on health behaviour is sometimes contradictory. This may be because, in some circumstances, social support may support the individual in dysfunctional as well as health promoting behaviours (Burg and Seeman, 1994). For example, Burg and Seeman suggest that social ties have been linked to non-compliance with medication. They argue that family members and other significant people have influence over lifestyle, for example as models and normative influences as well as by direct control, which can operate in both positive and negative directions.

Overall, therefore, it seems unlikely that the effect of social supports on health can be attributed solely to their influence on health behaviours.

Effects of individual differences

The use made of social supports and the benefits derived from it are clearly likely to vary between individuals. Some individual differences, such as those related to *age and gender* may also be difficult to disentangle from the effects of socio-cultural factors. The patterns of social networks available, and regarded as socially acceptable, for men and women of different age groups, is likely to vary greatly between different societies and at different historical periods. Leavy (1983) suggested that relationships are more important for women than men and that women use social support more (see also Box 8.2). However, we have also seen that social integration and marriage are less beneficial for women than for men.

Box 8.2   Adjustment to the first year of university life: individual differences, social support and coping with exam stress.

Halamandaris and Power (1999) look at psychosocial adjustment to university life in a sample of 182 students at a UK university. Students completed a questionnaire near the end of their first year. They completed personality measures including neuroticism, and extraversion and achievement motivation. Coping was assessed using the WOC (Folkman and Lazarus, 1980) completed in relation to coping with the exam stress of the previous few weeks (see Chapter 7). Functional social support was measured by asking them to rate perceptions of the availability of appraisal, belonging, tangible and esteem support. They also completed measures of loneliness and adaptation to university life. Academic performance information was also available for a subset of the students.

They found quite high negative correlations between social support and loneliness (−0.82). Personality variables were also highly related to social support. Extraversion was associated with perceiving more social support (0.53) and neuroticism with less social support (−0.43). In terms of achievement motivation, students who were high on social support and low on loneliness had greater hopes for success. Overall adjustment was related to social support (0.63), loneliness (−0.74), extraversion (0.46) and introversion (−0.41) as well as hopes for success (0.31). The measures of coping showed few significant correlations.

Although there were no gender differences in personality, women fared better in terms of reporting less loneliness and more social support and better overall adjustment to university life, while those with the poorest adjustment had lowest scores on social support and extraversion and the highest on neuroticism. However, looking on the bright side, these measures were not reflected in academic scores.

Social support accounted for significant extra variance in adjustment after personality variables were taken into account, suggesting that social support is not totally explained by personality.

All of this makes gender and age differences difficult to interpret. Such findings seem inconsistent but such crude relationships ignore complex underlying factors, for example the different roles and expectations of men and women in marriage and other social structures, and the different characteristics of men and women who chose to marry and those who do not. Comparisons between different ages and genders may therefore not be informative. A more constructive approach adopted by most researchers is to look at the patterns of relationships within particular subsamples. Thus a large literature exists looking at social support in women or in elderly people for example. Detailed consideration of this literature is beyond the scope of a single chapter but the frameworks offered here will help in understanding and evaluating this wider literature.

Personality factors and personal preferences are also clearly implicated in the extent to which people participate in social networks, the quality of their relationships, the use they make of supportive behaviours and the extent to which they perceive they are supported. We have already discussed the possibility that a 'sense of support' might be a personality variable implicated in people's perceptions of support. A number of researchers have also reported that self-esteem (e.g. Brown *et al.*, 1986; Hobfall and Liebermann, 1987) and neuroticism (e.g. Parkes, Mendham and von Rabenau, 1994) are correlated with social support. It has been suggested that these variables, as well as others such as extraversion and locus of control be included in studies of social support (Cohen and Wills, 1985; Parkes, Mendham and von Rabenau, 1994). These relationships are also explored in the study described in Box 8.2. However, Cohen and Wills (1985) go further in also suggesting that it is possible that social support is a 'proxy' for a personality variable (such as sociability or social competence) which is highly correlated with support. In support of this view, Winnubst *et al.* (1988) point out that social support, like personality variables, tends to remain stable over several years and that people with low social support are judged less attractive and socially skilled than those with more social support (Hansson, Jones and Carpenter, 1984).

IS SOCIAL SUPPORT ALWAYS A GOOD THING?

Although the concept of social support is conceptualised very widely to include social networks and family relationships, it seems only too obvious that such relationships can also be damaging. We saw in Chapter 4, the effects that poor marital relationships can have on immune functioning, as well as the negative effects that social support can have for the support provider caring for an Alzheimer's patient (Kiecolt-Glaser *et al.*, 1995). We have also seen in this chapter that social support may have negative (as well as positive) effects on health behaviours. Rook (1984) suggested that the enthusiasm for social support and the tendency to equate social interaction with social support has threatened to obscure recognition of the potential negative effects of social relationships.

Box 8.3   Social exchange theory and social support.

Social exchange theory has been useful in examining the processes of social support and the conditions under which social support is, or is not, helpful. This theory suggests that people evaluate relationships in terms of inputs and outcomes in a way that is similar to economic transactions. They also compare their inputs and outcomes to those of other parties in the transaction. Satisfaction with a relationship is considered likely where there is relative equality (or reciprocity) between the inputs and outcomes of both parties. Buunk et al. (1993) suggested that while receiving less social support than one gives is likely to be more negative than the perception of giving more than one receives, both are likely to be associated with more negative affect than reciprocal relationships. In a study in the workplace they found that relationships with colleagues were perceived to be more reciprocal than those with superiors. Feeling that relationships were not reciprocal (whether this was because more support was given than received or vice versa) was associated with greater negative affect. This effect was independent of job stress. However, the lack of reciprocity seems more important for some individuals than for others – specifically, the relationship between reciprocity and affect was moderated by an individual difference variable called 'exchange orientation' (the general expectation of immediate reciprocity).

Rook's study interviewed 120 widowed women who were between the ages of 60 and 89. They were asked about supportive and problematic social ties. Psychological well-being was measured using scales measuring life satisfaction, psychological well-being and loneliness scales. She found that the number of problematic ties was related to reduced well-being, while surprisingly the number of supportive ties was not related to improved well-being. These differences did not seem to be explained by individual differences in personal characteristics between those with more or less problematic ties, though there were some indications that those with problematic ties tended to have less egalitarian relationships that might suggest lower social competence.

While it is clear that social relationships can have a negative impact, it is perhaps less obvious that actual deliberate attempts to provide support might also have negative effects. However, we have already seen that some studies have reported that social supports are not always helpful (e.g. Dakof and Taylor, 1990; Kaufmann and Beehr, 1986). For one explanation of this effect see Box 8.3.

In real world research which seeks to explore ways of improving social support there is therefore a need to take into account the possibility of negative, as well as positive effects. This is illustrated further in the next section which looks in more detail at research focusing on social support for those suffering from one particular extreme stressor, that of suffering from cancer.

SOCIAL SUPPORT IN THE REAL WORLD – THE CANCER SUFFERER

Consideration of the situation of a person suffering from cancer helps to illustrate the very complex issues that come into play when looking at social support in a real situation. It helps highlight some of the limitations of frameworks focusing only on the types of support provided, ignoring the context in which the supportive behaviour takes place and the reactions of the support provider as well as the recipient.

Being diagnosed as having cancer is without doubt among the most stressful experiences most of us can envisage and it is not hard to imagine that we would like to think that we would get a great deal of social support. However, work by Wortman and Dunkel-Shetter (1987) suggests that people who have cancer actually find it difficult to get adequate support. The evidence suggests that communications between cancer patients and others are particularly problematic.

> The evidence suggests that cancer patients appreciate the opportunity to clarify their situation through discussion and supportive interactions with others. However, others often feel threatened, apprehensive and uncomfortable about the person's disease. Moreover, although their feelings about the patient's illness are largely negative, others appear to believe they should remain optimistic and cheerful in their interactions with the patient. The conflict between these feelings and beliefs may result in behaviours that are unintentionally harmful to the patient, such as physical avoidance, avoidance of open communication, and strained and uncomfortable interactions. The person with cancer often interprets these behaviours as evidence of rejection at the very time when support from others is especially important. (p. 67)

Thus they suggest that not only may social relationships fail to buffer the stress of cancer but they may also turn out to be an additional source of distress. Dakof and Taylor (1990) support this view in a study of cancer patients which found that avoidance of social contact was a commonly reported unhelpful action. However, this only occurred with friends and acquaintances, not family members. In the case of family members, attempts to minimise the impact of the disease or criticise the patient's handling of the situation were more problematic.

Wortman and Dunkel-Shetter highlight the need to look at what types of support are helpful for what types of problem. So, for example, at diagnosis, informational support may be important; during hospitalisation tangible help may be particularly valued but when seriously ill, emotional support may be more appreciated. Dakof and Taylor (1990) further suggest that different types of support will be experienced as helpful depending on the nature of the relationship with the support provider. For example, in intimate relationships esteem/emotional support are most valued. Other patients and physicians are more valued for informational support. Equally, a lack of these kinds of support from these individuals is perceived to be unhelpful.

It is, of course, also important to consider social support from the point of view of the support provider, particularly in such an emotive area as cancer, where there may be a lack of understanding or fear of the situation. Wortman and Dunkel-Shetter point out that a behaviour that is intended to be helpful may be perceived very differently by the recipient. This is vividly illustrated by a study by Peters-Golden (1982) of perceptions of social support in breast cancer patients. She interviewed 100 breast cancer patients and 100 disease-free individuals. Sixty one percent of the latter said that they might or would avoid contact with someone whom they knew had cancer. However, 66% also said 'they would go out of their way to cheer up a cancer patient'. The cancer patients confirmed that they were indeed ignored or that people were falsely cheerful. This made them feel 'less normal' and prevented them from discussing their illness. The healthy people felt that it was a bad thing for patients to discuss their feelings, but those with cancer were disturbed by the ban on communication. Overall, there was a lack of fit between the views of the disease-free and the support needs identified by the patients. However, the disease-free expressed confidence that if they did have cancer their support needs would be met. One third of the cancer sufferers, on the other hand, reported that they had no-one to turn to.

Social support in the area of breast cancer has attracted particular interest, and there is some evidence that social support is linked to survival. For example, a prospective study found that factors such as number of friends and extent of social networks at the time of diagnosis predicted survival four years later (Waxler-Morrison et al., 1991). Increasing the amount of support for women with breast cancer offers an interesting possibility for extending survival. To date some studies have shown promising results but have also been a source of some controversy. For example, a study by Spiegel et al. (1989) evaluated a supportive intervention in which 86 women with metastatic breast cancer were randomly allocated either to treatment groups attending weekly supportive group therapy meetings over a year, or to a control group. The intervention focused on encouraging discussion and expressing feelings and also taught self-hypnosis for pain relief. It aimed to address social isolation by developing relations among members. At 10-year follow-up only three of the patients were still alive but those in the treatment group survived significantly longer (a mean of 36.6 months compared with 18.9 months in the control). However, Fox (1998) suggests that biasing factors may have accounted for these results. For now, the jury seems to be out on this issue.

SUMMARY

This chapter has skimmed the surface of an extensive and complex area of research that spans a broad area, from the effects of general integration within social networks to the effects of very specific social relationships. Generally, there is evidence to support the benefits of social supports from a range of different approaches to the topic. However, the mechanisms whereby the different types of social support impact on well-being appear to be different.

173

Social support studies are often subject to the same criticisms as other areas discussed in this book, for example, a lack of conceptual clarity and the use of cross-sectional methods. However, social support research arguably has a longer history and has attracted researchers from a wider range of social science traditions. As a result it also has a larger number of well-conducted prospective studies providing convincing evidence of the benefits of social support for physical and psychological well-being. However, many studies fail to take into account the complexity of the process by which social supports and stressors may interact to affect health, by treating social support as an unchanging variable which is itself independent of stressors. For example, Brown *et al*. point out that

> relationships can undergo radical changes and . . . these may threaten the
> effectiveness of predictions made in prospective studies where there may be
> a considerable period between the initial assessment of support and the
> subsequent crisis. (Brown *et al*., 1986 p. 827)

In some cases it may even be the case that the person providing the social support at the start of a study may subsequently become the major source of stress, for example in the case of bereavement or marital disruption. Further research is needed to look at the processes by which social relationships influence well-being over time.

Future research into social support also has many new and interesting avenues to explore. There are ever expanding possibilities for remote or long distance communications and relationships via the internet and other new technologies such as video mobile phones. Little is known about the implications of such technology for social support and relationships generally. Use of the home computer is sometimes seen as an isolated and unsociable activity that possibly contributes to poorer family relationships. However, there are growing numbers of support and discussion groups on the internet that enable people to share experiences with others with similar problems and offer the potential to provide social contacts for housebound people. Only very recently have researchers become interested in the role of the internet in social support. For example, a study by Cody *et al*. (1999) provided training for older people (average age 80 years) to surf the internet. Training consisted of weekly meetings with a mentor over four months. They found that participation in the training programme was associated with significantly reduced computer anxiety and increased ratings of perceived social support and more positive attitudes to ageing. The nature of supports available on the internet and the processes by which they operate are, however, likely to be very different from those available in face to face contacts. For example, internet groups may greatly increase informational support and even provide some emotional support but be much less useful in providing instrumental support. It certainly seems the case that new technology is going to radically change social relationships in the future and the implications for well-being both positive and negative is something we are only beginning to investigate.

PART 4

A FOCUS ON STRESS AT WORK

Work stress merits a specific section because of the huge growth in research into the effects of work on psychological and physical well-being, as well as the popular interest in the topic. This is reflected in the volume of media coverage, for example, giving information about the latest occupations to claim crippling levels of stress.

Chapter 9 introduces important models and approaches to the study of stress at work. Some of the key findings are discussed and the merits of the different approaches are considered. Conducting an organisational 'stress audit' is now a popular form of applied research. For this reason this chapter pays particular attention to the problems of designing such an audit and considers the pros and cons of different approaches.

The interface between the work and non-work aspects of life are the focus of the second chapter of this section, Chapter 10. This considers the possible effects that work may have on home life and vice versa. It further considers the impact of work on home relationships and on the well-being of partners.

CHAPTER 9

WORK STRESS

This chapter focuses specifically on occupational stress. It introduces models and approaches that are specific to this area and reviews the value of different approaches. It further discusses practical issues concerning conducting stress audits in the workplace.

THE RISE IN CONCERN ABOUT WORK STRESS

It will be clear from the preceding chapters that the working environment is a major focus for stress research. Popular press and many academic articles lend credence to the view that work stress is greatly increasing. Undoubtedly, it is the case that the introduction of new technology, the emphasis on efficiency, downsizing and increasing numbers of short-term contracts certainly can make the workplace an insecure and rapidly changing environment. However, it seems hard to substantiate a claim that the modern Western workplace is more stressful than work in the past (e.g. in coal mines or cotton mills).

We have already discussed the problems inherent in the stress concept and the fact that people may mean many different things when they report experiencing stress. However, it is clear that many do perceive that they are experiencing excessive amounts. It is, nevertheless, necessary to treat with some caution claims that people are suffering much higher levels of stress than they did in a past where the concept of stress was not high on people's agendas. Chapter 1 demonstrated the difficulties in the interpretation of statistics showing that stress-related absence has increased and the difficulty in drawing conclusions about the extent to which stress is the cause. Our best estimates are therefore, as Cox (1993) suggests, no more than 'an educated guess' but are at least indicative of the growing concern about well-being at work. As we have seen in Chapter 1, reports of high levels of stress may also feed into and add to the view that work is stressful and help to increase the problem.

It is, of course, also likely that many recent workplace changes have had positive impacts for many, creating new opportunities and challenges and often eliminating work that was dirty and tedious. Little attention is given to these effects of work in either the popular or academic press. Few researchers have looked at the positive psychological effects, beyond suggesting that work is generally better for psychological well-being than being unemployed (Warr, 1987). However, a large study of the British adult population by Warr and Payne (1982) investigated experiences of pleasure and strain by asking about their feelings for the previous day. This found that 69% of men and 68% of women felt 'very pleased' for at least half of the previous day and that 24% of men and 19% of women who reported pleasure attributed it to work. In comparison only 13% of men and 18% of women reported feeling unpleasant emotional strain for half or more of the previous day and less than half of those who reported strain attributed it to work. So while work was clearly perceived as a source of strain it appeared to give even more pleasure – at least in the early 1980s. Nevertheless it is predominantly the negative aspects of work that been emphasised and studied.

Alongside the increased publicity and emphasis on the damage done by work, there has been increased legislation and litigation in this area in many countries. For example in the UK, the *Health and Safety at Work Act* (1974) spells out that the employer has a duty 'to ensure as far as is reasonably practicable, the health, safety, and welfare at work of all employees'. This is now clearly interpreted to include 'the demands of work, the way work is organised and the way people deal with each other' (HSE, 1995).

To enable employers to meet this increasing pressure to assess and respond to stress, they need good practical theories and methodologies. Much of the research (described below) conducted by occupational psychologists, working both in universities and in commercial organisations, has focused on identifying organisational stressors. However, when it comes to intervening to reduce stress, a clinical approach has dominated leading to an emphasis on treating the individual. Over the past 20 years organisations have increasingly made stress management training or counselling available to their employees. The success of these interventions is discussed in Chapter 11. It is likely that the provision of such services is cheaper and easier than paying real attention to changing the work environment. However, the simple provision of services to help the individual to cope, or to treat the damage once it has occurred, does not address problems in the work environment, and therefore may not address the causes of strain.

This chapter describes the types of theoretical approaches that have been taken by work stress researchers attempting to identify common factors across many organisations. It will then move on to practical methodologies used to examine stress where the focus of concern is a single organisation looking to address its problems.

——————

Traditional psychological approaches to work stress have tended to look for the characteristics of the work environment (stressors) that are related to strain in terms of diminished psychological well-being, physical well-being and in some cases performance. This has led to elaborate box and arrow diagrams linking large numbers of stressors, which seem to include most aspects of the work environment, to an equally diverse range of strains via various intervening variables. One such approach is that developed by Cooper, Sloan and Williams (1988) (see Figure 9.3 later in the chapter). These are general frameworks and are useful in illustrating the scope of the stress phenomenon (much like Box 1.1 in the first chapter of this book) rather than testable theories. This type of approach is criticised by Briner and Reynolds (1993) in assuming or suggesting relationships between a great many different phenomena. They suggest that:

> Such models are rag-bags, into which are thrown any or all of the things which, in general, people or organizations don't like (e.g. illness, absenteeism) and anything on which we might be able to blame any of these bad things (e.g. personality, job characteristics). (p. 3)

Their all-encompassing nature provides little in the way of clear guidance for practitioners. In contrast, the models described below all have limitations but go some way towards suggesting simple and testable hypotheses about the nature of relationships between stressors and strains.

One of the simplest approaches is Warr's vitamin model, the first approach described below. It identifies nine key features of the environment and hypothesises two different types of relationship between such features and psychological well-being. However, it ignores the ways stressors may combine together and interact and that they may affect different people in different ways. The interaction between different stressors and the person's individual characteristics is the focus of the interactional theories, the second type of approach described here.

Both the above approaches have been criticised by those who support a transactional view of stress – the third major approach discussed in this section. Whether an event is stressful depends on the properties of the transaction between the individual person and the work situation. Lazarus and Folkman (1984), for example, focus on the cognitive and emotional aspects of appraisal and coping with stress. So while the traditional approach might investigate the employee's perception of workload and the ways in which this correlates with outcome variables such as anxiety, Lazarus' approach would focus on the process of whether the person appraises the workload as exceeding their coping resources (see also Chapter 7).

Simple models of environmental characteristics – Warr's vitamin model

Warr (1987) conducted a comprehensive review of the literature and identified a number of environmental features that affect mental health. The importance of these features has primarily been studied in the context of work or unemployment, although they are relevant to all kinds of environment. They are as follows:

1. *Opportunity for control.* Mental health is likely to be affected by the extent to which situations offer opportunity for personal control over activities or events. Warr (1987) suggests that the 'opportunity for control has two main elements: the opportunity to decide and act in one's chosen way, and the potential to predict the consequences of action' (p. 4).
2. *Opportunity for skill use.* Mental health is likely to be affected by the extent to which the environment allows the opportunity to use existing skills or develop new skills.
3. *Externally generated goals.* Mental health is likely to be affected by the extent to which the environment makes demands or generates goals.
4. *Variety.* The extent to which environments offer variety will further influence mental health.
5. *Environmental clarity.* This includes three aspects:
    (i)   feedback about the consequences of one's own actions;
    (ii) the degree to which other people and things in the environment are predictable;
    (iii) the clarity of role requirements.
6. *Opportunity for interpersonal contact.* This is important in meeting needs for friendship and social support. In addition, many goals may only be achieved through group membership.
7. *Availability of money.* The availability of money is clearly a factor likely to influence mental health by causing anxiety about the individual's ability to provide for their own, or their family's basic needs. In addition, shortage of money is likely to influence the extent to which the individual may be able to gain access to sufficient levels of the other factors – such as variety or control.
8. *Physical security.* In the work context this would include such factors as job security and poor working conditions.
9. *Valued social position.* The final aspect considered important for mental health is that of having a position within a social grouping that leads to being held in esteem by others.

Warr uses the analogy of vitamins to explain the way that these work features affect mental health. Low levels of vitamins lead to poor physical health and, similarly, low levels of each of the listed environmental features will lead to poor mental health. As with vitamins, Warr suggests that above a certain level there is no added benefit if more of the feature is added. For example, above a certain level an increase in money or interpersonal contact will not lead to a further improvement in mental health. In the case of some vitamins (for example, Vitamins A or D) very large amounts may be harmful for health. Other vitamins (for example, C or E) can safely be consumed in large quantities. Similarly, Warr suggests that certain environmental features will be harmful if levels are very high. This is true of elements 1–6 listed above. The remaining three elements are not harmful at high levels. Thus, the model predicts that too much money or physical security will not be harmful, but too much control or variety may be.

Most studies have assumed linear relationships between stressors and strains and as a result the curvilinear relationship (suggested by this model) is seldom examined. Warr himself is one of the few researchers to find such relationships between stressors and strains (Warr, 1991). Such effects may be rare as studies seldom encompass a sufficient range of jobs to include both those where employees perceive too little control and those with too much control.

A basic assumption of the model is that variables act independently of each other. In fact the analogy to vitamins would assume that a deficiency or lack in just one area would cause serious problems. Warr acknowledges the analogy fails in this respect and that the way environmental features interact with each other and with individual difference variables is clearly important. More recently Warr (1994) has discussed how his model can account for interactions between the variables and individual differences. It is this aspect that is addressed by the interactional models.

Interactional approaches

Still very much within the same 'stressor–strain' tradition as the simpler models, a range of more complex models have been developed which place a heavy emphasis on environmental characteristics but include the possibility of interactions between different factors, and may take into account individual differences. Two such approaches are described below, the first is one of the most influential American models – the person–environment fit model. The second, which has arguably been more influential in the UK and the rest of Europe and Australia, is Karasek's model.

Person–environment fit theory

One of the most frequently cited models of occupational stress is the person–environment fit model (French, Caplan and Van Harrison, 1982). This is based on the view that job characteristics (such as role ambiguity or role conflict) are threatening because of a misfit between the abilities of the employee and the demands of the job or between the needs of the individual and the provision of rewards from the job. Thus people may be asked what level of workload they perceive and what level they prefer. As with many approaches to stress, the theory is very general and it is not clear exactly what variables in the person are critical and what features of the environment they should match. However, the theory has some support, where researchers have focused on specific relationships for which hypotheses can be formed. For example, Chelmers et al. (1985) found that university administrators whose personal leadership style fitted features of the environment (defined according to Fiedler's contingency model of leadership effectiveness, 1967) experienced less stress and fewer health problems.

Eulberg, Weekley and Bhagat (1988) evaluated this theory and compared it to a number of other theoretical approaches. They concluded that in addressing broad conceptual issues the model suffers from lack of clarity and specificity and is essentially not falsifiable. A model in the same tradition but which has much greater claims to specificity and testability is that of Karasek which will therefore be discussed in greater detail below.

Karasek's demand–control model

This model is one of the most well-known and influential approaches to occupational stress. It is sometimes regarded as a form of person–environment fit approach (Edwards and Cooper, 1990), though this is rather misleading since its core measures focus on essentially environmental features. It focuses on only two main aspects of work, job demands (by which he is referring to volume and pace of work and being subject to conflicting demands) and job control.

Karasek considers that the effects of job demands are moderated by decision latitude (which, roughly speaking, means the same as discretion or control). Figure 9.1 identifies the types of jobs that are thought to result from the various combinations of demands and control. The model predicts that a combination of high job demand and low levels of job control would lead to high levels of psychological and physical strain – a 'high strain' job. By contrast, low levels of demand and high levels of control would be 'low strain' jobs. High job demands combined with a high level of control make for 'active jobs' that are not unduly stressful because they allow the individual to develop protective behaviours (such as delegation). Jobs with low demands and low control, on the other hand, tend

Figure 9.1   Karasek's demand–control model. Reprinted from Karasek (1979).

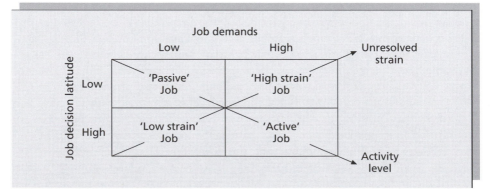

to be passive, resulting in learned helplessness and reduced activity. Active and passive jobs are regarded as intermediate in terms of strain and are comparatively rarely researched. A central feature of the model is the interactive (or moderated) effect, whereby a high level of demands coupled with low levels of control leads to a disproportionate amount of strain. This is typically tested by entering a multiplicative interaction term into a multiple regression equation predicting strain outcomes (as described for testing moderators in Chapter 6).

Much of Karasek's work has focused on demonstrating that there are increased risks of cardiovascular disease among those employed in 'high strain' jobs (e.g. Karasek *et al.*, 1982; Pieper, LaCroix and Karasek, 1989; see Chapter 3). However, the model has also been used to predict the more immediate impact on psychological well-being and job satisfaction. This approach may help to explain why high levels of heart disease are often found in the lower levels in organisational hierarchies in studies of a range of organisations including the British Civil Service (Marmot *et al.*, 1991). While there are clearly stressors associated with senior positions these are likely to be mitigated by greater control and ability to delegate. One clear practical implication of this model is that it suggests that work could be made less stressful, without reducing demand, merely by increasing control. Indeed, his own research (Karasek, 1990) has shown that where people had experienced company reorganisations in which they participated, and which resulted in increased job control, they showed lower levels of symptoms (including depression, exhaustion, heart problems, dizziness and headaches). While this study shows convincing evidence in terms of the importance of control it does not consider other aspects of the model and, in particular, the notion that there is a statistical interaction effect between demands and control. Many researchers, using a variety of different research methodologies, have attempted to test the full model, yet few have found the predicted interaction between demand and control. In general it seems to be the case that the evidence is stronger for the importance of control than it is for the full model (see Ganster and Fusilier, 1989; Jones and Fletcher, 1996b).

Karasek's narrow focus on demand and control and the interactions between the two has meant that this is a model that is relatively easily testable and has straightforward practical implications. This probably accounts for the dominance of this approach in both the psychological and medical literature (see Chapter 4). However, while it is a highly influential theory in terms of promoting research, the model has had limited impact on practice. This may be because its key variables are too general and non-specific to suggest practical interventions, but they also fail to incorporate many important factors such as job insecurity or aspects of new technology (Jones *et al.*, 1998).

An example of the limitations of the demand–control model is demonstrated by Wright and Cordery's (1999) study of production operators in a waste water treatment plant. This highlighted the need to consider (production) uncertainty as a key contextual variable in the demand–control equation. They found that when there was little production uncertainty, those employees with low job control reported higher levels of job satisfaction than those with high job control. However, when production uncertainty was high, the situation was reversed. Similar findings were reported for intrinsic motivation and, in both cases, the least satisfied employees were those that were given high control through the introduction of self-managed teams, but in fact found that there were few opportunities to exercise this control because production uncertainty was low. Their results demonstrate that job design interventions are more complex than just a consideration of demands and control, and that it is not always necessarily beneficial to provide greater control if in reality there is little opportunity to exercise this latitude. For instance, creating a 'self-managed' team on a production line may not be beneficial where in reality the production line may dictate the work processes and leave little room for discretion. In these kinds of circumstances, management intervention may raise employees' expectations only to dash them when it becomes clear that there is little scope for any real benefit.

Various extended versions of the model have been advocated and tested, for example, lack of social support is now widely recognised as a major contributor to stress at work and is frequently added to Karasek's model (e.g. Johnson and Hall, 1988). In addition, Karasek and Theorell (1990) further propose the addition of job insecurity and physical demands. Despite this, the demand and control dimensions alone are still used to define stressful work in many studies, an approach which offers limited guidance to practitioners.

However, an important attempt has been made by Wall and colleagues (e.g. Wall et al., 1990a, b) to develop a more practical theory to guide research and interventions. This builds on Karasek's model but Wall et al. suggest it is important to distinguish between several quite different forms of control. They suggest three types of control: method control (control over how to do the work); timing control (control over the timing of work), and boundary control (control over a range of peripheral activities, e.g. machine maintenance or ordering supplies). Similarly they distinguish between two different types of cognitive demand, that associated with monitoring of machines and that associated with problem solving (Wall et al., 1990a). They have produced a range of specific measures applicable to industrial jobs (Jackson et al., 1993). These measures are aimed to be useful both for theory development and for applied research and can be applied to test Karasek's hypothesis. For example, Wall et al. (1996) suggest that Karasek's predicted interaction effect is seldom demonstrated because the decision latitude measure used lacks specificity. They compared a measure of timing and method control with the conventional decision latitude measure in a study that aimed to predict psychological strain. They found a significant interaction effect with demand for the specific measure but not for the conventional measure. They point out that other studies finding interaction effects have also used more focused measures than Karasek's concepts (e.g. Dwyer and Ganster, 1991; Fox, Dwyer and Ganster, 1993).

Box 9.1   The role of individual differences.

The role of individual differences in stress was considered in Chapter 6 which particularly focused on the role of negative affect/neuroticism and Type A behaviour. Both these variables were examined in studies in the workplace. However, the notion of negative thinking has been further explored in the work context by researchers focusing on the tendency to be self-critical or hold oneself to high standards of perfection.

For example, Firth-Cozens (1992b) conducted a longitudinal study of 170 junior doctors that looked at both organisational and individual predictors of perceived job stress. She focused specifically on the tendency to be self-critical and dependent. Unusually, the study looked for the underlying mechanisms for these dispositional tendencies in early childhood experiences. She concluded that both individual and organisational factors were important. Childhood factors also had a demonstrable impact. For example, the level of stress caused by senior doctors was predicted both by the type of hospital and by relationships with fathers.

Judge and Locke (1993) also looked at the tendency to be self-critical in a study of a cluster of characteristics they label 'dysfunctional thought processes'. They found that people who feel dependent on others for their self-worth, who believe their work should be perfect, and who tend to generalise from single events (e.g. 'If I do something wrong, I am a bad person') will tend to have lower job satisfaction and to be more depressed.

Other researchers have sought to extend Karasek's approach to take into account individual differences such as personality which have been shown to be complicated in work stress (see Box 9.1 and Chapter 6). For example, Parkes (1991), in a study of civil servants, found that the interactive demand–control model predicted anxiety for people with external locus of control but not for those with internal locus of control. Furthermore, its very nature as a model focusing on job design, means Karasek's approach ignores issues related to how individuals differ in their appraisal of job characteristics. This is the focus of transactional approaches discussed below.

The transactional approach

While the transactional approach of Lazarus has dominated the wider stress literature, its impact has been much less marked in the occupational field. This may be because the main concern of occupational researchers has been to identify common work factors that can be modified to improve the general well-being of the workforce. They have therefore tried to either ignore or reduce the muddying effect of individual differences in perceptions of stressors rather than seeing these as themselves an interesting focus of research. Lazarus, however, argues that knowledge of stressful factors in the workplace, while it has value, 'misses the central point that the sources of stress are always, to some extent, individual, as are the ways people cope with stress . . . To describe and understand stress in the workplace requires that these individual patterns be studied' (Lazarus, 1995, p. 8). Furthermore he suggests that, since stress varies within the person in different circumstances over time, it cannot adequately be measured by a single assessment. The key features of Lazarus' general approach to stress are described in Chapters 2 and 7. However, fundamentally it suggests that a transaction between the person and the environment would be perceived as stressful to the extent that the individual evaluates the environment as presenting harm, threats and challenges (Lazarus, 1995). This evaluation is dependent on the individual's appraisal of both the environmental situation and their own resources to cope. The hassles and uplifts scale (Lazarus and Folkman, 1989), the major instrument traditionally used to measure perceptions of the environment by Lazarus and colleagues, is not specifically adapted to the workplace. However, some researchers have used qualitative approaches to gain information on appraisals of work stressors (Caspi, Bolger and Eckenrode, 1987; Dewe, 1992).

For example, Dewe (1992) looked at how individuals appraise and cope with work stressors. He used qualitative approaches to find out what situations people described as stressful and their primary appraisals of these situations, then more traditional rating methods to investigate secondary appraisal and coping (see Chapter 2). The work stressors most frequently raised were interpersonal relationships (47%) and work overload (39%). Primary appraisals included being made to feel uncomfortable or embarrassed or feeling that little support was available. Secondary appraisal included feeling constrained from doing what they wanted. Findings were overall very complex and detailed, for example, the coping strategy of 'trying not to let it get to you' was more likely to be used if a problem is appraised in terms of lack of support rather than lack of control. By their detailed focus such studies can start to give a more elaborated view of the processes whereby individuals come to feel they are stressed.

However, this kind of research (involving interviews, daily measures or both) is time consuming to conduct and complex to analyse and interpret and as a result has failed to win popular appeal in the work environment. Brief and George (1995) further suggest that Lazarus' approach, in emphasising the individual, ignores the basic agenda of occupational researchers that emphasises 'the development of theory to guide one to identify those conditions of employment likely to affect adversely the psychological well-being of most persons exposed to them'. They suggest that while they recognise that stress is an individual phenomenon, researchers have a responsibility to society to identify those conditions of work that are generally stressful and harmful to well-being. In general, therefore, researchers interested in exploring aspects of the workplace which cause strain in most people might be advised to use simple or interactional theories. Those wanting to find out

Figure 9.2   A general model of occupational stress. From Beehr and Newman (1978).
Reprinted with permission.

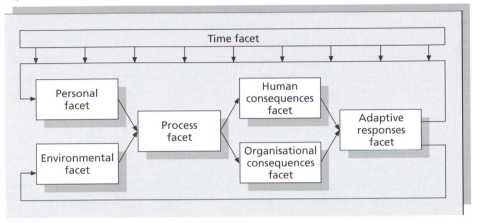

more about individual processes of stress appraisal and coping may do better with
the transactional approach.

Where should work stress theory go from here?

Some of the theories listed here are not inconsistent with each other but may be
criticised as only covering limited aspects of the topic. It is therefore not surprising
that attempts have been made to produce an overriding all-encompassing theory.
An example is the facet analytic approach of Beehr and Newman (1978). This
approach attempted to 'encompass not only all variables studied from the various
approaches to occupational stress, but also virtually all theories about the topic'
(Beehr, 1995, p. 12). As a result it includes over 150 variables which are classified into the seven facets listed shown in Figure 9.2 and incorporates elements of
the interactional and transactional approaches. The model has been criticised
(Eulberg, Weekley and Bhagat, 1988) as being too comprehensive to be of much
practical significance and not clear or specific enough to suggest practical relationships. The authors themselves accept that this model is not testable and have
focused on testing a more limited version.

   Clearly then, there is a problem in trying to produce an acceptable model of
stress that is both comprehensive and useful. Eulberg, Weekley and Bhagat suggest
that there is an inverse relationship between a model's breadth and its overall impact
on the field. They suggest that broad coverage such as offered by Beehr and Newman
is achieved by sacrificing conceptual tightness and falsifiability. Perhaps this also
explains why Karasek's demand–control model has had much greater impact
(on research if not in practice), as this is one of the few relatively well-specified
models which is testable, even though it is undeniably lacking in breadth.

So why is it so difficult to produce a theory of work stress? One problem appears to be that in seeking to explain stress we are seeking to explain a phenomenon that is too broad and diffuse for it to be possible to produce a satisfactory theory. Eulberg, Weekley and Bhagat (1988) suggested the solution may lie in the development of 'mid-range' theories which do not seek to explain stress but rather to examine the impact of perception of stress on some more limited outcomes, such as task performance (e.g. McGrath, 1976). One possible way forward, discussed in the next section, is to replace the study of work stress with the study of specific emotions at work.

Alternatives to the 'stress' concept?

Because of the difficulties in defining work stress and producing good theories, a number of writers have started to criticise the usefulness of the concept of stress in the occupational setting. Essentially the concerns expressed about the stress concept discussed in Chapter 1 (e.g. Pollock, 1988) have been taken up by those working in the occupational setting.

Briner and Reynolds (1993) suggest that it adds little to our understanding to label a person as stressed since the definition is so vague. There has been a move towards looking at emotion in the workplace as offering a much richer basis for understanding than the notion of stress (Ashforth and Humphrey, 1995; Weiss and Cropanzano, 1996). Ashforth and Humphreys, for example, criticise the concentration of research on the relatively general and stable affective states such as stress and satisfaction and suggest 'emotions are an integral and inseparable part of organisational life'. They further suggest that 'the experience of work is saturated with feeling' and that 'the relative neglect of the role of everyday emotion in mundane organisational life is surprising' (p. 98). They argue that emotions have been seen as essentially in conflict with the rationality that is fundamental to organisational effectiveness, and their expression is seen as something which should be regulated and controlled. They suggest that instead we should view emotion as inevitable and that sometimes effectiveness may be improved 'by celebrating rather than attempting to suppress emotion'. Given the diversity of emotional experiences associated with work, a focus studying stress and job satisfaction with a view to eliminating one and increasing the other is arguably naive and simplistic, denying the importance of complex emotional experiences.

Lazarus has also recently started to question the reliance on the concept of stress as a uni-dimensional variable. He now also suggests that we would gain much more information about the experience of work by a focus on emotions rather than stress alone (Lazarus, 1995). As discussed in Chapter 1, Lazarus suggests there are at least 15 different emotions. He identifies nine essentially negative emotions (anger, fright, anxiety, guilt, shame, sadness, envy, jealousy and disgust) and four positive emotions (happiness, pride, relief and love). In addition he suggests three more which might perhaps be regarded as more mixed (hope, compassion and gratitude) (Lazarus, 1993).

Many irritating obstructions and frustrations are commonplace and frequent experiences at work and may be major disruptions to organisational effectiveness. They may also be major factors in leading people to experience work as extremely stressful yet these stressors and the emotions they engender are seldom reflected in research studies. What contributes to positive feelings, well-being and determination is perhaps even less likely to be reflected in studies of job satisfaction. Lazarus' new approach seeks to remedy this. It is certainly the case that our existing concepts have failed to deliver unambiguous findings. Overall it seems that relationships between strain indicators (such as anxiety or psychological well-being) and physical illness are tenuous. It is tempting to hope that the study of emotion will contribute to the development of more focused and specific theories. Coupled with well-defined job characteristics and clear behavioural or disease outcomes it is possible to envisage a new wave of more usable theories of work and well-being. But there is equally a danger that this may lead to a multiplicity of highly complex theories that are difficult to translate into practical applications.

In the meantime, while researchers ponder these issues, there is a gulf between theories used predominantly for research purposes, e.g. to clarify understanding of stress, and the needs of practitioners seeking information to use to improve conditions in an organisation. Some approaches that could be used by practitioners are considered in the next section.

CONDUCTING OCCUPATIONAL STRESS AUDITS

It will be clear from Chapter 2 and from the above discussion that there is a range of conflicting views about stress measurement, corresponding to the different theoretical stances. In the area of work stress these become particularly problematic for those outside of academic research who wish to study stress in organisations with a view to improving the plight of those working there. Much published research is focused on esoteric theoretical concerns and is sometimes criticised as having little relevance to the practitioner (Jones, 1998). At the same time organisations are often criticised for introducing stress policies which are based on little evidence (Briner, 1997). This section constitutes an introductory guide to some approaches likely to be relevant to the student or practitioner involved in organisational stress assessment or 'stress audits', which might help them to develop better evidence on which to base policies and interventions.

The notion of the stress audit has become fairly widespread in recent years. Given the confusion about the causes of stress and the conflicting approaches it will not come as a surprise that any attempt to conduct an organisational audit of 'stress' is fraught with difficulty. It requires a clear definition of exactly what it is the investigator is choosing to measure – anxiety, psychological well-being, mood and emotion, etc. While the models and approaches discussed above provide some framework for applied researchers many will prefer 'off the peg' measures, which do not necessarily have their roots in tested theoretical approaches. There are undoubtedly a number of instruments available of varying quality. These can be assessed in the light of the issues raised in Chapters 1 and 2 of this book. The Job Stress Survey (Spielberger, 1994; Spielberger and Reheiser, 1995) for example, is based on a transactional approach to stress and thus is interested in the extent that people appraise work features as stressful. It therefore asks people to rate the severity of stress and the frequency of occurrence of various stressors (but see Box 2.1). Other audits try to look more objectively at perceptions of the existence of work stressors (e.g. by asking people to rate the extent they experience a demand, such as paperwork, rather than asking them to rate the severity of stress they experience due to paperwork). Scores for stressor items or groups of items are then correlated with measures of psychological or physical well-being. These aim to produce results which will be less dependent on the individual appraisal and more on the extent to which a relationship between work stressors and poor well-being can be demonstrated, regardless of whether people perceive the aspect of work as stressful. The following section considers one of the most well-known measures of occupational stress commonly used in the UK, the Occupational Stress Indicator.

An 'off the peg' measure – the Occupational Stress Indicator (OSI)

The Occupational Stress Indicator is a survey measure of stress designed by Cooper, Sloan and Williams (1988). Since this is a very popular measure of organisational stress in the UK, and has spawned many publications, it deserves some attention in this book. The OSI is based on a model of stress which incorporates a wide range of aspects of life (or sources of stress), individual and organisational effects, as well as numerous intervening variables including personality factors, perception of control and coping strategies. Many of the relationships implicit in the model are not clearly established by research. The full model is shown in Figure 9.3 below. This makes for a long questionnaire (over 150 questions) that combine into 28 different subscales measuring the key dimensions of the model.

A large number of studies have now been published based on this instrument (e.g. Bogg and Cooper, 1995; Bradley and Sutherland, 1995; Brown, Cooper and Kirkcaldy, 1996.) Studies have been conducted in many countries including Australia (Langan-Fox and Poole, 1995), Germany (Kirkcaldy and Cooper, 1992), India (Tharakan, 1992), Portugal (Cunha, Cooper, Moura et al., 1992) and Brazil (de Moraes, Swan and Cooper, 1993). These studies tell us about a mass of relationships between variables and comparisons between different work groups. These disparate findings are difficult to integrate without a more specific theory.

This type of model can be criticised for assuming relationships between work features and organisational outcomes that have not clearly been established. Newton (1995) further suggests that, by its emphasis on personality traits such as Type A, the model implies that stress is 'primarily about character defects of the individual worker' (p. 87). He suggests this kind of approach is essentially politically

190

Figure 9.3   Cooper's model.

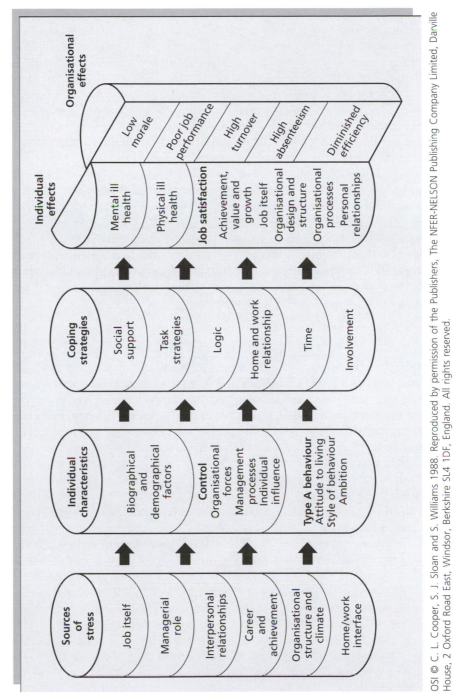

OSI © C. L. Cooper, S. J. Sloan and S. Williams 1988. Reproduced by permission of the Publishers, The NFER-NELSON Publishing Company Limited, Darville House, 2 Oxford Road East, Windsor, Berkshire SL4 1DF, England. All rights reserved.

conservative, diverting attention away from collective experiences of working life and issues relating to power and conflict. It further may be used to support individual treatments such as stress management. This criticism could of course apply to any approach to stress that seeks to incorporate individual characteristics or perceptions.

The OSI measure itself has been the subject of a number of studies of its reliability and validity mainly conducted by Cary Cooper and his colleagues. Davis (1996) highlights two particular issues. Firstly the internal validity of many of the scales is low (items within the scale may not be measuring the same construct) and secondly that both reliability and construct validity of the Type A and locus of control scale is problematic. Some of these problems may lie in the wide-ranging and ambitious nature of this measure. It could be argued that in trying to measure everything it does nothing very well. For example, there is little reason to believe it is possible to produce a useful measure of Type A using only six items. However, its broad brush approach may be useful to identify problem areas in an organisation that can then be investigated further using more focused approaches.

If time allows, it may be better to construct an audit which has been developed and tailored to meet the particular needs of the specific organisation. This kind of approach is discussed in the next section.

'Pick and mix' measures – constructing an audit from existing scales

In some instances, it may be more appropriate to develop an audit from existing measures, perhaps drawing on a theoretical framework such as Warr's vitamin model. For example, many organisations may contain stressors not readily assessed by off the peg measures or, in other circumstances, the researcher may wish to focus on a specific type of stressor using a shorter, more focused instrument. Here organisational researchers are often able to find valid and reliable but brief measures for some of the constructs they wish to measure. A number of useful scales are published in journal articles, for example, measures of job control (Jackson et al., 1993), role conflict and ambiguity (Rizzo, House and Lirtzman, 1970). Frequently, additional items or measures of stressors unique to a particular job or organisation may also need to be written.

The researcher constructing an audit will normally wish to include measures to assess occupational strains and possibly other outcomes such as job satisfaction (see Mullarkey et al., 1999). They may also wish to look at organisational outcomes such as performance, absenteeism or turnover. However, because of difficulties in obtaining satisfactory indicators of these dimensions, researchers often fall back on self-report measures. Anxiety or well-being measures (such as the GHQ, see Chapter 2) for which norms are available are frequently used in work stress research. However, well-being measures developed specifically for the workplace may also be used, for example, the Maslach Burnout Inventory (Maslach and Jackson, 1981; see Box 9.2).

Box 9.2   Maslach Burnout Inventory.

Burnout is a form of psychological reaction that is specific to the work situation. In particular, it has become a very popular way to examine stress in the caring professions in the US. The concept is operationalised in the Maslach Burnout Inventory (Maslach and Jackson, 1981) which consists of 22 items which require the respondent to rate how often they experience various feeling states (e.g. 'I feel emotionally drained by my work'). The inventory consists of scales measuring *emotional exhaustion*, *depersonalisation*, and *lack of personal accomplishment*. Emotional exhaustion is characterised by lack of energy and feeling that one's emotional resources are used up (Cordes and Dougherty, 1993). The key element in depersonalisation is a feeling of detachment, or treating clients as objects rather than people. A lack of personal accomplishment may be marked by feelings of failure. Emotional exhaustion is often regarded as the first stage of burnout and is primarily a response to excess demands especially from 'work overload, interpersonal interactions, role conflict and high levels of both personal and organisational expectations' (Cordes and Dougherty, 1993, p. 644).

Burnout has been linked to a wide range of negative outcomes including mental and physical health problems, adverse effects on social and family relationships, negative attitudes towards clients, increased turnover of labour and deterioration in performance. However, the three-dimensional aspect of burnout has been criticised (e.g. Garden, 1989), and it has been suggested that not all components are necessary for defining burnout, emotional and physical exhaustion being the key components. Garden suggests that the association of depersonalisation and lack of personal accomplishment with burnout could be the result of human service occupations attracting certain personality types who may be particularly prone to it.

The concept of 'burnout' has produced a substantial literature in the US, but the measure is also quite commonly incorporated in stress surveys in the UK and elsewhere.

As we have seen stress researchers have been criticised as focusing on a limited range of negative outcomes and Lazarus (1995) has recommended a focus on a wider range of emotions in the workplace including positive emotions. One approach to measurement appropriate to the work context is Warr's work-related well-being measure, which together with his non-work-related measure, is discussed in Box 9.3. Short job satisfaction measures such as that developed by Hackman and Oldham (1980) or Warr, Cook and Wall (1979) are also commonly incorporated.

The researcher using this approach, however, is likely to need to conduct some preliminary investigation into the organisational stressors prior to constructing a survey. Here the interview approaches used in the next section may be relevant.

Box 9.3   Warr's job- and non-job-related mental health.

Warr (1990) has produced measures of affective well-being that are specific to both job and non-job contexts. Unlike many other measures, they consider positive as well as negative affective reactions. In line with earlier work (e.g. Watson and Tellegen, 1985; Thayer, 1989), Warr views psychological well-being as comprising two orthogonal dimensions (pleasure and arousal) that are represented on three axes (pleasure to displeasure, anxiety to contentment and depression to enthusiasm – see Figure 9.4). In order to assess affective health, Warr's measure of job-related well-being concentrates on the two diagonal axes (anxiety–contentment and depression–enthusiasm). Respondents are presented with 12 adjectives, six positive and six negative. Respondents are asked how frequently their job has made them feel tense, contented, worried or enthusiastic, for example. Several studies have used this measure to assess patterns in work-related psychological health status. For example, Warr (1992) examined the relationship between employee age and job-related well-being with over 1,600 workers from a wide range of occupations. A U-shaped pattern was found, i.e. lower levels of contentment and enthusiasm were reported by middle-aged workers than by younger and older respondents.

Figure 9.4   Warr's axes for measuring affective well-being.

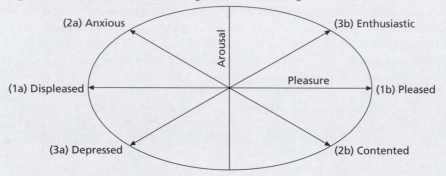

There is, however, a lack of consensus on the precise factor structure of the instrument and on the adjectives that should be used to assess each dimension. Some prefer to replace some adjectives (Sevastos, Smith and Cordery, 1992), whilst others consider the use of two dimensions as over-simplistic. Daniels et al. (1997), conclude that more complex multi-dimensional models are needed to capture the variety of affective experience in the workplace.

Interviews

A number of writers advocate the use of interviews for investigating work stress (Dewe, 1989; Keenan and Newton, 1985). Dewe (1989) suggests that traditional questionnaire measures of sources of stress may distort the importance of some items that may no longer be important while ignoring others. Keenan and Newton also found that the use of interviews in a study of engineers revealed the presence of stressors not emphasised in typical questionnaires, specifically interpersonal conflicts and time-wasting job demands. Role ambiguity and conflict, which feature a great deal in questionnaires, were seldom mentioned. Similarly, Dewe (1992) found that the events or situations most frequently described as stressful by employees in a large insurance company were related to interpersonal relationships. Not only do interviews reveal the existence of stressors, they can give information on the intensity, frequency and the meaning individuals attribute to stressful experiences (Dewe, 1989).

One useful approach used in interviews is to ask respondents to focus on a particular incident at work, for example Dewe used the question 'Can you think of a particular time at work when you felt under pressure, tension or stress? Can you tell me what happened?' This was followed up by questions about the intensity, frequency and direction of impact (positive and negative). This type of method is sometimes called the 'critical incidents' approach. Such interviews are clearly quite different from the kind of informal chat that may occur in some job interviews. Usually the interviewer would have a structured standard schedule of questions, but would have some flexibility to probe further to encourage the respondent to answer. This kind of interview enables the researcher to get stand-ard information from respondents which can be categorised and quantified (see Chapter 2). There are clear pros and cons to using interviews rather than ques-tionnaires. Questionnaire ratings allow the researcher to use a standardised instru-ment and get data easily from a representative sample. Powerful statistics can be applied to the results. Interviews, however, can give a greater depth of understanding but are more time consuming and difficult to analyse rigorously. Few attempts have been made to directly compare the two methods of assessing work stressors. However, Jex et al. (1997) compare questionnaire scale-based methods with written descrip-tions of critical incidents to measuring role ambiguity, role conflict and interpersonal conflict. For each of the stressors respondents were asked to write a description of a recent incident. Three trained independent raters were asked to rate the level of stress. They found a reasonable level of convergence between the two methods. However, there were differences between the two approaches. For instance, in look-ing at the relationship between stressors and strains, role conflict emerged as the most important predictor when the scale-based methods are used, whereas inter-personal conflict was more important when incidents were considered. They also found that while the questionnaire scale responses were related to self-esteem, the incidents were not, indicating that the former are more influenced by disposition. They conclude that each method has its place and that ultimately the best approach is to use multiple methods.

An integrated approach to measuring stress in practice

By now it may be apparent that there are pros and cons to all of the methods of measuring stressors and strains and that combining methods may be the best way forward. Cox and Griffiths (1996) use such a combination in an approach that is in line with the latest UK legislation. They view stressors as psychosocial hazards and talk in terms of developing a risk assessment strategy. The type of work features that may be hazards are presented in Box 9.4. They recommend a 'triangulation' approach to assessing hazards which involves 'collecting and cross-checking information from at least three separate domains'. This might encompass the following elements (taken from Cox and Griffiths, 1996):

- self-report measures of how people perceive their work and their (emotional) experience of stress. This might include ratings of perceptions of level, frequency and duration of work demands, perceptions of control and support and perceived ability to cope;
- objective antecedents of these perceptions;
- changes in behaviour, physiology and health of employees.

Cox describes a full approach to assessment that starts with familiarization with the organisation, perhaps involving discussions with management, observation of the workplace and data collection from management systems. This initial phase would be followed by in-depth interviews with a structured sample of employees to obtain both factual information and perceptions of work and health. These interviews form the basis for the design of questionnaires to obtain information on both work hazards and health status of employees. This may involve tailoring an established theoretically based generic survey to fit the needs of the organisation. Finally, for the purpose of making practical recommendations, formal audits of management controls are conducted. Thus the approach uses both qualitative and quantitative methods and may involve a multi-disciplinary approach with psychologists responsible for assessment of psychosocial hazards and medical and nursing staff involved in assessments of health.

Summary of measurement methods

It is clear that adequate assessment of work stress requires good theoretical frameworks and reliable and valid methods of measurement. It is equally clear that there is disagreement about which is the most appropriate theory and method. The purpose of the investigation will to some extent determine the methods used, and this in turn may be influenced by a range of assumptions about the nature of stress

Box 9.4   Psychosocial hazards of work (Shabracq, Winnubst and Cooper, 1996).

Category	Conditions
Content of work	
Job content	Lack of variety or short work cycles, fragmented or meaningless work, underuse of skills, high uncertainty.
Workload/work pace	Work overload or underload, lack of control over pacing, high levels of time pressure.
Work schedule	Shift working, inflexible work schedules, unpredictable hours, long or unsocial hours.
Interpersonal relationships at work	Social or physical isolation, poor relationships with superiors, interpersonal conflict, lack of social support.
Control	Low participation in decision making, lack of control over work (control, particularly in the form of participation, is also a context and wider organisational issue).
Context to work	
Organisational culture and function	Poor communication, low levels of support for problem solving and personal development, lack of definition of organisational objectives.
Role in organisations	Role ambiguity and role conflict, responsibility for people.
Career development	Career stagnation and uncertainty, underpromotion or over-promotion, poor pay, job insecurity, low social value to work.
Home–work interface	Conflicting demands of work and home, low support at home, dual career problems.

Reprinted by permission of John Wiley & Sons Limited.

and where the responsibility for its effects should lie, in the individual or in the organisation. These factors will ultimately be reflected in the choice of intervention used to combat stress.

CONCLUSION

This chapter has reviewed some of the theoretical approaches to studying stress and considered the issues that arise when trying to apply these in the workplace, both in measuring stress and in trying to reduce it. In stress research, as in other areas of applied psychology, there sometimes seems to be a conflict between the academic seeking to develop and refine theory and the more immediate practical need of practitioners seeking information on which to develop interventions. For example, approaches such as the OSI have sought to meet the needs of practitioners to measure diverse stressors and strains based on a theoretical framework that suggests possible relationships between a very large range of variables. This approach may be useful to explore organisational issues, but in terms of advancing theory it is of limited use, for example, it does not suggest clearly testable hypotheses or specify ways in which variables may interact. Testable theories for which we can develop good reliable measures consist of a much more limited number of variables (e.g. Karasek's model). Such theories, however, may not address all the issues organisations wish to explore. Indeed, an overemphasis on testing and retesting such models may distract researchers from looking at what is really going on in organisations in the new millennium. There is also a need for exploratory research (for example, using qualitative methods) to investigate the demands employees themselves perceive as stressful. The work environment is, for many people, changing out of all recognition with new technology, virtual offices, virtual teams and the blurring of home/work boundaries. It cannot therefore be assumed that the work stressors embodied in some to the models and measures described here, remain the most important factors in the changing work environment. Current theories tend to lag behind work practices so that occupational psychologists are ill-prepared to investigate the many changes that are going on in work environments. Psychologists need to expand their theories and research if they are to meet the challenge of managing stress and well-being at work.

CHAPTER 10

THE HOME–WORK INTERFACE

Gail Kinman and Fiona Jones

This chapter examines the idea that stressors experienced in working life may have an influence that extends to home life and vice versa. Research investigating whether work stress can affect marital functioning and even impact on other family members is emphasised.

STRESS IN DIFFERENT LIFE DOMAINS

WHEN considering the impact of stressors on the individual, some researchers have found it useful to divide up the individual's life into a set of different functional domains. The most common example of this approach is the division between home and work. During the course of one day, individuals are likely to move from home to work (and back again) and possibly also to leisure or other activities. Within each domain they may take on more than one role. For example, within the family they may have the roles of both spouse and parent, and within the workplace they may have several roles.

Researchers in this area examine the premise that each of these domains and roles may produce stressors and strains that have the potential to elicit reactions in other domains and roles. Thus, if a demanding job causes a person to become anxious whilst at work, it is plausible that this anxious state may be maintained when they leave work. Equally anxiety generated from difficulties in the home such as caring for relatives, or problems with relationships, may manifest itself in the workplace. This issue is frequently ignored by work stress researchers who typically make only passing reference to extra-organisational stressors. However, thinking about stress in these terms raises many research questions, e.g. Does work stress 'spill over' to affect the stressed worker in the home environment? Do home stressors influence the individual's work performance? Are work and home roles in conflict, and are these effects worse for men or for women? Do work stressors effect marital relationships and the well-being of other family members? Is it useful to compartmentalise stressors by domain and role, or would it be more sensible to consider all stressors experienced in life when trying to understand the predictors of strain? This chapter considers some of the theoretical approaches and considers studies addressing some of these key questions.

THEORETICAL APPROACHES TO THE STUDY OF HOME/WORK RELATIONSHIPS

This section introduces two main approaches to investigating the issue of stress in different life domains. The first attempts to describe the relationship and the impact of one domain on another (in terms of spillover or compensation). The second focuses more on the process of conflict between life domains.

Spillover, compensation and segmentation

Two major competing hypotheses have been proposed to explain the relationship between home and work. The *spillover hypothesis* suggests that there are no firm boundaries between life domains, and that work and non-work experiences will be positively related. Thus, individuals who have varied, stimulating and satisfying work experiences will have similarly varied, stimulating and satisfying non-work experiences. Equally, it is suggested that the strain produced by work and home stressors results in the individual experiencing negative emotional states not only in their original setting, but also in other domains. Thus stressful events experienced in the workplace might leave the individual feeling tired or preoccupied with work when at home which, in turn, makes it difficult to participate effectively in family, leisure or social life. Early work based on descriptive case studies tends to support this approach (Young and Wilmott, 1973; Piotrkowski, 1978).

The *compensatory hypothesis*, on the other hand, suggests that there will be a negative relationship between home and work: for example, an individual may compensate for boring, unstimulating work by seeking opposite experiences at home or from leisure activities (Wilensky, 1960; Rousseau, 1978). According to this hypothesis, someone highly involved at work would be uninvolved at home and vice versa.

A third and less important approach is the *segmentation hypothesis* which suggests that work and non-work domains are essentially independent, psychologically separate and serve different functions (Blood and Wolfe, 1960; Dubin, 1973). This was the earliest conceptualisation of the relationship between work and home but the 'myth of separate worlds' of work and family has generally been exposed (Kanter, 1977), and the segmentation model is now frequently discredited.

Testing these hypotheses is problematic – not least because of the diversity of the variables that are considered, and the variation in the ways that 'work' and 'family life' are defined (Kabanoff, 1980). None of the three models described above have been clearly formulated. For example, they can refer to the extent to which behaviour (such as engaging in risk taking activities) in one domain leads to similar or dissimilar behaviour in another, or the extent to which satisfaction or distress in one domain is related to the same feelings in another (Staines, 1980).

Research looking at the spillover and compensation hypotheses has frequently been based on cross-sectional studies in which, for example, feelings and reactions to work are correlated with feelings and reactions to home. However, the claim that positive correlations between home and work variables provides support for the spillover hypothesis should be viewed with caution for a number of reasons:

- They may use similar items to measure variables in the home and in work, so that correlations may be partially explained by common method variance (see Chapter 2).
- Social psychology theories suggest that people's attitudes tend to be consistent across settings rather than differ (Festinger, 1957). Yet a test of the compensation model requires that people show opposing attitudes towards different aspects of life.
- Correlations may be the result of individual differences. For example, personality, and not spillover may account for individuals being isolated both at home and at work.

Such methodological factors tend to bias results in such a way that it is much easier to gain evidence to support the spillover than the compensation hypothesis. This idea is developed further below.

Role conflict

A second theoretical approach to the study of work–family conflict derives from role theory. Role theory is based on the idea that individuals occupy different roles or social positions in different arenas of activity. Each role is associated with a particular pattern of expected behaviours which usually involve rights, obligations and duties which an individual occupying the role is expected to perform. Sometimes people experience conflict between two or more of these expectations. Role conflict has been defined as 'the simultaneous occurrence of two or more role expectations such that compliance with one would make compliance with the other more difficult' (Katz and Kahn, 1978, p. 204). Much early research on role conflict and role ambiguity focused primarily on *intra-role conflict* (specifically conflict within the work role). In recent years, however, *inter-role conflict*, more particularly work–family conflict, has generated a vast amount of research. Inter-role conflict is defined as 'a form of role conflict in which the sets of opposing pressures arise from participation in different roles'. Work–family conflict is a form of inter-role conflict in which the incompatible pressures are seen as 'arising simultaneously from work and family roles' (Greenhaus and Beutell, 1985, p. 77). Two factors may be responsible for the rise in concern about inter-role conflict. Firstly, increased levels of paid employment amongst women have resulted in less clarity in the work and family roles held by both women and men. Secondly, there is an increase in home working and the blurring of home/work boundaries for many employees. Both these factors may increase the potential for conflict.

Although occupying multiple roles can provide individuals with important psychological benefits (Gove, 1972; Repetti and Crosby, 1984; Baruch and Barnett, 1986), a number of studies have indicated that role conflict is commonly experienced by and is a source of psychological strain in married and cohabiting men and women (e.g. Wortman, Biernat and Lang, 1991). Research findings suggest that the strain of managing multiple roles is greatest when work and family role responsibilities are both onerous (Emmons *et al.*, 1990), and when work is perceived to be demanding but not rewarding (Piotrkowski, 1978).

Three possible forms such conflict might take are suggested by Greenhaus and Beutell (1985):

* *time-based* in which the time spent in one role makes it difficult to give time to another role: an example might be where long working hours or frequent business trips away from the home reduces the opportunity to participate in family life;
* *strain-based* in which strain experienced in one role overlaps into other roles: examples could include worrying about work during the time at home, or preoccupation with work leading to irritability with, or distancing from, family and friends;
* *behaviour-based* conflict in which the behaviours required in one role are incompatible with those required in another role. An example of this form of conflict could be that behaviours appropriate to dealing with a large team of subordinates are likely to be inappropriate in the family setting.

While some studies look specifically at time-based conflict most now view work–family conflict as a mixture of time- and strain-based conflict. There is little research on behaviour-based conflict. Conflict between work and family has been measured using general bi-directional measures, or separate measures of the extent to which work interferes with family (work–family conflict) and family interferes with work (family–work conflict). Generally, the separate unidirectional measures have proved more useful (Kossek and Ozeki, 1998).

Because of the different ways work–family and family–work conflict are conceptualised, and some lack of clarity in use of the terms, this is a difficult area in which to interpret findings or compare studies. For example, while some studies regard work–family conflict as an outcome measure and examine the predictors (Williams and Alliger, 1994) others view work–family conflict as a mediator between stressors and strains (e.g. Frone, Russell and Cooper, 1992a; Cooke and Rousseau, 1984). Common method variance problems are particularly likely in this area (see Chapter 2) where ratings of conflict inevitably are highly dependent on perceptions and may have similar content to measures of psychological well-being.

There are fundamental theoretical differences between role theory and spillover; the former model tends to conceptualise the relationship between work and home as more static and structural, in that 'roles' are treated as separate entities (albeit with reciprocal influences), whereas spillover implies that the different domains are more dynamically inter-related. In early research spillover and role conflict were often treated separately, however, more recent work tends to draw on both approaches. For example, Higgins and Duxbury (1992) compared the potential for inter-role conflict and negative spillover between men with a home-maker wife and those with a spouse in a career-oriented job. Although the role conflict model tends to predominate in recent empirical studies, it could be argued that spillover research has been highly influential in helping to achieve recognition of the fact that work and home life are not separate entities but are inextricably psychologically intertwined.

RESEARCH INTO THE RELATIONSHIPS BETWEEN HOME AND WORK

Do people engage in similar activities at home and at work?

Early research stemming from the spillover/compensation approach tended to focus on the relationship between work and home activities. In this context, the spillover hypothesis would suggest that those whose work involved mentally demanding and stimulating activities might seek equally challenging leisure activities, whereas the compensation hypothesis might suggest that they might opt for more passive and undemanding leisure activities such as watching television. One of the earliest empirical studies looking at this issue, Kornhauser's (1965) study of 400 Detroit factory workers, supported the spillover model by concluding that routine work was associated with routine and narrow leisure activities. Meissner (1971) extended spillover theory in a study of Canadian forestry workers by suggesting that it was necessary to specify the areas in which work and leisure may correspond. Meissner proposed three possible dimensions:

(i)   *high–low discretion dimension*. A spillover hypothesis would suggest that those with high discretion at work would take part in leisure activities which give scope for discretion, such as participating in voluntary work for charities rather than watching television;

(ii) *instrumental–expressive dimension*. Instrumental activities are those which lead to an output, e.g. DIY activities; expressive activities are an end in themselves, e.g. religious activities; here the spillover hypothesis could suggest that engineers, for example, would be unlikely to take part in expressive leisure activities;

(iii) *social interaction dimension*. Here spillover would suggest that isolation in the workplace would give rise to isolation in the home environment and vice versa.

Meissner found support for the spillover hypothesis in all these areas. He suggests for example that:

> When work is socially isolating, workers reduce their exposure to situations in which they have to talk and also spend less time in organised and purpose-directed activities. (p. 260)

This however implies that isolated work is the cause of isolated leisure and not vice versa, which is not a conclusion that can be reached from cross-sectional data of this nature. It further ignores the fact that individual personality characteristics might influence the choice of both work and leisure activities.

A similar approach, again supporting the spillover hypothesis, is adopted in a study by Rousseau (1978) who adapted a job characteristics questionnaire to measure both work and leisure on several dimensions: autonomy; feedback; skill variety; task identity; task significance and dealing with others (Hackman and Oldham, 1975). Results indicated positive relationships between 'work' and 'home' measures. It is clear, however (and acknowledged by the author), that problems of method variance may have influenced these results, since items measuring work and non-work attitudes were very similar and derived from the same questionnaire. It is perhaps unlikely that people would rate such items differently enough to support the compensation hypothesis.

Staines, in his 1980 review of this literature, concluded that the evidence in general was inclined to favour the spillover hypothesis, the only major exception being that those who use a lot of physical effort at work are less likely to be physically active away from work (Bishop and Ikeda, 1970; Staines and Pagnucco, 1977). However, perhaps because of the methodological difficulties as well as the limited practical implications of this research area, it has largely fallen out of fashion in more recent years.

Are ratings of satisfaction within different domains related?

As well as looking at work and leisure activities, early researchers also examined whether perceptions of different life domains were related: for example, was satifaction with work related to home satisfaction? Again, the available evidence predominantly supports the spillover hypothesis. Early work by Haavio-Mannila (1971) found a significant correlation between work satisfaction and family satisfaction, although these correlations were low (0.20 between job and home satisfaction for married men and 0.24 for married women). Similarly, a review by Near, Rice and Hunt (1980) also supports the view that there is a weak positive relationship. However, as we have seen, common method variance may inflate correlations. If this is the case then findings are indeed inconclusive. Such results would be expected if there were a range of contrasting satisfaction profiles for different people, which largely cancel each other out when all are put together. Shaffer (1987) investigated this possibility, by analysing a number of subgroups, and found that the largest subgroup were generally satisfied in both work and non-work; however a significant proportion had highly variable profiles and could be regarded as having a compensatory relationship between work and non-work domains.

In some studies, researchers have also focused on the relationship between job satisfaction and overall life satisfaction (rather than satisfaction with the non-work domain). In a meta-analysis of this literature, Tait, Padgett and Baldwin (1989) find a correlation of 0.44, indicating a moderate relationship, suggesting that work is fairly important for life satisfaction. They also found that the relationship between job and life satisfaction for women has become much stronger in recent years, and while the relationship was weaker for women than for men in studies conducted before 1974, there is no difference in the post 1974 studies. A survey by Judge and Watanabe (1994) confirmed the existence of a generally positive relationship between job satisfaction and life satisfaction but (like Shaffer, above) suggested that for a significant minority the relationship is negative or there is no relationship at all. Thus, they suggest that, while the spillover model is true for most, the segmentation and compensation models are also true for some.

It is perhaps not surprising that early attempts to uncover very simple relationships between home and work were largely fruitless. Perceptions of work and home are far too complex to be encapsulated in simple measures of satisfaction. It has also been suggested that the notions of job and family satisfaction examine only a small facet of well-being in these domains (Kline and Cowan, 1988), and that such measures should be extended to include perceived *quality* of work and family life which have been found to jointly predict life satisfaction (Higgins and Duxbury, 1992). Furthermore, these relationships may be confounded by other variables that are likely to influence home and work, for example, the role of personality factors such as negative affect (see Chapter 6).

Does strain come mainly from work or from family life?

The above studies required participants to rate the degree of satisfaction they experience from different domains, i.e. work, family, leisure, and/or life in general. Researchers have also sought to identify which life domains are the major source of any anxiety and depression. Establishing whether negative mood and psychological symptomatology are principally derived from 'work' and/or 'home/family' is, however, problematic. Depressed mood and anxiety may be prolonged and pervasive; i.e. both causes and effects are unlikely to be confined to one domain. Consequently it may be difficult for the individual to make accurate attributions about the source of negative mood. Thus it is no surprise that researchers who have used separate measures of job-related and home-related anxiety and depression have found positive correlations between the two measures; for example, Warr reports correlations of 0.34 for job-related and non-job-related anxiety and 0.58 for depression (Warr, 1990).

205

Although few studies have tried to isolate the relative effects of particular areas of life on psychological well-being, attempts have been made to assess individuals' perceptions of the general 'stressfulness' of their work and home lives, and sources of strain experienced in each domain. Warr and Payne (1982) in a study of 3,077 British adults found that 14% of men and 19% of women reported experiencing unpleasant emotional strain for at least half of the previous day. Of those in full-time work, 40% of men and 28% of women attributed the cause of strain to their work. In a further study by Payne, Lane and Leahy (1989), 308 participants were given a measure of psychological well-being (the GHQ) and asked to attribute any recent changes in health to either 'mainly work factors', 'mainly factors outside work' or 'a mixture of both'. Payne, Lane and Leahy found that, for all symptoms except sleep items, work alone or a mixture of work and non-work factors were the main perceived causes of symptoms. Recent work on specific occupational groups support these findings: for example, studies of social workers (Jones, Fletcher, and Ibbetson, 1991) and university lecturers (Abouserie, 1996) both reported that around 75% of respondents considered work to be the main cause of any strain they experienced.

These ratings no doubt reflect genuine beliefs about the dominance of work as a stressor and a source of strain; however a number of biasing influences have been proposed which might lead the individual to blame work as a source of negative feelings and so artificially inflate this relationship. Payne, Lane and Leahy (1989), for example, suggest that such results could be due to the well-established tendency to attribute negative outcomes to external causes. Work may be seen as more external to the individual than home and family factors. It may even be that the current publicity about occupational stress may make work a particularly likely candidate for blame for feelings of distress and strain (Briner, 1996).

What kind of effects does work have on home life and vice versa?

A number of studies have linked work stressors with a range of negative outcomes that are likely to impact on life outside work. These include negative mood and anxious and depressive symptomatology (e.g. Doby and Caplan, 1995; Leiter and Durup, 1996); maladaptive coping behaviours including alcohol abuse (Frone, Russell and Cooper, 1997; Steptoe, Lipsey and Wardle, 1998); physical ill health (e.g. see Chapters 4 and 9) and fatigue (Chan and Margolin, 1994; Rystedt and Johansson, 1998). For example, Rystedt and Johansson (1998) investigated links between the workload and health of urban bus drivers over a period of 18 months and found a range of negative outcomes that are likely to have a significant impact on workers' home lives. Increased workload was strongly associated with spillover of work fatigue and exhaustion to home and leisure, problems in unwinding after work, difficulties in coping with home demands and psychosomatic complaints (such as sleeping difficulties, nausea and headaches).

Although research on spillover has predominantly focused on psychological aspects, Frankenhaueser and colleagues (1989) have identified a physiological pattern, or an 'unwinding' process, that occurs at home after a stressful working day. This is characterised by a reduction in adrenaline secretion levels. They found certain work features, such as overload, underload and conflicting demands, lead to slower physiological unwinding which may be a threat to health.

Much less research has been conducted looking at the effects of home on working life. However, some evidence for spillover from home to work settings is provided by Harrell and Ridley (1975) who found that mothers' levels of satisfaction with childcare arrangements were positively related to their job satisfaction. However, while the woman with good childcare arrangements may be more satisfied with work, those who give greater priority to their family over their work roles may find their career development may suffer (Sekaran, 1986). Caring for elderly relatives may also have negative effects on work (Lee, 1997). Lee compared workers with elder care responsibilities to non-caregiving workers on a number of variables related to job performance. Findings indicated that carers were absent more often and gave less attention to the job, mainly because of fatigue and drowsiness.

Two longitudinal studies have looked at spillover in both directions and suggested complex bi-directional relationships between variables in the home and at work, but with a tendency for work effects on home life to be greater than vice versa (Leiter and Durup, 1996; Chan and Margolin, 1994).

What characteristics of work lead to spillover to the home?

Over the last two decades, studies have attempted to identify the working conditions and family characteristics that might affect the likelihood of spillover from work into the home domain (and vice versa). Not surprisingly, carrying out work tasks at home during evenings and weekends has been linked with perceptions of work interfering with family life (Kinman, 1996; Doyle and Hind, 1998). There is also evidence that the degree of flexibility in work scheduling, and the timing and number of hours worked outside the home (i.e. working long 'unsociable' hours with little choice or control) has a similar relationship with these perceptions (Staines and Pleck, 1983; Spitze and South, 1985). Barling (1994) maintains, however, that the increased implementation of flexible work schedules on the part of organisations is based on the belief that work exerts a negative effect on families only to the extent that it physically keeps workers away from the home and their families. He argues that this belief is erroneous, and suggests that the key to developing a greater understanding of the relationship between work and family life is through investigating employees' perceptions of the nature and features of the work itself.

Table 10.1   Examples of job characteristics and strain outcomes that have been linked with negative spillover from the workplace to the home.

Work features and outcomes	Examples of studies
Long working hours	Spitze and South (1985); Alexander and Walker (1996)
Work overload	Repetti (1989)
Shiftwork	Alexander and Walker (1996)
Lack of task variety	Kanter (1977)
Lack of leader support	Bowen (1998)
Lack of feedback	Doby and Caplan (1995)
Lack of social support	Greenhaus, Bedeian and Mossholder (1987); DeLongis, Folkman and Lazarus (1988)
Low levels of job autonomy	Kanter (1977)
Job insecurity	Piotrkowski and Crits-Christoph (1981)
Dangerous working conditions	Long and Voges (1987)
Inadequate salary	Pleck (1985)
Role ambiguity	Burke and Weir (1981); Doby and Caplan (1995)
Rapid pace of change	Burke and Weir (1981)
Interpersonal conflict	Bolger et al. (1989); Repetti (1994)
Training inadequacy	Doby and Caplan (1995)
Working with people in distress	Jackson and Maslach (1982)
Emotional labour	Wharton and Erickson (1995)
Burnout/emotional exhaustion	Jackson and Maslach (1982)
Threat to work reputation	Doby and Caplan (1995)
Low sense of professional efficacy	Leiter and Durup (1996)
Insignificance within work role	Schwartzberg and Dytell (1996)

Although little has been demonstrated conclusively, studies have begun to identify specific features of work likely to indirectly influence the non-work domain. Table 10.1 provides some examples of the range of job characteristics and working conditions that have been found to interfere with family functioning. As can be seen, jobs that lead to high levels of 'burnout' and/or emotional exhaustion are implicated, so also are jobs that require 'emotional labour' (Hochschild, 1983). This means the work involves the management of feelings: for example, receptionists who may be required to smile and be pleasant whatever they may really be feeling. A cross-sectional study conducted by Doby and Caplan (1995) suggested that job stressors that threaten employees' perceived reputations with their supervisors (i.e. how their line managers judge their abilities and performance) are particularly likely to result in anxiety and loss of self-esteem and subsequent spillover into the home domain. These authors suggest that job characteristics (such as lack of feedback, training inadequacy, role overload and role ambiguity) may also have the potential to increase spillover of emotional distress from work to home settings, whereas others (such as lack of control, lack of job meaningfulness and role conflict) have no such effects.

What characteristics of family life lead to spillover to work?

Considerably less attention has been given to the features of the non-work domain that are likely to impact on the individual in his or her working environment. Although marriage is generally considered to be a protective factor for men, early research tended to focus on the potential negative effects of marriage and children on women's job experiences and the difficulties they experience in combining work with family life. Research has focused on:

- *characteristics of the family*, for example: marital status, marital adjustment, presence, number and ages of children, child and elder care responsibilities;
- *characteristics of the spouse or partner*, for example: attitudes towards partners' work, and the extent to which availability and quality of emotional and practical support influence job-related outcomes (such as work performance or salary level) and experience of strain (such as role overload or job tension).

Examples of such research can be found in Table 10.2.

How do work roles and home roles conflict?

Whilst the above studies have helped describe some aspects of the relationship between work and home, they tell us little about the ways in which home and work interact. However, research on role conflict has helped shed some light on the processes whereby home and work affect each other. Greenhaus and Beutell (1985) reviewed a range of early studies which confirm the existence of time-based

Table 10.2   Characteristics of family life likely to impact on aspects of working life.

Family features	Work features	Reference
Marriage	Occupational attainment	Housenecht, Vaughan and Stratham (1987)
Good marital adjustment	Job satisfaction	Barling and Rosenbaum (1986)
Presence and number of children	Lower salary levels	Olson and Frieze (1987)
Satisfaction with childcare arrangements	Job satisfaction	Harrell and Ridley (1975)
Elder care responsibilities	Poorer work performance	Lee (1997)
Family cohesion	Positive social climate at work	Repetti (1987)
Time investment in family role	Lack of career development	Sekaran (1986)
Spouse's positive attitudes towards partner's work	Career development/work commitment	Sekaran (1986)
Availability of emotional/ practical support	Ability to deal with work stress	Repetti (1987)

conflict and its potential for negative outcomes. They suggest that time pressures may cause conflict either because they make it physically impossible for the person to participate in another role, or because, although physically present, they may be preoccupied. However, a more recent review (Barnett, 1998) failed to support the view that long working hours give rise to work–family conflict. They suggest that this may be because jobs that are often associated with long hours also have rewards such as high pay.

Whether or not time-based conflict leads to strain is likely to depend, to a large extent, on individual differences. One key factor that has been identified is the extent to which the individual is involved in their job or family (Frone and Rice, 1987). Research examining the influence of job and family involvement has yielded complex findings – not least because measuring involvement is itself not simple. For example, Frone and Rice distinguish between two types of family involvement: spouse and child involvement; similarly there is also the potential for job–spouse conflict and job–parent conflict. In each case the patterns of moderation are somewhat different. Later work by Frone, Russell and Cooper (1992a) proposes a model in which work–family and family–work conflict mediate the relationship between stressors/role involvement and psychological strain.

Williams and Alliger (1994) have extended this work by using a technique called experience sampling methodology (see Chapter 2). Participants are asked to give information about mood and activities *at that moment in time*, rather than providing retrospective accounts. Participants report experiences whenever prompted by a signal emitted from a pre-programmed watch (on eight occasions a day over a seven-day period). 'Role juggling' was assessed by asking people to report the extent to which they had been interrupted in the 30 minutes before the alarm, causing them to 'juggle' two tasks at once. They were also asked to indicate whether this had involved juggling work or family roles or both. Thus we get a very real indication of conflict. At the end of the day they were asked to rate their general perceptions of work–family conflict and measures of involvement. Findings revealed that daily levels of role involvement predicted individual's end-of-day ratings of conflict between work and family. The study also found some evidence of bi-directional spillover. Although the results indicated that unpleasant moods spill over from work to family and vice versa, it was generally perceived that work interfered with family to a greater extent than family interfered with work; i.e. moods and behaviours at work were more likely to influence moods and behaviours at home. However, females displayed stronger spillover effects (in terms of negative mood states) from family to work than their male counterparts.

Overall, studies on role involvement and conflict are generally consistent with those on spillover in reporting stronger effects of work on home than vice versa. Clearly role involvement is a factor to be considered in the study of role conflict. Evidence suggests that individuals who are highly involved with one role may find it difficult to put aside thoughts and feelings relating to that role, even when in a different situation.

Figure 10.1   (from MacEwen, Barling and Kelloway, 1992)

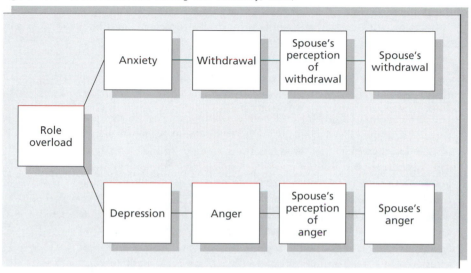

EFFECTS OF WORK ON FAMILY FUNCTIONING

How does work affect marital relationships?

In recent years, more sophisticated methodologies have been used to try to establish causation and examine processes. In this area, the use of daily questionnaires (referred to as diaries) has become an increasingly popular methodology (see Chapter 2). These are completed by couples over a period of weeks or even months. Using this type of methodology, researchers have found links between interpersonal problems or conflict at work and increased conflict at home (e.g. Bolger *et al.*, 1989). This is illustrated by a study by MacEwen, Barling and Kelloway (1992). They asked cohabiting student couples to complete daily diary questionnaires over a four-month period in order to examine the impact of role overload on couples' interactions. The study demonstrated that role overload was strongly related to anxiety but also correlated significantly with depression; anxiety predicted withdrawal from couples' interactions, whilst depression predicted anger in these interactions (see Figure 10.1).

The daily diary approach, although undoubtedly of value, has some drawbacks. As MacEwen, Barling and Kelloway's study indicated, data are often complex and analysis is a statistically challenging process. A further disadvantage of this method, which no doubt restricts the frequency with which it is used, is the fact that the process is highly demanding for participants, although it is unusual for daily reports to be collected for four months as in the study described above. Not surprisingly, it is difficult to recruit and retain participants for such studies, and

211

the kind of people willing to complete daily diaries may not be a typical sample of the population. Box 10.1 describes a study by Crouter *et al.* (1989) that examined the effects of work-related stressors on marital interactions and behaviour. As can be seen, participation was an onerous process.

Box 10.1   The demands of participating in longitudinal diary studies.

The demands that participants of longitudinal diary studies can face are well illustrated by the following study. Crouter *et al.* (1989) examined the impact of work-induced psychological states (i.e. stress, fatigue, arousal and depression) on subsequent marital interactions and involvement with household duties and leisure. Data were obtained from 29 young married, predominantly blue-collar, couples following the husbands' return from work. Findings indicated that husbands' reports of high levels of stress and fatigue after work were associated with their wives' reports of husbands' low involvement in household tasks. Similarly, higher levels of perceived work-related stress by husbands were associated with a greater number of subsequent negative marital interactions as reported by wives. These included social withdrawal, seeming bored, uninterested and distracted; expressions of anger such as shouting, and the use of sarcasm and criticism.

These are interesting findings; however, participation in this study was a time-consuming task and an intrusive process for the couples involved. The data collection process initially involved participant couples completing a variety of questionnaires and participating in face-to-face and telephone interviews in order to gather demographic information and assess lifestyles, relationships and family functioning. Subsequently, couples were telephoned separately on nine different evenings over a period of two or three weeks in order to systematically report on their family activities during the previous 24-hour period. Yet another data collection process assessed psychological spillover; husbands completed mood state questionnaires on their return from work; the objective being to link psychological state after work with wives' reports of their activities and moods. We can only speculate on the effects of the research process on marital interactions!

How does work affect parent–child relationships?

In comparison with studies that examine the impact of occupational stressors on marital functioning, those that focus on the effects of parental work stress on children are very rare. However, a few researchers have recently used longitudinal data to investigate how parental job-related stress and role conflict and/or overload impacts on younger and older children. The work of Repetti and her colleagues provides particularly good examples. Repetti and Wood (1997) studied 30 dyads (working mother with pre-school child) after work over five consecutive weekdays. The mothers made subjective ratings of the quality of mother–child interactions, but more objective ratings were also made by independent observers. Results indicated that mothers tended to be more emotionally and behaviourally withdrawn from their children on days where they reported a heavier workload, or where interpersonal conflict had occurred at work. This effect was particularly evident for mothers who were emotionally distressed, or who reported more Type A behaviours. In an earlier study, Repetti (1994) examined the quality of fathers' interactions with older children over three consecutive days and obtained results similar to the above, also underlining the impact of inter-personal conflict on family functioning. A relationship was also observed between father's stressful inter-personal experiences and subsequent expressions of anger to the child and greater use of discipline on the same day. Although the sample was small (i.e. 15 participants) and the ages of the 'children' ranged from 4 to 20, a particular strength of this study was that participants' assessments of the social climate at work were corroborated by co-workers' independent ratings.

Although little is yet known about the impact of parents' work on their children, the above findings are worrying. It is evident that more research is needed with larger samples over a longer time-scale that explores the effects of parental job-stress on children of all ages.

EFFECTS OF WORK ON OTHER FAMILY MEMBERS – TRANSMISSION/CROSSOVER

If stress can spill over into the home environment in ways described in the above section, then it is likely that it will also have an impact on the well-being of others sharing that environment. This hypothesised phenomenon has been labelled *stress contagion* (Wilkins, 1974), *crossover* (Bolger *et al.*, 1989) or *transmission* (Fletcher, 1991) and has been defined by Westman as: 'an inter-individual, inter-domain contagion of stress that is an unintended interpersonal process that manifests itself in certain ways' (Westman, 1997, p. 3). Thus it is postulated that one person's stressors and strains resulting from one domain (e.g. work) will impact on others in a different domain (usually, the family).

This area has not been as heavily researched as spillover and role conflict – perhaps because a good test of the transmission hypothesis is difficult. It may involve, for example, establishing that a measure of stressors (taken from one partner) is related to measures of strain (taken from the other). While it is not always easy to find couples that are both prepared to complete questionnaires (often over a period of time), this methodology offers the opportunity to overcome a number of the problems of cross-sectional studies which beset spillover and role conflict research. Unfortunately, conclusions are often drawn from data collected from one partner only (e.g. Pavett, 1986). It is also advisable to control for the partner's *own* life and/or work stress when investigating the transmission phenomenon, though this is seldom done. The importance of this practice is well illustrated by a study by Mitchell, Cronkite and Moos (1983). They found that transmission effects (e.g. depression) from the focal partner to the spouse disappeared when variables, such as the coping responses, extent of family support, life events and strain perceived by the spouse, were controlled.

Effects of men's work on their female partners

Research on transmission has focused predominantly on the effects of men's jobs on their wives. For example, Long and Voges (1987) found that wives of prison officers could accurately perceive the sources of their husbands' stress and that both husband and wife had reduced psychological well-being compared to norms. Research in this area has often focused on specialised occupations which are male-dominated, potentially highly stressful, and/or involve risk: e.g. police and correctional officers (Burke, Weir and Duwors, 1980; Jackson and Maslach, 1982), military personnel (Westman and Etzion, 1995; Morrison and Clements, 1997) and air traffic controllers (Repetti, 1989). Whilst findings from such studies may not be generalisable to the wider population, some work in this area has used more heterogeneous samples (e.g. Jones and Fletcher, 1993; Crossfield, 1999).

Burke, Weir and Duwors (1980) was one of the first studies of couples to collect data from both partners in order to look directly at the transmission effects of work stressors. Burke, Weir and Duwors found that specific occupational demands experienced by male administrators of 'correctional institutions' were correlated with greater levels of dissatisfaction and distress in their spouses, and that wives whose husbands experienced greater occupational demands were less likely to cope in constructive ways; e.g. they showed increased cigarette, alcohol and coffee consumption. Although this early study was undoubtedly influential, Barling (1990), however, suggests that Burke, Weir and Duwors' findings should be interpreted cautiously. The size of the relationship was modest, the number of correlations was large and the data was obtained at one point in time only, thus increasing the likelihood of error.

A more recent study by Morrison and Clements (1997) attempted to demonstrate causal relationships between one partner's job and the other partner's distress by using a longitudinal design where job characteristics were subject to controlled fluctuations. The sample comprised 82 Navy couples where the sea-going partner (male) was deployed during the course of the study, in comparison with controls who were shore-based. These conditions enabled assessment of the impact on partners of job characteristics that were both objective (i.e. the deployment) and subjective (i.e. male partners' perceptions of role ambiguity, role conflict and work overload). The well-being of partners was sampled on three occasions: before, during and after deployment. Results indicated that, after controlling for any work-related stress, physical illness and stressful life events that might have been experienced by the female partner who remained at home, the women's well-being fluctuated in direct relation to both deployment status and the sea-going partners' perceptions of their job characteristics. Whilst it could be argued that the sample was atypical, this study provided a fairly unique opportunity to explore the transmission process under relatively controlled but natural conditions. It also raises some interesting questions for further research: for example, why should it be that while the return home of the sea-going partner was associated with better mental health for their female partners, more physical health problems were also reported by females *after* their partners had returned home from deployment?

Bi-directional transmission in working couples

While the majority of studies in this area have examined the effects of men's work on women, a number have also looked at bi-directional effects in working couples. Jones and Fletcher (1993) in a cross-sectional study, examine bi-directional effects of one person's job on the other person's distress in couples who were both working. They found that while husbands' job stressors were related to levels of depression and anxiety in their wives (after controlling for wives' own job stressors), there were few relationships between wives' job stressors and husbands' strains.

Whilst this study reported few ill effects of women's work on men, there is how-ever some previous evidence that women's work may impact on men. Several studies found that females' employment status had small but significant negative effects on the well-being of their male partners (Burke and Weir, 1976; Staines, Pottic and Fudge, 1986; Parasuraman *et al.*, 1989; Kessler and McRae, 1982). For example, Galambos and Walters (1992) found that wives' long working hours were associated with husbands' anxiety and depression, but husbands' working hours and schedule inflexibility were unrelated to the psychological well-being of their wives.

Whether male to female or female to male transmission is the predominant effect is likely to be at least partially dependent on the relative job status of the individuals in the sample. Women, typically, have jobs which are of lower pay and prestige and therefore less central to family finances and security. Hence prob-lems in the male job inevitably have more impact on the family. This may explain the preponderance of transmission from male to female in studies such as Jones and Fletcher (1993) where this was not controlled. A recent replication of this study by Crossfield (1999) used data from 40 working couples who were more evenly matched in terms of salary and job status. Although, as anticipated, a relationship was found between male demands and female anxiety, this was only moderate. In contradiction to previous findings, however, the evidence of transmission from female to male partners was significantly stronger. Females' work demands were positively related to their male partners' levels of anxiety, depression and general negative mood, and females' negative perceptions of inter-personal work relationships were related to male depression. Moreover, evidence was provided of positive transmission; wives' job-related commitment and satisfaction was linked with their husbands' more positive general mood.

215

Westman and Etzion (1995) have also examined the transmission of burnout symptoms and coping resources between marital partners. Findings suggest a two-way relationship between male and female partners' sense of control and burnout; i.e. perceived control and burnout in one partner (conceptualised as physical, emotional and mental exhaustion) were positively related to those in the other, after controlling for their own job stress and resistance resources (that is social support from work and family).

Two-way transmission was also found by Chan and Margolin (1994) who gathered data from 529 working couples in order to investigate the spillover and transmission hypotheses as explanations for relationships between fatigue and negative mood experienced in the work and home domains. They asked couples to complete questionnaires on mood before leaving work and to write accounts of marital interactions in the evenings. The authors found evidence to support their hypotheses i.e. within-person *spillover* was demonstrated both by positive relationships between work-related fatigue and fatigue experienced later in the home, and by positive home affect predicting subsequent work moods. Support for *transmission* came from links between wives' fatigue and work mood and husbands' home affect.

Daily diaries have also been used by Jones and Fletcher (1996b) to try to shed light on the processes of transmission. This study examined the day-to-day fluctuations in perceptions of work and domestic stressors, physical and psychological well-being and mood. Although the study found that partners' moods tended to fluctuate in a similar manner, there was no evidence for a direct relationship between one individual's work stressors and their partner's. One difficulty highlighted in this study is the large number of potential relationships that could be examined, including temporal relationships (for example, will all work stressors affect individuals and their partners on the same day or might effects sometimes be delayed?). Jones and Fletcher further indicate that transmission may be the result of chronic stressors (such as overload) which may have long-term effects on partners' well-being and may not be reflected in daily fluctuations.

The study illustrates the fact that testing a hypothesis at different levels and looking at either proximal or more distal outcomes (see Chapter 2) can lead to different results. Relationships may not appear in daily fluctuations in mood which may be apparent when stressors and psychological strains are rated as a general summary over a longer period of time. Box 10.2 considers some more controversial studies on even more distal relationships between one partner's work and long-term health outcomes and mortality in partners.

Transmission to other family members

Few studies have looked at transmission processes involving other family members, particularly children. Thomson and Vaux (1986) is one such study which examined the transmission of stress within the family system. The sample consisted of 113 couples with one adolescent child. Whilst not specifically investigating work

Box 10.2   Can your work make your partner ill?

An extreme version of the transmission hypothesis is that proposed by Fletcher (1988, Jones and Fletcher, 1992). Fletcher suggested that not only could work have negative effects on an employee's physical well-being and mortality, but it can also make their partner ill and effect their partner's life expectancy. He drew this conclusion using data from occupational mortality statistics that indicated that some occupations have much higher mortality rates (both overall and for specific diseases) than others. For historic reasons, husband's occupations are recorded in married women's death certificates. This makes it possible to examine married women's mortality according to their husband's occupations. This analysis showed that where men work in specific occupations which have high mortality rates, women married to men in that occupation are also likely to have similarly high mortality rates, and for similar diseases. A range of alternative explanations for this finding have been considered and ruled out. For example, the relationship is not easily explained by social class or such factors as similar life style. The relationship is puzzling and remains largely unexplained (Jones and Fletcher, 1992). Fletcher (1988), therefore, proposed the controversial explanation that 'occupational risks are transmitted by psychological mechanisms to spouses through their shared domestic environment'. Spillover is one mechanism that might contribute to this transmission effect. However, this suggestion is speculative as the nature of the data does not enable any psychological mechanisms to be investigated.

The mortality data used in these studies are recorded in such a way that it is not possible to test whether male deaths are also related to female occupation. However, the suggestion that wives' work stressors may have health implications for husbands has been raised by evidence from the Framingham Heart Study (Haynes, Eaker and Feinleib, 1983). This found that men married to women with white collar jobs were over three times more likely to develop heart disease than those married to clerical workers, blue-collar workers or housewives (regardless of the husband's own social status and standard coronary risk factors). In addition, this study revealed that more highly educated wives whose husbands developed coronary heart disease were significantly more likely to have had a non-supportive boss and fewer job promotions. Haynes, Eaker and Feinleib suggest that such wives may have suffered stressful and frustrating work environments which influenced the home environment and impacted on their husbands' health. However, the validity of these findings has been criticised (Fletcher, 1991).

The conclusions of these studies may be open to a range of other explanations and are clearly speculative. They suggest relationships much more extreme than those found in other studies of transmission. However, if the findings are confirmed in further research, then it would appear that work has far greater implications for health than has been previously considered.

stressors, these authors looked for sources of stress that were *exogenous* to the family system (which included work, school, etc.) and *endogenous* stressors (which originated within the family). Thomson and Vaux found that exogenous stressors were 'imported' into the family and transmitted, such that the stressors reported by one family member were consistently associated with the distress of other family members. Micro-stressors (everyday demands) exerted a more powerful influence in this process than macro-stressors (life events). This study further reported that adolescents appeared to transmit more stress to their parents than vice versa, and that mothers bore the emotional brunt of this process. Mothers' reports of depressed mood and affect balance were related to both husbands' and children's stressors; however, whilst husbands were significantly affected by their wives' stressors they were less influenced by those of their children.

A more recent study of 48 couples by Almeida and McDonald (1998) came to different conclusions to those of Thomson and Vaux. Daily diaries which examined day-to-day variations in parent–adolescent conflict over 42 days indicated that parent–adolescent tension was particularly associated with mothers' work and home stress, which also predicted tension between father and adolescent. However, the results of these two studies cannot easily be compared; whilst Thomson and Vaux gathered data from all three family members (i.e. mother, father and child), Almeida and McDonald obtained reports of stressors and tension from parents only – children's perceptions were not assessed.

Potential mechanisms for transmission

Researchers have proposed various mechanisms for explaining the transmission phenomenon outlined above. These are summarised below:

- *Sympathy/empathy*. One suggestion is that strain might be directly transmitted from one partner to the other through some form of sympathetic reaction, or empathy, which increases the level of strain or distress perceived by the other partner (Riley and Eckenrode, 1986; Pavett, 1986). Using this explanation, one would expect that the closer the relationship the greater the concordance of strain that would be seen between partners.
- *Emotional contagion*. Hatfield, Caccioppo and Rapson (1994) have proposed that individuals transmit moods to each other in their day-to-day encounters by an automatic, unintentional and largely unconscious process – a form of 'social virus'. Gender differences have been found in the ability to 'send' and 'receive' emotions. Findings from studies of married couples by Noller (1982, 1987) suggest that men and women in happy marriages are skilled at sending emotional messages (mainly through facial expressions or gestures). However, Noller reports that wives find it easier than husbands to send, whilst husbands were less susceptible than wives at catching these emotions. Westman (1997) proposes that the contagion of negative affect may be particularly salient in

the transmission process, and Westman and Vinokur (1997) suggest that social undermining in the workplace may be especially implicated. Social undermining is defined as 'a behaviour directed toward the target person and displaying negative affect and negative evaluation of that person' (p. 4), and has been linked with depression (Vinokur and Van Rijn, 1993).

- *Modelling.* Westman and Etzion (1995) suggest that it is not possible to rule out modelling as an explanation, i.e. one partner imitates the other's reaction.

- *Transmission as a result of communication style.* According to this explanation, work-related stress experienced by one partner leads to strain, which results in a negative (or possibly conflictual) communication style or conversational content which, in turn, increases the other partner's stress and strain. Jones and Fletcher (1996b) and Crossfield (1999) suggest that the frequency and nature of couples' work-related discussion is likely to be a mediator in the transmission process.

- *Confounding by negative affect.* The relationship between one partner's stressors and strains and the self-reported well-being of the other partner might be due to the confounding effect of a third variable such as negative affect. This might be particularly an issue if individuals choose partners of similar disposition to themselves.

- *Confounding by social environment effects.* Westman (1997) suggests that what might appear to be a transmission or crossover effect between partners is merely the result of a shared social environment. Correlations between stress and strain within couples might be spurious, and at least partially attributable to common life events that the couple face and living conditions that they share.

- *Fatigue.* Work fatigue experienced by one partner, rather than emotional transmission, has been suggested as the key link between work-to-home spillover. Fatigue engendered by work is likely to have an impact on the individual's home mood as well as their partner's home affect (Chan and Margolin, 1994). An exhausted or depressed partner is unlikely to 'pull their weight' with domestic tasks and childcare, which might mean the other partner assuming a greater share of responsibility for these duties.

- *Social support.* Wives may act as 'stress buffers' for their husbands (Repetti, 1989) and tend to respond to husbands' work overload with supportive inter-personal behaviours (such as providing comfort, sympathy and appreciation) and more practical behaviours (such as increased housework) (Bolger *et al.*, 1989). Bolger *et al.* speculate that this may be why marriage is associated with greater emotional adjustment for husbands and not for wives. Most research on social support has focused on the recipient of this support, not on the provider. The role of the donor might be an important factor in the mechanisms of the transmission process that warrants further study (Westman, 1997). Recent studies have suggested that the erosion of support from wives in dual career couples may also be a factor implicated in the transmission of wives' work stressors to men.

219

SUMMARY

Overall, this chapter has reviewed psychological methods for conceptualising home–work relationships and presented evidence to suggest that the effects of work do spill over into the home environment and vice versa. Research also highlights the impact of work on family functioning and marital relationships. Potential mechanisms for the transmission process have been highlighted, several of which have not been researched in any depth. Many questions still remain to be answered about the extent of, and mechanism for, transmission of affect. New methodologies such as experience sampling techniques offer new possibilities. However, methodological developments in this area, as in many others, are leaping ahead of theoretical advances. Currently, many studies are exploratory and offer insights that are fragmentary and difficult to integrate and compare because of the diverse variables that are used. Thus it becomes difficult to build and extend a knowledge structure.

Despite the research challenges of this area, it is also an area of potential importance at a time when trends towards long hours and flexible working may mean that the boundaries between home and work become increasingly blurred.

PART 5

STRESS REDUCTION STRATEGIES

This section considers some of the many interventions that have been suggested to tackle the problem of stress both in the workplace and elsewhere. This includes interventions designed to change the environment (the stressor), those designed to change individual difference factors (e.g. by changing the individual's ability to cope) and those aimed at treating the individual suffering ill effects (e.g. by reducing levels of anxiety). Thus the chapter encompasses interventions aimed at removing stressors, various stress management training techniques and counselling schemes. The evidence related to the efficacy of these approaches is considered. Some less well-evaluated approaches such as neuro-linguistic programming are also briefly discussed.

The second part of the chapter discusses some specific intervention approaches developed to deal with particularly stressful situations including undergoing uncomfortable medical procedures or dealing with the stress of cancer. In the latter case this includes controversial work investigating whether such interventions may have far-reaching impacts in terms of increasing longevity.

STRESS INTERVENTIONS

This chapter examines the variety of interventions that have been designed to combat stress. This includes interventions designed to prevent stress by removing stressors, as well as stress management training courses and counselling. Do these interventions work?

IT should be apparent from the research presented in earlier chapters that stress covers a multitude of possible symptoms and that many different psychological and environmental factors have been implicated as causes. In the light of this perhaps we should not be surprised that many different interventions have been designed to reduce stress.

Despite the multi-faceted nature of stress, many of the interventions that have been reported appear to focus on particular symptoms using relatively narrow treatment regimes. We shall see that such interventions are unlikely to do more than provide some temporary relief of symptoms rather than tackling the root cause of the problem. However we should not dismiss such interventions on this basis, as in many situations it is not possible to attempt more extensive interventions aimed at removing stressors. Given the breadth of the construct of stress, even if some environmental stressors could be removed, it is hard to imagine a single intervention that could successfully tackle and eliminate 'stress'. Figure 11.1 illustrates the problem confronting the practitioner working in the stress intervention field.

There is no limit to the number of remedies that have been suggested for stress. These range from off-the-shelf products such as toiletries containing aromatherapy oils to a range of treatments including therapies based on complimentary medicine or psychotherapy, as well as activities such as juggling. There is little evidence related to some of these approaches. This chapter will focus predominantly on those interventions that have

Figure 11.1   The problem of addressing stress in an intervention.

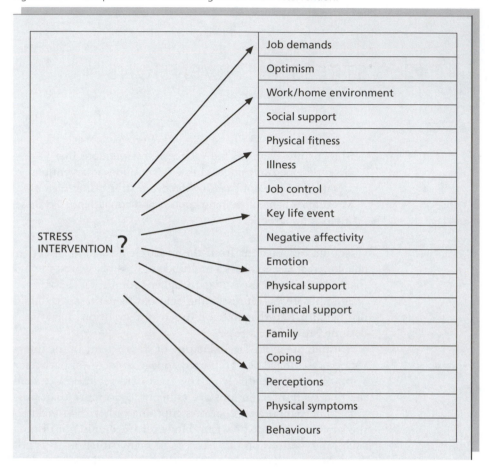

been to some extent evaluated. Examples will be drawn from two main areas where substantial research has been conducted, that is, the workplace and the medical setting.

The interventions discussed in this chapter can be viewed in terms of the three categories of stress reduction methods suggested by Murphy (1996).

- *Primary prevention*. This involves reducing the stressor at the source. This would include environmental interventions to remove stressors either in the workplace or elsewhere, for example by job redesign.
- *Secondary prevention*. This involves reducing the severity of symptoms before they lead to more serious problems. Stress management training (SMT) courses would come into this category.

- *Tertiary prevention*. This is arguably not so much prevention as treatment, as it involves such interventions as counselling aimed at alleviating a problem once it has occurred. In the workplace setting this is the most common approach.

Williamson (1994a, b), alternatively, focuses more specifically on the content of the technique, and argues that there are four main types of interventions:

- Changing the wider environment. This corresponds to primary prevention.
- Assisting people to reconstruct their views about particular situations or experiences. This might include cognitive techniques such as positive thinking.
- Assisting people to cope with particular stressors in the short or long term. Examples here might include interventions focusing on relaxing as a way of coping with a medical treatment or assertiveness training to deal with difficult people at work.
- Assisting people to adopt lifestyles that improve their ability to withstand the pressure of stressors. Exercise would come into this category.

The first section of this chapter will consider workplace and community interventions for dealing with the general stressors of life and work. Examples of primary, secondary and tertiary prevention methods will be considered. The particular focus on work stress reflects the increase in interest amongst employers in the use of stress management techniques. This reflects both an increased awareness of stress as a physical/psychological problem and a growing concern about legal liability.

The second half of the chapter moves on to look at some more specific interventions, developed to deal with the particular stressors of medical and surgical treatment and the extreme stress of the cancer sufferer.

WORKPLACE AND COMMUNITY INTERVENTIONS

Primary prevention

The removal of stressors where possible would appear to be both sensible and ethically desirable, yet the literature on stress management relating to primary prevention is surprisingly sparse, and where it exists relates primarily to the workplace. In the community at large, it is not difficult to think of examples of social policy changes that have been implemented with an intention to reduce psychological stress. For example, policies such as the abandonment of large residential institutions or asylums and the introduction of facilities to allow children to stay with parents in hospital can be seen in this light. Such changes drew on social science theory and research. However, such research was not couched in terms of stressors and stress management but rather in terms of theories of attachment or deprivation.

We therefore need to turn to the literature on work stress for examples of explicit stressor reduction interventions. In the workplace it is possible to envisage a wide range of interventions as having some role in primary prevention and reducing stressors. These potentially encompass most aspects of management (from recruitment and selection, supervision, staff development and health and safety issues).

Newman and Beehr (1979) suggest three possible types of primary intervention to reduce workplace stressors:

* changing organisational characteristics, e.g. training or selection procedures;
* changing role characteristics, e.g. increasing employees' participation in decisions;
* changing task characteristics, e.g. increasing method and timing control, see Chapter 9).

Evidence points to there being few primary interventions compared to secondary or tertiary interventions (Earnshaw and Cooper, 1996). Where they do exist they are primarily in the last two of Newman and Beehr's categories.

Before considering some specific examples of interventions, it is worth giving some consideration to why we have spent so long developing theories and conducting research pinpointing the importance of certain work stressors (as discussed in Chapter 9), only to find that in practice this information seems to be largely ignored. While much research is contradictory, there is now mounting evidence for the damaging effects on health of employment in work that is low in control. A risk factor of this nature, should, one would imagine, be taken seriously and lead to pressure on employers to increase control in the workplace. Instead, existing literature does not suggest any increase in the number of interventions to increase control, despite the rhetoric of empowerment. This may be because primary interventions are both difficult and costly to set up and difficult to evaluate. A further factor is that current stress theory does not offer good practical advice about how to intervene. For example, we may know that in general people seem to benefit from having control at work, but increasing control can mean many different things. We know little about what kind of control may be helpful and in what circumstances. We also know little about how one person's increased control may impinge on those around them, for example, increasing an employee's control may mean their supervisor has reduced control.

Where researchers have tried to apply theoretical models, the practical difficulties they encounter make it difficult to draw firm conclusions from even the most well-designed studies. For example, in the US, Landsbergis and Vivona-Vaughan (1995) used an intervention based on a range of approaches, including Karasek's model, to reduce stress in a public service agency. Two matched pairs of departments were assigned to either a treatment or a waiting list control group. The intervention involved employees participating in problem solving committees. They identified stressors and developed action plans to reduce stressors and encouraged and assisted management to implement changes. Priority stressors included such factors as uneven or repetitive workload and poor communication. At the end of one year there were mixed results in one department and negative or negligible impact in the other. It seems likely that the failure of the intervention can be attributed to the fact that the intervention was only department wide while workers were also affected by a range of organisational changes. In this case these included a major agency reorganisation without any employee or union involvement. This produced frustration and disappointment. Both departments lost directors who had supported the changes and some planned changes were not completed. This study clearly demonstrates the wide range of impediments to this kind of organisational change.

One of the few studies to demonstrate a positive impact of programmes to reduce work stressors is by Rose, Jones and Fletcher (1998). This is an example of a stress management programme being designed specifically to address the needs of a particular occupational group (direct care health staff). In their study, stress was measured using theoretically driven concepts of demands, supports and constraints. The intervention programme resulted in reduced anxiety and increased perceptions of social support in the treatment group compared to controls. Rose, Jones and Fletcher also managed to get some behavioural measures pre- and post-training that indicated that the treatment group increased their positive interactions and assistance given to clients. However, effects were small in this study and the treatment and control groups were not matched at the outset.

Overall, while some studies have succeeded in demonstrating limited improvements in mental health as a result of organisational changes (Rose, Jones and Fletcher, 1998; Wall and Clegg, 1981), many have also failed to do so (Kemp *et al.*, 1983). Some have found that while perception of pressure is reduced, measures of psychological well-being (such as the GHQ) are not reduced, e.g. Wall *et al.* (1990b).

In the face of this evidence it is perhaps not surprising that many turn to the easier strategies of secondary or tertiary interventions.

Secondary prevention

Stress management training courses are the clearest example of secondary prevention. Such courses may be workplace based or provided by colleges or other organisations in the community. Typically they incorporate a range of elements including information about stressors, cognitive strategies and relaxation but may also include aspects of other approaches, such as meditation, which are considered separately in the sections below.

Stress management training (SMT)

Stress management training is designed to equip people with a series of techniques that are designed to help prevent or minimise 'stress'. Sending employees on stress management training (SMT) courses is a measure frequently adopted by employers. In an Australian survey of 504 training managers (Bright, Gillam and Balaam, 1997), 32% said that they conducted stress management training courses. Furthermore, these trainers reported that even if they were not personally involved in stress management training some 42% of companies they work for conduct stress management training.

The literature on stress management training is subject to a number of limitations, which it shares with the evaluations of other types of training generally. There are few studies that use proper control groups, and much of the available evidence comes from those who conducted the training, who are therefore not strictly independent. With these shortcomings in mind, however, there does now appear to be mounting evidence to suggest that some of these programmes do have a small but positive impact on participants.

A typical course might include a diverse range of techniques including training about stressors, relaxation (or meditation) techniques and assertiveness (see Box 11.1). A key element is also likely to be the use of cognitive-behavioural techniques, based on the view that stress is often caused by negative 'self-talks'. Training would focus on replacing these with more positive internal dialogues. In terms of Lazarus' approach to stress, such techniques can be seen as having an impact on both appraisal and coping stages (see Chapter 7). A classic study by Ganster *et al.* (1982) provided a very thorough evaluation of a stress management programme in an American social services agency. Seventy-nine public service employees were randomly assigned to treatment and control groups (the control group were given the same training but later on). Training involved 16 hours of group activity over 8 weeks. The training was typical of many stress management training courses in consisting of a combination of different treatments. In this case this involved four sessions based around cognitive strategies involving recognising the emotional and physiological responses to stressful events at work, evaluating objective consequences of stressors and replacing self-defeating cognitions with more positive responses. The remainder of the sessions concentrated on various relaxation techniques.

The researchers found that after 16 hours of training, there were small reductions in depression, anxiety and adrenaline secretion in participants compared with a control group. These changes were maintained four months later. There has, as yet, been insufficient research to identify which of the diverse elements are particularly effective and what amount of training may be required to have a sustained effect. However, Ganster *et al.* suggest that many commercially available training programmes offer courses that are no more than half a day and are unlikely to produce noticeable improvements.

More recently, Garcia-Vera, Labrador and Sanz (1997) conducted an evaluation of a stress management programme aimed at reducing hypertension. Twenty-two patients with hypertension received a programme based on education, relaxation and problem-solving, and a further 21 patients were put on a waiting list. Significantly

Box 11.1   Five common components of stress management courses.

Relaxation
Relaxation involves attempting to 'slow down' and perhaps entering into a semi-sleeplike or hypnotic state. Exercises to achieve this might involve deep breathing, positive imagery, reducing external stimuli (e.g. darkening the room, lying down) or introducing soothing stimuli such as gentle music, pleasant aromas, pleasant pictures and photographs. Biofeedback devices are also sometimes used to give the individual feedback about physiological functions such as heart rate, muscle tension, etc.

Meditation
Meditation is another technique that attempts to calm the individual by focusing their thoughts on non-stressful stimuli. The aim of meditation is to focus so strongly on one particular stimuli that all other thoughts are shut out. The claim is that such a technique can provide the user with respite from their stressors, and so they can address them afresh with more vitality after the meditation session.

Cognitive restructuring
This is a cognitive behavioural technique that involves individuals changing the way they think about issues that make them stressed. This can take the form of trying to replace negative or irrational thoughts with more positive and constructive ones. The techniques are related to the well-established and researched cognitive behaviour therapy model used by many clinical psychologists in treating a range of behavioural problems.

Assertiveness training
Assertiveness training is a series of techniques aimed to improve a person's interaction with others, so that they are better able to manage the demands placed upon them by others, for instance, being able to say no to requests from other people. Thus assertiveness training aims to help people better manage demands, and it also aims to boost control by improving a person's chances of having their say.

Stress inoculation training (Meichenbaum, 1985)
This is an approach that combines a range of techniques including relaxation and cognitive strategies. It works on the principle that the individual can develop coping strategies and other techniques that will allow them to withstand more severe stressors in the future. In the first phase of the training, patients are taught the rationale of the method and given information about the effects of cognition on behaviour. In phase two they are taught a number coping techniques (including cognitive restructuring) and in the third phase they rehearse these techniques.

more patients in the treatment group achieved a reduction in blood pressure greater than 5 mm of mercury. In addition, significantly more patients achieved a normotensive (i.e. normal) level of blood pressure. Although the effects were smaller for self-measured blood pressure, the differences were still significant and remained so after four months. In another report Garcia-Vera, Sanz and Labrador (1998) reported that individuals in the treatment group improved their problem solving abilities.

While a number of studies have looked at the success of SMT, few have looked at the specific characteristics of the intervention that contribute to that success. This includes factors such as *leadership*, the *size* of the group and the specific *content*. Information about such factors may be crucial for those looking to run such interventions and some clues can be found from the literature.

* *Leadership*. Most stress management training programmes are led by a trainer or expert in the field. However, this may not be necessary. Fontana *et al.* (1999) suggest that peers may also successfully lead groups. They report on a controlled study of a peer-led stress inoculation programme. The 18 male teenagers in the treatment group received six sessions of peer-led stress inoculation, compared to 18 individuals in a control group. The treatment led to lower heart rate, and state anxiety compared to the controls immediately after the six sessions, and the heart rates remained lower six months later.
* *Size*. We know little about the optimum size of a group but Brown *et al.* (1998) compared large one-off public workshop-style stress management one-day programmes with small weekly stress training groups for referred clients. Thirty-six people in large groups and the same number in small groups were compared to a control group of 52 people who were on a waiting list for group membership. Counter-intuitively, the large group one-day programme proved to be as effective as the small weekly sessions. Given the large literature on small group counselling, this one result should be treated with caution, but it does provide a further degree of general support for the stress management training programme approach.
* *Content*. Most courses have a range of different types of approach but evaluation studies usually evaluate the entire course. This means that if they are successful, we do not know why. Unfortunately, where researchers have compared different types of stress management strategy, they have found that all elements have tended to find similar outcomes (e.g. Sallis *et al.*, 1987; Higgins, 1986; see also Box 11.2). Reynolds, Taylor and Shapiro (1993a) refer to this phenomenon as the 'equivalence paradox'. One possibility is that all components are effective because of some common factor such as social support. Reynolds *et al.*, however, suggest that different components do have differential effects. They designed a course consisting of six two-hour

workshops each consisting of a different element (e.g. relaxation, assertiveness, cognitive strategies, etc.). After each session participants rated the impacts on a range of dimensions including experience of insight, support or problem definition. They found that different components did have different impacts. They suggest therefore that a range of different approaches may be effective via different mechanisms, rather than some feature they share in common.

Overall, therefore, it appears that stress management courses can have at least small short-term effects on well-being. Exactly what it is about them that helps is not yet clear.

Meditation

Meditation is a technique that is sometimes used for stress management, either alone or together with other strategies. Essentially meditation is assumed to work by relaxing the individual. Meditation can take a variety of different forms, but common to most approaches are a series of techniques that are aimed at focusing attention away from immediate worries or concerns. This may be achieved through focusing all of one's attention on a neutral or relaxing stimulus.

Murphy (1996) reviews four studies from the 1970s and 1980s evaluating meditation as an intervention in the workplace. He reports uniformly positive results with outcomes including reduced blood pressure, anxiety and somatic complaints following meditation. More recent research by Winzelberg and Luskin (1999) compared trainee teachers who were allocated to either meditation training or a control group. After four 45-minute meditation training sessions, the participants reported less gastronomic distress, and less emotional and behavioural manifestations of stress compared to the control group.

Despite these positive findings meditation has not proved a popular strategy for stress reduction (Murphy, 1996). This may be because the association of meditation with Eastern religions and with alternative lifestyles is not seen as consistent with the ethos of modern organisations.

Exercise

Exercise as a form of stress management is becoming increasingly popular. A number of possible benefits of exercise for psychological well-being as well as physical health have been widely promoted and investigated by researchers. Research has focused on two types of hypothesis. The first suggests that exercise may have protective effects in terms of increasing physiological stress resistance. Fit individuals have less sympathetic nervous system activation to a physical workload than the unfit, including less adrenaline secretion and lower increases in heart rate.

231

It has therefore been hypothesised that this may also have a beneficial impact on responsivity to stress (Van Doornen, de Geus and Orlbeke, 1988). However, the many studies that exist show conflicting results. De Geus and Van Doornen (1993) review laboratory studies and conclude that intensive fitness programmes of up to eight months do not change physiological reactivity to stress. However, they do reduce absolute levels of heart rate and blood pressure, which are likely to protect against the impact of stressors on health. Thus, while a fit individual may show as great an increase in pulse and blood pressure in the face of stressors as the unfit person, he or she will be starting from a lower base line. Kremer and Skully (1994) similarly conclude that there is little evidence for fitness related improvements in stress reactivity in response to laboratory stressors. However, they suggest that this may not be true of real life stressors.

The second hypothesis is that exercise has psychological benefits in terms of improving psychological well-being in terms of moods and emotions. Studies looking at the psychological benefits of exercise range from those looking at the effects of one bout of exercise on mood (often measured using the POMS rating scale, described in Chapter 2), to those looking at the effects of regular exercise on anxiety and depression in clinical populations.

Many studies and a number of reviews of this research now exist (e.g. Tuson and Sinyor, 1993). A recent review by Biddle (2000) concludes that moderate levels of physical activity are consistently associated with improved mood. This includes reduced levels of tension, depressed mood, fatigue, confusion and to a small extent anger, as well as increased feelings of vigour. However, he also makes the point that many studies are flawed. We cannot be sure that the association is causal and we do not yet understand the mechanisms. Similar findings in relations to anxiety are reported in a review by Taylor, A. (2000), and self-esteem (Fox, 2000).

Somewhat stronger evidence exists in relation to depression (e.g. Craft and Landers, 1999; Mutrie, 2000). Mutrie's review concludes that numerous studies have found that exercise can result in reductions in depression, and that the effect can be comparable to psychotherapeutic interventions.

A popular explanation for the positive psychological effects of exercise is that they can be attributed to the effect of endorphins. These are opiate-like chemicals that are associated with elevated mood. Exercise is associated with raised levels of endorphins in the blood stream. Hence they appear to offer an explanation of the observed exercise related mood improvements. They have also become associated with the notion of 'exercise addiction'. However, Kremer and Skully (1994) point out that this argument is flawed. They suggest that whilst there is evidence that levels of endorphins rise after exercise, this is observed in the blood stream rather than the brain itself. As endorphins cannot cross the blood-brain barrier, it seems unlikely that this effects psychological state.

A range of alternative explanations has been suggested. Physiological explanations include the effects of exercise on core temperature and effects on neurotransmitters (e.g. see Murphy, 1994). Psychological explanations include exercise functioning as a distractor, exercise bringing about improvements in self-confidence and self-esteem or improving social support. Further research is inevitably needed.

However, research in this area is difficult, not least because people cannot be made to exercise. Adherence is a problem and typically more than 50% drop out of any exercise intervention (Dishman, 1982). This makes it very difficult to be sure that the effects of exercise are not attributable to individual differences, for example, in personality, between people who exercise and those who do not. This often makes it difficult to draw conclusions from studies. This is illustrated by Jex (1991), in his evaluation of the benefits of exercise for work stress. He found that studies generally report positive results. However, there may be alternative explanations for the findings. Jex proposes that part of the difficulty in establishing the link between exercise and psychological benefits has been the failure to consider the role of individual difference variables. Specifically, those who are self-motivated, optimistic, have internal locus of control and are low in negative affectivity (see Chapter 6) are more likely to exercise and more likely to report more positive reactions to work.

Nevertheless, the results of research in this area are at least encouraging and suggest the potential of exercise as a stress management intervention. Long and Flood (1993) suggest that exercise can be used as a coping strategy viewed in terms of Lazarus' theory. Thus it may be used as an emotion focused coping strategy, for example, because of its distracting or relaxing effects. It may also act as a coping resource influencing primary appraisal of stressors, for example, because of its effects on self-esteem and feelings of confidence. How exercise compares with other stress management strategies is as yet unclear, A study in Box 11.2 looks at this issue in the work setting.

Alternative strategies

The area of stress management has inevitably spawned many alternative approaches. Because of the breadth of the concept of stress, it is likely that many of the suggested stress-reducing activities may be helpful for some of the difficulties people are experiencing. Activities such as juggling may be distracting, alternative therapies such as laughter therapy may at the very least offer social support. Many strategies recommended in the media, however, have had little evaluation. Two strategies, neuro-linguistic programming and sunlight, are discussed further below.

Broadly speaking *neuro-linguistic programming (NLP)* is a set of beliefs concerning the relationship between thinking and communication. It makes a series of assumptions about mental capacity and claims that rapid acceleration in learning are possible by following the NLP techniques. Many of the techniques associated with rapid learning tend to emphasise some form of relaxation technique (see Depamo and Job, 1990). Given the central role of relaxation techniques, it is plausible that these approaches may provide some benefits. Konefal and Duncan (1998) evaluated a 21-day residential training course using NLP techniques to

Box 11.2   Comparing the effects of exercise, relaxation and management skills training on stress in workers.

Bruning and Frew (1987) conducted a study of the impact of different stress reduction interventions used by managers in a large manufacturing organisation. The organisation in which the study was completed did not appear to have any particular work stress problems, and none were identified by the managers. They recruited their participants at a lunch time seminar on stress at work. Sixty-two people were included in the final study sample, a further 21 having withdrawn during the study for personal or job-related reasons.

Participants were randomly allocated into one of four groups of 15 or 16. The four groups consisted of management skills training, meditation, exercise and a control group. Management skills training consisted of encouraging participants to explore work and personal values and then to set personal goals. Participants were given training in goal setting, goal prioritisation, communication, listening skills, skill development and empathy.

The meditation group had to sit quietly and meditate for 15–20 minutes once or twice a day. After calming and relaxing their bodies, participants listened to meditation sounds to assist them in focusing. The exercise group were instructed to do 30 minutes of aerobic exercise three times per week, on alternate days. The type of exercise was up to the individual's discretion and included running, walking, cycling, etc. Their goal was to raise their pulse rate by 15% of their usual resting pulse rate. All the above groups received 10–12 hours of training. The control group were given some general information pertaining to stress.

After 13 weeks three original groups were split and assigned a second treatment (with a further 10–12 hours of training). At this point the control group had to be abandoned. Due to pressure from the participants, those in this group were given all three types of training. Physiological measures (including blood pressure and pulse rates) were taken at the outset and at two-week intervals throughout the study.

Over a period of six months, all three intervention methods had led to a significant reduction in pulse and systolic blood pressure compared to the control group but there were no significant differences between the different interventions themselves. The dual combinations also led to a reduction in pulse and blood pressure but again no combination was significantly superior to the others. Results suggest that a range of interventions in the workplace may have some benefits.

reduce social anxiety. They found scores for social anxiety were reduced both after training and at six-months' follow-up; however, there was no control group in this study. Currently, there seems to be no evidence based on rigorously conducted and controlled studies.

Sunlight has been linked to mood disorders, and in particular, seasonally affective disorder (SAD), a condition regarded as more likely to occur in the Northern Hemisphere countries where sunlight is severely limited at different times of the year, e.g. countries such as the United Kingdom and Scandinavian countries. Whilst there is evidence linking sunlight to depression (e.g. Wehr and Rosenthal, 1989), the relationship is not clearly understood. For example, there are no clear links with latitude and it has been suggested that socio-cultural context, genetic predisposition and climate may be important (Mersch *et al.*, 1999). Light therapy does appear to have benefits (Terman *et al.*, 1989) but the underlying physiological mechanisms are unclear. It has also been suggested that many studies are flawed by using retrospective measures which may be biased by people's beliefs and that the number of people genuinely affected by SAD may be small (Hardt and Gerbershagen, 1999).

Any stress reduction benefits of sunlight may also be unrelated to SAD. Sunshine is generally regarded as pleasurable and creates opportunities for relaxation and distraction that are highly likely to improve mood and perceptions of well-being.

Self-help books

Probably one of the most popular approaches to stress management is the self-help book and there has been a proliferation of titles available in recent years written by both lay people and by psychologists. The use of written materials for therapeutic purposes is also sometimes called bibliotherapy. Stress management is only one of the many topics addressed by this literature. Much of the information and guidance in the popular self-help literature is not based on research findings. Rosen (1987) has been particularly critical of this development suggesting that psychologists have 'published untested material, advanced exaggerated claims and accepted the use of misleading titles that encourage unrealistic expectations'. However, despite this, self-help literature is extremely popular among both lay people and health professionals (Fried, 1994). Starker (1986), for example, found that almost 90% of psychologists and 60% of psychiatrists in a US sample recommend such books.

There are a few studies showing benefits for various forms of self-help literature (see Fried, 1994) but little specifically related to stress management. However, Register *et al.* (1991), found that stress management materials were effective in reducing test anxiety in college students. Written materials that focused on relaxation, coping strategies and 'positive self-talk' were given to two treatment groups of students. These materials were to be used over a four-week period during which participants were asked to record answers to questions about the content. One of the treatment groups was also contacted weekly by a therapist to try to increase adherence to the materials. Measures of anxiety and worry were reduced in the treatment group compared to control groups and these improvements were maintained one month later, though therapist's phone calls made no difference.

Overall, given the amount of self-help literature published, we really know little about whether it helps and, if so, in what circumstances it can be useful. However, the development of the internet means there are now also a range of stress management websites and the scope for this kind of approach is expanding.

Summary

Overall, there is evidence that some interventions (particularly stress management training courses, relaxation, meditation and exercise) can show some short-term benefits. Less is known about long-term effects. It is also not clear how these approaches work or which is most effective.

In the absence of hard evidence, the type of interventions commonly used is likely to depend greatly on experts' perceptions of which is most effective. Bellarosa and Chen (1997) surveyed 96 stress management subject matter experts who were asked to review six widely used stress management interventions (relaxation, physical fitness, cognitive restructuring, meditation, assertiveness training and stress inoculation) in terms of practicality and effectiveness. Relaxation was rated as the most practical technique, whereas exercise was seen as the most effective. Meditation was poorly rated in terms of practicality and effectiveness as a technique to manage stress.

Tertiary prevention – counselling

Over the past few years there has been a growth in the number of organisations providing counselling services for their employees. These may take the form of in-house confidential counselling services, as provided by some large organisations such as the Post Office (Cooper and Sadri, 1995), perhaps located within personnel or occupational health departments. Alternatively, a number of independent companies offering Employee Advice Programmes (often referred to as EAPs) are increasingly being used to provide counselling services. Typically, the latter offer advice and counselling for a wide range of problems, from minor consumer or legal issues to more serious psychological problems.

For EAPs to be effective it is widely accepted that there must be commitment and support from management for the goals of the EAP. Employees need to be reassured as to the role and limits of the EAP through a clear set of written policies including confidentiality, which may require close cooperation with unions. Within the organisation EAP effectiveness can be enhanced if supervisors are given training to spot the tell-tale signs of stress. The EAP needs to have the capability to refer clients with serious problems to the appropriate services and records need to be kept so the EAP can be appropriately evaluated.

Given all this interest in EAPs there is little hard evidence in the form of properly controlled studies to support them. In terms of financial savings a number of studies in the states have indicated that EAPs are a worthwhile investment. For example, the large McDonnell-Douglas (1989) study looked at costs of healthcare claims and absenteeism over a four-year period before and after an EAP intervention. Each person attending counselling was matched on demographic variables with other employees who formed a control group. They found an overall saving of US$5.1 million for those attending the EAP compared with controls.

There remain calls for more evidence, based on well-controlled studies. However, Highley-Marchington and Cooper (1997a) argue that it is virtually impossible to randomly allocate people to workplace counselling schemes which operate on the basis of self-referral and immediate access to counselling. They conducted an evaluation of EAPs in the UK (Highley-Marchington and Cooper; 1997b) involving clients of nine different counselling services collecting data pre-counselling, post-counselling and three-to-six months later. The study used an unmatched control group of people not referring themselves for counselling. However, as they point out, such a control is not ideal as those not seeking help are more likely to be psychologically healthy to begin with and therefore less likely to improve. They found that mental and physical well-being and absenteeism of those counselled improved between the pre- and post-counselling time points, although there was no change in job satisfaction or perception of stress at work. The control group showed no changes on any of these variables over the same time period. A further survey of workplace counsellors by Highley and Cooper (1996) also suggests that the quality of counselling is likely to vary greatly as they found that 11% of counsellors had no formal counselling qualifications.

Similar methodological problems beset the study of in-house counselling schemes. For example, an evaluation of a Post Office counselling scheme in the UK showed improvements in psychological well-being and sickness-absence after counselling though no significant changes in job satisfaction or organisational commitment were found (Cooper and Sadri, 1995). While this study did have a control group, it was unfortunately not strictly comparable, having better levels of well-being and lower levels of absence. A more rigorously designed and controlled study by Firth and Shapiro (1986) found large reductions in symptoms after 16 hours of therapy for work-related distress. This study compared two different types of therapy: prescriptive therapy (utilising cognitive-behavioural approaches similar to those often used in stress management training), and exploratory (relationship oriented) therapy. While both approaches produced a reduction in distress, the reduction in overall symptoms was greater amongst those who had prescriptive therapy. Firth and Shapiro suggest that 16 hours spent treating distressed individuals may be a more useful and cost-effective way of stress management than an equivalent time providing stress management training as a preventative measure.

In recent years, the development of the world-wide web creates both new opportunities and new problems. Already it is possible to find employee advisory and counselling programmes on the internet, by which means people can discuss problems on line with a counsellor, either by email or by meeting in a chat room. The fee may be based on a set fee for 15 minutes of keyboard work, for example.

Clearly the quality of such services is likely to be highly variable. As yet little is known about whether the internet could provide an acceptable substitute for face-to-face counselling. However, it is likely that the ease of access and anonymity of this form of therapy may appeal to people who might hesitate to seek conventional therapy.

Workplace and community interventions – the way forward

It is clear that there is a big growth in stress management interventions within organisations. Most are secondary or tertiary and few are based on good assessment of need or subject to rigorous evaluation. It is often stated that the most ethical and desirable approach is to remove the stressors, that is to use primary prevention (e.g. Ganster *et al.*, 1982). Although such approaches are seldom used in practice, many writers remain optimistic about their benefits. For example, Cooper and Cartwright (1994) reviewed the literature and, despite citing few examples of stressor reduction interventions leading to improved psychological well-being, they claim:

> As has been hopefully demonstrated, primary level interventions and the diagnostic stress audit is a potentially more cost-effective and more focused way of reducing stress in the workplace. It is an old but true adage that 'prevention is better than cure'. (p. 468)

One study by Reynolds (1997) actually compared a primary with a tertiary intervention. She used a quasi-experimental design to compare an organisational intervention (increasing employees' control) with a counselling intervention and a non-intervention control. She found that only the counselling service was effective in reducing psychological and physical symptoms.

Briner and Reynolds (1999) are very critical of the tendency in the occupational stress literature to continue to advocate organisation level (primary) remedies as a simple answer. They review existing evidence and suggest that the effects of such interventions on illness, performance and absence are either 'weak (explaining 2–3% of the variance), or non-existent, or difficult to interpret causally'. This however, should not be taken as indicating that individual interventions are more effective, rather, they suggest that the choice should be based on thorough assessment. Briner and Reynolds (1999) conclude that it is perhaps time that we redirected energies away from such interventions and instead work towards answering basic theoretical and empirical questions about occupational stress and that until we

> know and understand the causes of negative employee states and behaviors, and know and understand how and if organizational interventions work, our interventions will continue to be simple and clear – but also hopelessly wrong. (p. 15)

Briner (1997) further advocates the need for an evidence-based approach to stress intervention based on good research designs that can show causal relationships. He suggests more sophisticated measurements may show that job conditions (such as autonomy) affect different people in different ways and hence more sophisticated interventions may be needed.

INTERVENTIONS IN THE MEDICAL CONTEXT

The medical environment is fraught with stressors both acute and chronic. These range from going to the dentist or enduring an unpleasant investigative procedure to facing a diagnosis of cancer or living with coronary heart disease. In addition, the many new techniques of genetic screening mean that people will increasingly be faced with anxiety-provoking and difficult decisions that provide new challenges for stress management practitioners. Compared to the often diffuse stressors dealt with in the sections above, many of these situations offer opportunities for more focused interventions addressing particular stressors. Such interventions are easier to evaluate, particularly where they are aiming to reduce stress in a very specific situation and the outcome of interest is clear (such as enhanced recovery from an operation or increased relaxation during an investigative procedure). The types of intervention used in this context include many of those discussed above (particularly relaxation and cognitive behavioural techniques) but is also likely to include interventions focusing on information giving and social support. Some examples of the use of stress management in the medical context are discussed in this section.

Dealing with the stress of facing major life threatening diseases is an obvious focus for a range of psychosocial interventions, providing information, social support and various forms of SMT. A considerable literature is now developing around the value of such interventions in the cases of cancer and CHD. This focuses on both whether interventions can reduce distress and whether they can have implications for improving medical outcomes and even extending life.

Stress management for people suffering from cancer

One of the best-known studies of a psychosocial intervention for cancer patients was that by Spiegel *et al.* (1989). The authors expected that their intervention would improve the quality of life without affecting the quantity, but they found that it led to unexpected improvements in life expectancy. This is discussed further in Box 11.3.

Other studies have not always produced results consistent with Spiegel *et al.* For example, Gellert, Maxwell and Siegel (1993) also followed up breast cancer patients for 10 years after involvement in a psychosocial support programme. Here they found no significant differences in survival between treatment and control groups.

Box 11.3   Effects of a psychosocial intervention on survival of breast cancer patients.

One of the most well-known interventions studies was conducted by Spiegel *et al.* (1989). A sample of women with metastatic breast cancer were randomly allocated to either treatment or control groups. Both groups received routine oncological care, but in addition the intervention groups met for 90 minutes weekly over a one-year period for group meetings led by a psychiatrist or social worker with a therapist who had breast cancer in remission. The focus was on coping and social support. Participants were encouraged to discuss their feelings about the illness and its effects. Self-hypnosis was taught as a strategy for pain control and the formation of relationships was encouraged to prevent isolation. Participants were not led to believe that the intervention would alter the course of the disease. In fact the authors were not expecting the intervention to effect survival. They state that they started with the belief that 'positive psychological and symptomatic effects could occur without affecting the course of the disease' (p. 888).

Thirty (out of the 34) women in the treatment group and all 24 control women survived long enough to complete at least one follow-up during the first year of the study. At the end of one year there were no indications that the treatment group were surviving longer. In fact 30% of the treatment group died versus 20% of the control. Participants were then followed up to check their survival time. After 10 years only three patients were still alive, all of whom were in the treatment group. Mean survival time from the start of the intervention was 36.6 months for the intervention group and 18.9 months for the treatment group. This difference between the two groups did not start to appear until eight months after the intervention finished. The difference did not seem to be accounted for by methodological flaws such as participants in the treatment group by chance being less ill than those allocated to the control group.

The explanation for the effect of the intervention on survival is unclear but the authors speculate that involvement in the groups increased social support and enabled patients to mobilise resources better.

Meyer and Mark (1995) conducted a meta-analysis of a range psychosocial interventions for cancer sufferers. They included 45 studies that randomly allocated patients to treatment and control groups. These spanned the following types of interventions:

- cognitive behavioural interventions, including SMT and relaxation techniques;
- information and education;
- counselling and psychotherapy;
- social support (by non-professionals), including patient support groups;
- unusual treatments (e.g. music therapy) or those combining dissimilar approaches.

Overall, they found that the interventions had a positive effect on emotional adjustment, behavioural functioning and symptoms. As with other research discussed earlier, there was no significant difference between the different types of interventions. However, as there were few studies in each type, the meta-analysis lacked statistical power. The analysis also did not show any overall significant improvement in medical outcomes (for example, in measures such as tumour response to chemotherapy and physician ratings of disease progression). However, few of the studies looked at these variables, so again the study lacked power to detect such effects. Overall, they conclude that there is strong evidence for generally beneficial effects of psychosocial interventions on emotional and functional adjustment and symptoms. Further research is needed before we can conclude what elements of treatment lead to positive outcomes and particularly why some treatments seem to lead to increased survival and others do not.

Stress management for CHD

In rehabilitating CHD patients a range of interventions may be used, including smoking cessation and exercise, as well as SMT techniques and techniques to modify Type A behaviour. These may focus primarily either on the long-term aim of reducing risk factors or the more immediate aim of relieving anxiety and distress in the period after a myocardial infarction.

In the former category exercise is the most commonly used on the basis that it reduces risk factors such as weight and blood pressure (Bennett and Carroll, 1994). However, exercise, as we have seen, is also relevant to reducing distress. Stress management interventions are less frequently used to reduce risk factors though some studies have incorporated stress management with other lifestyle changes. For example, Ornish et al. (1990) randomly allocated patients with coronary artery disease to either a control group or a treatment group consisting of exercise, low-fat vegetarian diet (no caffeine, limited alcohol), stress management (relaxation and imagery) and smoking cessation. The intervention consisted of a week-long residential training followed by eight hours per week of group support meetings. At the end of the year coronary artery lesions in the intervention group patients had regressed but had progressed in the control group. However, while this study shows that life style changes can have a dramatic effect on medical outcomes in a short period, it is not clear that stress reduction played a central role. The intervention in this study was also much more ambitious than is normally practicable.

More specific, cognitive behavioural interventions have tended to focus on reducing risk factors such as Type A behaviour (see Chapter 6). For example a study by Roskies et al. (1986) found that cognitive-behavioural stress management training was more effective than exercise in reducing Type A behaviour. More recently attention has focused on hostility, which is now considered to be the major risk component in Type A behaviour. A study by Gidron, Davidson and Bata (1999) suggests that hostility reduction is a promising approach. An intervention for men who were suffering from CHD and were high in hostility was able to reduce hostility and lower blood pressure in comparison to an information only control group. However, it is not known whether this will lead to improved medical outcomes in the longer term.

Stress management interventions are much more commonly used with the short-term focus of reducing stress during recovery from CHD. Such interventions may be fairly minimal. For example, Thompson and Meddis (1990) evaluated an intervention consisting of four 30-minute sessions of counselling conducted by nurses shortly after admission to hospital following a myocardial infarction. The intervention included aspects of education, social support and increasing coping strategies. After the intervention and at six-months' follow-up, the treatment group were found to have lower anxiety and depression than the control group who received routine care.

Bennett and Carroll (1994) review a number of studies and suggest that there is evidence that cognitive-behavioural interventions may help reduce distress and improve coping in the short term but that typically there are no longer-term benefits.

Overall, we can conclude that many psychosocial interventions can have short-term benefits for well-being but we cannot say with any confidence that we can reduce mortality from either cancer or coronary heart disease. However, those studies producing positive outcomes give grounds for some optimism that this may be an important area to pursue.

Hospital stressors – facing surgery and medical procedures

The stress of facing often routine medical or surgical procedures is an area that has stimulated research interest. Stress and anxiety management in hospital settings is likely to be important in circumstances where people are facing unpleasant medical procedures for which tension (or in some cases real fear) may increase the pain or even make a procedure impossible. It is also important if we accept the mounting evidence that stress does effect the immune system and damages physical health (see Chapter 4). Any increased risk of infection, for example, needs to be avoided in surgical patients or in any patients who may already be in a weakened state. Some research has also indicated that pre-operative anxiety may be associated with poorer recovery and increased pain (Kincey and Saltmore, 1990).

Research in this area has the advantage of focusing on a much more limited and clearly focused stressor than interventions focusing on stress in work or life in general. It is also possible to specify more clearly defined outcomes in terms of improvements in recovery time or reductions in hospitalisation as well as reduction in fear about surgery. In this area it has therefore been easier to conduct rigorous evaluations using quasi-experimental designs. The interventions evaluated also have tended to include clearly defined elements, rather than the mixture of different approaches seen in the wider field of stress. Even so the area is complex and findings are often conflicting.

242

Psychologists' primary contribution has been the development of interventions for patients/clients which have aimed to reduce stress by altering the way a patient perceives the environment (that is, secondary interventions). This may be by the provision of information or assistance in developing appropriate coping strategies. While these may not change objective features of the external environment they may have the effect of making the environment more controllable by making treatment predictable. This may allow the patient to make informed choices where possible, and encouraging the patient to engage in active coping strategies.

A particular focus of research has been the evaluation of stress management procedures for unpleasant medical procedures. Four particular types of approach that have been commonly investigated are information provision, relaxation, cognitive behavioural approaches and modelling. The evidence for their effectiveness has been reviewed by Ludwick-Rosenthal and Neufeld (1988) and Kendall and Epps (1990) and is summarised below.

Information provision

A large number of studies have focused on the effects of providing information about medical treatments. Two main types of information have been considered: (i) procedural, which gives factual information about the sequence of events that the patient is likely to experience, and (ii) sensory information about the sorts of feelings and sensations that the patient is likely to experience. Results of such studies have been complex, contradictory and have not resulted in clear guidelines for the practitioner.

Studies that take account of individual differences in personality or coping style help to account for some of the inconsistent effects. For example, Kendall and Epps (1990) draw on the distinction between avoidant and non-avoidant coping styles discussed in Chapter 7. Those with avoidant styles, sometimes known as blunters or repressors, may deal with stressful situations by denying the information or distancing themselves from it. Those with a non-avoidant style, sometimes known as monitors or sensitisers, cope by seeking information and preparing plans of action. Kendall and Epps suggest that information should be given in a manner consistent with the preferred coping style of the patient. Thus non-avoiders may benefit from specific procedural and sensory information. Avoiders may prefer more general information.

Relaxation approaches

A number of studies have taught patients techniques such as progressive relaxation to deal with medical procedures; these involve concentrating on tensing and relaxing different groups of muscles in turn. The intention of such interventions is to replace the anxious response with a response that is incompatible with anxiety. These techniques have been found to be effective for a wide variety of situations from childbirth to chemotherapy and are frequently used in conjunction with other approaches (e.g. cognitive-behavioural approaches). For example, training in progressive muscle relaxation combined with therapist guided imagery has reduced anticipatory nausea in chemotherapy patients and led to better performance on a range of physiological measures of anxiety (Burish and Lyles, 1981; Lyles *et al.*, 1982).

Cognitive–behavioural approaches

Approaches such as stress inoculation training (Meichenbaum, 1985) have also been used to improve coping with medical procedures. This technique is described in further detail in Box 11.1. The majority of studies have shown benefits of these types of approaches (e.g. Kendall and Epps, 1990; Kaplan, Atkins and Reinsch, 1984).

Modelling

This approach stems from the work of Bandura (1969). It is based on the view that exposure to a model (for example, on a video) who is coping successfully with a particular experience can teach the patient to utilise similar appropriate coping strategies. In one study patients undergoing gastrointestinal endoscopy were shown a film of individuals undergoing similar treatment (Shipley *et al.*, 1978). A control group were shown an unrelated video. Those exposed to the model had significantly lower levels of anxiety during the medical procedure. Overall, studies reviewed by Ludwick-Rosenthal and Neufeld (1988) provide strong support for modelling interventions.

So which approach is best for hospital stressors?

Ludwick-Rosenthal and Neufeld (1988) conclude that there is some evidence that all of the above interventions can reduce patient stress during aversive medical procedures. While modelling and cognitive-behavioural approaches have generally demonstrated more positive effects, this may be at least partly due to the fact that these interventions are likely to include elements of information giving or relaxation. As with studies investigating the effects of occupational stress management interventions, there has been insufficient research to identify which of the particular elements are most useful. The best current advice to practitioners would be to provide a broad range of support, taking into account the needs, wishes and preferred coping styles of the individual patient.

While the above approaches have focused on medical interventions, it is recognised that surgical interventions are likely to be particularly stressful (Volicer, Isenberg and Burns, 1977). Surgery, in many cases has more long-term effects than the types of procedures discussed above. Nevertheless similar approaches have been found to be useful in dealing with stress. Wells *et al.* (1986) found that stress inoculation training reduced anxiety and pain and improved post-operative adjustment. Generally approaches aimed at reducing anxiety (for example, relaxation and emotional support) have been more effective than those simply aimed at education (Mumford, Schlesinger and Glass, 1982).

CONCLUSION

It should be clear by now that the evidence for the success of stress management interventions is at best sketchy and incomplete. In the medical context, where interventions are more focused and may have quite specific goals the utility is more easily established. In the occupational context it seems likely that the demand to tackle the perceived problem of 'stress' may lead to people rushing to find solutions to this 'problem' without first attempting to identify the causes. Some authors have suggested that a critical factor in the success of a stress management programme in the workplace is the degree of understanding and support provided for the programme by the managers who commissioned it. Managers may commission stress management programmes without really understanding what problems exist within their organisation and that such programmes may be irrelevant and therefore inevitably ineffective (Briner, 1997).

CONCLUSIONS: MYTHS, THEORY AND RESEARCH

This final chapter aims to address the issue of stress myths in the light of evidence presented in preceding chapters and highlights emerging theoretical and research issues.

THIS final chapter draws together strands from preceding chapters to try to identify some of the commonly held beliefs about stress that might be regarded as myths. These beliefs will be briefly evaluated in the light of the available evidence and their impact before pinpointing theoretical and research issues and future directions.

WHAT DO WE MEAN BY MYTHS?

The term 'mythology' derives from two words, mythos and logos, that describe the complementary forms of knowledge we possess. Logos refers to sense and reason, and in this context to the scientific evidence-based form of knowledge, whereas mythos refers to knowledge held typically in the narrative form, not based upon evidence and reason, perhaps better referred to as folk knowledge or even folklore. Although the term 'mythology' is commonly used in a pejorative sense to describe something fictitious, it may also encompass accounts of something commonly held, but held in the absence of current scientific evidence. In the case of stress it would appear that society has built up a complex folklore about stress which is reinforced by popular culture and the media. This folklore is likely to be influenced by research findings but also contains many myths. In the next section some of the popular beliefs about stress are described and assessed drawing on evidence discussed throughout the book. In some cases these beliefs may clearly be myths (in the sense of being untrue). In others they may have some foundation, but at this stage there is insufficient scientific evidence to promote them to the status of fact. Many of these deserve more rigorous investigation. Some myths are controversial in the sense that, although large bodies of evidence have been presented in their support, the variety of conceptual and methodological shortcomings provide sufficient reason for caution about the claims made.

WHAT ARE THE MYTHS ABOUT STRESS?

- Stress leads to illness

One of the recurring themes in this book is the lack of clarity surrounding the definition of stress. One particular problem has been the tendency to use the term to describe both a stressor and the strain reaction. Thus, in the question of whether stress leads to illness or not, it is necessary to be very clear about what psycho-social factors researchers are studying when the term 'stress' is used.

In Chapter 4, the evidence linking stress and illness was reviewed and the work of Cohen *et al.* was introduced. They use the term 'stress' to include both life events and perceptions of being distressed as a result. Taking this broad view of stress it was clear that the evidence for a relationship with the illnesses considered was variable. We do have evidence of links to some aspects of immune functioning (e.g. Herbert and Cohen, 1993) but, while research in this area is developing rapidly, we do not yet know whether they have significance in terms of causing serious illness. Evidence also exists to support the view that job control is implicated in heart disease (Schnall, Landsbergis and Baker, 1994). However, evidence in relation to many other diseases is weak or inconclusive. For example, it seems likely that the widespread belief that breast cancer is caused by stressful life events is no more than a myth (e.g. McKenna *et al.*, 1999; Petticrew, Fraser and Regan, 1999).

Nevertheless, the lack of evidence has not prevented researchers from making the assumption that the link is already established and claiming that, for example, if work stress leads to distress then this will inevitably have consequences for employees' health.

- Executive stress leads to heart disease

The view that heart disease is caused by work stress, and particularly by executive stress, is pervasive. Evidence that this association has been taken seriously in medical circles, for example, is illustrated by an entry in *Black's Medical Dictionary* (Thompson, 1981). This states that coronary thrombosis goes together with stress and strain 'particularly that to which those in authority and with responsibility, such as business executives, are subject'.

However, the research discussed in Chapters 4 and 9 has suggested that, while work stressors are implicated to some extent in heart disease, the relationship is rather different from that implied above. The influential work of Karasek and

248

colleagues (e.g. Karasek *et al.*, 1981; Karasek, 1990) investigating the concept of control or decision latitude indicates that there is now considerable evidence that a lack of control is implicated in heart disease. This offers one potential explanation for the fact that higher levels of illness, including heart disease, have been found at lower organisational levels in a study of UK Civil Servants (Bosma *et al.*, 1997). Thus our particular concerns about the stressed executive may be unfounded.

• People's reactions to stressors vary considerably as a result of individual differences in personality

In Chapter 6, a variety of different individual difference factors were examined to see whether they influenced reactions to stressors. Certainly there is some good evidence to suggest that people vary in their *experience* of stressors, both in terms of whether a stimulus is perceived as stressful and the perceived intensity of the stressor. This can perhaps most clearly be seen in the research on negative affectivity (NA) where people who are high on negative affectivity appear to over-report the intensity of stressors (Stone and Costa, 1990).

However, good evidence that people vary in their reactions to stressors, as opposed to their appraisal of stressors, is harder to come by. The evidence reviewed for the Type A concept did not provide a convincing basis for accepting that people are differently reactive. Furthermore, the evidence that other variables such as NA influence reaction to stressors is equally weak. However this is an area that probably deserves greater attention, as relatively few studies have treated variables such as NA as anything other than a methodological nuisance.

So, evidence that people differ in their reactions to stress on the basis of psychological factors such as traits is not particularly strong. On the other hand, there is stronger evidence that some situational and demographic individual difference factors such as age, education and social support do seem likely to influence people's reactions to stress (see Chapters 6 and 7).

• Stress can be measured using a simple questionnaire scale

There are many measures of stress, some of which are described in Chapters 2 and 9. These range from inventories of psychological or physical symptoms, life event check-lists and scales assessing the number or intensity of stressors in the work environment. These assess diverse factors which, while they may come under the umbrella term of stress, cannot be said to be measuring 'stress' itself. However, a measure which actually asks people directly to rate their level of stress would be open to a wide range of different interpretations and would therefore not be meaningful (see Chapter 2). Hence, even the measure called 'The Perceived Stress Scale' (Cohen, Kamarck and Mermelstein, 1983) actually mentions the word stress only once. Measures such as the Occupational Stress Indicator (Cooper, Sloan and Williams, 1988) designed as comprehensive surveys of stress in the workplace consist of a large number of scales measuring different dimensions (see Chapter 9).

Even these however may omit important stressors for many specialised occupational groups In fact, it is doubtful whether it is possible to develop a valid or reliable questionnaire of anything like a reasonable length that will encompass everything that different people mean when they refer to 'stress'.

• Stress can be cured or managed through relaxation, meditation, exercise, etc.

In Chapter 12, stress management interventions were considered. From the evidence reviewed there is some reason to believe that some interventions of the types mentioned may have some beneficial effect (e.g. Ganster *et al.*, 1982). For instance, there would appear to be some evidence that both exercise and stress management courses may lead to improvements on specific mood (such as anxiety) and physiological indicators (such as blood pressure). However, we do not know the mechanisms for the effects, which may be due to relaxation, distraction or social support, nor do we know for how long such mood effects last. Even if effects were demonstrated to be long term they could only be said to be curing 'stress' if stress is regarded as a disorder which is manifested in such symptoms. Furthermore, while some interventions can be shown to have benefits, it is not entirely clear that this has anything to do with improved ability to manage in the face of stressors.

• Stress can be cured by changing the way we work

A myth to which stress researchers themselves seem particularly keen to subscribe is that job design is the most effective way to tackle the problem of 'stress'. The idea of preventing stress by removing the stressors (e.g. by reducing demand and increasing control) is certainly logical and would seem to have both moral and ethical advantages over the alternative of training people to tolerate stressful environments. However, what evidence we have suggests that these interventions seldom work (see Chapter 11). Briner and Reynolds (1999) suggest this may be because of the limitations of the current research and its theoretical bases, which limit our ability to develop interventions that are relevant to organisations' needs (Briner and Reynolds, 1999). While we may hope that, in future, it may be possible to redesign work so that people do not experience distress, we currently do not seem to be able to do it.

• Stress is increasing

It is fitting that our list of myths is concluded with this one, as this is perhaps the most popular starting point for many stress management programmes and newspaper articles on stress. We have all read about the 'increasing pace of life', 'increased job insecurity', the 'lack of the old certainties', etc. Those few commentators who actually try to justify such remarks tend to turn to figures for compensation claims and the like. However, whether such figures genuinely represent a rising tide of stress problems or merely increasing awareness of both the concept of stress and the availability of litigation is difficult to determine.

Whether we are really working longer hours than before, or are experiencing more job insecurity or less control over our work (or indeed, other aspects of our lives) seems to be open to question. Typically, this myth is supported by its exponents by listing a variety of stressors from modern life, but how can the impact of the telephone ringing all day be compared, say, with the risk of contracting a potentially fatal infectious disease or losing a child? Rates of both infectious diseases and infant mortality are both lower today than in the past. This is not necessarily to suggest that people experience less stress today than say a hundred years ago, merely that comparisons between then and now are highly likely to be unreliable, and may lead to over-simplistic theorising about both the causes of stress and rates of stress.

WHERE NOW FOR THEORY?

Throughout this book the point has been made that there seems to be a shortage of adequate models and theories to guide research and practice. This can perhaps best be illustrated with examples taken from the areas of work stress and coping. Here there are some quite simple theoretical approaches such as the demand-control theory of work stress (Karasek, 1979) and the monitoring-blunting approach to coping (Miller and Mangan, 1983). Both of these offer useful, but somewhat limited, insights. However, when researchers attempt to produce models that are better reflections of the complexity of the phenomenon (for example, the facet model of work stress by Beehr and Newman, 1978, or the theory of coping by Lazarus and Folkman, 1984) then we find the theories are too complex to be easily testable or to be used in the design of interventions.

At this point it is worth giving further consideration to the criteria for an acceptable theory. Eulberg, Weekley and Bhagat (1988) suggest seven criteria for evaluating stress theories which, though they refer to theories and models of work stress, have much wider relevance. These are shown in Box 12.1.

Box 12.1 Eulberg, Weekley and Bhagat's (1988) criteria for evaluating stress theory presented in order of importance.

- *Clarity* – Is the model clear and are its components specific and conceptually distinct?
- *Internal consistency* – Does it have logical contradictions or inconsistencies?
- *Falsifiability* – Can it be tested?
- *External consistency* – Is it compatible with existing theories and research findings?
- *Comprehensiveness* – Does it cover the range of stress phenomena?
- *Parsimony* – Is it economical and uncluttered by unnecessary concepts and interrelationships?
- *Originality* – Does it lead to new predictions and hypotheses?

While many of the criteria listed here go hand in hand with each other, some appear to be incompatible. It is difficult to develop a comprehensive model or theory of stress that is also clear and parsimonious. In fact, the evidence seems to suggest that there is an inverse relationship between a model's breadth and its overall impact in the field (Eulberg, Weekley and Bhagat, 1988). Eulberg, Weekley and Bhagat suggest that broad coverage such as that offered by the facet model of Beehr and Newman can only be achieved by sacrificing conceptual tightness. The same can be said for Lazarus' theory of coping.

One of the reasons for the difficulty seems to lie in the broadness of the concept of stress. We expect a single job stress model to encompass a wide range of stressors and to predict a range of very diverse outcomes, including mood, job satisfaction and heart disease. Similarly, coping theorists aimed to develop theories that would enable identification of the most effective ways to cope with diverse stressful situations. Possibly the only workable solution to the need to develop theories that are both parsimonious and comprehensive is to break down the stress concept and then develop theories relevant to specific stressors and strains, in other words, develop theories to explain the microphenomena. It is already clear, for example, that the same variables and combinations of variables do not predict anxiety, dissatisfaction and performance (Wall *et al.*, 1990a).

It may also be desirable to develop theories specific to a range of different emotional states. Lazarus (1993) has suggested that each emotion has its 'core' relational theme: for example, anger is in response to appraisals of a 'demeaning offence against me and mine', whilst an individual who perceives that he or she is facing 'an uncertain existential threat' will feel anxiety.

In addition to theories specific to particular strain outcomes, it may also be necessary to develop theories relevant to specific stressful situations. For example, in the context of coping research, Somerfield (1997) has suggested that this may be necessary in order to develop comprehensive models that encompass all the relevant factors. The development of such theories would help guide practitioners conducting applied research and designing interventions. However, in Chapter 8, we also discuss the need for broader theoretical frameworks. Smith and Wallston (1997) suggest meta-analysis can be used to integrate these findings so that they feed into more general over-arching theories (meta-theories).

Thus, in order to explain the complex phenomena in this area, we might foresee a future of micro- and meta-theories, less driven by the construct of stress. Rather they might use a large number of different variables for which it might benefit researchers to draw on knowledge from other areas of clinical, social and cognitive psychology as well as from other disciplines such as sociology or anthropology.

WHERE NOW FOR RESEARCH?

The theoretical issues discussed above clearly have had implications for research, and some, though by no means all, of the limitations of the research discussed in this book are the result of atheoretical approaches or an over reliance on a few popular theories. Furthermore, much of the research in this book has been criticised for its use of a limited range of methodologies and approaches. Again, this is well-illustrated using examples from the coping and work stress literature. In the coping literature, research has too often been dominated by the use of a small number of standard coping questionnaires (e.g. Lazarus' Ways of Coping inventory). Similarly, work stress research is dominated by cross-sectional studies – very frequently based on a limited range of work stressors (e.g. drawn from Karasek's models). Both areas have been criticised for failing to provide the information useful to guide interventions. Various ways forward have been suggested:

- Multiple methods

We have seen that research in the real world setting is frequently flawed and subject to a range of confounding variables. Equally, research in the laboratory can be controlled but lacks ecological validity and may not readily be generalisable to the real world. A solution is to use a range of approaches and seek converging evidence. Thus it can be valuable to test ideas about, for example, the effects of work stressors in the laboratory so that causes and effects relationships can be identified and hypotheses refined. These can then be tested further in studies conducted in real world settings.

- Multiple sources of information on stressors and strains

In the field of stressors and strains, people's subjective reports of both stressors and strains are inevitably important. Yet examples of the ways in which these reports may be biased are frequently encountered. In the case of stressors it is sometimes possible to obtain objective validation as well as self-reports (e.g. for life events such as bereavement). Even for feelings such as anxiety or mood, where it may at first seem difficult to identify alternatives to the self-report measure, behavioural observations and ratings from family members or colleagues as well as physiological measures may be possible (Marsella, 1994). Diener *et al.* (1999) recommend the use of a range of such approaches to assess psychological well-being.

- Multiple occasions

Most research considered in this book has looked at stressors and strains on one or two occasions only. These can shed little light on the processes involved. However, there is some evidence that minor stressors and hassles may be important for health and well-being and a few studies have been discussed which demonstrate the potential of daily diaries (e.g. Repetti, 1989; Caspi, Bolger and Eckenrode, 1987) or experience sampling (Marco and Suls, 1993). These can overcome the memory biases inherent to studies using retrospective recall and can track fluctuations in relationships in short-term moods and emotions. Furthermore they can examine the time frame of effects. This kind of approach however needs to be underpinned by clear and specific theoretical frameworks if researchers are to avoid being bogged down in a mass of data.

CONCLUSION

Thus, there is scope for re-evaluating myths, expanding our theories and our methods but also focusing in on narrower and more clearly defined phenomena, in terms of either specific stressful situations or specific psychological and physical outcomes. We have seen that some researchers wish to abolish the concept of stress and while this may seem extreme, it is possible to envisage a future in which the concept of stress has become largely redundant amongst a broad range of specific theories. These might, for example, include theories that address the psychosocial effects of cancer (incorporating aspects of emotions, adaptation and social supports) or theories of the occupational predictors of anger and frustration or boredom.

GLOSSARY

autonomic nervous system   Part of the peripheral nervous system that regulates our internal organs and is not (normally) under our conscious control

adrenaline   Also known as epinephrine, stimulates the sympathetic nervous system. It is released by the adrenal glands as part of the stress response, leading to an increase in available glucose in the blood

age – chronologic   Measured in time since birth, e.g. what one would generally refer to as one's age

age – physiologic   Measured in terms of body condition relative to chronologic age norms; thus a 35-year-old could have the body of an average 50-year-old

ambiguity   In the stress context, normally means that there is no clear course of action to take in the face of a stressor, e.g. an employee given unclear and confusing instructions about how to complete a task experiences ambiguity

anxiety   The collection of psychological and behavioural responses normally associated with responses to threats

anxiety state   The individual's current level of anxiety

anxiety, trait   The individual's relatively stable tendency to experience anxiety

big five   The five factors commonly measured by personality inventories – extraversion, agreeableness, conscientiousness, emotional stability and culture

blood pressure   A physiological measure that has two components, systolic and diastolic. Systolic pressure is measured when the heart contracts and pumps blood out, the diastolic reading is when the heart expands and blood flows in

blunters   People who will avoid threat-relevant information

buffer   A moderator that decreases the strength of the stressor–strain relation

burnout   A psychological state of mental exhaustion usually associated with prolonged exposure to high levels of work stressors

caseness The degree to which an individual matches clinical diagnostic criteria on a particular measure

central nervous system Comprises the brain and spinal cord

confound model Suggests that self-report measures of stressors and strains are not measuring separate, meaningful constructs but instead are measuring indirectly a third independent dispositional trait such as NA

control The degree to which an individual has freedom to use their resources to meet demands placed upon them

coping – emotion-focused Coping which is directed at dealing with the emotion caused by the stressor

coping – problem-focused Coping which is aimed at actually managing or dealing with the stressor

coronary heart disease (CHD) A collection of diseases involving degradation of heart and blood vessel function, also known as circulatory diseases in some official statistics. The degradation can involve blocked arteries, muscle damage, and enlargement

daily hassles A variant on life events but more focused on everyday niggles and little pleasures in life and their severity

decision latitude A variable which corresponds to job control. Typically it includes two components decision authority (or amount of control people have over decision making) and skill discretion (encompassing levels of skill and creativity used)

demand A load placed upon an individual or perceived to be placed upon an individual, something that requires a response

depression A negative psychological state with common behavioural features such as withdrawal, lethargy, despondency and hopelessness

diathesis An individual predisposition to diseases

direct effects These occur when the individual difference variable has a direct effect on the level of strain regardless of the level or intensity of stressors

discretion Like control, and decision latitude, the degree to which an individual is free to decide how to meet demands

double hermeneutic Describes a situation where a social scientist who studies a behavioural phenomenon alters the nature of the phenomenon by raising awareness of it. For instance, scientists studied stress, which made the public more interested in stress, and thus stress in people became a slightly altered phenomenon

downsizing A euphemistic term meaning to reduce the size of an organisation usually through sacking staff or making them redundant, voluntarily or involuntarily

embeddedness The degree to which an individual is part of a social group or environment (see also social integration)

employee assistance programmes (EAPs)   Work-sponsored programmes consisting typically of counselling to assist employees with a variety of psychological problems that may be affecting their performance at work

epidemiology   The study of the presence and cause of disease in the community

etiology/aetiology   The study of the causes of disease. Thus a factor having an 'aetiological role' in disease means the factor has a role in causing the disease

eustress   Pressure that has positive effects on performance or well-being

fight or flight   The view that reactions to stressors involve two mechanisms, the first to try to combat the stressor through a dynamic response, and the second to try to avoid the stressor by getting away from the source of the stressor.

GHQ   General Health Questionnaire. A commonly used scale measuring general well-being

heart disease   See CHD

hypothalamic–pituitary–adrenal (HPA) axis system   The integrated response system that involves the hypothalamus, the pituitary gland and the adrenal glands

interaction   A statistical term that indicates that the effect of two (or more) variables on a third variable has to be considered by looking at the effects of each level of every variable on the other variables because the size or direction of the effect will differ at different levels. For instance if one considers the effect of heat (hot or cold) and light (light or dark) on the growth of a tomato, we might find that the variables heat or light alone have no effect on growth, and that growth is only observed when it is hot and it is light

intervening variables   An intervening variable is one that sits between an independent variable and a dependent variable. This encompasses both moderators and mediators

life event   An external (i.e. not psychological) change in a person's life such as marriage, divorce, moving house, death of a friend, etc.

limbic system   The system that is responsive for directing behaviours required for survival e.g. sexual reproduction, fear and aggression

locus of control   A construct that describes an individual's attributional style depending on whether a person tends to attribute events to causes beyond themselves (external locus of control) or they attribute events to themselves (internal locus of control)

main effects   A statistical term that indicates that the presence of a factor has a reliable effect on a dependent variable and that this effect occurs across all levels of a second variable

mediators   A mediator is an intervening variable via which one variable effects another. For example, workload may lead to excessive drinking which then leads to ill health. Alcohol consumption is the mediator

memory bias   The phenomenon that previously stored memories will influence the recognition, recall, or understanding of newly presented stimuli. So it is suggested that anxious people may more readily process threatening words such as 'knife', etc.

moderators   Intervening variables that can influence either the strength or direction of the stressor–strain relationship

monitors   People who will seek out threat-relevant information

mucosal surfaces   The linings of the passageways that run through the body, e.g. the gastrointestinal and urinogenital tracts

myocardial infarction   Sudden loss of blood to the myocardium, caused by a blocked artery – commonly called a heart attack

negative affect   The dispositional tendency to experience negative emotions and a negative self-concept

neuroticism   Personality dimension characterised by a tendency to experience emotional instability. Negative effects including anxiety.

noradrenaline   The neurotransmitter released by the SNS to activate the internal body organs

PANAS   Positive and negative affect scale developed by Watson, Clark and Tellegen (1988)

peripheral nervous system   Projects to and from the central nervous system connecting all other parts of our bodies, the internal organs and glands as well as skeletal muscles

primary appraisal   The process whereby the person evaluates the potential harm, loss, threat or challenge imposed by the stressor

primary prevention   Interventions aimed at reducing or removing the stressor before it becomes serious, such as reducing job demands, or increasing decision latitude

proximal–distal   Something that immediately impacts upon you is proximal, whereas something that is less immediate is distal

psychiatric disorders   A collection of symptoms and behaviours that match a standard classification of an observed disorder usually as set out in the *American Diagnostic and Statistical Manual (DSM)*

psychophysiologists   Scientists interested in the relationship between psychological states and corresponding physiological states

psychosocial factors   This is a global term used to encompass both social and psychological matters. In stress research the term may be used to refer to both social variables such as work and family stressors and psychological reactions to them such as depression and anxiety

repressors   Repressors react to anxiety-arousing stimuli and their consequences by avoidant behaviour (including repression, denial and rationalisation)

schema   A term used in cognitive psychology to refer to a stereotypical memory. For instance, a schema for a dog may include attributes such as four legs, barks, needs walking, retrieves sticks, etc.

secondary appraisal   This is the process whereby the person evaluates what can be done to overcome or prevent harm or improve benefits, i.e. coping options are evaluated

secondary prevention   Interventions aimed at reducing or removing the symptoms of the strain reaction, perhaps through relaxation, meditation, etc. before they become serious

secretory immunoglobulin A (sIgA)   The main antibody to protect the mucosal surfaces. Collected levels in saliva reflect immune system functioning

sensitisers   Attempt to reduce anxiety by approaching or controlling threats (e.g. by intellectualisation, obsessive behaviours and ruminative worrying)

situational constraints   Limits that the immediate environment places upon one's ability to meet demands, e.g. inability to delegate some work to colleagues due to a lack of staff

social integration   The degree to which an individual has connections (social relationships) with other people

social support – perceived   Satisfaction, adequacy and availability of supportive relationships, rather than the mere existence of social contact

strain   In this book the term 'strains' is used as a general shorthand term to cover a range of negative physical and psychological states and behaviours. Generally, the term is vague and often used to refer to any ill effects of stressors. Where 'stress' is defined as a stimulus, 'strains' becomes the results of 'stress'. When 'stress' is defined as a response, then 'stress' and 'strains' become synonymous. The use of the term 'strain' implies that these states are known to be the direct effect of some stressor – in fact these are more likely to be hypothesised relationships

stress   The word 'stress' is used in many ways, e.g. it is sometimes used to refer to an environmental stimulus (stressor) and sometimes as the response to that stimulus (strain). It may also be defined in terms of a relationship between the environment and the person that is appraised as exceeding their ability to cope. In this book , unless otherwise stated, it is used as a rubric or umbrella term which includes a range of potentially demanding environmental stimuli (often known as 'stressors'), stress responses and various variables that influence the relationship between the two (including personality factors)

stressor   In this book the term stressor may be used as shorthand to include a range of potentially demanding stimuli, most frequently conceptualised in terms of life events, chronic job stressors, or minor daily hassles. These are the variables that are hypothesised to be related to various forms of lack of well-being and are commonly perceived by people as being sources of pressure. Stressors are sometimes defined as anything that causes 'stress'. This definition has been criti-cised as circular, since stress can be defined as a response to stressors

survey – cross-sectional   Collection of data by questionnaire and other methods on one occasion only

survey – longitudinal   Repeated collection of data from the same people by ques-tionnaire or other methods over a period of time, e.g. six-month follow-up

sympathetic adrenal medullary system (SAM)   The system that releases adrenaline into the bloodstream

tertiary prevention   Interventions aimed at reducing strain through methods such as counselling. This approach aims to prevent serious strain by looking at the prob-lem in a more general sense than secondary prevention

transactional theories   The view that the reaction to a stressor is a function of the environment and the individual's response to that environment, especially their appraisal of the stressor

turnover   The number of people leaving an organisation (usually voluntarily) in a set period. Strictly speaking it should also include the number of staff subsequently recruited to make up for the losses. This variable is often taken as an indicator of employee satisfaction

Type A   A behaviour pattern characterised by impatience, irritability, hostility, competitiveness, job involvement and achievement striving

Type B   A behaviour pattern characterised by a relative lack of Type A characteristics

voluntary nervous system   Part of the peripheral nervous system that controls our skeletal muscles that we have conscious control over

vulnerability model   A model which proposes that individuals are considered to have a heightened reactivity (or stronger reaction) to stressors

well-being   A broad term used to include a range of factors related to positive psychological health. It spans the range from poor well-being, which may include negative states such as psychiatric or physical illness or feelings of negative mood, to positive states. Thus the term 'well-being' has the advantage over the term 'strain' in that it is bi-polar, ranging from feeling bad to positive feelings such as happiness and elation. It has the further benefit over the term 'stress response' or 'strain' in that it is not defined as a response to a stressor (i.e. it avoids circularity)

working memory   A model of memory developed by Alan Baddeley and colleagues that describes the relationship, structure, function and capacity of short and long term memory encoding systems. It is often used as a framework for exploring the effects of heavy demands upon performance by 'loading' working memory

REFERENCES

Abouserie, R. (1996). Stress, coping strategies and job satisfaction in university academic staff. *Educational Psychology*, **16**, 49–56.

Ader, R. (1981). Psychosomatic and psychoimmunological research. Presidential address. *Psychosomatic Medicine*, **42**, 307–321.

Adler, S., Skov, R. B. and Salvemini, N. J. (1985). Job characteristics and job satisfaction: when causes become consequences. *Organizational Behavior and Human Decision Processes*, **35**, 266–278.

Alfredsson, L., Karasek, R. and Theorell, T. (1982). Myocardial infarction risk and psychosocial work environment: an anlysis of the male Swedish working force. *Social Science and Medicine*, **16**, 463–467.

Alexander, D. A. and Walker, L. G. (1996). The perceived impact of police work on police officers' spouses and families. *Stress Medicine*, **12**, 239–246.

Alloy, L. B. and Abramson, L. Y. (1979). Judgment of contingency in depressed and nondepressed students: Sadder but wiser? *Journal of Experimental Psychology: General*, **108**, 441–485.

Almeida, D. M. and McDonald, D. (1998). Weekly rhythms of parents' work stress, home stress, and parent–adolescent tension. In A. C. Crouter and R. Larson *et al.* (Eds.) (1998). *Temporal rhythms in adolescence: Clocks, calendars, and the co-ordination of daily life. New directions for child and adolescent development, No. 82.* San Francisco, CA, USA: Jossey-Bass Inc, Publishers.

Alterman, T., Shekelle, R. B., Vernon, S. W. and Burau, K. D. (1994). Decision latitude, psychologic demand, job strain, and coronary heart disease in the Western Electric Study. *American Journal of Epidemiology*, **139**, 620–627.

Amick, B. C., Kawachi, I., Coakley, E. H., Lerner, S., Levine, S. and Colditz, G. A. (1998). Relationship of job strain and iso-strain to health status in a cohort of women in the United States. *Scandinavian Journal of Work and Environmental Health*, **24**, 54–61.

Andrews, F. M. and Withey, S. B. (1974). *Social Indicators of Well-being: Americans Perceptions of Life Quality*. New York: Plenum Press.

Asendorpf, J. B. and Scherer, K. R. (1983). The discrepant repressor: differentiation between low anxiety, high anxiety, and repression of anxiety by autonomic-facial-verbal patterns of behavior. *Journal of Personality and Social Psychology*, **45**, 1334–1346.

Ashforth, B. E. and Humphrey, R. H. (1995). Emotion in the workplace: A reappraisal. *Human Relations*, **48**, 97–124.

Asmundson, G. J. G. and Stein, M. B. (1994). Selective processing or social threat in patients with generalized social phobia: Evaluation using a dot-probe paradigm. *Journal of Anxiety Disorders*, **8**, 107–117.

Aspinwall, L. G. and Taylor, S. E. (1992). Modeling cognitive adaptation: a longitudinal investigation of the impact of individual differences and coping on college adjustment and performance. *Journal of Personality and Social Psychology*, **63**, 989–1003.

Aukett, R., Ritchie, J. and Mill, K. (1988). Gender differences in friendship patterns. *Sex Roles*, **19**, 57–66.

Averill, J. R. (1989). Stress as fact and artifact: an inquiry into the social origins and functions of some stress reactions. In C. D. Spielberger, I. G. Sarason and J. Strelay (Eds), *Stress and Anxiety (Vol. 12)*. New York: Hemisphere.

Baddeley, A. D. (1986). *Working Memory*. Oxford: Clarendon Press.

Baddeley, A. D. (1990). *Human Memory: Theory and Practice*. Hove: Lawrence Associates.

Baddeley, A. D. and Hitch, G. (1974). Working Memory. In G. H. Bower (Ed.), *The Psychology of Learning and Motivation*, Volume 8. London: Academic Press.

Baghurst, K. I., Baghurst, P. A. and Record, S. J. (1992). Public perceptions of the role of dietary and other enviornmental factors in cancer causation and prevention. *Journal of Epidemiology and Community Health*, **46**, 120–126.

Bandura, A. (1969). *Principles of Behavior Modification*. New York: Holt, Rinehart & Winston.

Banks, M. H., Clegg, C. W., Jackson, P. R., Kemp, N. J., Stafford, E. M. and Wall, T. (1980). The use of the General Health Questionnaire as an indicator of mental health in occupational studies. *Journal of Occupational Psychology*, **53**, 187–194.

Banks, M. H. and Jackson, P. R. (1982). Unemployment and risk of minor psychiatric disorder in young people: cross-sectional and longitudinal evidence. *Psychological Medicine*, **12**, 789–798.

Barley, S. R. and Knight, D. B. (1992). Towards a cultural theory of stress complaints. *Research in Organizational Behavior*, **14**, 1–48.

Barling, J. (1990). *Employment, Stress and Family Functioning*. Chichester: Wiley.

Barling, J. (1994). Work and family: in search of more effective workplace interventions. In C. Cooper and D. Rousseau (Eds), *Trends in Organisational Behaviour*. Chichester: Wiley.

Barling, J. and Macintyre, A. T. (1993). Daily work role stressors, mood and emotional exhaustion. *Work and Stress*, **7**, 315–325.

Barling, J. and Rosenbaum, A. (1986). Work stressors and wife abuse. *Journal of Applied Psychology*, **71**, 346–348.

Barnett, R. C. (1998). Towards a review and reconceptualisation of the work/family literature. *Genetic, Social and General Psychology Monographs*, **124**, 125–182.

Baron, R. M. and Kenny, D. A. (1986). The moderator–mediator variable distinction in social psychological research: Conceptual, strategic, and statistical considerations. *Journal of Personality and Social Psychology*, **51**, 1173–1182.

Barrera, J. M. (1986). Distinctions between social support concepts, measures and models. *American Journal of Community Psychiatry*, **14**, 413–445.

Barrera, M. (1981). Preliminary development of a measure of scale of social support. *American Journal of Community Psychology*, **9**, 435–447.

Bartlett, F. C. (1932). *Remembering: a Study in Experimental and Social Psychology*. Cambridge: Cambridge University Press.

Baruch, G. K. and Barnett, R. C. (1986). Role quality, multiple role involvement, and psychological well-being in midlife women. *Journal of Personality and Social Psychology*, **51**, 578–585.

Bayne, R., Horton, I. and Bimrose, J. (1996). *New Directions in Counselling*. London: Routledge.

Beck, A. T. and Clark, D. A. (1988). Anxiety and depression: an information processing perspective. *Anxiety Research*, **1**, 23–36.

Beck, A. T. and Emery, G. (1985). *Anxiety Disorders and Phobias: A Cognitive Perspective*. New York: Basic Books.

Beck, A. T., Mendelson, M., Mock, J. *et al.* (1961). Inventory for measuring depression. *Archives of General Psychiatry*, **4**, 561–571.

Beekman, A. T. F., Copeland, J. R. M. and Prince, M. J. (1999). Review of community prevalence of depression in later life. *British Journal of Psychiatry*, **174**, 307–311.

Beehr, T. (1995). *Psychological Stress in the Workplace*. London: Routledge.

Beehr, T. A. and Newman, J. E. (1978). Job stress, employee health and organizational effectiveness: a facet analysis, model and literature review. *Personnel Psychology*, **31**, 665–699.

Bellarosa, C. and Chen, P. Y. (1997). The efffectiveness and practicality of occupational stress management interventions: A survey of subject matter expert opinions. *Journal of Occupational Health Psychology*, **2**, 247–262.

Bennett, P. and Carroll, D. (1994). Cognitive-behavioural interventions in cardiac rehabilitation. *Journal of Psychosomatic Research*, **38**, 169–182.

Berger, B. G., Owen, D. R., Motl, R. W. and Parks, L. (1998). Relationship between expectancy of psychological benefits and mood alteration in joggers. *International Journal of Sport Psychology*, **29**, 1–16.

Berkman, L. F. (1995). The role of social relations in health promotion. *Psychosomatic Medicine*, **57**, 245–254.

Berkman, L. F. and Syme, S. L. (1979). Social networks, host resistance, and mortality: a nine year follow-up study of Alameda County residents. *American Journal of Epidemiology*, **109**, 186–204.

Biddle, S. (in press). Emotion, mood and physical activity. In S. J. H. Biddle, K. R. Fox and S. H. Boutcher (Eds), *Physical Activity and Psychological Well-being*. London: Routledge.

Birley, J. L. and Brown, G. W. (1970). Crises and life changes preceding the onset or relapse of acute schizophrenia: clinical aspects. *British Journal of Psychiatry*, **116**, 327–333.

Bishop, D. W. and Ikeda, M. (1970). Status and role factors in the leisure behavior of different occupations. *Sociology and Social Research*, **54**, 190–208.

Blair, S. N., Kohl, H. W., Paffenbarger, R. S., Clark, D. G., Cooper, K. H. and Gibbons, L. W. (1989). Physical fitness and all cause mortality: A prospective study of healthy men and women. *Journal of the American Medical Association*, **262**, 2395–2401.

Blood, R. O. and Wolfe, D. M. (1960). *Husbands and Wives*, New York: Macmillan.

Boffetta, P. and Garfinkel, L. (1990). Alcohol drinking and mortality among men enrolled in an American Cancer Society prospective study. *Epidemiology*, **1**, 342–348.

Bogg, J. and Cooper, C. (1995). Job satisfaction, mental health, and occupational stress among senior civil servants. *Human Relations*, **48**, 327–341.

Bolger, N. (1990). Coping as a personality process: A prospective study. *Journal of Personality and Social Psychology*, **59**, 525–537.

Bolger, N. and Schilling, E. A. (1991). Personality and the problems of everyday life: The role of neuroticism in exposure and reactivity to daily stressors. *Journal of Personality*, **59**, 355–386.

Bolger, N., DeLongis, A., Kessler, R. C. and Schilling, E. A. (1989). Effects of daily stress on negative mood. *Journal of Personality and Social Psychology*, **57**, 808–818.

Bolger, N., DeLongis, A., Kessler, R. C. and Wethington, E. (1989). The contagion of stress across multiple roles. *Journal of Marriage and the Family*, **51**, 175–183.

Bonner, K. (1967). Industrial implications of stress. In L. Levi (Ed.), *Emotional Stress*. New York: American Elsevier Publishing Co.

Booth-Kewley, S. and Friedman, H. S. (1987). Psychological predictors of heart disease: A quantitative review. *Psychological Bulletin*, **101**, 343–362.

Bornstein, R. F. (1991). Manuscript review in psychology: Psychometrics, demand characteristics and an alternative model. *Journal of Mind and Behavior*, **12**, 429–467.

Bosma, H., Marmot, M. G., Hemingway, H., Nicholson, A. C., Brunner, E. and Stansfeld, S. A. (1997). Low job control and risk of coronary heart disease in Whitehall II (prospective cohort) study. *British Medical Journal*, **314**, 558–565.

Bowen, G. L. (1998). Effects of leader support in the work unit on the relationship between work spillover and family adaptation. *Journal of Family and Economic Issues*, **19**, 25–52.

Bower, G. H. (1981). Mood and memory. *American Psychologist*, **36**, 129–148.

Bowling, A. (1998). *Measuring Health: A Review of Quality of Life Measurement Scales*. Buckingham: Open University Press.

Bowling, A. P., Edelmann, R. J., Leaver, J. and Hoekel, T. (1989). Loneliness, mobility, well-being and social support in a sample of over 85 year olds. *Personality and Individual Differences*, **10**, 1189–1192.

Bradley, J. and Sutherland, V. (1995). Occupational stress in social services: a comparison of social workers and home help staff. *British Journal of Social Work*, **25**, 313–331.

Brandt, L. P. A. and Nielsen, C. V. (1992). Job stress and adverse outcome of pregnancy: A causal link or recall bias? *American Journal of Epidemiology*, **135**, 302–311.

Brett, J. F., Brief, A. P., Burke, M. J. and George, J. M. *et al.* (1990). Negative affectivity and the reporting of stressful life events. *Health Psychology*, **9**, 57–68.

Brief, A. P. and George, J. M. (1995). Psychological stress and the workplace: a brief comment on Lazarus' outlook. In R. Crandall and P. L. Perrewe (Eds), *Occupational Stress: A Handbook*. Bristol: Taylor and Francis.

Brief, A. P., Burke, M. J., George, J. M., Robinson, B. S. and Webster, J. (1988). Should negative affectivity remain an unmeasured variable in the study of job stress? *Journal of Applied Psychology*, **73**, 193–198.

Brief, A. P., Butcher, A. H. and Roberson, L. (1995). Cookies, disposition, and job attitudes: The effects of positive mood inducing events and negative affectivity on job satisfaction in a field experiment. *Organizational Behavior and Human Decision Processes*, **62**, 55–62.

Bright, J. E. H., Gillam, B. and Balaam, C. (1997). *A survey of managment training practices in New South Wales*. Presented to the Australian Academy of Social Sciences Symposium on Training. June. Melbourne.

Briner, R. B. (1996). Stress talk: sociocultural approaches to understanding organizational stress (Abstract only published). Paper presented at the Annual Conference of the British Psychological Society, Brighton.

Briner, R. B. (1997). Improving stress assessment: toward an evidence-based approach to organizational stress interventions. *Journal of Psychosomatic Research*, **43**, 61–71.

Briner, R. B. and Reynolds, S. (1993). Bad theory and bad practice in occupational stress. SAPU memo 1405. Sheffield University.

Briner, R. and Reynolds, S. (1998). The costs, benefits, and limitations of organizational level interventions. *Journal of Organizational Behavior*, **20**, 647–664.

Briner, R. B. and Reynolds, S. (1999). The costs and limitations of organizational level interventions. *Journal of Organizational Behavior*, **20**(5), 647–664.

Brisson, C., Laflamme, N., Moisin, J., Milot, A., Masse, B. and Vezina, M. S. O. (1999). Effect of family responsibilities and job strain on ambulatory blood presure among white collar women. *Psychosomatic Medicine*, **61**, 205–131.

Brodman, K., Erdmann, A. J. J., Lorge, I. and Wolff, H. G. (1949). The Cornell Medical Index: An adjunct to medical interview. *Journal of the American Medical Association*, **140**, 530–534.

Brown, G. W. (1974). Meaning, measurement and stress of life events. In B. S. Dohrenwend and B. P. Dohrenwend (Eds), *Stressful Life Events: Their Nature and Effects*. London: John Wiley.

Brown, G. W. (1990). What about the real world? Hassles and Richard Lazarus. *Psychological Inquiry*, **1**, 19–22.

Brown, G. W. and Harris, T. O. (1978). *Social Origins of Depression: A Study of Psychiatric Disorder in Women*. London: Tavistock Publications.

Brown, G. W. and Harris, T. O. (1989). *Life Events and Illness*. New York: Guilford.

Brown, G. W., Andrews, B., Harris, T., Adler, Z. and Bridge, L. (1986). Social support, self-esteem and depression. *Psychological Medicine*, **16**, 813–831.

Brown, J. A. C. (1964). *Freud and the Post-Freudians*. Harmondsworth: Penguin.

Brown, J. S. L., Cochrane, R., Mack, C. F., Leung, N. and Hancox, T. (1998). Comparisons of effectiveness of large scale stress workshops with small stress/anxiety management training groups. *Behavioural and Cognitive Psychotherapy*, **26**, 219–235.

Brown, J., Kranzler, H. R. and Delboca, F. K. (1992). Self-reports of alcohol and drug-abuse patients – factors affecting reliability and validity. *British Journal of Addiction*, **87**, 1013–1024.

Brown, J., Cooper, C. and Kirkcaldy, B. (1996). Occupational stress amongst senior police officers. *British Journal of Psychology*, **87**, 31–41.

Bruning, N. S. and Frew, D. R. (1987). Effects of Exercise, relaxation, and management skills training on physiological stress indicators: a field experiment. *Journal of Applied Psychology*, **72**, 515–521.

Bryant, F. B. and Marquez, J. T. (1986). Educational status and the structure of subjective well-being in men and women. *Social Psychology Quarterly*, **49**, 142–153.

Buck, N., Gershuny, J., Rose, D. and Scott, J. (1994). *Changing Households: The British Household Panel Survey, 1990–1992*. ESRC Research Centre on Microsocial Change, University of Essex, Colchester.

Bunce, D. and West, M. (1994). Changing work environments: innovative coping responses to occupational stress. *Work and Stress*, **8**, 319–331.

Burg, M. M. and Seeman, T. E. (1994). Families and health: the negative side of social ties. *Annals of Behavioral Medicine*, **16**, 109–115.

Burish, T. G. and Lyles, J. N. (1981). Effectiveness of relaxation training in reducing adverse reactions to cancer chemotherapy. *Journal of Behavioral Medicine*, **4**, 65–78.

Burke, M. and Mathews, A. (1992). Autobiographical memory and clinical anxiety. *Cognition and Emotion*, **6**, 23–35.

Burke, M. J., Brief, A. P. and George, J. M. (1993). The role of negative affectivity in understanding relations between self-reports of stressors and strains: A comment on the applied psychology literature. *Journal of Applied Psychology*, **78**, 402–412.

Burke, R. J., Weir, T. and Duwors, R. E. J. (1980). Work demands on administrators and spouse wellbeing. *Human Relations*, **33**, 253–278.

Burke, R. J. and Weir, T. (1981). Impact of occupational demands on nonwork experiences. *Group and Organization Studies*, **6**, 472–485.

Burke, R. J. (1988). Type a behavior, occupational and life demands, satisfaction, and well-being. *Psychological Reports*, **63**, 451–458.

Buunk, B. P., Doosje, B. J., Jans, L. G. J. M. and Hopstaken, E. M. (1993). Perceived reciprocity, social support and stress at work: the role of communal orientation. *Journal of Personality and Social Psychology*, **65**, 801–811.

Byrne, D. (1961). The repression-sensitization scale: Rationale, reliability and validity. *Journal of Personality*, **29**, 334–349.

Byrne, D. (1964). Repression-sensitization as a dimension of personality. In B. A. Maher (Ed.), *Progress in Experimental Personality Research*. San Diego, CA: Academic Press.

Caldwell, J. (1995). Assessing the impact of stressors on performance. *Biological Psychology*, **40**, 197–208.

Caldwell, M. A. and Peplau, L. A. (1982). Sex differences in same-sex friendship. *Sex Roles*, **8**, 721–732.

Calnan, J. (1984). *Coping with research: the complete guide for beginners*. Heinemann Medical.

Caplan, R. D., Cobb, S., French, J. R. P., Harrison, R. V. and Pinneau, S. R. (1975). *Job Demands and Worker Health*. HEW Publication No. 75160 (NIOSH), Washington, DC.

Carver, C. (1997). You want to measure coping but your protocol's too long: Consider the brief COPE. *International Journal of Behavioral Medicine*, **4**, 92–100.

Carver, C. S. and Scheier, M. F. (1994). Situational coping and coping dispositions in a stressful transaction. *Journal of Personality and Social Psychology*, **66**, 184–195.

Carver, C. S., Scheier, M. F. and Weintraub, J. K. (1989). Assessing Coping Strategies: A theoretically based approach. *Journal of Personality and Social Psychology*, **56**, 267–283.

Caspi, A., Bolger, N. and Eckenrode, J. (1987). Linking person and context in the daily stress process. *Journal of Personality and Social Psychology*, **52**, 184–195.

Cassell, J. (1976). The contribution of the social environment to host resistance. *American Journal of Epidemiology*, **104**, 107–123.

Cattell, R. B., Eber, H. W. and Tatsuoka, M. M. (1970). *Handbook for the Sixteen Personality Factor Questionnaire*. Champaign, Illinois: Institute for Personality and Ability Testing.

Caughey, J. (1996). Psychological distress in staff of a social services district office: A pilot study. *British Journal of Social Work*, **26**, 389–398.

Ceci, S. J. and Peters, D. (1984). How blind is blind review? *American Psychologist*, **39**, 1491–1494.

Chan, C. and Margolin, G. (1994). The relationship between dual earner couples daily work mood and home affect. *Journal of Social and Personal Relationships*, **11**, 573–586.

Chaplin, J. P. (1985). *Dictionary of Psychology. (2nd revised ed.).* New York: Dell Publishing.

Charlesworth, K. (1996). *Are Managers under Stress?* London: Institute of Management.

Chelmers, M. M., Hays, R. B., Rhodewalt, F. and Wysocki, J. (1985). A person–environment analysis of job stress: a contingency model explanation. *Journal of Personality and Social Psychology*, **49**, 628–635.

Chen, C. C., David, A. S., Nunnerley, H., Mitchell, M., Dawson, J. L., Berry, H., Dobbs, J. and Fahy, T. (1995). Adverse life events and breast cancer: case-control study. *British Medical Journal*, **311**, 1527–1530.

Chen, P. Y. and Spector, P. E. (1991). Negative affectivity as the underlying cause of correlations between stressors and strain. *Journal of Applied Psychology*, **76**, 398–407.

Clover, R. D., Abell, T., Becker, L. A., Crawford, S. and Ramsey, C. N. J. (1989). Family functioning and stress as predictors of influenza B infection. *Journal of Family Practice*, **28**, 535–539.

Cobb, S. (1976). Social support as a moderator of life stress. *Psychosomatic Medicine*, **38**, 300–314.

Cody, M. J., Dunn, D., Hoppin, S. and Wendt, P. (1999). Silver surfers: Training and evaluating internet use among older adult learners. *Communication Education*, **48**, 269–286.

Cohen, F. (1987). Measurement of Coping. In S. V. Kasl and C. L. Cooper (Eds), *Stress and Health: Issues in Research Methodology*. Chichester: John Wiley and Sons.

Cohen, S. and Edwards, J. R. (1989). Personality characteristics as moderators of the relationship between stress and disorder. In R. W. J. Neufeld *et al.* (Eds), *Advances in the Investigation of Psychological Stress. Wiley Series on Health Psychology/Behavioral Medicine* (pp. 235–283). New York: John Wiley and Sons.

Cohen, S. and Manuck, S. B. (1995). Stress, reactivity and disease. *Psychosomatic Medicine*, **57**, 427–435.

Cohen, S. and Williamson, G. M. (1991). Stress and infectious diseases in humans. *Psychological Bulletin*, **109**, 5–24.

Cohen, S. and Wills, T. A. (1985). Stress, social support and the buffering hypothesis. *Psychological Bulletin*, **98**, 310–357.

Cohen, S., Kamarck, T. and Mermelstein, R. (1983). A global measure of perceived stress. *Journal of Health and Social Behavior*, **24**, 385–396.

Cohen, S., Schwartz, J. E., Bromet, E. J. and Parkinson, D. K. (1991a). Mental health, stress and poor health behaviors in two community samples. *Preventive Medicine*, **20**, 306–315.

Cohen, S., Tyrell, D. A. J. and Smith, A. P. (1991b). Psychological stress and susceptibility to the common cold. *New England Journal of Medicine*, **325**, 606–612.

Cohen, S., Tyrell, D. A. J. and Smith, A. P. (1993). Negative life events, perceived stress, negative affect and susceptibility to the common cold. *Journal of Personality and Social Psychology*, **64**, 131–140.

Cohen, S., Frank, E., Doyle, W. J., Skoner, D. P., Rabin, B. S. and Gwaltney, J. M. (1998). Types of stressors that increase susceptibility to the common cold in healthy adults. *Health Psychology*, **17**, 214–223.

Cooke, R. A. and Rousseau, D. M. (1984). Stress and strain from family roles and work-role expectations. *Journal of Applied Psychology*, **69**, 252–260.

Cooper, C. L. and Cartwright, S. (1994). Healthy mind, healthy organization – a proactive approach to occupational stress. *Human Relations*, **47**(4), 455–468.

Cooper, C. L. and Marshall, J. (1976). Occupational sources of stress: a review of the literature relating to coronary heart disease and mental health. *Journal of Occupational Psychology*, **49**, 11–28.

Cooper, C. L. and Payne, R. (Eds) (1988). *Causes, Coping and Consequences of Stress at Work*. Chichester: John Wiley and Sons.

Cooper, C. L. and Sadri, G. (1995). The impact of stres counseling at work. In R. Crandall and P. L. Perrew (Eds), *Occupational Stress: A Handbook*. London: Taylor and Francis.

Cooper, C. L., Sloan, S. J. and Williams, S. (1988). *The Occupational Stress Indicator*. Windsor: NFER-Nelson.

Cooper, C. L., Cooper, R. and Faragher, E. B. (1989). Incidence and perception of psychosocial stress: the relationship with breast cancer. *Psychological Medicine*, **19**, 315–318.

Cordes, C. and Dougherty, T. W. (1993). A review and integration of research on job burnout. *Academy of Management Review*, **18**, 621–656.

Corr, C. (1993). Coping with dying: Lessons that we should and should not learn from the work of Elisabeth Kubler-Ross. *Death Studies*, **17**, 69–83.

Costa, J. P. T., Somerfield, M. R. and McRae, R. R. (1996). Personality and coping: a reconceptualization. In M. Zeidner and N. S. Endler (Eds), *Handbook of Coping*. New York: John Wiley and Sons.

Costa, P. T. and McRae, R. R. (1987). Neuroticism, somatic complaints and disease: Is the bark worse than the bite? *Journal of Personality*, **55**, 299–316.

Costa, P. T. and McCrae, R. R. (1990). Personality: another 'hidden factor' in stress research. *Psychological Inquiry*, **1**, 22–24.

Costa, P. T., McCrae, R. R. and Zonderman, A. B. (1987). Environmental and dispositional influences on well-being: Longitudinal follow-up of an American national sample. *British Journal of Psychology*, **78**, 299–306.

Courtney, J. G., Longnecker, M. P. and Peters, R. K. (1996). Psychosocial aspects of work and the risk of colon cancer. *Epidemiology*, **7**, 175–181.

Cox, T. (1993). *Stress Research and Stress Management: Putting Theory to Work*. (Health and Safety Executive Contract Research Report No 61/1993). Suffolk, UK: Health and Safety Executive.

Cox, T. and Griffiths, A. (1996). Assessment of psychosocial hazards at work. In M. J. Schabracq, J. A. M. Winnubst and C. L. Cooper (Eds), *Handbook of Work and Health Psychology*. Chichester: Wiley and Sons.

Coyne, J. C. (1997). Improving coping research: raze the slum before any more building. *Journal of Health Psychology*, **2**, 153–172.

Coyne, J. C. and Gottlieb, B. H. (1996). The mismeasure of coping by checklist. *Journal of Personality*, **64**, 957–989.

Craft, L. L. and Landers, D. M. (1999). The effect of exercise on clinical depression and depression resulting from physical illness: a meta-analysis. *Journal of Exercise and Sports Psychology*, **20**, 339–357.

Cropanzano, R. and James, K. (1993). Dispositional affectivity as a predictor of work attitudes and job performance. *Journal of Organizational Behavior*, **14**, 595–606.

Crossfield, S. (1999). *An Investigation into the Transmission of Occupational Stress in Full-Time Working Couples*, BSc dissertation, University of Hertfordshire, UK.

Crouter, A. C., Perry-Jenkins, M., Huston, T. L. and Crawford, D. W. (1989). The influence of work-induced psychological states on behaviour at home. *Basic and Applied Social Psychology*, **10**, 273–292.

Crown, S. and Crisp, A. H. (1979). *Manual of the Crown–Crisp Experiential Index*. London: Hodder and Stoughton.

Crowne, D. P. and Marlowe, D. A. (1964). *The Approval Motive: Studies in Evaluative Dependence*. New York: Wiley.

Cunha, R. C., Cooper, C. L., Moura, M. I., Reis, M. E. *et al.* (1992). Portuguese version of the OSI: a study of reliability and validity. *Stress Medicine*, **8**, 247–251.

Cutrona, C. E. and Russell, D. W. (1990). Type of social support and specific stress: toward a theory of optimal matching. In B. R. Sarason, I. G. Sarason and G. R. Pierce (Eds), *Social Support: An interactional View*. New York: Wiley.

Dakof, G. S. and Taylor, S. E. (1990). Victims perceptions of social support: What is helpful and from whom? *Journal of Personality and Social Psychology*, **58**, 80–89.

Daniels, K., Brough, P., Guppy, A., Peters-Bean, K. M. and Weatherstone, L. (1997). A note on modification to Warr's measures of affective well-being at work. *Journal of Occupational and Organisational Psychology*, **70**, 129–138.

Davey, G. C. L., Tallis, F. and Hodgson, S. (1993). The relationship between information-seeking and information-avoidant coping styles and the reporting of physical and psychological symptoms. *Journal of Psychosomatic Research*, **37**, 333–344.

Davis, A. J. (1996). A re-analysis of the Occupational Stress Indicator. *Work and Stress*, **10**, 174–182.

De Geus, E. J. C. and Van Doornen, L. J. P. (1993). The effects of fitness training on the physiological stress response. *Work and Stress*, **7**, 141–159.

de Moraes, L. F., Swan, J. A. and Cooper, C. L. (1993). A study of occupational stress among government white collar workers in Brazil using the Occupational Stress Indicator. *Stress Medicine*, **9**, 91–104.

Deary, I. J., Blenkin, H., Agius, R., Endler, N. S., Zealley, H. and Wood, R. (1996). Models of job-related stress and personal achievement among consultant doctors. *British Journal of Psychology*, **87**, 3–29.

DeFrank, R. S., Jenkins, C. D. and Rose, R. M. (1987). A longitudinal investigation of the relationships among alcohol consumption, psychosocial factors, and blood pressure. *Journal of Psychosomatic Medicine*, **49**, 236–249.

DeLongis, A., Coyne, J. C., Dakof, G., Folkman, S. and Lazarus, R. S. (1982). Relationships of daily hassles, uplifts, and major life events to health status. *Health Psychology*, **1**, 119–136.

DeLongis, A., Folkman, S. and Lazarus, R. S. (1988). The impact of daily stress on health and mood: psychological and social resources as mediators. *Journal of Personality and Social Psychology*, **54**, 486–495.

Dembroski, T. M., MacDougall, J. M., Costa, P. T. and Grandits, G. A. (1989). Components of hostility as predictors of sudden death and myocardial infarction in the Multiple Risk Factor Intervention Trial. *Psychosomatic Medicine*, **51**, 514–522.

Denollet, J. (1998). Personality and risk of cancer in men with coronary heart disease. *Psychological Medicine*, **28**, 991–995.

Depamo, B. and Job, R. F. S. (1990). An evaluation of SALT (Suggestive-accelerative learning and teaching) techniques. *Australian Journal of Educational Technology*, **6**, 36–55.

Depue, R. A. and Monroe, S. M. (1986). Conceptualization and measurement of human disorder in life stress research. *Psychological Bulletin*, **99**, 36–51.

Derakshan, N. and Eysenck, M. W. (1997). Interpretive biases for one's own behavior and physiology in high-trait-anxious individuals and repressors. *Journal of Personality and Social Psychology*, **73**, 816–825.

Derakshan, N. and Eysenck, M. W. (1998). Working memory capacity in high trait-anxious and repressor groups. *Cognition and Emotion*, **12**, 697–713.

Derogatis, L. R. and Coons, H. L. (1993). Self-report measures of stress. In L. R. Goldberger and S. Breznitz (Eds), *Handbook of Stress: Theoretical and Clinical Aspects*. New York: The Free Press.

Dewe, P. J. (1989). Examining the nature of work stress: individual evaluations of stressful experiences and coping. *Human Relations*, **42**, 993–1013.

Dewe, P. J. (1992). Applying the concept of appraisal to work stressors: some exploratory analysis. *Human Relations*, **45**, 143–164.

Dewe, P., Cox, T. and Ferguson, E. (1993). Individual strategies for coping with stress at work: a review. *Work and Stress*, **7**, 5–15.

Dhabhar, F. S. and McEwan, B. S. (1997). Acute stress enhances while chronic stress suppresses cell-mediated immunity in vivo: a potential role for leukocyte trafficking. *Brain, Behaviour and Immunity*, **11**, 286–306.

Diener, E., Suh, E. M., Lucas, R. E. and Smith, H. L. (1999). Subjective well-being: Three decades of progress. *Psychological Bulletin*, **125**, 276–302.

Dinan, T. G. (1994). Glucocorticoids and the genesis of depressive illness: a psychobiological model. *British Journal of Psychiatry*, **164**, 365–371.

Dishman, R. K. (1982). Compliance/adherence in health related exercise. *Health Psychology*, **1**(13), 237–267.

Doby, V. J. and Caplan, R. D. (1995). Organisational stress as threat to reputation: effects on anxiety work and at home. *Academy of Management Journal*, **38**, 1105–1123.

Dohrenwend, B. P. (Ed.) (1998). *Adversity, Stress and Psychopathology*. New York: Oxford University Press.

Dohrenwend, B. S. and Dohrenwend, B. P. (1974). Overview and prospects for research on stressful events. In B. S. Dohrenwend and B. P. Dohrenwend (Eds), *Stressful Life Events: their Nature and Effects*. London: John Wiley and Sons.

Dohrenwend, B. P. and Shrout, P. E. (1985). 'Hassles' in the conceptualization and measurement of life stress variables. *American Psychologist*, **40**, 780–785.

Dohrenwend, B. S., Dohrenwend, B. P., Dodson, M. and Shrout, P. E. (1984). Symptoms, hassles, social supports, and life events: Problem of confounded measures. *Journal of Abnormal Psychology*, **93**, 222–230.

Dohrenwend, B. P., Link, B. G., Kern, R., Shrout, P. E. and Markowitz, J. (1990). Measuring life events: the problem of variability within event categories. *Stress Medicine*, **6**, 179–187.

Dohrenwend, B. P., Raphael, K. G., Schwarz, S., Stueve, A. and Skodol, A. (1993). The structured event probe and narrative rating method for measuring stressful life event. In L. Goldberger and S. Breznitz (Eds), *Handbook of Stress: Theoretical and Clinical Aspects*. New York: The Free Press.

Doyle, C. and Hind, P. (1998). Occupational stress, burnout and job status in female academics. *Gender, Work and Organisation*, **5**, 67–82.

Dubin, R. (1973). Work and non-work: Institutional perspectives. In M. D. Dunnette (Ed.), *Work and Non-Work in the Year 2001*. Monterey, CA: Brookes/Cole.

Dunkel-Shetter, C., Feinstein, L. G., Taylor, S. E. and Falke, R. L. (1992). Patterns of coping with cancer. *Health Psychology*, **11**, 79–87.

Dunn, M. R., Fargher, B., Thorogood, M., De-Caestecker, L., MacDonald, T. M., McCollum, C., Thomas, S. and Mann, R. (1999). Risk of myocardial infarction in young female smokers. *Heart*, **82**, 581–3.

Durkheim, E. (1952). *Suicide: A Study in Sociology*. London: Routledge and Kegan Paul.

Duxbury, L. E. and Higgins, C. A. (1991). Gender differences in work–family conflict. *Journal of Applied Psychology*, **76**, 60–73.

Dwyer, D. J. and Ganster, D. C. (1991). The effects of job demands and control on employee attendance and satisfaction. *Journal of Organizational Behaviour*, **12**, 595–608.

Earnshaw, J. and Cooper, C. (1996). *Stress and Employer Liability*. London: Institute of Personnel and Development.

Easterbrook, J. A. (1959). The effect of emotion on cue utilization and the organization of behavior. *Psychological Review*, **66**, 183–201.

Edwards, J. R. and Cooper, C. L. (1990). The person–environment fit approach to stress: recurring problems and some suggested solutions. *Journal of Organizational Behavior*, **11**, 293–307.

Edwards, J. R., Baglioni, A. J. and Cooper, C. L. (1990). Stress, Type A, coping, and psychological and physical symptoms: a multi-sample test of alternative models. *Human Relations*, **43**, 919–956.

Emmons, C., Biernat, M., Tiedge, L. B., Lang, E. L. and Wortnman, C. (1990). Stress, support and coping among women professionals with preschool children. In J. Eckenrode and S. Gore (Eds), *Stress Between Work and Family*. New York: Plenum Press.

Esterling, B. A., Kiecolt-Glaser, J. K., Bodnar, J. C. and Glaser, R. (1994). Chronic stress, social support, and persistent alterations in the natural killer cell response to cytokines in older adults. *Health Psychology*, **13**, 291–298.

Eulberg, J. R., Weekley, J. A. and Bhagat, R. S. (1988). Models of stress in organizational research: a metatheoretical perspective. *Human Relations*, **41**, 331–350.

Evans, P. D. and Edgerton, N. (1991). Life-events and mood as predictors of the common cold. *British Journal of Medical Psychology*, **64**, 35–44.

Evans, P. D., Doyle, F., Hucklebridge, F. and Clow, A. (1996). Positive but not negative life-events predict vulnerability to upper respiratory illness. *British Journal of Health Psychology*, **1**, 339–348.

Evans, P., Clow, A. and Hucklebridge, F. (1997). Stress and the immune system. *The Psychologist*, **10**, 303–307.

Evans, P., Hucklebridge, F. and Clow, A. (2000). *Mind, Immunity and Health*. London: Free Association Books.

Eysenck, H. J. (1953). *The Structure of Personality*. London: Methuen.

Eysenck, H. J. (1990). *The Decline and Fall of the Freudian Empire*. Washington, DC: Scott-Townsend Publishers.

Eysenck, H. J. and Eysenck, S. B. G. (1964). *Manual for the Eysenck Personality Inventory*. London University Press: London.

Eysenck H. J. and Eysenck, S. B. G. (1976). *Psychoticism as a Dimension of Personality*. London: Hodder and Stoughton.

Eysenck, M. W. (1982). *Attention and Arousal: Cognition and Performance*. Berlin: Springer.

Eysenck, M. W. (1983). Anxiety and individual differences. In G. R. J. Hockey (Ed.), *Stress and Fatigue in Human Performance*. Chichester: Wiley and Sons.

Eysenck, M. W. (1992). *Anxiety: The Cognitive Perspective*. Hove: Lawrence Erlbaum Associates.

Eysenck, M. W. (1997). *Anxiety and Cognition: A Unified Theory*. Hove, England UK: Psychology Press/Erlbaum (UK) Taylor and Francis.

Eysenck, M. W. and Derakshan, N. (1997). Cognitive biases for future negative events as a function of trait anxiety and social desirability. *Personality and Individual Differences*, **22**, 597–605.

Eysenck, M. W. and Graydon, J. (1989). Susceptibility to distraction as a function of personality. *Personality and Individual Differences*, **10**, 681–687.

Eysenck, M. W., Mogg, K., May, J., Richards, A. and Mathews, A. (1991). Bias in interpretation of ambiguous sentences related to threat in anxiety. *Journal of Abnormal Psychology*, **100**, 144–150.

Feldman, P. J. and Cohen, S. (1999). The impact of personality on the reporting of unfounded symptoms and illness. *Journal of Personality and Social Psychology*, **77**, 370–378.

Ferrie, J. E., Shipley, M. J., Marmot, M. G., Stansfeld, S. and Smith, G. D. (1998). The health effects of major organisational change and job insecurity. *Social Science and Medicine*, **46**, 243–254.

Festinger, L. (1957). *A Theory of Cognitive Dissonance*. Stanford, CA: Stanford University Press.

Fiedler, F. E. (1967). *A Theory of Leadership Effectiveness*. New York: McGraw-Hill.

Firth, J. and Shapiro, D. A. (1986). An evaluation of psychotherapy for job-related distress. *Journal of Occupational Psychology*, **59**, 111–119.

Firth-Cozens, J. (1992a). The role of early family experiences in the perception of organizational stress: Fusing clinical and organizational perspectives. *Journal of Occupational and Organizational Psychology*, **65**, 61–75.

Firth-Cozens, J. (1992b). Why me? A case study of the process of perceived occupational stress. *Human Relations*, **45**, 131–141.

Firth-Cozens, J. and Hardy, G. E. (1992). Occupational stress, clinical treatment and changes in job perceptions. *Journal of Occupational and Organizational Psychology*, **65**, 81–88.

Fischer, C. L., Gill, C., Daniels, J. C., Cobb, E. K., Berry, C. A. and Ritzmann, S. E. S. O. (1972). Effects of space flight environment on man's immune system. I. Serum proteins and immunoglobins. *Aerospace Medicine*, **43**, 856–891.

Fletcher, B. (C.) (1988). Occupation, marriage and disease-specific mortality concordance. *Social Science and Medicine*, **27**, 515–622.

Fletcher, B. (C.) (1991). *Work, Stress, Disease and Life Expectancy*. Chichester: Wiley and Sons.

Fletcher, B. C. and Jones, F. (1993). A refutation of Karasek's demand–discretion model of occupational stress with a range of dependent measures. *Journal of Organizational Behaviour*, **14**, 319–330.

Folkman, S. (1997). Holistic approaches: appealing but unwieldy. *Journal of Health Psychology*, **2**, 153–172.

Folkman, S. and Lazarus, R. (1980). An analysis of coping in a middle-aged community sample. *Journal of Health and Social Behavior*, **21**, 219–239.

Folkman, S. and Lazarus, R. S. (1985). If it changes it must be a process: study of emotion and coping during three stages of a college examination. *Journal of Personality and Social Psychology*, **48**, 150–170.

Folkman, S. and Lazarus, R. (1988). *Manual for the Ways of Coping Questionnaire*. Palo Alto, California: Consulting Psychologists Press.

Folkman, S., Lazarus, R. S., Gruen, R. J. and DeLongis, A. (1986). Appraisal, coping, health status and psychological symptoms. *Journal of Personality and Social Psychology*, **50**, 571–579.

Fontana, A. M., Hyra, D., Godfrey, L. and Cermak, L. (1999). Impact of a peer-led stress innoculation training intervention on state anxiety and heart rate in college students. *Journal of Biobehavioral Research*, **4**, 45–63.

Forgas, J. P. (1995). Mood and judgement: the affect infusion model. *Psychological Bulletin*, **117**, 39–66.

Fox, B. H. S. O. (1998). A hypothesis about Spiegel *et al.*'s 1989 paper on psychosocial intervention and breast cancer survival. *Psychooncology*, **7**, 361–370.

Fox, K. R. (In press). The effects of exercise on self-perception and self-esteem. In S. J. H. Biddle, K. R. Fox and S. H. Boutcher (Eds), *Physical Activity and Psychological Well-being*. London: Routledge.

Fox, M. L., Dwyer, D. J. and Ganster, D. C. (1993). Effects of stressful job demands and control on physiological and attitudinal outcomes in a hospital setting. *Academy of Management Journal*, **36**, 289–318.

Frankenhaueser, M., Lundberg, U., Fredrikson, M., Melin, B. *et al.* (1989). Stress on and off the job as related to sex and occupational status in white-collar workers. *Journal of Organizational Behavior*, **10**, 321–346.

French, J. R. P., Caplan, R. D. and Van Harrison, R. (1982). *The Mechanisms of Job Stress and Strain*. Chichester: John Wiley and Sons.

Frese, M. (1985). Stress at work and psychosomatic complaints: a causal interpretation. *Journal of Applied Psychology*, **70**, 314–328.

Frese, M. and Zapf, D. (1988). Methodological issues in the study of work stress: objective versus subjective measurement of work stress and the question of longitudinal studies. In C. L. Cooper and R. L. Payne (Eds), *Causes, Coping and Consequences of Stress at Work*. Chichester: John Wiley and Sons.

Freud, A. (1946). *The Ego and Mechanisms of Defence*. New York: International Universities Press.

Fried, S. B. (1994). *American Popular Psychology: an Interdisciplinary Research Guide*. New York: Garland Publishers.

Fried, Y., Rowland, K. M. and Ferris, G. R. (1984). The physiological measurement of work stress: a critique. *Personnel Psychology*, **37**, 583–615.

Frone, M. R. and Rice, R. W. (1987). Work–family conflict: the effect of job and family involvement. *Journal of Occupational Behaviour*, **8**, 45–53.

Frone, M. R., Russell, M. and Cooper, M. L. (1992a). Antecedents and outcomes of work–family conflict: testing a model of the work–family interface. *Journal of Applied Psychology*, **77**, 65–78.

Frone, M. R., Russell, M. and Cooper, M. L. (1992b). Prevalence of work–family conflict: Are work and family boundaries assymetrically permeable? *Journal of Organizational Behavior*, **13**, 723–729.

Frone, M. R., Russell, M. and Cooper, M. L. (1997). Relation of work–family conflict to health outcomes: A four-year longitudinal study of employed parents. *Journal of Occupational and Organizational Psychology*, **70**, 325–336.

Fuhrer, R., Stansfeld, S. A., Chemali, J. and Shipley, M. J. (1999). Gender, social relations and mental health: prospective findings from an occupational cohort (Whitehall II study) Social *Science and Medicine*, **48**, 77–87.

Fujita, F., Diener, E. and Sandvik, E. (1991). Gender differences in negative affect and well being: the case for emotional intensity. *Journal of Personality and Social Psychology*, **61**, 427–434.

Funk, S. C. and Houston, B. K. (1987). A critical analysis of the Hardiness Scale's validity and utility. *Journal of Personality and Social Psychology*, **53**, 572–578.

Furnham, A. and Henderson, M. (1983). Response bias in self-report measures of general health. *Personality and Individual Differences*, **4**, 519–525.

Fuster, V., Badimon, L., Badimon, J. and Chesebro, J. (1992). The pathogenesis of coronary artery disease and the acute coronary syndromes. *New England Journal of Medicine* **326**, 242–248.

Galambos, N. L. and Walters, B. J. (1992). Work hours, schedule inflexibility and stress in dual-earner spouses. *Canadian Journal of Behavioural Science*, **24**, 290–302.

Ganster, D. C. and Fusilier, M. R. (1989). Control in the workplace. In C. L. Cooper and I. Robertson (Eds), *International Review of Industrial and Organizational Psychology*. Chichester: Wiley and Sons.

Ganster, D., Mayes, B. T., Sime, W. E. and Tharp, G. D. (1982). Managing organizational stress: a field experiment. *Journal of Applied Psychology*, **67**, 533–542.

Ganster, D. C. and Schaubroeck, J. (1991) Work Stress and Employee Health. *Journal of Management*, **17**, 235–271.

Garcia-Vera, M. P., Labrador, F. J. and Sanz, J. (1997). Stress-management training for essential hypertension: A controlled study. *Applied Psychophysiology and Biofeedback*, **22**, 261–283.

Garcia-Vera, M. P., Sanz, J. and Labrador, F. J. (1998). Psychological changes accompanying and mediating stress-management training for essential hypertension. *Applied Psychophysiology and Biofeedback*, **23**, 159–178.

Garden, A. (1989). Burnout: The effect of psychological type on research findings. *Journal of Occupational Psychology*, **62**, 223–234.

Gellert, G. A., Maxwell, R. M. and Siegel, B. S. S. O. (1993). Survival of breast cancer patients receiving adjunctive psychosocial support therapy: a 10-year follow-up study. *Journal of Clinical Oncology*, **11**, 66–91.

George, J. M. (1992). The role of personality in organizational life: Issues and evidence. *Journal of Management*, **18**(2), 185–213.

Gerin, W., Milner, D., Chawla, S. and Pickering, T. G. (1995). Social support as a moderator of cardiovascular reactivity in women: a test of the direct effects and buffering hypothesis. *Psychosomatic Medicine*, **57**, 16–21.

Geyer, S. (1991). Life events prior to the manifestation of breast cancer: a limited prospective study covering eight years before diagnosis. *Journal or Psychosomatic Research*, **35**, 355–363.

Giddens, A. (1984). *The Constitution of Society*. Berkeley, CA: University of California Press.

Gidron, Y., Davidson, K. and Bata, I. (1999). Short-term effects of a hostility-reduction intervention on male coronary heart disease patients. *Health Psychology*, **18**, 416–420.

Glaser, R., Kiecolt-Glaser, J. K., Malarkey, W. B. and Sheridan, J. F. (1998). The influence of psychological stress on the immune response to vaccines. *Annals of the New York Academy of Science*, **840**, 649–651.

Glassner, B. and Moreno, J. D. (Eds) (1989). *The Qualitative–Quantitative Distinction in the Social Sciences (Vol. 112)*. Dordrecht: Kluwer Academic Publishers.

Goldberg, A. (1978). *Manual for the General Health Questionnaire*. Windsor, England: National Foundation for Educational Research.

Goldberg, D. P. (1972). *The Detection of Psychiatric Illness by Questionnaire*. London: Oxford University Press.

Goldberg, D. P. (1978). *General Health Questionnaire*. Windsor: NFER.

Goldberg, D. P. and Williams, P. (1988). *A User's Guide to the General Health Questionnaire*. Windsor: NFER-NELSON.

Gove, W. (1972). Sex, marital status and mental illness, *Social Forces*, **51**, 34–55.

Graham, N. M., Douglas, R. M. and Ryan, P. (1986). Stress and acute respiratory infection. *American Journal of Epidemiology*, **124**, 340.

Grant, T. (2000). *Physical Activity and Mental Health. National Consensus Statements and Guidelines for Practice*. Taunton: Somerset Health Authority.

Graydon, J. and Eysenck, M. W. (1989). Distraction and cognitive performance. *European Journal of Cognitive Psychology*, **1**, 161–179.

Greer, S. and Morris, T. (1975). Psychological attributes of women who develop breast cancer: A controlled study. *Journal of Psychosomatic Research*, **19**, 147–153.

Greenhaus, J. H. and Beutell, N. J. (1985). Sources of conflict between work and family roles. *Academy of Management Review*, **10**, 76–80.

Greenhaus, J. H., Bedeian, A. G. and Mossholder, K. W. (1987). Work experiences, job performance, and feeling of personal and family well-being. *Journal of Vocational Behavior*, **31**, 200–215.

Gruen, R. J. (1993). Stress and depression: toward the development of integrative models. In L. Goldberger and S. Breznitz (Eds), *Handbook of Stress: Theoretical and Clinical Aspects.* New York: The Free Press.

Guppy, A. and Marsden, J. (1997). Assisting employees with drinking problems: changes in mental health, job perceptions and work performance. *Work and Stress*, **11**, 341–350.

Haavio-Mannila, E. (1971). Satisfaction with family, work, leisure and life among men and women. *Human Relations*, **24**, 585–601.

Hackman, J. R. and Oldham, G. R. (1975). Development of the Job Diagnostic Survey. *Journal of Applied Psychology*, **60**, 159–170.

Hackman, J. R. and Oldham, G. R. (1980). *Work Redesign.* London: Addison-Wesley.

Hahn, S. E. and Smith, C. S. (1999). Daily hassles and chronic stressors: conceptual and measurement issues. *Stress Medicine*, **15**, 89–101.

Halamandaris, K. F. and Power, K. G. (1999). Individual differences, social suport and coping with the examination stress: A study of the psychosocial and academic adjustment of first year home students. *Personality and Individual Differences*, **26**, 665–685.

Haley, G. A. (1974). Eye movement responses of repressors and sensitizers to a stressful film. *Journal of Research in Personality*, **8**, 88–94.

Halperin, J. M. (1986). Defensive style and the direction of gaze. *Journal of Research in Personality*, **20**, 327–337.

Hampson, S. E. (1988). *The Construction of Personality: an Introduction.* London: Routledge.

Hansson, R. O., Jones, W. H. and Carpenter, B. N. (1984). Relational competence and social support. *Review of Personality and Social Support*, **5**, 265–284.

Hardt, J. and Gerbershagen, H. U. (1999). No changes in mood with the seasons: observations in 3000 chronic pain patients. *Acta Psychiatrica Scandinavica*, **100**, 288–294.

Harrell, J. E. and Ridley, C. A. (1975). Substitute child care, maternal employment and the quality of mother-child interaction, *Journal of Marriage and the Family*, **37**, 556–564.

Hart, C. L., Davey Smith, G., Hole, D. J. and Hawthorne, V. M. (1999). Alcohol consumption and mortality from all causes, coronary heart disease, and stroke: results form a prospective study of Scottish men with 21 years of follow-up. *British Medical Journal*, **318**, 1725–1729.

Hatfield, E., Cacioppo, J. T. and Rapson, R. L. (1994). *Emotional Contagion.* Cambridge: University of Cambridge Press.

Haynes, G., Eaker, E. D. and Feinleib, M. (1983). Spouse behaviour and coronary heart disease. *American Journal of Epidemiology*, **118**, 1–41.

Health and Safety at Work Act (1974). HMSO: London.

Heitzmann, C. A. and Kaplan, R. M. (1988). Assessment of methods for measuring social support. *Health Psychology*, **7**, 75–109.

Hellerstedt, W. L. and Jeffrey, R. W. (1997). The association of job strain and health behaviours in men and women. *International Journal of Epidemiology*, **26**, 575–583.

Hendrix, W. H. (1987). *Organizational and Individual Assessment Survey*. Clemson, SC: Clemson University.

Herbert, T. B. and Cohen, S. (1993). Stress and immunity in humans: a meta-analytic review. *Psychosomatic Medicine*, **55**, 364–379.

Hewitt, P. L. and Flett, G. L. (1996). Personality traits and the coping process. In M. Zeidner and N. S. Endler (Eds), *Handbook of Coping: Theory, Research, Applications*. Wiley: New York.

Hiatt, R. A. (1990). Alcohol consumption and breast cancer. *Med-Oncol-Tumor-Pharmacother.*, **7**, 143–151.

Higgins, C. A. and Duxbury, L. E. (1992). Work–family conflict: a comparison of dual-career and traditional-career men. *Journal of Organisational Behaviour*, **13**, 389–411.

Higgins, N. C. (1986). Occupational stress and working women: the effectiveness of two stress reduction programmes. *Journal of Vocational Behavior*, **29**, 66–78.

Highley, J. C. and Cooper, C. L. (1996). Counselling in the workplace. In R. Bayne, I. Horton and J. Bimrose. *New Directions in Counselling*. Routledge: London.

Highley-Marchington, C. and Cooper, C. L. (1997a). Evaluating and auditing workplace counselling schemes. In M. Carroll, M. Walton *et al.* (Eds), *Handbook of Counselling in Organisations*. London: Sage Publications.

Highley-Marchington, C. and Cooper, C. L. (1997b). An evaluation of employee assistance and workplace counselling programmes in the UK. In M. Carroll, M. Walton *et al.* (Eds), *Handbook of Counselling in Organisations*. London: Sage Publications.

Hinkle, L. E. (1973). The concept of 'stress' in the biological and social sciences. *Science, Medicine and Management*, **1**, 31–48.

Hitchcock, P. B. and Mathews, A. (1992). Interpretation of bodily symptoms in hypochondriasis. *Behaviour Research and Therapy*, **30**, 223–234.

Hlatky, M. A., Lam, L. C., Lee, K. L., Clapp-Channing, N. E., Williams, R. B., Pryor, D. B., Califf, R. M. and Mark, D. B. (1995). Job strain and the prevalence and outcome of coronary artery disease. *Circulation*, **92**, 327–333.

Hobfall, S. E. (1986). The ecology of stress and social support in women. In S. E. Hobfall (Ed.), *Stress, Social Support and Women*. Washington, DC: Hemisphere.

Hobfall, S. and Leibermann, J. R. (1987). Personality and social resources in immediate and continued stress resistance among women. *Journal of Personality and Social Psychology*, **52**, 18–26.

Hochschild, A. R. (1983). *The Managed Heart: Commercialisation of Human Feeling*. California: University of California Press.

Holahan, C. J. and Moos, R. H. (1981). Social support and psychological distress: A longitudinal analysis. *Journal of Abnormal Psychology*, **90**, 365–370.

Holmes, D. S. (1994). *Abnormal Psychology* (2nd edition). New York: HarperCollins.

Holmes, T. H. and Masuda, M. (1974). Life change and illness susceptibility. In B. S. Dohrenwend and B. P. Dohrenwend (Eds), *Stressful Life Events: their Nature and Effects*. John Wiley: London.

Holmes, T. H. and Rahe, R. H. (1967). The social readjustment rating scale. *Journal of Psychosomatic Research*, **11**, 213–218.

House, J. S., Robbins, C. and Metzner, H. M. (1982). The association of social relationships and activities with mortality: prospective evidence from the Tecumseh Community Health Study. *American Journal of Epidemiology*, **116**, 123–140.

House, J. S., Landis, K. R. and Umberson, D. (1988). Social relationships and health. *Science*, **241**, 540–545.

Housenecht, S. K., Vaughan, S. and Stratham, A. (1987). The impact of single-hood on career patterns of professional women. *Journal of Marriage and the Family*, **49**, 353–366.

HSE (1995). *Stress at Work: A Guide for Employers*. Suffolk: HSE Books.

HSE (1998). *Self-Reported Work Related Illness: Results from a Household Survey*. London: Government Statistical Service.

Hultman, C. M., Wieselgren, I. M. and Oehman, A. (1997). Relationships between social support, social coping and life events in the relapse of schizophrenic patients. *Scandinavian Journal of Psychology*, **38**, 3–13.

Hurrell, J. J. (1985). Machine-paced work and the Type A behaviour pattern. *Journal of Occupational Psychology*, **58**, 15–25.

Ingledew, D. K., Hardy, L. and Cooper, C. L. (1996). Health behaviors reported as coping strategies: A factor analytic study. *British Journal of Health Psychology*, **1**, 263–281.

Ivancevich, J. M. and Matteson, M. T. (1980) Stress and Work: A managerial perspective. Glenview, IL: Scott Foreman.

Ivancevich, J. M., Matteson, M. T., Preston, C. (1982). Occupational stress, Type A behavior, and physical well being. *Academy of Management Journal*, **25**, 373–391.

Jackson, P. R., Wall, T. D., Martin, R. and Davids, K. (1993). New measures of job control, cognitive demand, and production responsibility. *Journal of Applied Psychology*, **78**, 753–762.

Jackson, S. E. and Maslach, C. (1982). After-effects of job related stress: families as victims. *Journal of Occupational Behaviour*, **3**, 63–67.

Jamner, L. D. and Leigh, H. (1999). Repressive defensive coping, endogenous opioids and health: how a life so perfect can make you sick. *Psychiatry Research*, **85**, 17–31.

Jamner, L. D., Schwartz, G. E. and Leigh, H. (1988). The relationship between repressive and defensive coping styles and monocyte, eosinophile and serum glucose levels: support for the opiod peptide hypothesis of repression. *Psychosomatic Medicine*, **50**, 567–575.

Jandorf, L., Deblinger, E., Neale, J. M. and Stone, A. A. (1986). Daily versus major life events as predictors of symptom frequency. *The Journal of General Psychology*, **113**(3), 205–218.

Jemmott, I. J. B. and Magloire, K. (1988). Academic stress, social support and secretory immunoglobin. *A Journal of Personality and Social Psychology*, **55**, 803–810.

Jenkins, R. (1985). Minor Psychiatric Morbidity in employed young men and women and its contribution to sickness absence. *British Journal of Industrial Medicine*, **42**, 147–154.

Jenkins, R., Harvey, S., Butler, T. and Lloyd-Thomas, R. (1996). Minor psychiatric morbidity, its prevalence and outcome in a cohort of civil servants – a seven-year follow-up study. *Occupational Medicine*, **46**, 209–215.

Jensen, A. B. (1991). Psychological factors in breast cancer and their possible impact upon prognosis. *Cancer Treatment Reviews*, **18**, 191–210.

Jensen, M. R. (1987). Psychobiological factors predicting the course of breast cancer. *Journal of Personality*, **55**, 317–342.

Jex, S. M. (1991). The psychological benefits of exercise in work settings: a review, critique, and dispositional model. *Work and Stress*, **5**, 133–147.

Jex, S. M. and Beehr, T. A. (1991). Emerging theoretical and methodological issues in the study of work-related stress. In G. R. Ferris and K. W. Rowland (Eds), *Research in Personnel and Human Resources Management* (Vol. 9). Greenwich, CT: JAI Press.

Jex, S. M. and Spector, P. E. (1996). The impact of negative affectivity on stressor-strain relations: A replication and extension. *Work and Stress*, **10**, 36–45.

Jex, S. M., Beehr, T. A. and Roberts, C. K. (1992). The meaning of occupational stress items to survey respondents. *Journal of Applied Psychology*, **77**, 623–628.

Jex, S. M., Adams, G. A., Elacqua, T. C. and Lux, D. J. (1997). A comparison of incident-based and scale-based measures of work stressors. *Work and Stress*, **11**, 229–238.

Jimmieson, N. L. and Terry, D. J. (1998). An experimental study of the effects of work stress, work control, and task information on adjustment. *Applied Psychology: An international review*, **47**, 343–369.

Johansson, G., Johnson, J. V. and Hall, E. M. (1991). Smoking and sedentary behavior as related to work organization. *Social Science and Medicine*, **32**, 837–846.

Johnson, J. V. and Hall, E. M. (1988). Job strain, work place social support and cardiovascular disease: a cross-sectional study of a random sample of the working population. *American Journal of Public Health*, **78**, 1336–1342.

Johnson, J. V., Hall, E. M. and Theorell, T. (1989). Combined effects of job strain and social isolation on cardiovascular disease morbidity and mortality in a random sample of the Swedish male working population. *Scandinavian Journal of Work and Environmental Health*, **15**, 271–279.

Jolley, M. T. and Spielberger, C. D. (1973). The effects of locus of control and anxiety on verbal conditioning. *Journal of Personality*, **41**, 443–456.

Jones, D. R., Goldblatt, P. O. and Leon, D. A. (1984). Bereavement and cancer: Some data on deaths of spouses from the longitudinal study of the OPCS. *British Medical Journal*, **289**, 461–464.

Jones, F. (1998). The divide between practitioners and researchers. *The Psychologist*, **11**, 204–205.

Jones, F. and Fletcher, B. C. (1992). Disease concordances amongst marital partners: not 'way of life' or mortality data artefact. *Social Science and Medicine*, **35**, 1525–1533.

Jones, F. and Fletcher, B. C. (1993). An empirical study of occupational stress transmission in working couples. *Human Relations*, **46**, 881–903.

Jones, F. and Fletcher, B. C. (1996a). Taking work home: A study of daily fluctuations in work stressors, effects on moods and impacts on marital partners. *Journal of Occupational and Organizational Psychology*, **69**, 89–106.

Jones, F. and Fletcher, B. C. (1996b). Job control and health. In M. J. Schabracq, J. A. Winnubst and C. L. Cooper (Eds). *Handbook of Work and Health Psychology*. Chichester: Wiley and Sons.

Jones, F., Fletcher, B. C. and Ibbetson, K. (1991). Stressors and strains amongst social workers: demands, supports, constraints, and psychological health. *British Journal of Social Work*, **21**, 443–469.

Jones, F., Bright, J. E. H., Searle, B. and Cooper, L. (1998). Modelling occupational stress and health: The impact of the demand-control model on academic research and on workplace practice. *Stress Medicine*, **14**, 231–236.

Jones, H. (1997). *I'm Too Busy to be Stressed*. London: Hodder and Stoughton.

Judge, T. A. and Locke, E. A. (1993). Effects of dysfunctional thought processes on subjective well-being and job satisfaction. *Journal of Applied Psychology*, **78**, 475–490.

Judge, T. A. and Watanabe, S. (1994). Individual differences in the nature of the relationship between job and life satisfaction. *Journal of Occupational and Organizational Psychology*, **67**, 101–107.

Judge, T. A., Erez, A. and Thoresen, C. J. (2000). Why negative affectivity (and self-deception) should be included in the job stress research: bathing the baby with the bath water. *Journal of Organizational Behavior*, **21**, 101–111.

Kabanoff, B. (1980). Work and nonwork: a review of models, methods and findings. *Psychological Bulletin*, **88**, 60–77.

Kabanoff, B. and O'Brien, E. (1986). Stress and the leisure needs and activities of different occupations. *Human Relations*, **39**, 903–916.

Kamen-Siegel, L., Rodin, J., Seligman, M. E. and Dwyer, J. (1991). Explanatory style and cell-mediated immunity in elderly men and women. *Health Psychology*, **10**, 229–235.

Kanner, A. D., Coyne, J. C., Schaefer, C. and Lazarus, R. S. (1981). Comparison of two modes of stress measurement: Daily hassles and uplifts versus major life events. *Journal of Behavioral Medicine*, **4**, 1–39.

Kanter, R. (1977). *Work and Family in the United States: A Critical Review and Agenda for Research and Policy*. New York: Sage.

Kaplan, R. M., Atkins, C. J. and Reinsch, S. (1984). Specific efficacy expectations mediate exercise compliance in patients with COPD. *Health Psychology*, **3**, 223–242.

Karasek, R. A. (1979). Job demands, job decision latitude and mental strain: implications for job design. *Administrative Science Quarterly*, **24**, 285–308.

Karasek, R. A. (1990). Lower health risk with increased job control among white collar workers. *Journal of Organisational Behavior*, **11**, 171–185.

Karasek, R. A. and Theorell, T. (1990). *Healthy Work. Stress, Productivity and the Reconstruction of Working Life*. New York: Basic Books.

Karasek, R. A., Baker, D., Marxer, F., Ahlbom, A. and Theorell, T. S. O. (1981). Job decision latitude, job demands and cardiovascular disease: a prospective study of Swedish men. *American Journal of Public Health*, **71**, 694–705.

Karasek, R. A., Theorell, T. G. T., Schwartz, J., Pieper, C. and Alfredsson, L. (1982). Job, psychological factors and coronary heart disease. *Advanced Cardiology*, **29**, 62–67.

Kasl, S. V. (1978). Epidemiological contributions to the study of work stress. In C. L. Cooper and R. L. Payne (Eds), *Stress at Work*. Chichester: Wiley and Sons.

Katz, D. and Kahn, R. L. (1978). *The Social Psychology of Organizations*. (2nd ed.). New York: Wiley.

Kaufmann, G. M. and Beehr, T. A. (1986). Interactions between job stressors and social support: Some counterintuitive results. *Journal of Applied Psychology*, **71**, 522–526.

Keenan, A. and McBain, G. D. (1979). Effects of Type A behaviour, intolerance of ambiguity, and locus of control on the relationship between role stress and work-related outcomes. *Journal of Occupational Psychology*, **52**, 277–285.

Keenan, A. and Newton, T. J. (1985). Stressful events, stressors and psychological strains in young professional engineers. *Journal of Occupational Behavior*, **6**, 151–156.

Kelly, J. E. (1992). Does job re-design theory explain job re-design outcomes? *Human Relations*, **45**, 753–774.

Kemp, N. J., Wall, T. D., Clegg, C. W. and Cordery, J. L. (1983). Autonomous work groups in a greenfield site: A comparative study. *Journal of Occupational Psychology*, **56**, 271–278.

Kendall, P. C. and Epps, J. (1990). Medical treatments. In M. Johnston and L. Wallace (Eds), *Stress and Medical Procedures*. Oxford: Oxford University Press.

Kennedy, S., Kiecolt-Glaser, J. K. and Glaser, R. (1988). Immunological consequences of acute and chronic stressors: Mediating role of interpersonal relationships. *British Journal of Medical Psychology*, **61**, 77–85.

Kessler, R. C. and McRae, J. A. (1982). The effect of wives' employment on the mental health of married men and women. *American Sociological Review*, **47**, 216–227.

Kiecolt-Glaser, J. K. and Glaser, R. (1993). Mind and immunity. In D. Goleman and J. Gurin (Eds), *Mind, Body Medicine*. Yonkers, NY: Consumer Reports Books.

Kiecolt-Glaser, J. K., Ogrocki, P., Stout, J. C., Speicher, C. E. and Glaser, R. (1987). Marital quality, marital disruption and immune function. *Psychosomatic Medicine*, **49**, 13–34.

Kiecolt-Glaser, J. K., Dura, J. R., Speicher, C. E., Trask, O. J. and Glaser, R. S. O. (1991). Spousal caregivers of dementia victims: longitudinal changes in immunity and health. *Psychosomatic Medicine*, **53**, 345–362.

Kiecolt-Glaser, J. K., Marucha, P. T., Malarkey, W. B., Mercado, A. M. and Glaser, R. (1995). Slowing of wound healing by psychological stress. *The Lancet*, **346**, 1194–1196.

Kiecolt-Glaser, J., Glaser, R., Cacioppo, J. T. and Malarkey, W. B. (1998). Marital stress: immunologic, neuroendocrine, and autonomic correlates. *Annals of the New York Academy of Science*, **1**, 656–663.

Kincey, J. and Saltmore, S. (1990). Surgical treatments. In M. Johnston and L. Wallace (Eds), *Stress and Medical Procedures*. Oxford: Oxford University Press.

Kinman, G. (1996). *Stress, Health and Sense of Coherence in the Lecturing Profession*, BSc. Dissertation, University of Luton.

Kirkcaldy, B. D. and Cooper, C. L. (1992). Managing the stress of change: Occupational stress among senior police officers in Berlin. *Stress Medicine*, **8**, 219–231.

Kirschbaum, C. and Hellhammer, D. H. (1989) Salivary cortisol in psychobiological research: an overview. *Neuropsychobiology*, **22**, 150–169.

Kirschbaum, C., Pike, K.-M. and Hellhammer, D. H. (1993). The 'Trier Social Stress Test' – a tool for investigating psychobiological stress responses in a laboratory setting. *Neuropsychobiology*, **28**, 76–81.

Kline, M. and Cowan, P. A. (1988). Re-thinking the connections among 'work' and 'family' well-being. *Journal of Social Behavior and Personality*, **3**, 61–90.

Kobasa, S. C. (1979). Stressful life events, personality and health: An inquiry into hardiness. *Journal of Personality and Social Psychology*, **37**, 1–11.

Konefal, J. and Duncan, R. C. (1998). Social anxiety and training in neuro-linguistic programming. *Psychological Reports*, **8**, 1115–1122.

Kornhauser, A. W. (1965). *Mental Health of the Industrial Worker*. New York: Wiley.

Kossek, E. and Ozeki, C. (1998). Work-family conflict, policies, and the job-life satisfaction relationship: A review and directions for organizational behavior-human resources research. *Journal of Applied Psychology*, **83**, 139–149.

Kozlowski, L. T. and Heatherton, T. F. (1990). Self-report issues in cigarette smoking: State of the art and future directions. *Behavioral Assessment*, **12**, 53–75.

Krantz, D. and Manuck, S. (1984). Acute psychophysiologic reactivity and risk of cardiovascular disease: a review and methodological critique. *Psychological Bulletin*, **96**, 435–439.

Krause, N., Ragland, D. R., Geiner, B. A., Syme, L. and Fisher, J. M. (1997). Psychosocial job factors associated with back and neck pain in public transit operators. *Scandinavian Journal of Environmental Health*, **23**, 179–186.

Kremer, J. and Skully, D. (1994). *Psychology in Sport*. London: Taylor and Francis.

Kristensen, T. S. (1995). The demand-control-support model: methodological challenges for future research. *Stress Medicine*, **11**, 17–26.

Kristensen, T. S. (1996). Job stress and cardiovascular disease: A theoretical critical review. *Journal of Occupational Health Psychology*, **1**(3), 246–260.

Krohne, H. W. (1996). Individual differences in coping. In M. Zeidner and N. S. Endler (Eds), *Handbook of Coping*. New York: John Wiley and Sons.

Kubler-Ross, E. (1970). *On Death and Dying*. London: Tavistock.

Kuby, J. (1997). *Immunology*. Third edition. New York: Freeman and Co.

Kugelmann, R. (1992). *Stress: The Nature and History of Engineered Grief*. Westport, CT: Praeger.

Kupfersmid, J. (1988). Improving what is published: A model in search of an editor. *American Psychologist*, **43**, 635–642.

Landsbergis, P. A. and Vivona-Vaughan, E. (1995). Evaluation of an occupational stress intervention in a public agency. *Journal of Organizational Behavior*, **16**, 29–48.

Landy, F. J. and Trumbo, D. A. (1976). *Psychology of Work Behaviour*. Homewood, Ill: Dorsey Press.

Langan-Fox, J. and Poole, M. E. (1995). Occupational stress in Australian business and professional women. *Stress Medicine*, **11**, 113–122.

Last, J. M. (1983). *A Dictionary of Epidemiology*. New York: Oxford University Press.

Lazarus, R. S. (1992). Four reasons why it is difficult to demonstrate psychosocial influences on health. *Advances*, **8**, 6–7.

Lazarus, R. S. (1993). Coping theory and research: Past, present and future. *Psychosomatic Medicine*, **55**, 234–247.

Lazarus, R. S. (1990). Theory-based stress measurement. *Psychological Inquiry*, **1**, 3–13.

Lazarus, R. S. (1993). From psychological stress to the emotions: A history of changing outlooks. *Annual Review of Psychology*, **44**, 1–21.

Lazarus, R. S. (1995). Psychological stress in the workplace. In R. Crandall and P. L. Perrewe (Eds), *Occupational Stress: A Handbook*. Bristol: Taylor and Francis.

Lazarus, R. S. and Folkman, S. (1984). *Stress, Appraisal and Coping*. New York: Springer.

Lazarus, R. S. and Folkman, S. (1989). *Manual for the Hassles and Uplifts Scale*. Palo Alto, CA: Consulting Psychologists Press.

Lazarus, R. S., DeLongis, A., Folkman, S. and Gruen, R. (1985). Stress and adaptational outcomes: the problem of confounded measures. *American Psychologist*, **40**, 770–779.

Leavy, R. S. (1983). Social support and psychological disorder. *Journal of Community Psychology*, **11**, 3–21.

Lee, J. A. (1997). Balancing elder care responsibilities and work: Two empirical studies. *Journal of Occupational Health Psychology*, **2**, 220–228.

Lee, M. and Reason, L. (1988). *Action on Stress at Work*. London: Health Education Authority.

Leiter, M. P. and Durup, M. J. (1996). Work, home and in-between: A longitudinal study of spillover, *Journal of Applied Behavioural Science*, **32**, 29–47.

LeShan, L. (1959). Psychological states as factors in the development of malignant disease. *Journal of the National Cancer Institute*, **22**, 1–18.

LeShan, L. and Worthington, R. E. (1956). Loss of cathexes as a common psychodynamic characteristic of cancer patients. An attempt at clinical validation of a clinical hypothesis. *Psychological Reports*, **2**, 183–193.

Leventhal, E. A., Hansell, S., Deifenbach, M., Leventhal, H. and Glass, D. (1996). Negative affect and self-report of physical symptoms: Two longitudinal studies of older adults. *Health Psychology*, **15**, 193–199.

Leventhal, H., Patrick-Miller, L. and Leventhal, E. (1998). It's long term stressors that take a toll: Comment on Cohen *et al.* (1998). *Health Psychology*, **17**, 211–213.

Levine, D. M., Green, L. W., Deeds, S. G., Chwalow, J., Russell, R. P. and Finlay, J. (1979). Health education for hypertensive patients. *Journal of the American Medical Association*, **241**, 1700–1703.

Levy, E. A. and Mineka, S. (1998). Anxiety and mood-congruent autobiographical memory: A conceptual failure to replicate. *Cognition and Emotion*, **12**, 625–634.

Light, K. C., Dolan, C. A., Davis, M. R. and Sherwood, A. (1992). Cardiovascular responses to an active coping challenge as predictors of blood pressure 10–15 years later. *Psychosomatic Medicine*, **54**, 217–239.

Livingston Booth, A. (1985). *Stressmanship*. London: Severn House Publishers.

Logie, R. H. (1999). Working memory. *Psychologist*, **12**, 174–178.

Long, B. C. and Flood, K. R. (1993). Coping with work stress: Psychological benefits of exercise. *Work and Stress*, **1**, 109–119.

Long, N. R. and Voges, K. E. (1987). Can wives perceive the source of their husbands' occupational stress? *Journal of Occupational Psychology*, **60**, 235–242.

Luborsky, L., Blinder, B. and Schimek, J. (1965). Looking, recalling and GSR as a function of defence. *Journal of Abnormal Psychology*, **70**, 270–280.

Lucas, R. E. and Gohm, C. L. (1999). Age and sex differences in subjective well-being across cultures. In E. Diener and E. M. Suh (Eds), *Subjective Well-being Across Cultures*. Cambridge, MA: MIT Press.

Ludwick-Rosenthal, R. and Neufeld, R. W. J. (1988). Stress management during noxious medical procedures: an evaluative review of outcome studies. *Psychological Bulletin*, **104**, 326–342.

Lyles, J. N., Burish, T. G., Krozely, M. G. and Oldham, R. K. (1982). Efficacy of relaxation training and guided imagery in reducing the aversiveness of cancer chemotherapy. *Journal of Consulting and Clinical Psychology*, **50**, 509–524.

MacEwen, K. E., Barling, J. and Kelloway, K. (1992). Effects of short-term role overload on marital interactions. *Work and Stress*, **6**, 117–126.

Mackay, C. J., Cox, T., Burrows, G. and Lazzerini, A. J. (1978). An inventory for the measurement of self-reported stress and arousal. *British Journal of Social and Clinical Psychology*, **17**, 361–367.

MacLeod, C. (1990). Mood disorders and cognition. In M. W. Eysenck (Ed.), *Cognitive Psychology: An International Review*. Chichester: Wiley and Sons.

MacLeod, C. and Cohen, I. L. (1993). Anxiety and the interpretation of ambiguity: A text comprehension study. *Journal of Abnormal Psychology*, **102**, 238–247.

MacLeod, C. and Donnellan, A. M. (1993). Individual differences in anxiety and the restriction of working memory capacity. *Personality and Individual Differences*, **15**, 163–173.

MacLeod, C., Mathews, A. and Tata, P. (1986). Attentional bias in emotional disorders. *Journal of Abnormal Psychology*, **95**, 15–20.

Maddi, S. R. and Kobasa, S. C. (1991). 'The development of hardiness', in A. Monat and R. S. Lazarus (Eds) *Stress and Coping: An Anthology* (3rd Edition). Columbia University Press.

Mahoney, M. J. (1977). Publication predjudices: an experimental study of confirmatory bias in the peer review system. *Cognitive Therapy and Research*, **1**, 161–165.

Mahoney, M. J. (1987). Scientific publication and knowledge politics. *Journal of Social Behavior and Personality*, **2**, 165–176.

Mair, S. F. and Watkins, L. R. (1998). Cytokines for psychologists: implications for bidirectional immune to brain communication for understanding behaviour, mood and cognition. *Psychological Reviews*, **105**, 83–107.

Malarkey, W. B., Kiecolt-Glaser, J. K., Pearl, D. and Glaser, R. (1994). Hostile behavior during marital conflict alter pituitary and adrenal hormones. *Psychosomatic Medicine*, **56**, 41–51.

Marcenes, W. S. and Sheiham, A. (1992). The relationship between work stress and oral health status. *Social Science and Medicine*, **12**, 1511–1520.

Marco, C. A. and Suls, J. (1993). Daily stress and the trajectory of mood; spillover, response assimilation, contrast and chronic negative affectivity. *Journal of Personality and Social Psychology*, **64**, 1053–1063.

Marmot, M. G., Smith, G. M., Stansfield, S., Patel, C., North, F., Head, J., White, I., Brunner, E. and Feeney, A. (1991). Health inequalities among British Civil Servants: the Whitehall II study. *The Lancet*, **337**, 1387–1393.

Marsella, A. J. (1994). The measurement of emotional reactions to work: conceptual and methodological and research issues. *Work and Stress*, **8**, 153–176.

Martin, M. (1978). Speech recoding in silent reading. *Memory and Cognition*, **6**, 108–114.

Martin, M., Williams, R. M. and Clark, D. M. (1991). Does anxiety lead to selective processing of threat-related information? *Behaviour Research and Therapy*, **29**, 147–160.

Martin, R., Davis, G. M., Baron, R. S., Suls, J. and Blanchard, E. B. (1994). Specificity in social support: perceptions of helpful and unhelpful provider behaviors amongst irritable bowel syndrome, headache and cancer patients. *Health Psychology*, **13**, 432–439.

Marucha, P. T., Kiecolt-Glaser, J. K. and Favegehi, M. (1998). Mucosal wound healing is impaired by examination stress. *Psychosomatic Medicine*, **60**, 362–365.

Maslach, F. and Jackson, S. E. (1981). *The Maslach Burnout Inventory*: Research Edition. Palo Alto, California: Consulting Psychologists Inc.

Mason, J. W. (1975). A history of the stress field. *Journal of Human Stress*, **1**, 6–12, 23–36.

Mathe, A. A. and Knapp, P. H. (1971). Emotional and adrenal reactions to stress in bronchial asthma. *Psychosomatic Medicine*, **33**, 323–340.

Mathews, A. and MacLeod, C. (1985). Selective processing of threat cues in anxiety states. *Behaviour Research and Therapy*, **23**, 563–569.

Mathews, A. and MacLeod, C. (1986). Discrimination of threat cues without awareness in anxiety states. *Journal of Abnormal Psychology*, **95**, 1–8.

Mathews, A. and MacLeod, C. (1994). Cognitive approaches to emotion and emotional disorders. *Annual Review of Psychology*, **45**, 25–50.

Mathews, A., May, J., Mogg, K. and Eysenck, M. W. (1990). Attention bias in anxiety: selective search or defective filtering. *Journal of Abnormal Psychology*, **99**, 166–173.

Matthews, K. (1988). Coronary Heart Disease and Type A behavior: Update on an alternative to the Booth-Kewley and Friedman (1987) quantitative review. *Psychological Bulletin*, **104**, 373–380.

Matthews, K. A. and Haynes, S. G. (1986). Type A behavior pattern and coronary risk: update and critical evaluation. *American Journal of Epidemiology*, **6**, 923–960.

McCrae, R. R. and Costa, P. T. (1985). Updating Norman's 'adequacy taxonomy': intelligence and personality dimensions in natural language and in questionnaires. *Journal of Personality and Social Psychology*, **49**, 710–721.

McCrae, R. R. and Costa, P. T. (1991). Adding liebe and arbeit: The full five factor model and well-being. *Personality and Social Psychology Bulletin*, **17**, 227–232.

McDonnell-Douglas (1989). McDonnell Douglas Corporations EAP produces hard data. *The Almanac*, August, 18–26.

McGee, R. (1999). Does stress cause cancer? *British Medical Journal*, **319**, 1015–1016.

McGrath, J. E. (1976). Stress and behavior in organizations. In M. Dunnette (Ed.), *Handbook of Industrial and Organizational Psychology*. Chicago: Rand McNally.

McGrath, J. E. and Beehr, T. A. (1990). Time and the stress process: some temporal issues in the conceptualisation and measurement of stress. *Stress Medicine*, **6**, 93–104.

McKenna, M. C., Zevon, M. A., Corn, B. and Rounds, J. (1999). Psychosocial factors and the devleopment of breast cancer: A meta-analysis. *Health Psychology*, **18**, 520–531.

McNair, D. M., Lorr, M. and Droppleman, L. F. (1981). *Profile of Mood States*, San Diego, CA: Educational and Industrial Testing Service.

Meichenbaum, D. (1985). *Stress Inoculation Training*. New York: Pergamon.

Meissner, M. (1971). The long arm of the job: a study of work and leisure. *Industrial Relations*, **10**, 239–260.

Menaghan, E. G. and Merves, E. S. (1984). Coping with occupational problems: the limits of individual efforts. *Journal of Health and Social Behavior*, **25**, 406–423.

Merletti,F., Boffetta, P., Ciccone, G., Mashberg, A. and Terracini, B. (1989). Role of tobacco and alcoholic beverages in the etiology of cancer of the oral cavity/oropharynx in Torino, Italy. *Cancer Research*, **49**, 4919–4924.

Mersch, P. P. A., Middendorp, H. M., Bouhuys, A. L., Beersma, D. G. and van-den-Hoofdakker, R. H. (1999). Seasonal affective disorder and latitude: a review of the literature. *Journal of Affective Disorders*, **53**, 35–48.

Mestecky, J. (1993). Saliva as a manifestation of the common mucosal immune system. *Annals of the New York Academy of Science*, **694**, 184–194.

Meyer, T. J. and Mark, M. M. (1995). Effects of psychosocial interventions with adult cancer patients: a meta-analysis of randomized experiments. *Health Psychology*, **14**, 101–108.

Meyerson, D. E. (1994). Interpretations of stress in institutions: the cultural production of ambiguity and burnout. *Administrative Science Quarterly*, **39**, 628–653.

Miller, S. M. (1987). Monitoring and Blunting: Validation of a questionnaire to assess styles of information seeking under threat. *Journal of Personality and Social Psychology*, **52**, 345–353.

Miller, S. M. and Mangan, C. E. (1983). Interacting effects of information and coping style in adapting to gynaecologic stress: Should the Doctor tell all. *Journal of Personality and Social Psychology*, **45**, 223–236.

Miller, S. M., Summerton, J. and Brody, D. S. (1988). Styles of coping with threat: implications for health. *Journal of Personality and Social Psychology*, **54**, 142–148.

Miller, S. M., Rodoletz, M., Schroeder, C. M., Mangan, C. E. and Sedlacek, T. V. (1996). Applications of the monitoring process model to coping with severe long-term medical threats. *Health Psychology*, **15**, 216–225.

Miller, T. Q., Turner, C. W., Tindale, R. S., Posavac, E. J. and Dugoni, B. L. (1991). Reasons for the trend towards null findings in research on Type A behavior. *Psychological Bulletin*, **110**, 469–485.

Miller, T. Q., Smith, T. W., Turner, C. W., Guijarro, M. L. and Hallet, A. J. (1996). A meta-analytic review of research on hostility and physical health. *Psychological Bulletin*, **119**, 322–348.

Miller, T. W. (Ed.) (1989). *Stressful life events*. Madison, Ct: International Universities Press.

Mitchell, R. E., Cronkite, R. C. and Moos, R. H. (1983) Stress, coping and depression among married couples. *Journal of Applied Psychology*, **92**, 433–448.

Mogg, K. and Bradley, B. P. (1998). A cognitive-motivational analysis of anxiety. *Behaviour Research and Therapy*, **36**, 809–848.

Mogg, K., Mathews, A. and Weinman, J. (1987). Memory bias in clinical anxiety. *Journal of Abnormal Psychology*, **96**, 94–98.

Mogg, K., McNamara, J., Powys, M., Rawlinson, H., Seiffer, A. and Bradley, B. P. (2000). Selective attention to threat: A test of two cognitive models of anxiety. *Cognition and Emotion*, **14**, 375–399.

Morisky, D. E., DeMuth, N. M., Field-Fass, M., Green, L. W. and Levine, D. M. (1985). Evaluation of family health education to build social support for long-term control of high blood pressure. *Health Education Quarterly*, **12**, 35–50.

Morrison, D. L. and Clements, R. (1997). The effect of one partner's job characteristics on the other partner's distress: A serendipitous, but naturalistic, experiment. *Journal of Occupational and Organisational Psychology*, **70**, 307–324.

Morrison, D. L., Dunne, M. P., Fitzgerald, R. and Gloghan, D. (1992). Job design and levels of physical and mental strain among Australian prison officers. *Work and Stress*, **6**, 13–31.

Motowidlo, S. J., Packard, J. S. and Manning, M. R. (1986). Occupational Stress: its causes and consequences for job performance. *Journal of Applied Psychology*, **71**, 618–629.

Moyle, P. (1995a). The role of negative affectivity in the stress process: Tests of alternative models. *Journal of Organizational Behavior*, **16**, 647–668.

Moyle, P. J. (1995b). 'The Stress Process in Occupational Settings: The Role of Psychosocial Factors'. Ph.D. Dissertation, Oxford University.

MSF (1997). *What is Making us Stressed at Work?* London: MSF.

Mullarkey, S., Wall, T. D., Warr, P. B., Clegg, C. W. and Stride, C. B. (1999). *Measures of job satisfaction, mental health and job-related well-being: A benchmarking manual*. Institute of Work Psychology: Sheffield.

Mumford, E., Schlesinger, H. J. and Glass, G. V. (1982). The effects of psychological intervention on recovery from surgery and heart attacks: an analysis of the literature. *American Journal of Public Health*, **72**, 141–151.

Muntaner, C. and O'Campo, P. J. (1993). A critical appraisal of the demand/control model of the psychosocial work environment: epistomological, social and class considerations. *Social Science and Medicine*, **36**, 1509–1517.

Murphy, L. R. (1996). Stress management techniques: secondary prevention of stress. In M. J. Schabracq, J. A. M. Winnubst and C. L. Cooper (Eds), *Handbook of Work and Health Psychology*. Chichester: Wiley and Sons.

Murphy, M. H. (1994). Sport and drugs and runner's high. In J. Kremer and D. Sk (Eds), *Psychology in Sport*. London: Taylor and Francis.

Muslin, H. L., Gyarfas, K. and Pieper, W. J. (1966). Separation experience and cancer of the breast. *Annals of the New York Academy of Science*, **125**, 802–806.

Mutrie, N. (In press). Physical activity and clinically defined depression. In S. J. H. Biddle, K. R. Fox and S. H. Boutcher (Eds), *Physical Activity and Psychological Well-being*. Routledge: London.

290

Myers, L. B. (2000). Identifying repressors: a methodological issue for health psychology. *Psychology and Health*, **5**, 205–214.

Myers, L. B. and Brewin, C. R. (1996). Illusions of well-being and the repressive coping style. *British Journal of Social Psychology*, **35**, 443–457.

Myers, L. and Vetere, A. (1997). Repressors responses to health related question-naires. *British Journal of Health Psychology*, **2**, 245–257.

Myrtek, M. (1995). Type A behaviour pattern, personality factors, disease and physiological reactivity: A meta-analytic update. *Personality and Individual Differences*, **18**, 491–502.

Near, J. P., Rice, R. W. and Hunt, R. G. (1980). The relationship between work and nonwork domains: a review of empirical research. *Academy of Management Review*, **5**, 415–429.

Neuliep, J. W. and Crandall, R. (1993a). Everyone was wrong: there are lots of replications out there. Replication research in the social sciences (Special Issue). *Journal of Social Behavior and Personality*, **8**, 1–8.

Neuliep, J. W. and Crandall, R. (1993b). Reviewer bias against replication research. Replication research in the social sciences (Special Issue). *Journal of Social Behavior and Personality*, **8**, 21–29.

Newman, J. E. and Beehr, T. A. (1979). Personal and organisational strategies for handling job stress: A review of research and opinion. *Personnel Psychology*, **32**, 1–43.

Newton, T. (1995). *Managing Stress: Emotion and Power at Work*. London: Sage.

Newton, T. J. (1989). Occupational stress and coping with stress: a critique. *Human Relations*, **42**, 441–461.

Newton, T. J. and Keenan, A. (1985). Coping with work-related stress. *Human Relations*, **2**, 107–126.

Newton, T. L. and Contrada, R. J. (1992). Repressive coping and verbal – autonomic response dissociation: the influence of social context. *Journal of Personality and Social Psychology*, **62**, 159–167.

Niaura, R., Herbert, P. N., McMahon, N. and Sommerville, L. (1992). Repressive coping and blood lipids in men and women. *Psychosomatic Medicine*, **54**, 698–706.

Nishanian, P., Aziz, N., Chunh, J., Detels, R. and Fahey, L. (1998). Oral fluids as an alternative to serum for measurement of markers of immune activation. *Clinical and diagnostic laboratory Immunology*, **5**, 507–512.

Noller, P. (1982). Couple communication and marital satisfaction. *Australian Journal of Sex, Marriage and the Family*, **3**, 69–75.

Noller, P. (1987). Non-verbal communication in marriage. In D. Perlman and S. Duck (Eds), *Intimate Relationships: Development, Dynamics and Deterioration*, London: Sage.

Norman, W. T. (1963). Toward an adequate taxonomy of personality attributes: replicated factor structure in peer nomination personality ratings. *Journal of Abnormal Social Psychology*, **66**, 574–588.

Nugent, K. and Mineka, S. (1994). The effect of high and low trait anxiety on implicit and explicit memory tasks. *Cognition and Emotion*, **8**, 147–163.

O'Brien, W. H., Vanegeren, L. and Mumby, P. B. (1995). Predicting health behaviors using measures of optimism and risk. *Health Values*, **19**, 21–28.

O'Driscoll, M. P. (2001). Moderators of stressor-strain relationships. In C. Cooper, P. Dewe and M. O'Driscoll. *Organizational Stress: A Review and Critique of Theory, Research and Applications*. Thousand Oaks, CA: Sage Publications.

O'Driscoll, M. P. and Beehr, T. (2000). Moderating effects of perceived control and need for clarity on the relationship between role stressors and employee affective reactions. *Journal of Social Psychology*, **140**, 151–159.

O'Leary, A. (1990). Stress, emotion and human immune function. *Psychological Bulletin*, **108**, 363–382.

Oakland, S. and Ostell, A. (1996). Measuring coping: A review and critique. *Human Relations*, **49**, 133–154.

Ogden, J. and Mtandabari, T. (1997). Examination stress and changes in mood and health related behaviours. *Psychology and Health*, **12**, 289–299.

Olson, J. E. and Frieze, I. H. (1987). Income determinants for women in business. In A. H. Stromberg, L. Larwood and B. A. Gutek (Eds), *Women and Work: An Annual Review*, Vol. 2. Sage: Newbury.

Ornish, D., Brown, S. E., Scherwitz, L. W. *et al.* (1990). Can lifestyle changes reverse coronary heart disease? *The Lancet*, **336**, 129–133.

Osterweis, M., Solomon, F. and Green, M. (Eds). (1984). *Bereavement: Reactions, Consequences and Care*. Washington, DC: National Academy Press.

Palinkas, L. A., Suedfeld, P. and Steel, G. D. (1995). Psychological functioning among members of a small polar expedition. *Aviation, Space, and Environmental Medicine*, **66**, 943–950.

Parasuraman, S., Greenhaus, J. H., Rabinowitz, S., Bedeian, A. G. *et al.* (1989). Work and family variables as mediators of the relationship between wives' employment and husbands' well-being. *Academy of Management Journal*, **32**, 185–201.

Parker, J. D. A. and Endler, N. S. (1996). Coping and defense: A historical overview. In M. Zeidner and N. S. Endler (Eds), *Handbook of Coping*. New York: John Wiley and Sons.

Parkes, C. M. (1972). *Bereavement. Studies of Grief in Adult Life*. Harmondsworth: Penguin Books.

Parkes, K. R. (1986). Coping in stressful episodes: the role of individual differences, environmental factors, and situational characteristics. *Journal of Personality and Social Psychology*, **51**, 1277–1292.

Parkes, K. R. (1990). Coping, negative affectivity, and the work environment: Additive and interactive predictors of mental health. *Journal of Applied Psychology*, **75**, 399–409.

Parkes, K. R. (1991). Locus of control as a moderator: an explanation for additive versus interactive findings in the demand-discretion model of work stress? *British Journal of Psychology*, **82**, 291–312.

Parkes, K. R. (1994). Personality and coping as moderators of work stress process: Models, methods and measures. *Work and Stress*, **8**, 110–129.

Parkes, K. R., Styles, E. A. and Broadbent, D. E. (1990). Work preferences as moderators of the effects of paced and unpaced work on mood and cognitive performance: A laboratory simulation of mechanized letter sorting. *Human Factors*, **32**, 197–216.

Parkes, K. R., Mendham, C. A. and von Rabenau, C. (1994). Social support and the demand-discretion model of job stress: tests of additive and interactive effects in two samples. *Journal of Vocational Behavior*, **44**, 91–113.

Paulhus, D. L. and Lim, T. K. (1994). Arousal and evaluative extremity in social judgements: A dynamic complexity model. *European Journal of Social Psychology*, **24**, 89–100.

Pavett, C. M. (1986). High stress professions: Satisfaction, stress, and the well-being of spouses of professionals. *Human Relations*, **39**, 1141–1155.

Paykel, E. S. and Rao, B. M. (1984). Methodology in study of life events and cancer. In C. L. Cooper (Ed.), *Psychosocial Stress and Cancer*. Chichester: John Wiley and Sons.

Payne, R. (1988). Individual differences in the study of occupational stress. In C. L. Cooper and R. Payne (Eds), *Causes, Coping and Consequences of Stress at Work*, Chichester: John Wiley and Sons.

Payne, R., Lane, D. and Leahy, M. (1989). Work and non-work factors as perceived causes of symptoms of psychological strain. *Work and Stress*, **3**, 347–351.

Pearlin, L. (1989). The sociological study of stress. *Journal of Health and Social Behavior*, **30**, 241–256.

Pearlin, L. I. and Schooler, C. (1978). The structure of coping. *Journal of Health and Social Behavior*, **19**, 2–21.

Peirce, R. S., Frone, M. R., Russell, M. and Cooper, M. L. (1996). Financial stress, social support, and alcohol involvement: A longitudinal test of the buffering hypothesis in a general population survey. *Health Psychology*, **15**, 38–47.

Perrewe, P. L. and Ganster, D. C. (1989). The impact of job demands and behavioural control on experienced job stress. *Journal of Organizational Behaviour*, **10**, 213–229.

Peters, D. P. and Ceci, S. J. (1982). Peer-review practices of psychological journals: The fate of published articles, submitted again. *Behavioral and Brain Sciences*, **5**, 187–255.

Peters-Golden, H. (1982). Breast cancer: varied perceptions of social support in the illness experience. *Social Science and Medicine*, **16**, 483–491.

Peterson, C., Seligman, M. E. P. and Vaillant, G. E. (1988a). Pessimistic explanatory style is a risk factor for physical illness: a thirty-five-year longitudinal study. *Journal of Personality and Social Psychology*, **55**, 23–27.

Peterson, C., Seligman, M. E., Yurko, K. H., Martin, L. R. and Friedman, H. S. (1998b). Catastrophizing and untimely death. *Psychological Science*, **9**, 127–130.

Petrovsky, N. and Harrison, L. C. (1995). Th1 and Th2: swinging to a hormonal rhythm. *Immunology Today*, **16**, 605.

Petticrew, M., Fraser, J. M. and Regan, M. F. (1999). Adverse life events and risk of breast cancer: A meta-analysis. *British Journal of Health Psychology*, **4**, 1–17.

Phares, E. J. (1976). *Locus of Control in Personality*. New Jersey: General Learning Press.

Pieper, C., LaCroix, A. Z. and Karasek, R. A. (1989). The relation of psychosocial dimensions of work with CHD risk: a meta-analysis of five united states data bases. *American Journal of Epidemiology*, **129**, 483–494.

Pierce, G. R., Sarason, I. G. and Sarason, B. R. (1991). General and relationship-based perceptions of social supports: Are two constructs better than one? *Journal of Personality and Social Psychology*, **61**, 1028–1039.

Piotrkowski, C. S. (1978). *Work and the Family System*. New York: The Free Press.

Piotrkowski, C. S. and Crits-Christoph, P. (1981). Women's job and family adjustment, *Journal of Family Issues*, **32**, 126–147.

Pleck, J. (1977). The work–family role system. *Social Problems*, **24**, 417–427.

Pleck, J. (1985). *Work Wives, Working Husbands*. Beverly Hills: Sage.

Polani, P. E., Briggs, J. N., Ford, C. E., Clarke, C. M. and Berg, J. M. (1960). A mongol girl with 46 chromosomes. *Lancet*, **1**, 721–724.

Pollard, T., Ungpakorn, G., Harrison, G. A. and Parkes, K. R. (1996). Epinephrine and cortisol responses to work: a test of the models of Frankenhaueuser and Karasek. *Annals of Behavioral Medicine*, **18**, 229–237.

Pollock, K. (1988). On the nature of social stress: production of a modern mythology. *Social Science and Medicine*, **26**, 381–392.

Popper, K. R. (1959). *The Logic of Scientific Discovery*. New York: Basic Books.

Powell, L. H. (1987). Issues in the measurement of Type A behaviour pattern. In S. V. Kasl and C. L. Cooper (Eds), *Stress and Health: Issues in Research Methdology*. Chichester: John Wiley and Sons.

Pressner, J. C., Wolf, O. T., Hellhammer, D. H., Buske-Kishbaum, A., von Auer, K., Jobst, S., Kaspers, F. and Kirschbaum, C. (1997). Free cortisol levels after awakening: a reliable marker for assessment of adrenocortical activity. *Life Sciences*, **61**, 2530–2549.

Protheroe, D., Turvey, K., Horgan, K., Benson, E., Bowers, D. and House, A. (1999). Stressful life events and difficulties and onset of breast cancer: case control study. *British Medical Journal*, **319**, 1027–1030.

Rabkin, J. G. (1993). Stress and Psychiatric Disorders. In L. Goldberger and S. Breznitz (Eds), *Handbook of Stress: Theoretical and Clinical Aspects*. New York: The Free Press.

Rabkin, J. G. and Struening, E. L. (1976). Life events, stress and illness. *Science*, **194**, 1013–1020.

Raeikkoenen, K., Matthews, K. A., Flory, J. D., Owens, J. F. and Gump, B. B. (1999). Effects of optimism, pessimism, and trait anxiety on ambulatory blood presure and mood during everyday life. *Journal of Personality and Social Psychology*, **76**, 104–113.

294

Rahe, R. H. (1974). The pathway between subjects' recent life changes and their near-future illness reports: representative results and methodological issues. In B. S. Dohrenwend and B. P. Dohrenwend (Eds), *Stressful Life Events: their Nature and Effects*. London: John Wiley and Sons.

Rahe, R. H. and Lind, E. (1971). Psychosocial factors and sudden cardiac death. *Journal of Psychosomatic Research*, **8**, 487–491.

Rahe, R. H. and Paasikivi, J. (1971). Psychosocial factors and myocardial infarction. II. An outpatient study in Sweden. *Journal of Psychosomatic Research*, **8**, 35–44.

Raymond, M. W. and Moser, R. (1995). Aviators at risk. *Aviation, Space, and Environmental Medicine*, **66**, 35–391.

Register, A. C., Beckham, J. C., May, J. G. and Gustafson, D. J. (1991). Stress inoculation bibliotherapy in the treatment of test-anxiety. *Journal of Counseling Psychology*, **38**, 115–119.

Repetti, R. L. (1987). Linkages between work and family roles. In S. Oskamp (Ed.), *Applied Social Psychology Annual, Vol. 7: Family Processes and Problems*. Beverley Hills: Sage.

Repetti, R. L. (1989). Effects of daily workload on subsequent behaviour during marital interaction: roles of social withdrawal and spouse support. *Journal of Personality and Social Psychology*, **57**, 651–659.

Repetti, R. L. (1994). Short-term and long-term processes linking job stressors to father–child interaction. *Social Development*, **3**, 1–15.

Repetti, R. L. and Crosby, F. (1984). Gender and depression: Exploring the adult-role explanation. *Journal of Social and Clinical Psychology*, **2**, 57–70.

Repetti, R. L. and Wood, J. (1997). Effects of daily stress at work on mothers' interactions with preschoolers. *Journal of Family Psychology*, **11**, 90–108.

Reynolds, S. (1997). Psychological well-being at work: is prevention better than cure? *Journal of Psychosomatic Research*, **43**, 92–102.

Reynolds, S., Taylor, E., *et al.* (1993a). Session Impact in stress management training. *Journal of Occupational and Organizational Psychology*, **66**, 99–113.

Reynolds, S., Taylor, E. and Shapiro, D. (1993b). Session impact and outcome in stress management training. *Journal of Community and Applied Social Psychology*, **3**, 325–337.

Richards, A. and Whittaker, T. M. (1990). Effects of anxiety and mood manipulation in autobiographical memory. *British Journal of Clinical Psychology*, **29**, 145–153.

Ridder, D. T. D. (1996). Social status and coping: An exploration of the mediating role of beliefs. *Social Psychiatry and Psychiatric Epidemiology*, **31**, 309–315.

Riley, D. and Eckenrode, J. (1986). Social ties: costs and benefits within different subgroups. *Journal of Personality and Social Psychology*, **51**, 770–778.

Rizzo, J., House, R. and Lirtzman, S. (1970). Role conflict and ambiguity in complex organizations. *Administrative Science Quarterly*, **15**, 150–163.

Robson, C. (1993). *Real World Research*. Oxford: Blackwell.

Romagnani, S. (1997). The Th1/Th2 paradigm. *Immunology Today*, **18**, 263–266.

Roncolato, W. G. and Huon, G. F. (1998). Subjective well-being and dieting. *British Journal of Psychology*, **3**, 375–386.

Rook, K. S. (1984). The negative side of social interaction: impact on psychological well-being. *Journal of Personality and Social Psychology*, **46**, 1097–1108.

Rose, J., Jones, F. and Fletcher, B. C. (1998). The impact of a stress management programme on staff well-being and performance at work. *Work and Stress*, **12**, 112–124.

Rosen, G. (1987). Self-help treatment books and the commercialization of psychotherapy. *American psychologist*, **42**, 46–51.

Rosenbaum, M. and Piamenta, R. (1998). Preference for local or general anaesthesia, coping dispositions, learned resourcefulness and coping with surgery. *Psychology and Health*, **13**, 823–845.

Rosenman, R. H., Friedman, M. and Straus, R. *et al.* (1964). A predictive study of coronary heart disease. *Journal of the American Medical Association*, **189**, 15–22.

Roskies, E., Seraganian, P., Oseasohn, R., Hanley, J. A., Collu, R., Martin, N. and Smilga, C. (1986). The Montreal type A intervention project: Major findings. *Health Psychology*, **5**, 45–69.

Rotter, J. B. (1966). Generalized expectancies for internal versus external control of reinforcement. *Psychological Monographs*, **91**, 482–497.

Rousseau, D. M. (1978). Relationship of work to non-work. *Journal of Applied Psychology*, **63**, 513–517.

Rowlison, R. T. and Felner, R. D. (1988). Major life events, hassles, and adaptation in adolescence: Confounding in the conceptualization and measurement of life stress and adjustment revisited. *Journal of Personality and Social Psychology*, **55**, 432–444.

Russo, R., Fox, E. and Bowles, R. J. (1999). On the status of implicit memory bias in anxiety. *Cognition and Emotion*, **13**, 435–456.

Rydstedt, L.-W. and Johansson, G. (1998). A longitudinal study of workload, health and well-being among male and female urban bus drivers. *Journal of Occupational and Organizational Psychology*, **71**, 35–45.

Sallis, J. F., Trevorrow, T. R., Johnson, C. C. and Hovell, M. F. *et al.* (1987). Worksite stress management: A comparison of programs. *Psychology and Health*, **1**, 237–255.

Sarason, I. G., Johnson, J. H. and Siegel, J. M. (1978). Assessing the impact of life changes: development of the life experiences survey. *Journal of Consulting and Clinical Psychology*, **46**, 932–946.

Sarason, I. G., Levine, H. M., Basham, R. B. and Sarason, B. R. (1983). Assessing social support: the Social Support Questionnaire. *Journal of Personality and Social Psychology*, **44**, 127–139.

Saunders, T., Driskell, J. E., Johnston, J. H. and Salas, E. (1996). The effect of stress inoculation training on anxiety and performance. *Journal of Occupational Health Psychology*, **1**(2), 170–186.

Schaubroeck, J. and Ganster, D. C. (1991). Associations among stress-related individual differences. In C. L. Cooper, R. Payne *et al.* (Eds), *Personality and Stress: Individual Differences in the Stress Process. Wiley Series on Studies in Occupational Stress* (pp. 33–66). Chichester: Wiley and Sons.

Schaubroeck, J., Ganster, D. C. and Fox, M. L. (1992). Dispositional affect and work related stress. *Journal of Applied Psychology*, **77**, 322–335.

Scheier, M. F. and Carver, C. S. (1988). A model of behavioral self-regulation: Translating intention into action. In L. Berkowitz (Ed.), *Advances in Experimental Social Psychology*. New York: Academic Press.

Schnall, P. L., Landsbergis, P. A. and Baker, D. (1994). Job strain and cardiovascular health. *Annual Review of Public Health*, **15**, 381–411.

Schoenbach, V. J., Kaplan, B. H., Fredman, L. and Kleinbaum, D. G. (1986). Social ties and mortality in Evans County, Georgia. *American Journal of Epidemiology*, **123**, 577–591.

Schwartz, J. E., Pieper, C. F. and Karasek, R. A. (1988). A procedure for linking psychosocial job characteristics data to health surveys. *American Journal of Public Health*, **78**, 904–909.

Schwartz, J. E., Neale, J., Marco, C., Shiffman, S. S. and Stone, A. A. (1999). Does trait coping exist? A momentary assessment approach to the evaluation of traits. *Journal of Personality and Social Psychology*, **77**, 350–369.

Schwartz, M. D., Lerman, C., Miller, S. M., Daly, M. and Masny, A. (1995). Coping disposition, perceived risk, and psychological distress among women at increased risk for ovarian cancer. *Health Psychology*, **14**, 232–235.

Schwarzer, R. and Schwarzer, C. (1996). A critical survey of coping instruments. In M. Zeidner and N. S. Endler (Eds), *Handbook of Coping: Theory, Research, Applications*. Chichester: John Wiley and Sons.

Schwartzberg, N. S. and Dytell, R. S. (1996). Dual-earner families: The importance of work stress and family stress for psychological well-being. *Journal of Occupational Health Psychology*, **1**, 211–223.

Searle, B. J., Bright, J. E. H. and Bochner, S. (1999). Testing the three-factor model of occupational stress: the impacts of demands, control and social support on a mail sorting task. *Work and Stress*, **13**, 268–279.

Sekaran, U. (1986). *Dual-Career Families*. San Francisco: Jossey Bass.

Selye, H. (1976). *The Stress of Life* (revised edition). New York: McGraw-Hill.

Selye, H. (1993). History of the stress concept. In L. Goldberger and S. Breznitz (Eds), *Handbook of Stress: Theoretical and Clinical Aspects* (2nd edition). New York: The Free Press.

Sevastos, P., Smith, L. and Cordery, J. L. (1992). Evidence on the reliability and construct validity of Warr's (1990) well-being and mental health measures. *Journal of Occupational and Organisational Psychology*, **65**, 33–49.

Sexton-Radek, K. (1994). The nature of recurrent tension-type headache and stress experiences. *Psychotherapy in Private Practice*, **13**, 63–72.

Shaffer, G. S. (1987). Patterns of work and nonwork satisfaction. *Journal of Applied Psychology*, **72**, 115–124.

Shea, J., Clover, K. and Burton, R. (1991). Relationships between measures of acute and chronic stress and cellular immunity. *Medical Science Research*, **19**(7), 221–222.

Shipley, R. H., Butt, J. H., Horwitz, B. and Farbry, J. E. (1978). Preparation for a stressful medical procedure: Effect of stimulus pre-exposure and coping style. *Journal of Consulting and Clinical Psychology*, **46**, 499–507.

Skov, T., Borg, V. and Orhede, E. (1996). Psychosocial and physical risk factors for musculoskeletal disorders of the neck, shoulders, and lower back in sales-people. *Occupational and Environmental Medicine*, **53**, 351–356.

Smith, C. A. and Wallston, K. A. (1997). The 3Ms: Macroanalysis, microanalysis and meta-analysis. *Journal of Health Psychology*, **2**, 166–167.

Smith, C. A., Wallston, K. A. and Dwyer, K. A. (1995). On babies and bathwater – disease impact and negative affectivity in the self-reports of persons with rheumatoid arthritis. *Health Psychology*, **14**, 64–73.

Smith, R. E., Leffingwell, T. R. and Ptacek, J. T. (1999). Can people remember how they coped? Factors associated with discordance between same-day and retrospective reports. *Journal of Personality and Social Psychology*, **76**, 1050–1061.

Snow, H. (1893). *Cancer and the Cancer Process*. London: J and A Churchill.

Somerfield, M. R. (1997). The utility of systems models of stress and coping for applied research. *Journal of Health Psychology*, **2**, 133–151.

Spector, P. E. (1987). Method variance as an artifact in self-reported affect and perceptions at work: myth or significant problem. *Journal of Applied Psychology*, **72**, 438–443.

Spector, P. E. and Jex, S. M. (1991). Relations of job characteristics from multiple data sources with employee affect, absence, turnover intentions, and health. *Journal of Applied Psychology*, **76**, 46–53.

Spector, P. E., Zapf, D., Chen, P. Y. and Frese, M. (2000). Why negative affectivity should not be controlled in job stress research: don't throw the baby out with the bath water. *Journal of Organisational Behavior*, **21**, 79–95.

Spiegel, D., Bloom, J. R., Kraemer, H. C. and Gottheil, E. (1989). Effect of psycho-social treatment on survival of patients with metastatic breast cancer. *Lancet*, **2**, 888–891.

Spiegel, D., Sephton, S. E., Terr, A. I. and Stites, D. P. S. O. (1998). Effects of psychosocial treatment in prolonging cancer survival may be mediated by neuroimmune pathways. *Annals of the New York Academy of Science*, **840**, 674–683.

Spielberger, C. D. (1983). *Manual for the State trait anxiety questionnaire*. Odessa, FL: Psychological Assessment Resources.

Spielberger, C. D. and Reheiser, R. C. (1995). Measuring occupational stress: The Job Stress Survey. In R. Crandall and P. L. Perrewe (Eds), *Occupational Stress: A handbook*. Washington, DC: Taylor and Francis.

Spielberger, C. D. (1983). *Manual for the State-Trait Anxiety Inventory*. Palo Alto, CA: Consulting Psychological Press.

Spitze, G. and South, S. (1985). Women's employment, time expenditure and divorce. *Journal of Family Issues*, **6**, 307–329.

Staines, G. L. (1980). Spillover versus compensation: a review of the literature on the relationship between work and non-work. *Human Relations*, **33**, 111–129.

Staines, G. L. and Pagnucco, D. (1977). Work and non-work: Part II – An empirical study. In *Effectiveness in Work Roles: Employee Responses to Work Environments (Vol. 1)*. University of Michigan: Survey Research Center.

Staines, G. and Pleck, J. (1983). *The Impact of Work Schedules on the Family*. Ann Arbor: Institute for Social Research.

Staines, G. L., Pottic, K. G. and Fudge, D. A. (1986). Wives' employment and husbands' attitudes toward work and life satisfaction. *Journal of Applied Psychology*, **71**, 118–128.

Stansfeld, S. A. and Marmot, M. G. (1992). Social class and minor psychiatric disorder in British civil servants: a validated screening survey using the GHQ. *Psychological Medicine*, **22**, 739–749.

Stansfield, S., Feeney, A., Head, J., Canner, R., North, F. and Marmot, M. (1995). Sickness absence for psychiatric illness: the Whitehall II study. *Social Science and Medicine*, **40**, 189–197.

Starker, S. (1986). Promises and prescriptions: Self-help books in mental health and medicine. *American Journal of Health Promotion*, **1**, 19–24.

Staw, B. M., Bell, N. E. and Clausen, J. A. (1986). The dispositional approach to job attitudes: A lifetime longitudinal test. *Administrative Science Quarterly*, **31**, 56–77.

Steenland, K., Johnson, J. and Nowlin, S. (1997). A follow-up study of job strain and heart disease among males in the NHANES1 population. *American Journal of Industrial Medicine*, **31**, 256–260.

Stein, M., Miller, A. H. and Trestman, R. L. (1991). Depression, the immune system, and illness. *Archives of General Psychiatry*, **48**, 171–177.

Steptoe, A. (1991). The links between stress and illness. *Journal of Psychosomatic Research*, **35**, 633–644.

Steptoe, A. and O'Sullivan, J. (1986). Monitoring and blunting coping styles of women prior to surgery. *British Journal of Clinical Psychology*, **25**, 143–144.

Steptoe, A. and Wardle, J. (1994). What the experts think: a European survey of expert opinion about the influence of lifestyle on health. *European Journal of Epidemiology*, **10**, 195–203.

Steptoe, A., Fieldman, G., Evans, O. and Perry, L. (1993). Control over work pace, job strain and cardiovascular responses in middle aged men. *Journal of Hypertension*, **11**, 751–759.

Steptoe, A., Wardle, J., Pollard, T. M. and Canaan, L. (1996). Stress, social support and health related behavior: A study of smoking, alcohol consumption and physical exercise. *Journal of Psychosomatic research*, **41**, 171–180.

Steptoe, A., Lipsey, Z. and Wardle, J. (1998). Stress, hassles and variations in alcohol consumption, food choice and physical exercise: A diary study. *British Journal of Health Psychology*, **3**, 51–63.

Stolbach, L. L. and Brandt, U. C. (1988). Psychosocial factors in the development and progression of breast cancer. In C. L. Cooper (Ed.), *Stress and Breast Cancer*. Chichester: Wiley and Sons.

Stone, A. A., Bovbjerg, D. H., Neale, J. M., Napoli, A., Valdimarsdottir, H., Cox, D., Hayden, F. G. and Gwaltney, J. M. J. (1992). Development of common cold symptoms following experimental rhinovirus infection related to prior stressful events. *Behavioral Medicine*, **18**, 115–120.

Stone, A. A. and Neale, J. M. (1982). Development of a methodology for assessing daily experiences. In A. Baum and J. Singer (Eds), *Advances in Environmental Psychology: Environment and Health*. Hillsdale, NJ: Erlbaum.

Stone, A. A. and Neale, J. M. (1984). New measure of daily coping: Development and preliminary results. *Journal of Personality and Social Psychology*, **46**, 892–906.

Stone, A. A., Greenberg, M. A., Kennedy-Moore, E. and Newman, M. G. (1991). Self-report, situation-specific coping questionnaires: What are they measuring? *Journal of Personality and Social Psychology*, **61**, 648–658.

Stone, S. V. and Costa, P. T. (1990). Disease-prone personality or distress-prone personality? In H. S. Freedman (Ed.), *Personality and Disease*. Chichester: Wiley and Sons.

Storr, C. J., Trinkoff, A. M. and Anthony, J. C. (1999). Job strain and non-medical drug use. *Drug and Alcohol Dependence*, **55**(1–2), 45–51.

Stueve, A., Dohrenwend, B. P. and Skodol, A. E. (1998). Relationships between stressful life events and episodes of major depression and non-affective disorders: Selected results from a New York risk factors study. In B. P. Dohrenwend (Ed.), *Adversity, Stress and Psychopathology*. New York: Oxford University Press.

Tait, M., Padgett, M. Y. and Baldwin, T. T. (1989). Job and life satisfaction: a reevaluation of the strength of the relationship and gender effects as a function of the date of the study. *Journal of Applied Psychology*, **74**, 502–507.

Tattersall, A. and Farmer, E. (1995). The regulation of work demands and strain. In S. L. Sauter and L. R. Murphy (Eds), *Organizational Risk Factors for Job Stress*. Washington, DC: American Psychological Association.

Taylor, A., In S. J. H. Biddle, K. R. Fox and S. H. Boutcher (Eds), *Physical Activity and Psychological Well-being*. Routledge: London.

Taylor, S. E. and Brown, J. D. (1988). Illusion and well-being: the social psychological perspective on mental health. *Psychological Bulletin*, **103**, 193–210.

Terman, M., Terman, J. S., Quitkin, F. M., McGrath, P. J., Stewart, J. W. and Rafferty, B. S. O. (1989). Light therapy for seasonal affective disorder. A review of efficacy. *Neuropsychopharmacology*, **2**, 1–22.

Tharakan, P. N. (1992). Occupational stress and job satisfaction among working women. *Journal of the Indian Academy of Applied Psychology*, **18**, 37–40.

Thayer, R. E. (1989). *The Biophysiology of Mood and Arousal.* Oxford University Press: Oxford.

Theorell, T. and Rahe, R. H. (1971). Psychosocial factors and myocardial infarction. *Journal of Psychosomatic Research,* **15**, 25–31.

Thomson, B. and Vaux, L. (1986). The importation, transmission, and moderation of stress in the family system. *American Journal of Community Psychology,* **14**, 39–57.

Thompson, D. R. and Meddis, R. (1990). A prospective evaluation of in-hospital counselling for first time myocardial infarction men. *Journal of Psychosomatic Research,* **34**, 237–248.

Thompson, W. R. (Ed.). (1981). *Black's Medical Dictionary.* A. C. Black: London.

Thorstiensson, E. B. and James, J. E. (1999). A meta-analysis of the effects of experimental manipulations of social support during laboratory stress. *Psychology and Health,* **14**, 869–886.

Toates, F. (1995). *Stress: Conceptual and Biological Aspects.* Chichester: Wiley and Sons.

Tokar, D. M., Fischer, A. R. and Subich, L. M. (1998). Personality and vocational behavior: A selective review of the literature, 1993–1997. *Journal of Vocational Behavior,* **53**, 115–153.

Turner, R. J. and Noh, S. (1983). Class and psychological vulnerability about women: The significance of social support and personal control. *Journal of Health and Social Behavior,* **24**, 2–15.

Tuson, K. and Sinyor, D. (1993). On the affective benefits of acute aerobic exercise: taking stock after twenty years of research. In P. Seraganian (Ed.), *Exercise Psychology: The Influence of Physical exercise on Psychological Processes.* Chichester: Wiley and Sons.

Tyler, P. and Cushway, D. (1995). Stress in nurses: The effects of coping and social support. *Stress Medicine,* **11**, 243–251.

Uchino, B. N., Cacioppo, J. T. and Kiecolt-Glaser, J. K. (1996). The relationship between social support and physiological processes. a review with emphasis on underlying mechanisms and implications for health. *Psychological Bulletin,* **119**, 488–531.

Van der Doef, M. and Maes, S. (1998). The job demand-control (-support) model and physical outcomes: a review of the strain and buffer hypotheses. *Psychology and Health,* **13**, 909–936.

Van Doornen, L. J. P., de Geus, E. C. B. and Orlbeke, J. E. (1988). Aerobic fitness and the physiological stress response: A critical evaluation. *Social Science and Medicine,* **26**, 303–307.

Van Maanen, J. and Barley, S. R. (1984). Occupational communities: Culture and control in organizations. In B. Staw and L. Cummings (Eds), *Research in Organizational Behavior* (Vol. 6, pp. 287–365). Greenwich, CT: JAI Press.

Vedhara, K., Cox, N. K., Wilcock, G. K., Perks, P., Hunt, M., Anderson, S., Lightman, S. L. and Shanks, N. M. (1999). Chronic stress in elderly carers of dementia patients and antibody response to influenza vaccine. *Lancet*, **353**, 627–631.

Vinokur, A. and Van Rijn, M. (1993). Social support and undermining in close relationships: Their independent effects on mental health of unemployed persons. *Journal of Personality and Social Psychology*, **54**, 350–359.

Volicer, B. J., Isenberg, M. and Burns, M. (1977). Medical-surgical differences in hospital stress factors. *Journal of Human Stress, June*, 3–13.

Wall, T. D. and Clegg, C. W. (1981). A longitudinal field study of group work redesign. *Journal of Occupational Behaviour*, **2**, 31–49.

Wall, T. D., Corbett, J. M., Clegg, C. W., Jackson, P. R. and Martin, R. (1990a). Advanced manufacturing technology and work design: Towards a theoretical framework. *Journal of Organizational Behavior*, **11**, 201–219.

Wall, T. D., Corbett, J. M., Martin, R., Clegg, C. W. and Jackson, P. (1990b). Advanced manufacturing technology, work design and performance: a change study. *Journal of Applied Psychology*, **75**, 691–697.

Wall, T. D., Jackson, P. R., Mullarkey, S. and Parker, S. K. (1996). The demand-control model of job strain. A more specific test. *Journal of Occupational and Organisational Psychology*, **62**, 153–166.

Wall, T.-D., Bolden, R. I., Borrill, C. S., Carter, A. J., Golya, D. A., Hardy, G. E., Haynes, C. E., Rick, J. E., Shapiro, D. A. and West, M. A. (1997). Minor psychiatric disorder in NHS trust staff: Occupational and gender differences. *British Journal of Psychiatry*, **171**, 519–523.

Warr, P. (1987). *Work, Unemployment and Mental Health*. Oxford: Oxford University Press.

Warr, P. (1990). The measurement of wellbeing and other aspects of mental health. *Journal of Occupational Psychology*, **63**, 193–210.

Warr, P. B. (1991). Decision latitude, job demands and employee well-being. *Work and Stress*, **4**, 285–294.

Warr, P. (1992). Age and occupational well-being. *Psychology and Aging*, **7**, 37–45.

Warr, P. (1994). A conceptual framework for the study of work and mental health. *Work and Stress*, **8**, 84–97.

Warr, P. B. and Payne, R. L. (1982). Experiences of strain and pleasure among British adults. *Social Science and Medicine*, **16**, 1691–1697.

Warr, P., Cook, J. and Wall, T. (1979). Scales for the measurement of some work attitudes and aspects of psychological well-being. *Journal of Occupational Psychology*, **52**, 129–148.

Watson, D. (1967). Relationship between locus of control and anxiety. *Journal of Personality and Social Psychology*, **6**, 91–92.

Watson, D. and Clark, L. A. (1984). Negative affectivity: The disposition to experience aversive emotional states. *Psychological Bulletin*, **96**, 465–490.

Watson, D. and Pennebaker, J. W. (1989). Health complaints, stress and distress: Exploring the central role of negative affectivity. *Psychological Review*, **96**, 234–254.

Watson, D. and Tellegen, A. (1985). Toward a consensual structure of mood. *Psychological Bulletin*, **98**, 219–235.

Watson, D., Clark, L. A. and Tellegen, A. (1988). Development and validation of brief measures of positive and negative affect: the PANAS Scales. *Journal of Personality and Social Psychology*, **54**, 1063–70.

Waxler-Morrison, N., Hislop, T. G., Mears, B. and Kan, L. S. O. (1991). Effects of social relationships on survival for women with breast cancer: a prospective study. *Social Science and Medicine*, **33**, 178–183.

Wehr, T. A. and Rosenthal, N. E. (1989). Seasonality and affective illness. *American Journal of Psychiatry*, **146**, 829–839.

Weidner, G., Boughal, T., Pieper, C., Connor, S. L. and Mendell, N. R. (1997). Relationship of job strain to standard coronary rusk factors and psychological characteristics in women and men of the family heart study. *Health Psychology*, **3**, 239–247.

Weinberger, D. A. and Schwartz, G. E. (1990). Distress and restraint as super-ordinate dimensions of self-reported adjustment: A typological perspective. *Journal of Personality*, **58**, 381–417.

Weinberger, D. A., Schwarz, G. E. and Davidson, R. J. (1979). Low anxious, high anxious and repressive coping styles: psychometric patterns and behavioral responses to stress. *Journal of Abnormal Psychology*, **88**, 369–380.

Weinstein, N. D. (1980). Unrealistic optimism about future life events. *Journal of Personality and Social Psychology*, **39**, 806–820.

Weinstein, N. D. (1983). Reducing unrealistic optimism about illness susceptibility. *Health Psychology*, **2**, 11–20.

Weiss, H. M. and Cropanzano, R. (1996). Affective events theory: a theoretical discussion of the structure, causes and consequences of affective experiences at work. *Research in Organizational Behavior*, **18**, 1–74.

Wells, J. K., Howard, G. S., Nowlin, W. F. and Vargas, M. J. (1986). Presurgical anxiety and postsurgical pain and adjustment: Effects of a stress inoculation procedure. *Journal of Consulting and Clinical Psychology*, **54**, 831–835.

West, M., Arnold, J., Corbett, M. and Fletcher, B. C. (1992). Editorial: Advancing understanding about behaviour at work. *Journal of Occupational and Organizational Psychology*, **65**, 1–3.

Westman, M. (1997). A model of stress crossover, *Working Paper No. 15/97*, The Israel Institute of Business Research, Tel Aviv.

Westman, M. and Etzion, D. (1995). Crossover of stress, strain and resources from one spouse to another. *Journal of Organisational Behaviour*, **16**, 169–181.

Westman, M. and Vinokur, A. D. (1997). Unravelling the relationship of distress levels within couples: Common stressors, empathic reactions, or crossover via social interaction? *Human Relations*, **50**, 137–156.

Wharton, A. S. and Erickson, R. J. (1995). The consequences of caring: Exploring the links between women's job and family emotion work. *Sociological Quarterly*, **36**, 273–296.

Wilensky, H. (1960). Work, careers and social integration. *International Social Science Journal*, **12**, 543–560.

Wilkins, W. (1974). Social stress and illness in industrial society. In E. Grunderson and R. Rahe (Eds), *Life Stress and Illness*. Springfield, IL: Thomas.

Wilkinson, R. (1997). Socioeconomic determinants of health: Health inequalities: relative or absolute material standards? *British Medical Journal*, **314**, 591.

Willemsen, G., Ring, C., Carroll, D., Evans, P., Clow, A and Hucklebridge, F. (1998). Secretory immunoglobulin A. and cardiovascular reactions to mental arithmetic and cold pressor. *Psychophysiology*, **35**, 252–259.

Williams, J. M. G., Watts, F. M., Macleod, C. and Mathews, A. (1988). *Cognitive Psychology and Emotional Disorders*. Chichester: Wiley and Sons.

Williams, J. M. G., Ellis, N. C., Tyers, C., Healy, H., Rose, G. and MacLeod, A. K. (1996). The specificity of autobiographical memory and imageability of the future. *Memory and Cognition*, **24**, 116–125.

Williams, J. M. G., Watts, F. M., Macleod, C. and Mathews, A. (1997). *Cognitive Psychology and Emotional Disorders*, 2nd edition. Chichester: Wiley and Sons.

Williams, K. J. and Alliger, G. M. (1994). Role stressors, mood spillover and perceptions of work-family conflict in employed parents, *Academy of Management Journal*, **37**, 837–868.

Williams, L. J., Cote, J. A. and Buckley, M. R. (1989). Lack of method variance in self-reported affect and perceptions at work: reality or artefact? *Journal of Applied Psychology*, **74**, 462–468.

Williams, L. J., Gavin, M. B. and Williams, M. L. (1996). Measurement and nonmeasurement processes with negative affectivity and employee attitudes. *Journal of Applied Psychology*, **81**, 88–101.

Williamson, A. M. (1994a). Managing stress in the workplace: Part I. Guidelines for the practitioner. In A. Kilbom and A. Mital (Eds), *Industrial Ergonomics: Special Issue: 'Guidelines'*, **14**, 161–170.

Williamson, A. M. (1994b). Managing stress in the workplace: Part II. The scientific basis (knowledge base) for the guide. In A. Kilbom and A. Mital (Eds), *Industrial Ergonomics: Special Issue: 'Guidelines'*, **14**, 171–196.

Wills, T. A. (1990). Stress and coping factors in the epidemiology of substance use. In L. T. Kozlowski, H. M. Annis, H. D. Capell, F. B. Glaser, M. S. Goodstadt, Y. Israel, H. Kalant, E. M. Sellers and E. R. Vingilis (Eds), *Research Advances in Alcohol and Drug Problems*. New York: Plenum Press.

Winnubst, J. A. M., Buunk, B. P. and Marcelissen, F. H. G. (1988). Social support and stress: perspectives and processes. In S. Fisher and J. Reason (Eds), *Handbook of Life Stress, Cognition and Health*. Chichester: Wiley and Sons.

Winzelberg, A. J. and Luskin, F. M. (1999). The effect of a meditation training in stress levels in secondary school teachers. *Stress Medicine*, **15**, 69–77.

Wortman, C. B. and Dunkel-Shetter, C. (1987). Conceptual and methodological issues in the study of social support. In A. Baum and J. Singer (Eds), *Handbook of Psychology and Health*. Hillsdale, NJ: Erlbaum.

Wortman, C., Biernat, M. and Lang, E. (1991). Coping with role overload. In M. Frankenhaeuser, U. Lundberg and M. Chesney (Eds), *Women, Work and Health: Stress and Opportunities*. New York: Plenum.

Wright, B. M. and Cordery, J. L. (1999). Production uncertainty as a contextual moderator of employee reactions to job design. *Journal of Applied Psychology*, **84**, 456–463.

Young, M. and Wilmott, P. (1973). *The Symmetrical Family: a Study of Work and Leisure in the London Region*. London: Routledge and Kegan Paul.

Zajonc, R. B. (1965). Social facilitation. *Science*, **149**, 269–274.

Zapf, D., Dormann, C. and Frese, M. (1996). Longitudinal studies in organizational stress research: a review of the literature with reference to methodological issues. *Journal of Occupational Health Psychology*, **1**, 145–159.

Zedeck, S. (1992). Introduction: Exploring the domain of work and family concerns. In S. Zedeck (Ed.), *Work, Families and Organisations*. San Francisco: Jossey Bass.

INDEX